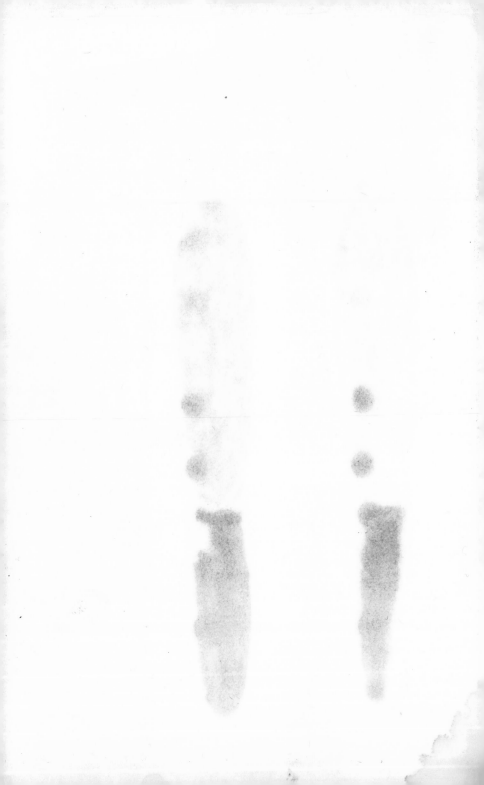

TELEVISION TODAY: A CLOSE-UP VIEW

TELEVISION TODAY: A CLOSE-UP VIEW

Readings from *TV Guide*

Edited by

BARRY COLE

OXFORD UNIVERSITY PRESS
Oxford New York Toronto Melbourne
1981

Library of Congress Cataloging in Publication Data

Main entry under title:
Television today.

Includes index.
1. Television broadcasting—United States—
Addresses, essays, lectures. I. Cole, Barry G.
II. TV guide.
PN1992.3.U5T43 1981 791.45'0973 80-16079
ISBN 0-19-502798-1
ISBN 0-19-502799-X (pbk.)

Printed in the United States of America

Introduction

In the vernacular of *Star Wars* television can be described as "The Force" of today. It is the frame in which we view the dimensions of our society. It reflects the quality of our culture and the character of our priorities. It is a determining influence on our politics, our economics, our ethics, our aesthetics, as well as our psychological and social perceptions.

Larry Grossman, President,
Public Broadcasting Service

TV Guide has published over 11,000 articles and features on almost every aspect of television since 1953. The sixty-four articles in this collection and my introductions to them are designed to provide an overview of today's television: that is, the content of television and how it is determined, the audience and its importance in affecting what's on the air, the role and significance of television in our society, the regulation and control of television programming, and television's future in an emerging, so-called "video revolution."

Throughout, I have attempted to keep editing to a minumum. I have updated information, enclosing it in brackets, when I thought it useful. It has sometimes been advisable to delete material from individual articles when the material was dated or when the subject was covered in greater detail and more appropriately placed in other portions of the book. These deletions are formally noted by ellipses. In some instances excerpts from articles are used, and this is noted as well, at the bottom of the page on which those articles begin.

Some of the more lengthy articles included in this collection were originally published as separate parts in two or more issues of *TV Guide.* In these cases the articles have been edited to delete information that was repetitive.

Because the articles are not reproduced in chronological order, there are some apparent inconsistencies in the titles of industry personnel. The references to executives and personnel are sufficiently numerous that in most instances I felt it inadvisable to tamper with these titles and risk interfering with the reader's concentration.

I am indebted to the contributors and to *TV Guide*; especially to Helene Curley, director of *TV Guide*'s Readers Service, for her help with locating some of the articles and to Margie Cantwell and Peter Obel for their aid in communicating with the contributors. Mary Lou Sutter, my wife Fran and my daughter Tracy were of great assistance in preparing and proofreading the manuscript. Harold Simpson of the Television Bureau of Advertising and Alan Pearce helped me in obtaining updated industry statistics, and Bill Behanna and W. S. Hamell of the A. C. Nielsen Company provided recent audience figures. My graduate assistants at the Annenberg School, Mary Beth Crowley-Ferrell and Nancy Csaplar, read and commented on portions of the volume.

To Merrill Panitt, editorial director of *TV Guide,* my sincere appreciation for his full cooperation and help whenever it was requested.

McLean, Va. B. C.
August 1980

Contents

TELEVISION TODAY: A CLOSE-UP VIEW

PROGRAMMING

To most people in this country, television programming is synonymous with network programming. There are roughly 750 commercial television stations in the United States, and about six of every seven are affiliated with one of the three major commercial television networks—ABC, CBS or NBC. These three networks provide programming that occupies two-thirds of all the hours broadcast by their affiliated stations. Nonaffiliated independent stations also depend on the networks for much of their schedules in the form of off-network programs, that is, syndicated programs that formerly appeared on the network.

The three networks virtually control what is seen on commercial television and go to great expense to capture large shares of the audience. According to CBS president John Backe, the cost of operating and programming the CBS television network more than doubled between 1973 and 1978. By 1980 the three networks together were spending $3.5 billion for their programming, about 5000 hours for each network. The cost of prime-time evening programming alone jumped forty per cent between 1978 and 1980, to a combined cost of $40 million each week. Program promotion is also a major expense. In 1979 each network spent several million dollars to promote its fall program schedule, including commercial advertising time.

The least expensive type of show is the situation comedy produced with simple sets and filmed or recorded indoors. According to

Broadcasting, the price for a segment of a situation comedy in early 1980 ranged from $190,000 for *Hello Larry* (NBC) to $475,000 for *Happy Days* (ABC). An hour-long program segment cost anywhere from $400,000 for *The Misadventures of Sheriff Lobo* (NBC) to $800,000 for *Buck Rogers in the 25th Century* (also NBC). ABC paid $750,000 for an episode of *Charlie's Angels,* and an episode of *Dallas* cost CBS $660,000. Most hour-long series cost at least $500,000 per segment. In 1979, *Centennial,* a twelve-part, twenty-six-hour production based on the James Michener novel was priced at $30 million or more than $1,350,000 per hour. The cost of *The Winds of War,* a mini-series of twelve one-hour segments based on the Herman Wouk novel, shown in 1980, was $25 million, which averages out to over $2 million an hour.

The networks themselves do not produce most entertainment programs. Independent producers charge the networks a fee for a license to show an individual program two or three times a year. In the spring of 1980, the two biggest producers of television shows, Aaron Spelling and Universal Television, were receiving between them more than $8 million per week from the networks. ABC was paying Aaron Spelling about $4,525,000 for seven one-hour program segments, including *Love Boat, Fantasy Island* and *Charlie's Angels.* For its weekly contribution of six and a half hours of programming for all three networks, Universal was receiving $3,665,000.

The real gamble, however, is in the development of new programs, and network investments in that activity have more than tripled between 1973 and 1980. CBS president Gene Jankowski told the press in early 1980 that a single one-hour pilot film cost CBS $1 million. For the fall of 1980, the networks financed approximately one hundred pilot shows of which only twenty to twenty-five were expected to become series. Historically, no more than one in every four new series is renewed by the networks for a second year. Furthermore, the average lifetime of even the biggest hit series is short. Of all the prime-time series that were on the air in 1970, only two survived through the 1979-80 season: *The Wonderful World of Disney* and *60 Minutes,* and *60 Minutes* has not been shown steadily during these years, having been preempted by other types of programming, such as football games.

The networks are constantly seeking new series to replace those that do badly in the ratings, and evolving new programs has become a "year-round continuum," according to Tom Werner, ABC vice president on series development. Fall has traditionally been the time to introduce new network offerings, and the official television season consists of thirty weeks beginning in September and ending in April. The summer months are typically devoted to reruns and new show try-outs. In recent years, however, programs have been put on and yanked off the air so frequently that by the 1979-80 season there were, in effect, four seasons, including the summer reruns. Over half of the new programs in the 1979-80 fall schedule were off the air by Christmas and CBS announced its earliest second season ever was to begin on December 17. *Variety* set the beginning of the second season at January 7 with the proviso that with all the constant changing, the date picked was arbitrary, but "some week must be designated and . . . [that week] is as good as any." In March 1980, seventeen new series appeared—the third season began.

CBS programming chief Donald (Bud) Grant discussed the networks' practice of introducing new shows in the spring: "What we're doing is bringing the audience into the decision-making process for setting our fall schedule. If they see a show and like it and tell us they like it through the rating services, we'll bring it back in the fall." NBC's programming chief stated that testing new shows in the spring is "just a little bit more life insurance. . . . The fewer shows you have to cancel in the fall, the better off you are." *Dallas, Family* and *Real People* are recent hit shows that were introduced in the spring and then retained in the fall schedule.

Television producers take a dim view of the networks' scheduling policies. They feel that many programs are not given a chance to settle in. Grant Tinker, a major producer of programs and chairman of the Caucus for Producers, Writers and Directors, complains that the networks have a "prove-yourself-in-three-weeks mentality." He points out that some quality programs may be slow starters: *All in the Family* (now *Archie Bunker's Place*), the original *Dick Van Dyke Show* and his own *The Mary Tyler Moore Show*—three of the most successful and critically praised situation comedies in the history of television—are examples. According to Tinker, if the networks had had their current attitude toward ratings when these shows were introduced, all three probably would have been cancelled within a few weeks.

Lee Rich, producer of *The Waltons* and *Eight Is Enough*, feels that "television has changed from a program business to a ratings business." The ratings are an estimate of how many television homes are viewing which programs (see pp. 185–209), and a single rating point represents approximately 763,000 homes. The number of advertisers the network can obtain, how much these advertisers can be charged for air time and, ultimately, what profits the networks will make depend on how many rating points the network's programs can attract. Former CBS program chief Mike Dann estimated in August 1979 that the number one-ranked network, ABC, could realize $75 million in pre-tax profits for every new rating point for 1979-80.

The network audience ratings not only determine the financial success of the network, they also have a considerable effect on the economic well-being of network affiliates. ABC had so many hit shows in the 1978-79 season that in February 1979, ABC affiliates were the number one-rated stations in twenty-four of the twenty-five largest television markets. ABC affiliates also had the highest audience in forty-two of the fifty largest markets, which represent about 70 per cent of all television households. As a result, ABC affiliates had higher revenues overall than did CBS and NBC affiliates.

ABC's own figures indicated the network tied with CBS for first place in the 1979-80 prime-time ratings race. Figures released by CBS and NBC showed CBS the winner by only one-tenth of a point or 76,300 homes. The variance was due to a difference of opinion between ABC and the other two networks as to which week in September was the start of the official season.

The higher the stakes, the more the networks scramble to gain the extra rating point and the more frenetic the program scheduling becomes. CBS president James Rosenfield told his affiliates in 1979 that "only the public is more confused about the schedule than the network and affiliate." He admitted that CBS often waited until the last moment to announce program specials in attempts to forestall counterprogramming by the other networks because "in the wildly competitive battle it behooves us [CBS] to play checkers a little more than you [the affiliates] or we would like."

One ploy the networks use in attempts to neutralize the ratings is to schedule blockbusters opposite each other, a frustrating experience for the television audience. This type of maneuver is most common when network competition is at its fiercest, during the ratings sweep periods (see pp. 186–88) which occur in February, May, July and November. On February 11, 1979, *Gone with the Wind* was scheduled opposite *One Flew over the Cuckoo's Nest* (Academy Award-winning picture of 1975) and *Elvis* (a made-for-TV movie about Elvis Presley). This effort cost the networks $13 million, more than three times the cost of programs on a typical night. *Elvis* received the highest ratings, but the networks did stay competitive.

Placing programs that most everyone wants to watch on television at the same time quite naturally raises some eyebrows and generates a certain amount of criticism. However, the networks do not need to apologize, as far as ABC programming chief Andres Thomopoulos is concerned:

> That's just good business. We're in a competitive situation. If Chrysler brings out a new small car, the other car companies don't all sit back and say, "okay, we're not going to bring out a small car to compete." Television is very competitive, and the excitement that results from that is beneficial to the viewer. If we were all docile and laid-back, the viewer would suffer. People like television and they know that competition is the best stimulus for improvement.

The networks have no wish to jeopardize their ratings positions or to take any unnecessary chances. Consequently, the formula already proven successful will invariably defeat new ideas which may or may not catch on. Of course this practice leads to duplication of effort: for example, all three networks aired new series based on college life for the 1978-79 second season, after *National Lampoon*'s movie *Animal House* became a big box-office hit. However, when Joseph Papp and Norman Lear, two of the most successful producers/creators in show business, offered the networks a twenty-four-part dramatic series of great American plays, the series was turned down. NBC, reportedly, would have bought the series had the network been first in the ratings, but it was not. ABC was number one and for this reason, the producers were told, there was no need for the network to take a chance on such a series.

The need to stay competitive in the ratings may at times even require an expensive "cutting of losses." When Fred Silverman became NBC president, he decided that a series called *Coast to Coast,* scheduled for the 1978–79 season, could not succeed because of projected bad ratings. Silverman concluded that the show was so poor that NBC could not dare to run *Coast to Coast,* even as a summer replacement. NBC had contracted for 13 episodes at a cost of $4.5 million and no filming had yet been done. The producer was paid $4 million by NBC and not a single segment was filmed.

The fierce competition in the ratings game has resulted in some practices which distress the producers. For many years fall schedules were announced as early as Washington's Birthday; in 1980 the producer could only hope the schedules would be announced by the end of April. Also, because of the rapid turnover of shows not up to snuff, new shows are often needed throughout the year and on short notice. During the 1978–79 season, one NBC program was delivered just an hour before it was scheduled to be telecast. The first episode of *Supertrain,* a series which cost a reported $12 million to get into production and was supposed to be the big hit for NBC for 1978–79, was completed so close to air time that satellites rather than the usual landlines had to be used to broadcast the show simultaneously around the country. After all that, *Supertrain* did not live up to expectations and NBC cancelled it.

The producers claim that the current state of affairs results in quality sacrificed for speed. Independent producer David Levy claims, "a lot of new programs turn out badly because they have to be produced in a hurry." Levy is a former NBC vice president and currently the executive director of the Caucus for Producers, Writers and Directors in Hollywood. The Caucus has demanded that the networks announce their fall schedules by March 15.

Ed Montanus, president of MGM television, summed up the entire situation as follows: "We're working in a Barnum & Bailey atmosphere, and the guy with the strongest stomach is going to win."

MERRILL PANITT

Network Power—Is It Absolute?

The power of the networks has grown to such an extent that they "dominate the television industry; they influence overall advertising rates and practices; they absorb a disproportionate share of revenue and profits; and they work a major impact on economic conditions in the industry." This is the opinion of Westinghouse Broadcasting Company (Group W), which owns television stations in five of the largest markets and has affiliates with all three networks.

The power accrued by the networks has not gone uncontested. Merrill Panitt discusses network power from the point of view of the participants in the industry who are most affected—the advertisers, the stations and the Hollywood creative community.

At the heart of most of the achievements—and the failures—of the communications medium that pervades nearly every aspect of American life is the television network.

Once a convenient arrangement that permitted stations to broadcast quality programming they could not afford individually, and permitted advertisers to reach across the country with their programs and commercial messages, the networks now stand in absolute control of the medium. They determine what programs Americans will see, who will make them, who will perform in them and what their content will be.

In the final analysis, network executives say, the public determines what will be on the air. In truth, what the public determines is

This essay first appeared February 26, 1977.

what will *not* be on the air. If the audience refuses to watch one network offering, another is submitted. The same men who selected the original program decide upon its replacement. The same thinking that brought about the first decision brings about the second. And, if necessary, the third and fourth and fifth.

The power of the networks brings them into conflict with other segments of the television business—with advertisers and agencies that buy commercial time from the networks; with local station affiliates that carry network programs; with producers who sell programs to the networks.

There was a time when advertisers selected programs, had them made and sponsored them on the air. Then, in 1958, the quiz scandals broke. A number of sponsored big-money quiz shows were caught playing hanky-panky to boost ratings, indulging in such practices as giving contestants answers to questions. The networks pleaded innocence, blamed it all on sponsors and announced firmly that they would now take charge of the programs they put on the air.

In short order it was all but impossible for a sponsor to buy a show from a producer. Instead he had his pick of several programs offered to him by the network. These programs, as it happened, were partly owned by the network. It had provided funds to make the pilot show and in return had an interest in the program. Before long, networks owned, at least in part, nearly every show they telecast. They thus received money from advertisers not only for the air time but also for the programs themselves. As prices rose, fewer and fewer advertisers could afford to sponsor programs. They found it more expedient, and profitable, to spread their commercials among a number of programs and thus reach more viewers.

Eventually, however, the Federal Communications Commission forced the networks out of major involvement in entertainment-program ownership.[1]

1. The FCC now prohibits networks from acquiring any interest in a program produced by an outside party beyond the right to network exhibition. Networks may no longer acquire distribution rights or profit shares in such programs or engage in selling (syndicating) them to anyone, anywhere in the world. Pending the outcome of a Justice Department suit, the networks are still permitted to produce their own entertainment programs, if the network is the sole producer and assumes the financial

Instead of sponsoring programs, most network advertisers now buy one-minute or 30-second commercials in various programs. The one-minute spots usually amount to two 30-second commercials devoted to different products owned by the same advertiser. These are called "piggyback" commercials.[2]

Television is a seller's market now. Available time—in prime time [which in 1979–80 sold] at an average rate of [about $80,000 per 30 seconds][3] is so scarce that a number of advertising agencies and production companies are speaking seriously about trying to form a fourth network. . . .

Some national commercials are placed directly on local stations, and, of course, the local stations sell commercial time to local advertisers. Estimates for [1979] have network income from advertising [at $4.5] billion, national commercials placed on local stations [at $2.9] billion and local advertising [at $2.8] billion.

Business is good. Advertisers who used to wait until Friday of each week to buy next week's unsold time from the networks at distress rates are now committing millions of dollars for commercial time months in advance.

Advertisers are generally unhappy because they have little to say about the kinds of programs on the air. They want their commercials on popular shows, but some express discomfort about being associated with programs that feature violence. A number of them,

risk. Even with their own shows, however, the networks can not engage in off-network distribution within the United States, nor retain the rights to share the revenues or profits from such distribution.

2. In 1979, 83.3 per cent of network advertising consisted of 30-second ads; 30-second piggybacks (two 30-second ads together) made up another 12.3 per cent. Sixty-second commercials for a single product accounted for only 2.8 per cent of network advertising; 10-second commercials, 0.6 per cent; and 45-second ads, 0.8 per cent. Also in 1979, 83.9 per cent of nonnetwork advertising was in the form of 30-second commercials or 30-second piggybacks. Another 8.4 per cent consisted of 10- and 20-second commercials, and 60-second (or longer) ads accounted for 7.6 per cent.

Until 1968, 10- and 20-second commercial spots were more common than 30-second ads, and until 1970 the most common type of television advertising was the 60-second commercial.

3. The cost of network commercials can vary tremendously, depending upon the program during which the commercial is broadcast. In the 1979–80 season, the cost of a 30-second commercial in prime time ranged from $45,000 to $150,000.

including General Foods, have refused to buy time in such programs.

Other advertisers are eager to sponsor documentaries, dramas or other programs of superior quality but find little of such programming available on the networks. These advertisers—Exxon, IBM, Mobil, Xerox, Gulf and others—contribute money to public broadcasting to get such programs on the air, to relatively small audiences, even though on public broadcasting they are not permitted to advertise.

Another sore point with advertisers is the number of commercials the networks lump together during commercial breaks. Advertisers prefer more interruptions in a program and few commercials during each interruption. Viewers apparently prefer fewer interruptions. The networks try to offer a compromise, but the results for viewers are chopped-up programs and a bombardment of hard sell; for advertisers, skyrocketing costs at a time when their commercials are all but lost in the cacophony of other commercials.

There are complaints from Madison Avenue, but not much more than that. The three networks are in the driver's seat. Their chief problem now is to try to allocate what commercial time is still available to advertisers who will be back when business may not be so good. Proctor & Gamble, which [in 1979 spent] nearly [$463] million on television, has little difficulty picking up a few more minutes for commercials. An advertiser who spends less than a million a year is less likely to be favored.

Viewers are being subjected to more and more television advertising. . . . Among the effects of so many commercials are the restrictions on writers. An hour-long program must have four breaks and must be written so that action reaches a high point before each commercial break. Producer-writer Richard Alan Simmons said of series writing: "There's no such thing as sitting down to a blank piece of paper. You start with characters probably invented by someone else, whose background and reactions are set in previous episodes. You've got to fill in the plot around these characters—and see to it that the action peaks every 15 minutes to provide a lead-in to the commercials."

The station conflict with networks is a quiet one, attracting attention usually when the networks appear to be ready to encroach on station time, as was the case in the networks' campaign to expand their news shows to an hour.

But one station group, Westinghouse's Group W (which owns stations affiliated with each of the three networks), [in 1976] petitioned the FCC to conduct an investigation into the network-station relationship. Some 100 stations have written Don McGannon, Group W president, that they support his position, although most of them will not risk saying so publicly. The Justice Department *has* said so publicly. Its antitrust division filed a petition with the FCC supporting a broad inquiry into network practices. Justice went even further, in suggesting that the FCC consider whether the networks shouldn't be required to divest themselves of some or all of the [five] stations they [each] own. The FCC agreed to conduct an investigation [which is scheduled for completion in 1980].

McGannon's position is that the networks treat the stations cavalierly, that networks reimburse stations for carrying network shows at what [in 1976 amounted] to about 13.8 per cent of the station's regular rate, that the networks increased their programming on local stations 22 per cent between 1960 and 1976, that their sales increased 92 per cent between 1964 and 1974 but payments to stations increased only 15 per cent.

The Group W chief, an outspoken critic of sex and violence on network programs, also wants the networks to provide station operators an opportunity to see programs well in advance of air date so that they can decide whether to carry the shows.

While McGannon, whose company owns stations in large cities, is publicly critical of the networks, his fellow broadcasters are, if not entirely satisfied with the healthy profits their network affiliations bring them, hardly willing to endanger those profits by indulging in intramural squabbling.

The money, in brief, is good. For the stations it could, and possibly should, be better, but most of them are not complaining—out loud. The networks say the stations are well paid for what amounts to using some electricity to keep the station on the air. McGannon says his company spends money on local news and other programming so that the network programs appear on respected stations that can guarantee high ratings. A number of stations and station groups do as much local programming as Group W, but too many stations depend largely upon inexpensive reruns of old network comedy and game shows to fill the time between network offerings.

There are [about 120] independent stations not affiliated with networks.[4] These operate under the handicap of having no regular source of big-time programming and make do with schedules that usually emphasize local sports and syndicated shows that already have appeared on the networks. . . .

Network difficulties with the program producers fall into two categories—money and creative problems. The Hollywood producers complain about "deficit financing," which means the programs they produce cost more than the networks pay for them.

Grant Tinker, whose company [has produced *Lou Grant* and] *The Mary Tyler Moore, Bob Newhart, Rhoda, Phyllis* and *Tony Randall* shows, said that he might be forced out of business because each episode of his programs cost more than the networks paid him. "They just don't understand how impossible this business is," he said.

The networks have been increasing measurably their payments to producers. They also point to the rather large salaries some producers draw—from the program budgets—and hint that perhaps they're not quite approaching penury. "They're drawing salaries of thousands of dollars a week," said one network head, "living in mansions with swimming pools and a flock of fancy cars. It's hard to feel too sorry for them." Since the producers remain in business year after year, and fight to get new shows on the air, it would appear that "deficit financing" is not yet breaking them.

Creative arguments between producers and networks center around network insistence on supervising stories and casting, and ordering series tailored to network needs. The network has the last word in determining which performers are used. The decisions sometimes depend upon surveys purportedly proving which actors are recognized by the audience, which are popular. One such survey, TvQ (for television quotient) reportedly is used extensively by the networks, especially in approving casts of movies made for television. And it is true that the same faces are seen again and again in

4. As of March 1980, ABC claimed 204 affiliated stations while CBS and NBC claimed 213 affiliates. Affiliate counts are a matter of controversy because the networks (and stations) do not always agree on the criteria by which a station becomes an affiliate.

TV-movies. Such decisions leave little room for producers to develop new talent, to employ their own experience and judgment.

Stories must be discussed with network programming executives, and scripts are approved by them, sometimes with extensive changes. Scripts must also be approved by network censors, euphemistically known as "Program Practices" people. The decisions of these departments, which have chiefly to do with just how far a script can go in portraying sex and violence and in use of mild obscenities, are frequently baffling to Hollywood writers [see pp. 322–29]. . . .

It is an expensive, nerve-racking, highly competitive business. It is a business controlled by three networks whose top executives usually hold their jobs for relatively short periods, but who during those short periods exercise an effect upon their country and its people rarely equaled—even by the President of the United States.

NEIL HICKEY

It's Being Called a "Dance of Death"

The power of the networks is most pervasive during the prime-time evening hours. On a typical fall or winter evening, two-thirds of the 76.3 million television households in this country are watching television. Each of these households has at least one set turned on, and 90 per cent of these sets are tuned to network programs. Naturally, the advertisers want the greatest possible percentage of this huge audience; about two-thirds of network advertising revenue comes from ads scheduled during prime time.

Altogether, the networks order about 2000 hours of original prime-time programming from outside suppliers during the course of a year. Neil Hickey discusses how the networks decide which programs to order and when they should be scheduled.

So you want to program a television network, be No. 1 in the ratings and get rich? You're certain you'd do it better than "those idiots in New York and Hollywood" who are always canceling your favorite show and replacing it with one you hate. Well, then you'll have to absorb a few simple rules about TV's martial arts: how to jab and counterpunch, how to keep your opponents off balance, how to exploit their weaknesses.

You'll need to know, first of all, that 30 per cent of the adults in America's [76.3] million television homes are between the ages of 18 and 34; that only [23] per cent are 35 to 54; and that [21] per cent of them are over 55. Those 18-34s are the big spenders, so you'll get more money from advertisers from delivering them (as much as $13 per thousand head) than for the over-50s ([$5] a thousand, or less) even

This essay first appeared April 29, 1978.

though the latter group watches more TV than anybody else.[1] And don't forget that Sunday and Monday nights are the week's heaviest prime-time viewing periods, and that [Thursday] and Friday nights are the lightest.

Those are a few rules of thumb to get you started. The rest you can pick up as you go along: how to establish a "flow" from one program to another through the evening; how to attack your enemies' weak flanks with strong "counterprogramming"; how and when to shift a failing show to a stronger slot in the schedule to give it a new lease on life; how to salt and pepper your schedule with mini-series, novels and specials to grab ratings points with preemptive attractions.

Having learned the rules of the game, you then must learn how to keep score. It's simple, really. The object is to win more ratings points and share points than the other two players. One ratings point equals one per cent of those [76.3] million TV homes, so if your show gets a 10 rating it was seen in [7,630,000] homes; and if you win 30 share points, you were watched by 30 per cent of all the homes whose TV sets were switched on. Most of the time, if your series doesn't get at least a 30 share you'll have to junk it as a weak competitor and put on something else.

And those scores are computed a lot faster than they used to be: the morning after your prime-time show is broadcast, the Nielsen ratings service will tell you how it fared in New York, Los Angeles, [San Francisco] and Chicago; and 24 hours after that, they'll give you the full, nationwide results based on their famous sample of 1200 homes having meters hooked up to Nielsen computers. (If you're the trigger-happy type, though, or don't have strong nerves, those speedy scores may cause you to cancel potential hits before they can show their stuff: *All in the Family,* for example, was a very slow starter when it first came on in 1971.)

1. Michael Drexler of the Doyle, Dane and Bernbach advertising agency says that women over 50 are "a segment to be reckoned with" by advertisers. They "view the golden years as the last chance to buy and do all the things they denied themselves before." There is more leisure time to think about their health and grooming.

There are now 22 million women between the ages of 50 and 75 and this group will soon outnumber the under-18 group. Almost 40 per cent of all 50- to 54-year-olds have household incomes of $20,000 or more. Eleven per cent have incomes over $35,000.

One-time specials you should know, usually do a little better in the ratings than the regular series they preempt; but unless you're some kind of do-gooder (or don't *want* to get rich and famous), you'll lay off documentaries, which (in one period [studied]) did 29 per cent worse in the ratings (than regular series) while variety specials were doing 18 per cent better. Mini-series, on the other hand, haven't scored as well on the average as the shows they preempt. *Roots,* of course, did, but that was TV's biggest all-time smash; it not only attracted a 137 per cent bigger audience than regular prime-time shows, but brought to the TV set, in large numbers, people who normally would be doing something else—one of the few times in TV history that such an increase can be documented.[2] So dream up another *Roots,* if you can. . . .

Programming a TV network, says ABC executive Seymour Amlen "is not a science, but it is something of an art." He ought to know: he's on the winningest team in the industry. . . . As far back as the early 1960s, ABC moguls were already mapping the master strategy that would lead them from the Egypt of ignominy (in which they appeared permanently encamped) right through the Red Sea of strife between CBS and NBC, to the Promised Land of fat ratings. They rightly perceived that the only major segment of TV watchers not adequately served were young marrieds, young singles and teenagers; and they perceived it at a time when the average age of Americans was dipping sharply down.

So they fabricated shows like *Hootenanny, Batman, Peyton Place, The Partridge Family, The Brady Bunch* and scores of others in the attempt to ride the youthquake to riches. Unexpected help came from two quarters: in 1971, the FCC removed from network control a half hour of prime time each night, thereby neutralizing part of

2. A total of 130 million viewers were estimated to have seen at least one episode of the six-part *Roots I,* which was first broadcast in January 1978. ABC had expected only about a 28–31 share of the audience and had charged advertisers only $120,000–$150,000 per minute for commercials—the most expensive were for the final segment. Because *Roots I* attracted a much larger share than expected, ABC was able to charge sponsors of the seven-part *Roots II* (broadcast in February 1979) $210,000–$260,000 per minute. *Roots II* raised $21 million in advertising for ABC. An estimated 110 million people saw all or part of *Roots II,* which cost a reported $16 million to produce.

CBS's and NBC's advantage in the early evening;[3] and in 1975 something called Family Viewing Time (misguidedly concocted by CBS) was born, aimed at defusing criticism of TV sex and violence by providing a *cordon sanitaire* from 7 to 9 P.M., ET, each night, inside which practically no program having any adult interest whatsoever could be broadcast [see pp. 307–8 and 331–36].

A light bulb flashed on over ABC's head; its vice presidents stared at each other and said, "Hell, we've got *plenty* of that kind of stuff." Their clear passage from Tap City to Easy Street was assured. Onward came shows like *The Six Million Dollar Man, Happy Days, Welcome Back, Kotter, Eight Is Enough* and *Donny & Marie.* By 1976, ABC stood astride Parnassus while its enemies were openly, indeed loudly, contemptuous of the "junk," the "bubble-gum shows" and the "kiddy porn" that were the foundation of ABC's success.

Their contempt, however, did not deter them from competing, eyeball to eyeball, using the weapons of ABC's choosing. Thus we [had] *Wonder Woman, The Amazing Spider-Man, The Incredible Hulk, The Return of Captain Nemo, The Human Torch, Project U.F.O., Quark, Buck Rogers* and *The Chuck Barris Rah Rah Show.* It's hard to overestimate at this point in television's history the degree to which the ABC sensibility—devised in cold blood all those years ago—has saturated broadcasting. Gone perhaps forever from prime-time commercial television are anthology dramas and other traditional forms of adult TV fare; the staple now is featherweight comedy and pulp action-adventure fiction, mitigated at intervals by mini-series and other preemptive material (of uncertain quality)—overlaid with heavy-handed gobs of sex as extra-added enticement. (One station owner, Ted Turner of Atlanta's [WTBS] says: "Most of what the masses watch is garbage. Most of the programs that get the ratings are garbage. Quality is how much money we made off it.")

On that playing field, this bizarre, three-sided scrimmage is being enacted with grim seriousness. Some experts call it a dance of death. One advertising executive wrote in *Advertising Age*: "Specials and

3. The FCC's Prime-Time Access Rule limits the amount of programming that may be carried in prime time from a single network by network affiliates in the fifty largest television markets. The practical effect of the rule is that every evening except Sunday, the three networks fail to offer programming between 7:30 and 8:00 P.M., ET.

mini-series of the same low quality as regular series are . . . clear benchmarks of how stagnant the TV industry has become. . . .It's pitiful that so far the only thing this multibillion-dollar enterprise has come up with to follow violence is sex."

The stakes are high. [Thirty] affiliated stations recently have defected to ABC [between January 1976 and July 1979] in search of higher profits—[18] of them from CBS and [12] from NBC.[4] A network that can't keep all its horses in the corral soon has no herd. No herd, no network. Big stockholders in top management are quick to wield their terrible swift sword on program executives when stock prices go down. If you owned [about 2 million] shares of CBS stock (as corporate chairman William Paley [did in 1979]), you'd lose over [$2] million every time it declined a point on the market.[5] So Paley and his peers aren't playing beanbag. They know that Wall Street knows that a single ratings point can be worth as much as [$75] million to a network over a season.

CBS's Bud Grant pondered all this recently in response to a question about the three-network struggle for dominance. "Do you remember," he inquired, "the Vince Lombardi remark about football? 'Winning isn't everything; it's the only thing'."

He wasn't smiling.

4. Some of those affiliates had been with CBS or NBC for more than twenty years. The importance to the networks of these switchers was reflected in the comments made by ABC officials after KSTP-Minneapolis decided to join their ranks. The station (which had been an NBC affiliate for thirty years) had the top-rated local news show in Minneapolis. ABC executives suggested that because of the larger lead in audience which KSTP's local news would provide, ABC's network news audience in Minneapolis might be doubled. After losing KSTP, NBC president Fred Silverman stated: "The greatest pressure I feel now is to keep our affiliate lineup."

5. Mr. Paley owns 1,971,286 shares of CBS stock. In 1979 his dividends from that stock were $5,224,000.

DICK HOBSON

ABC's Quarter Million Dollar Man Performs Heroics Too

The master practitioner of the art of programming a network during recent years has been Fred Silverman, currently president of NBC. In 1975, Silverman left CBS as head of programming—CBS was number one in the ratings at the time—and went to work for ABC, which then had its turn to be number one. In 1978, Silverman moved to NBC, a move which the network deemed worth a $1 million-a-year salary. RCA president Edgar Griffiths (NBC is a subsidiary of RCA) said that "Fred Silverman certainly has a proven track record of being the best there is in the country." Even the stock market takes notice of Fred Silverman's whereabouts. When he went to ABC, ABC stock rose two points and by the end of the year when ABC led the ratings, its stock doubled. Within one week of the announcement that he had joined NBC, RCA stock jumped $1.25 and ABC stock fell $1.75.

Silverman has been colorfully referred to as "the man with the golden gut" who seems to know just what the public wants to watch. However, by the summer of 1979, NBC was still a poor third in the ratings; in fact, its ratings for 1978–79 had dropped one point from those for 1977–78. More important, NBC's pre-tax profits were down by 20 per cent. Fred Silverman's image was a little tarnished. Bob Hope referred to him as "the only man in America who knows what it feels like to rearrange the deck chairs on the Titanic." In defense, Griffiths emphasized that the "fall 1979 represents Fred Silverman's first true opportunity to select the programming." The

This essay first appeared May 7, 1977.

fall 1978 schedule was set before Silverman came to NBC and "the prospects of 1979 relate very heavily on his ability to be a good program selector."

Silverman has predicted that NBC will be in first place by Christmas of 1980, but the 1980 spring prime-time rating figures showed NBC trailing both CBS and ABC by at least two rating points; and the viewing momentum and promotional advantages that were expected to accrue from NBC's coverage of the Moscow 1980 Summer Olympics have been eliminated by the U.S. boycott of the games. While NBC's position in the ratings has improved since 1978, for Silverman's prediction to come true, the network's new fall shows for 1980 will have to be very successful. Even if Silverman's goal is not achieved, he is still the best known and heretofore most successful programmer in network television. Dick Hobson describes Silverman's philosophy of programming while he was putting ABC in the lead.

The hypertensive, flash-tempered, unpredictable and fiercely competitive Fred Silverman ("Freddie" in the business) . . . was expostulating on the failure of a visiting contingent of fifty-two TV editors and columnists to comprehend the audience appeal of *Laverne & Shirley*—providing our first ingredient in what might be called "Freddie's Formula":

Maxim 1: "Make people laugh. There's enough tragedy in the world." Or, as he was saying: "The primary purpose of putting a comedy show on the air is to entertain people. And anybody who approaches half-hour comedy or television entertainment of any kind in any other manner is stupid! You must first get the people into the store."

Maxim 2: "People tune in to see a star." Silverman is always telling the creators of new shows: "Stop inventing these wonderful characters that are impossible to cast. Television is a personality medium. Start out with a piece of talent." If writers' intentions get bent out of shape by Freddie's Formula, they're expendable. Take *Kojak,* initially based on Abby Mann's Emmy-winning TV-movie, *The Marcus-Nelson Murders,* in which the writer said he "wanted people to understand that cops are human beings like everybody else." But Silverman's "people over premises" maxim required that *Kojak* be tailored to fit its stolid star, Telly Savalas. The result, according to Mann: "Kojak is imperturbable; he's always right. He has become exactly the reverse of what I intended."

Maxim 3: "Stress the positive, not the negative." Like MGM's Louis B. Mayer, Silverman cloaks himself in the good old apple-pie values. "God knows, somebody's got to do it! Pick up any newspaper these days and it's just terrible! The news programs on television dwell on crime. I think we should provide positive models for the audiences that we serve. I feel strongly that there should be many different places in the schedule where the family unit is presented in a positive way."

Maxim 4: "The common man is more appealing." Silverman has a predilection for shows with an earthy ambience, possibly reflecting his "blue-collar" childhood (his father was a TV repairman). "I think Freddie always felt that characters in the blue-collar or lower-class TV series were more appealing to America in a lot of ways," *Happy Days* producer Garry Marshall says. "That's the whole Fonzie character. He's uneducated; he's got nothing; but he's not giving up. It's the whole thing of *Laverne & Shirley*—two lower-class bimbos who work in a brewery and struggle and try to get in love and get hurt and who nevertheless are happy and full of dreams. These are real people to Freddie."

Maxim 5: "It's up to me to find new stars." TV stars are a rare and special breed, Silverman contends, and he is constantly prowling around unlikely places looking for new ones. There was the famous night he called an old friend, producer Fred Baum, from Las Vegas; "I just saw an act I'm going to make a star—Sonny and Cher." Baum reacted: "Are you nuts? They're on the downslide!" And the rainy night Freddie drove out to the end of Long Island for a look at a record act in a leaky tent and signed Tony Orlando & Dawn to a CBS contract. "Nobody in his right mind would do that!" was the consensus—even after he pulled it off. Over at ABC he persevered, and when *Donny & Marie* clicked, there were still the nervous jokes: "At least they won't get a divorce."

Maxim 6: "Familiarity breeds acceptability." Producer Marshall airily gives away the secret of Silverman's success: "Fred's theory, which I agree with, is that if you go to a cocktail party and you don't know anybody, which is an uncomfortable situation, your tendency always will be to gravitate to somebody you know rather than to this terribly exciting, wonderful person over here whom you don't know and you're a little afraid to go up to and try to start a conversation with."

Ergo: give the viewers somebody they know. Which explains Freddie's "spin-offs," "crossovers" and "crosspromotions." [It was] all part of Freddie's Formula to make "The ABC Family" seem just like kissin' cousins.

Maxim 7: "Take chances and run scared." For all his hot rolls of 7s and 11s, Silverman regards hit-picking as the biggest throw of the dice ever. "The shows that are the riskiest are also the shows that have got the potential to be the biggest hits." There are those who say that he's not really that good a gambler when it comes to picking programs; that he left the CBS schedule a shambles; that he inherited a brilliant development slate at ABC.

His megagamble—*Roots*—was not in program-picking (its inception is credited to his predecessor, Martin Starger, and programming executive Brandon Stoddard), but in serializing it on an unprecedented eight successive nights. Insiders say that Silverman and other ABC executives were so skeptical of the genealogical epic's pulling power that they ordered it "aired and over with" one week prior to the crucial [February] "sweep week"—when viewer ratings determine ad rates for local stations.

Maxim 8: "It's not only the show but how the audience is told about the show." Silverman's canny concept of "audience expectation" helped him decipher the inner workings of The Viewer Mind, which he manipulates shamelessly. His victory in some "very bitter fights" at CBS unleashed a blizzard of promotional blurbs, leading to the usual jokes: "Tony Orlando is on two hours a week, one hour for the show and one hour for the promos." At ABC where he calls all the shots, Freddie's promos are pandemic.

"Grabbers" are a Silverman trademark. As MTM Enterprises' Grant Tinker recalls: "When Fred heard about *Rhoda*'s wedding, he said, 'Let's clear an hour and make it like Lucy's baby!' And it got a hell of an audience."

Maxim 9: "Work the viewer mind." Freddie became the Dr. Strangelove of program tactics [in fall 1975] when he unleashed a form of Orwellian warfare—with unexpected results. NBC started it by suddenly announcing a blockbuster movie. *Airport 1975,* starring Charlton Heston, to kick off the new season on a Monday night, threatening to eclipse ABC's *The Captain & Tennille* debut. What could he do to take the sock out of *Airport*?

He could schedule a couple of air-disaster movies—*Murder on Flight 502* and *Sky Terror*—over the preceding weekend, specifically to mislead viewers into thinking they'd already seen *Airport 1975.* "Now that really is a form of genius, you know," marveled one of Hollywood's Freddie-watchers, "for him to think that he could work the viewer mind that way." His ploy wasn't entirely successful—*Airport*'s draw proved too powerful—but his disaster flicks over the final weekend of the old season pulled enough viewers to help give ABC the overall ratings title for 1975–76.

Maxim 10: "Keep a hard-action line." As bad money drives out good, according to Freddie's Formula, "hard" shows drive out "soft." At one point [in 1976], *The Bionic Woman* had in work an episode, "Claws," about a mountain lion jeopardizing schoolchildren. "You can't do this episode!" he told the puzzled producer. "You're competing with *Little House on the Prairie* and you've got to keep a hard-action line or the viewers will switch over."

It was too late to change the storyline and when "Claws" aired, true to Freddie's warning, the series dipped from fourth to nineteenth in the ratings. Executive producer Harve Bennett got Silverman on the phone: "I salute your instinct! We won't do that kind of show again." How did Freddie know that "Claws" would be perceived by the viewers as too soft? Because the "audience expectation," as implanted by program announcements, would perforce invoke the innocuous images of "kids and cuddly animals."

Maxim 11: "Cartoons aren't only for kids." For Freddie, the much-bruited-about "family hour" came as a lucky break. As Filmways TV chief Perry Lafferty tells it: "Most comedy has gotten too sophisticated now for 8 P.M., so you're limited to things like *Happy Days* and *Laverne & Shirley,* which are Freddie's. And you can't do shows with violence, so there you have Freddie's *Six Million Dollar Man* and *Bionic Woman*—a lot of flying around and derring-do but no shooting. See how clever it was to think of that solution? He has lined up shows that have almost cartoon overtones."

But it's not only kids who are watching these programs, according to Silverman: "I have to say that the shows with 'cartoon overtones' are among the most popular television programming for adults in the whole country."

Maxim 12: "Grab 'em while they're young." There have been jibes about Silverman's "Saturday morning mentality," but that infamous "daypart" is where he learned how to attract audiences. *Shazzan! The Herculoids! The New Adventures of Superman!* For seven years [as CBS daytime programming chief] he fired off such a barrage of "hard-action" shows for kids that alarmed parents finally got together to protest.

Silverman feels he's gotten a bum rap: "Well, it's just better copy to say, 'He brought the monsters to Saturday morning,' because that's provocative. But I was also the first to move into live action. I put *Children's Film Festival* on the air, which won a Peabody Award. I was the one who put the *CBS Children's Hour* on. I was the one who brought Dr. Seuss to CBS."

There are perhaps other ingredients to "Freddie's Formula," but by the time they're articulated, the prodigious programmer will be someplace else, chortling yet another maxim: "*Don't copy yourself.*"

Yet, isn't Silverman's game, when you get to the bottom line, simply a prescription for maximizing viewers, maximizing ratings, maximizing revenues? Is it all that hard to picture Silverman delivering Faye Dunaway's bravura speech in the movie *Network*? "I'm talking about a $6 cost-per-thousand show! I'm talking about a $130,000 minute! Figure out the revenues of a strip show[1] that sells for 130,000 bucks a minute!"

Bob Wood, the former CBS president who made Fred Silverman his programming chief, who fought the rating battles alongside him for five years said it all: "If you consider the system as a given, then Freddie is merely one helluva practitioner."

1. A strip show is one that typically appears every Monday through Friday at the same time each day.

LIZA BERCOVICI

The Moving Needle Stops

Beyond the expertise of a Fred Silverman, the networks depend on research to test audience reactions to programs before they appear on the air. Audience Studies Incorporated (ASI) does much of the testing of pilots and special episodes of existing series for the networks, for a fee. NBC's vice president for research, William Rubens, claims that paying ASI $5000 for screening and testing is "cost efficient" when the financial stakes of putting a show on the air are considered.

Each season ASI tests 20 to 30 shows for NBC during the "big testing push," four consecutive weeks in late March and early April. Although ASI will also provide data analysis, NBC claims that it analyzes its own data. ABC also uses ASI to test pilots for new program series, but CBS has its own method of pre-testing programs.

ASI's testing results, of course, do not provide a guarantee for the nervous programmer. However, as Liza Bercovici shows, the results of a screening by ASI can be crucial to the network's decision about the probable success of the projected series, much to the irritation of producers and writers.

It's 8 P.M. at Preview House, off the Sunset Strip. Inside, 400 persons, culled by invitation from local shopping centers and by tele-

This essay first appeared December 21, 1974.

phone[1] are watching a pilot for one of the fall's possible new series. It stars Karen Valentine, playing a Portland girl in the final stages of divorce.

Each of these 400 viewers holds a dial with five markings, reading Very Good, Good, Fair, Dull and Very Dull. If the viewer likes what he sees on the screen, up goes the dial to Very Good. If he doesn't, down it comes—possibly to Very Dull. As the dials are turned, these audience reactions are being fed into a giant computer at the back of the theater.[2]

Upstairs, unseen by the audience, network and studio executives are anxiously waiting to see how that computer curve develops.[3] Within minutes, the machine will feed out a number: an average of the audience's composite reaction to the show. How high that number is will be important in determining whether the pilot is to be signed as a new series.

In the case of "The Karen Valentine Program," the curve slowly begins to slip. The network executives nod apprehensively: the audience is not responding as hoped for. The final computer number is a low 62. The questionnaire results, filled out afterward by the audience, are largely negative, though they affirm the star's popularity. Weeks later, ABC rejects the show.

For the record, ABC executives explain that the series wasn't picked up because the pilot hadn't fulfilled what they had in mind for Karen Valentine. But David Davis, who co-produced the pilot, thinks he knows why the network didn't buy it. "I am a victim of the tests," says he. "If we had tested high, we'd be on the air." Everyone knows how avidly network research departments reach for the weekly Nielsen rating charts. Less well known is this other aspect of network research—program testing; that is, the testing of pilots for

1. The audiences are selected to conform with national demography. Age, sex, income and TV-viewing habits are determined before anyone receives a written invitation to attend any of the "Network Television Program Previews."

2. Ushers walk up and down the aisles throughout the screening, and if any viewer doesn't appear to be taking his or her task seriously, the control booth is notified and the culprit is "electronically removed" from the audience.

3. Garry Marshall, producer of *Laverne & Shirley, Happy Days* and *Mork & Mindy,* sits in the theater rather than the control room during screenings in order to get "the feel" of the audience. He has found this very helpful in determining reaction to pilots of his comedy series because "A 'ha ha' isn't something you need a dial to hear."

new series. With few exceptions, before any pilot is bought as a series, it must first win the audience's seal of approval in such testing.

Understandably, producers and writers hate the whole business. In Hollywood, the very mention of network research is sure to provoke a strong reaction. With obvious restraint, most producers frown and mutter darkly at its name. When the conversation turns to network research, Jim Brooks, the bearded young co-creator/executive producer of *The Mary Tyler Moore Show* and others, leaps up and angrily paces his office floor. "You're not going to find anybody who says it's terrific," he says bitterly. "I find there is nothing testing can tell you that you couldn't tell yourself looking at a film."

Another opponent of the testing system, producer Norman Lear [*Archie Bunker's Place, The Jeffersons, Different Strokes*], says, "For my part, and the part of every producer and director in this town, we would sign a paper tomorrow to do away with those research [departments]. Research is trivial and useless and doesn't function as well as simple human instinct and good taste."

Much of the testing is done at Preview House, which is run by ASI Market Research, Inc. ABC and NBC use it. Before each screening, ASI, seeking audiences that are fairly representative of the mass American viewing public, shows the group a seven-minute Mr. Magoo cartoon—"Magoo Goes Skiing." If an audience responds either too critically or too enthusiastically to the cartoon, the results of that test are adjusted accordingly.[4]

Across the continent, CBS, interestingly, doesn't bother going after carefully picked sample audiences. The network invites its audiences in right off the streets of midtown Manhattan. The practice "is not very scientific," acknowledges Arnold Becker, CBS's assistant director of television network research. "[For] people tend to think that blacks and diverse groups have diverse tastes. In fact, there is a great deal of similarity. Everybody watches everything. The notion that poor blacks like different types of entertainment—that's just not true. *People* like the same kinds of programs."

4. ASI has used the same Magoo cartoon since 1964. Through repeated usage, a typical audience response profile has been developed. Every audience is measured against that standard.

It is this attitude that so upsets TV producers. Opposition to program-testing is based on two arguments:

Argument No. 1. Shows can be made to produce high test scores. "You can cut for ASI, to make sure you build an audience reaction," says Andrew Siegel, ABC's director of comedy programs. "Some producers will have chase scenes and cop scenes and dinosaurs coming out of the walls, and the needle goes up very high."

Argument No. 2. The use of test results in making programming decisions is simply not valid. Reliance on the numbers means that honest programs, which require slow acclimatizing by the audience, won't have time to prove themselves. "The really breakthrough shows will not test well because breakthrough shows require change," agrees Marvin Antonowsky, NBC's vice president of program administration.

In the eyes of Hollywood producers there is one thing even more insidious than program-testing: concept-testing. Concept-testing means handing out one-paragraph descriptions of possible series to a sampling of viewers for their opinions. The reaction this practice provokes in Hollywood can be alarming even in normally quiet, gentle men.

Roy Huggins, [producer] of *The Rockford Files,* joins the dissent. He [wrote] a TV-movie, *The Case Against McCreed,* about the Un-American Activities Committee, only to see it rejected by ABC after poor concept-testing. "Naturally it concept-tested poorly," says he with some asperity. "It's like being asked to say what a cake will be like by tasting the dough."

Still, every once in a while some producers are willing to use testing. *Columbo's* producers wanted to know if viewers were getting tired of Peter Falk's trench coat. (The answer was no.) The producers of *Adam-12* wondered if they should be showing more of the personal life of their police officers. (Answer: No, people tune in to watch the characters perform as policemen.) Research is often used in selecting a title for a series. NBC changed the title of "In Tandem" to *Movin' On.* Research had showed that viewers were more likely to turn to the latter title.[5] . . .

5. *Movin' On* was broadcast on NBC between September 1974 and December 1976. The network grossed a total of $23.1 million in advertising revenues from the series.

In Hollywood, the pervading sentiment is that when a show doesn't make the fall lineup, a poor test score is often to blame; and that network executives are prone to rely on test scores when they are dealing with an innovative, untried story format. Catch-22, add the Hollywood types sardonically, is that most innovative shows (*All in the Family, Mary Tyler Moore, Batman*) produce terrible tests. And in the Russian-roulette world of TV, no network executive wants to be the guy who stakes his career on a daring new show that can't produce a high test score.

It would be unfair to imply that network executives are robots who execute programming decisions according to computer scores. . . . *All in the Family,* as noted above, tested badly at both ABC and CBS but, despite low scores, made it to the air—thanks largely to the audacity of CBS president Robert Wood.[6]

In the same vein, a high test score doesn't necessarily mean a pilot will be picked up by the network. Producer Sherwood Schwartz is still trying to figure out why a spin-off of *The Brady Bunch*—"Kelly's Kids," which grabbed an astonishingly high 86 at Preview House—wasn't used by ABC. "The Preview House number is quite important, but it doesn't sell a show," says Schwartz ruefully.

But in Hollywood, where it all happens, they still wish that testing business would go away. "We've grown up. TV has grown up," says MTM's Jim Brooks. "We're too big for that silliness any more."

6. NBC's vice president of research suggests *All in the Family* was an unusual case. He stated in 1979 that, in his nine years at NBC, "I can't remember even one show testing poorly and then doing well on the air."

BOB MACKENZIE

I'll Have Two Martinis and 52 Weeks of Name That Tune

Independent stations profit from the best audience test of all—was the show popular?—because most of their programming consists of off-network syndications, that is, series previously shown on the networks. Any series that beats the odds, about 35 to 1, and lasts long enough to provide a sufficient number of episodes for syndication can be profitable. It is through syndication that the producer of a popular series makes the money to keep his company going; the vast majority of network shows are produced at a loss. *The Mary Tyler Moore Show* lasted on CBS for eight years, yet reportedly barely broke even. When the show was syndicated, the profits were substantial.

In recent years, the inflated economics of television have made successful syndicated shows more profitable than ever. In 1976, a Nashville, Tenn., station paid $450 an episode for exclusive rights to show in its viewing area the successful off-network comedy series, *The Brady Bunch.* The same station was charged $4750 in 1977 for a segment of another comedy series, *Happy Days.* ABC sold *Laverne & Shirley* to the station in 1978 for $9100 per episode, with the provision that syndication would not begin before 1981 (to protect the first-run segments still playing). The prices became even more inflated in the big cities: a Los Angeles station was reported to have paid $7,370,000 for 134 episodes of *Laverne & Shirley,* or $61,500 an episode. The cost of the show was only slightly lower in New York and in Philadelphia it went for $37,000 an episode.

This essay first appeared May 22, 1976.

Network affiliates buy off-network shows for morning, late afternoon or late night broadcast. Also, rather than produce their own programming, most affiliates purchase shows to fill the prime-time access period before 8:00 P.M., ET. These shows as well as off-network offerings are exhibited at the annual convention of the National Association of Television Program Executives, at which many of the purchases are made. The February 1980 NATPE convention attracted 251 distributors, one of whom had more than sixty program series for sale to station representatives. How a potential buyer might go about making a purchase is described in Bob MacKenzie's article.

Well, Chief, I'm in my third day of the NATPE convention and I'm still standing upright. Either that or someone has laid my room on its side.

You may have to overlook a few typing errors here. This is not because I have been offered four-dozen alcoholic drinks in the past three days and refused more than half of them, or because I have put away enough hors d'oeuvres to feed every refugee in Guatemala, or because there are so many sexy hostesses here that my eyes hurt from too-close focusing.

I'm just tired, Chief, tired. Have you ever watched seven new television programs in one day? Have you ever had your ear bent by six fired-up syndication salesmen in one afternoon? . . .

The NATPE convention, as you know, is the annual marketplace of the television-syndication business. It is the most concentrated confluence of hard sell and hard partying in an industry known for fervor in both departments. This year's convention is in San Francisco, which is a beautiful city if anybody ever goes outside. But the lobby, the bars, and three floors of rooms and suites are jammed with program buyers and sellers—wheeling and dealing, wining and dining, and talking shop at a prodigious rate.[1]

Let me paint a typical picture for you. We step into the suite of

1. This article discusses a traditionally important aspect of the NATPE Annual Convention—the selling of syndicated programming. It should be noted that the NATPE convention also includes various programming workshops and seminars.

Worldvision Enterprises, a giant packager that handles 150 shows turned out by sixty independent producers. A salesman greets us at the door. We unclench our fingers momentarily and a glass of Scotch appears in them. The main room of the suite looks something like the floor of the Stock Exchange, except stockbrokers don't drink while they work. The salesman guides us to a couch just as another salesman bursts from an adjoining room. "Where are those order forms?" he barks. He has just sold 128 half-hours of *The Doris Day Show* to a big station; in his excitement he has taken the customer into the hors d'oeuvres room instead of the closing office.

Over in the corner, Monty Hall of *Let's Make a Deal* is shaking hands with station managers and program directors. On the couch next to us, a Worldvision vice president tries a sincere pitch on a visitor. "There are only three comedies coming off network. *My Three Sons, The Odd Couple, The Doris Day Show.* And *Doris* represents more value. The demographics are abundant on this. *Sons* is going to show more kids. Do you want kids or do want women 18 to 49?" Another Worldvision man yells, "OK, who wants to see *Rising Star*?" During the rush we make our escape.

As you know, network programming has filled a decreasing share of prime-time television hours, since the [FCC's Prime-Time Access Rule] turned back a [portion] of prime time to the affiliate stations. Nonnetwork programs are sold to individual stations or station groups by independent distributors and production companies. The NATPE convention brings buyers and sellers together. Program buyers from some 250 stations across the country are roaming through the suites in various states of curiosity and wariness. With almost 1000 shows for sale here, the competition is fierce and the pitch vigorous.

The salespeople offer lavish giveaways. Tomorrow afternoon the wives of the station execs will be treated to a special, nontelevised session of *Let's Make a Deal,* with Monty Hall in person handing out $10,000 in prizes.

Even the smaller syndicators offer lures to draw the strolling trade. At the door of Bill Burrud Productions' tiny suite, a sign proclaims: "Win a Round-the-World Cruise." Once in the door, a prospect will get a ticket in a drawing, a sales talk and a look at a Burrud nature-show pilot on a cassette player. At Yongestreet Program Services the visitor gets to pan for gold with a magnet in a small sandbox; if he picks up a nugget he wins a Polaroid camera. If he misses the nugget he'll probably get a camera anyway. *Hee Haw* is sold in almost every available market, but Yongestreet, which syndicates the show, likes to keep the customers happy.

A small but deliciously tense drama has been acted out here these past three days. The NBC O&O (owned-and-operated stations) group came to the convention with one of its prime-time-access half hours still available. That news electrified the suppliers—those, at least, who had a big half hour to sell.

For an independent producer, the key to getting a prime-time-access show off the ground is a sale to a station group—the four or five stations owned and operated by a network or other big company, such as Metromedia or Group W. These stations, and network O&O's, are usually big-city stations. With such a group paying the ground-floor costs, the producer has his basics just about covered and can go on to sell other stations. But if he doesn't land a station group, he might just as well scrap the pilot and start over. His chances of syndicating it at a profit in prime time are about the same as his chances of striking oil in his back yard.

Some syndicators, with not much investment at stake, seemed philosophical about their chances of nabbing the NBC half hour. Alan Courtney of Yongestreet, the *Hee Haw* packager, was offering a new half-hour version of *The Hollywood Palace.* Courtney, a big, hearty sort, told me, "They'll either take it or they won't. And they probably won't."

Courtney could afford to be casual, having invested only in a brief demo tape and a brochure. But up in Time-Life Television's princely suite, where a buffet spread included 100 kinds of imported cheese, and a buxom waitress in a low-cut gown leaned forward elaborately as she served drinks, there was tension in the air. Time-Life had invested much money and effort in a finished half-hour pilot for *People Cover Story*, a show spotlighting a different celebrity each week. The pilot subject was Ann-Margret. The ABC O&O group had helped finance the pilot, but then had changed its corporate mind and bought *The Gong Show,* another new show, instead. Time-Life would make a last-ditch effort to sell *People Cover Story* to the NBC representatives.

Inside bettors were giving a fighting chance to *Hollywood Palace,* no chance at all to *People Cover Story,* and a long-shot possibility to Worldvision's *Rising Star,* a half-hour game-panel show featuring amateur talent. But the really likely contenders, insiders knew, were two half hours about strange phenomena: *The Unexplained,* a Wolper series being pitched by Columbia Pictures Television, and *In Search of . . . ,* an Alan Landsburg series financed by Bristol-Myers.

While the contenders sweated it out, happy was the syndicator who came to the convention with a station group already in his pocket. In the cramped two-room suite of Firestone Program Syndication, a dozen station reps squeezed into a small bedroom to see the *Gong* pilot, one of the runaway hits of the convention. They sprawled on the bed or squatted on the floor as Len Firestone, a handsome, winning chap with a deep California tan, gave a preliminary spiel.

"First of all, let me tell you this is a definite go. It's been sold to the ABC O&O's. Now, what you'll see is a rough pilot, not the finished product. We'll be asking for input from you. It's a game, it's a variety show. It's zany, it's crazy, it's kooky."

The cassette of *Gong* unwound. It was crazy all right. A panel of celebrities judged a succession of amateur performers, most of them awful. Occasionally the panelists rang a gong to express their disapproval. The performers included an Elvis Presley imitator and a lady who played the cello while singing "Blue Moon." I swear it.

As the tape ended, Firestone got up in front again. "Lemme ask you now: who wants to buy it?"

There was a pregnant silence. Finally a program director from a Washington, D.C., station spoke up. "We're interested enough to think about it," he said.

Firestone responded instantly, "You know, we're talking to your pals at Post-Newsweek. They're very interested." This was a gentle reminder to the Washington man that Post-Newsweek, which owns a competing station in D.C., might move first. [It did.]

The Washington man was playing it cool, but obviously he felt the squeeze. If a station man passes up a show that becomes a hit for a competitor, his stock can go down pretty fast.

This sort of action was proceeding on a hundred fronts all weekend. Monday, the tension declined to a mild fever as some large hopes were abruptly dimmed. Hardly anybody had actually seen the NBC O&O people, but they had what you might call an almost tangible omnipresence. Today they made their move; they closed the last prime-time-access spot by buying *In Search of.* . . . The word went around quickly; a lot of syndicators resignedly got out the red ink.

But the beat goes on: from the mightiest suites to the dinkiest rooms. Wanta buy *The Six Million Dollar Man*? So does everybody else. Sure it won't be available [for off-network play for two years], but if you don't buy it now, the other guy will. Don't you need 147 half hours of *Dobie Gillis*? Sorry, *Medical Center* is sold out. How about 29 hardly used episodes of *Then Came Bronson*?

There's more to tell, but I think my eyes are beginning to cross. I'm going to go find a nice, quiet place where nobody ever heard the terms "audience skew," "access" or "demographics."

Goodnight, Chief.

EDITH EFRON

What Makes a Hit?

What elements combine to make a television series successful? The answer to this question, if there is one, is vital, given the financial risks of producing a show that may place high in the ratings or may be at the bottom of the heap. Producer David Gerber has said, "television has become a land rush for a hit show."

Edith Efron interviewed four of television's most successful producers in pursuit of key values or central ideas common to top-rated series. The producers interviewed were: Lee Rich (*The Waltons, Eight Is Enough*); Grant Tinker (*The Mary Tyler Moore Show, Lou Grant*); Quinn Martin (*Barnaby Jones, The FBI*); and Gene Roddenberry (*Star Trek*).

EFRON: You are all producers of top TV hits, series that [were] acclaimed by the mass audience. Can you tell me, briefly, what values you try to project in your work? Mr. Martin, would you start?

MARTIN: Well, let me put it in a very corny phrase. I am a patriot. In the police stories that I do, I show the police in an idealized way. Without respect for the police, I think we'd have a breakdown in our society. If I were to make shows that just capitalized on the nitty-gritty, dirty side of police work, there would be a very negative effect. That doesn't mean that we wouldn't do a show portraying a corrupt policeman. But 90 per cent of the time or more, we show the police as idealistic.

EFRON: You're not in the least abashed about creating heroes?

This essay first appeared April 27, 1974.

MARTIN: No. I've been in the business for quite a few years. I know that the antiheroic shows like *East Side/West Side*[1] have lost—because the protagonist never won. We're hitting the great heartland of America, and they want shows where the leading man does something positive, and has a positive result. Every time you go against that, you can almost automatically say you are going to fail.

EFRON: Do you, yourself, share "heartland America's" love for heroes?

MARTIN: Yes, I believe in heroes myself. And I know that people sitting in American living rooms will just not accept an antihero, or a bad protagonist.

EFRON: OK, what about you, Mr. Rich? What values do you try to project in *The Waltons*?

RICH: I approach things from a realistic point of view. But I don't mean the nitty-gritty *East Side/West Side* realism, either. By realism, I mean a full characterization in which the people have flaws as well as virtues, anchored in a specific time and place. There's no need for cardboard heroes. People are willing to see protagonists make mistakes. But they do want to see them correct those mistakes and solve their problems and progress.

MARTIN: Yes, I agree. Karl Malden (*Streets of San Francisco*) may lose his head because his daughter is being attacked, and may overstep his bounds as a policeman. But before the show is over, he will do the right thing. So I think we are saying the same thing.

RICH: Yes. Actually, something odd goes on in *The Waltons*. The mother is really a zealot. She's a Baptist minister's daughter who will not allow whisky or bad words in the house. She's a zealot—and the grandmother is a bigot.

EFRON: Is it for their zealotry and bigotry that they're loved?

RICH: Oh, no! I sincerely believe that the Waltons are loved because fundamentally they are good honest people. The family is a loving family, and everyone in it has respect for the others. We find that people say, "Yes, that's *exactly* what my family was like"—or

1. *East Side/West Side* starred George C. Scott and Cecily Tyson as New York social workers dealing with problems of the indigent. Its standing with critics was far higher than its standing in the ratings and the show only lasted for the 1963–64 season.

"That *wasn't* what my family was like, but I wish it were." I think part of the success of this series is because of what is going on in the country today, the loss of values. Many people see ethical qualities in this family that they hope they can get back to.

EFRON: By ethical qualities, you mean such things as responsibility, courage in the face of adversity?

RICH: Yes, definitely.

EFRON: Then you are projecting an ethical ideal in *The Waltons* just as Mr. Martin is projecting an ideal in his police shows?

RICH: Yes. Absolutely.

EFRON: How about you, Mr. Roddenberry? What values made *Star Trek* such a hit?

RODDENBERRY: Well, a couple of things are obvious, particularly from the college response at that time. *Star Trek* was telling the kids: it's *not* all over, there *is* a tomorrow, the challenges are *not* all gone, there *is* heroism. It's really just the beginning for us, if we want to be brave about it. To young-minded people, that was extraordinarily important. Also *Star Trek* was saying that diversity is a value . . . that to be different is not necessarily to be bad. That we don't have the right to interfere with or kill other people . . . and finally, *Star Trek* stressed the idea that people cared for each other, that there were rules, that discipline, bravery and decency were rewarded.

EFRON: Why was everyone so smitten with Mr. Spock?

MARTIN: Because he stood for loyalty and reliability!

EFRON: Did his seriousness about life and his rationality cause any of the audience response?

RODDENBERRY: Oh yes, I think so. When I created him, I said to myself: "If I could just get rid of the emotions that plague me, and work things out logically—ah, the things I could do!" That's what Spock represented.

EFRON: Finally, how about your shows, Mr. Tinker? What are their values?

TINKER: Well . . . the qualities in our shows—*The Mary Tyler Moore Show,* for example—are not as important, perhaps, as those we've been discussing. These are comedies, after all—and if the theme were too serious, we'd lose the comedic element.

RODDENBERRY: You're underestimating them, Grant. Don't you realize that Mary is a hero?

EFRON: Yes. She does project something very sturdy. She has a tenacious gaiety in the face of her dilemmas.

TINKER: Yes, I agree. She does come close, in her 1970s version, to the good old-fashioned virtues we find in *The Waltons.* In fact, now that I think of it, in its own way the show is projecting all the different values we have been talking about. The show appears to be rather hip for TV, but in fact she and all the characters in that show—forgetting their comedic eccentricities—are all four-square people.

RODDENBERRY: You know, this is interesting. All of our shows are very different, and yet I realize there's a great deal in common among them. They all have straight heroes, family groups, rules and order. They all have squarish values. They attract audiences from the youngest viewers to the oldest. And all were hits. That's exciting. It seems to reveal something very important about the nature of our country.

TINKER: When you get right down to it, has there ever been a big hit in TV that was anything *but* that?

MARTIN: Never.

RICH: No, never.

RODDENBERRY: And they offer quite a contrast with the shows that come and go every year, where the only principle behind the hero is to win a million dollars, or to put someone in jail. Those shallow-motive heroes come and go. But the ones with the solid values stay. They're the big hits.

RICH: There's another interesting contrast—between the hits and the imitations. People are always trying to imitate the solid-value hits. But these imitations generally do not work. Why don't they work? My belief is that they spend so much time trying to copy the original that they lose something in the copy.

EFRON: Don't you think that the *kind* of person who copies is exactly the kind of person who *couldn't* project the values you are talking about?

RICH: Yes, exactly.

TINKER: Yes.

MARTIN: That takes care of *that* question!

EFRON: How would you tie all this to the "scoundrel-with-the-heart-of-gold" shows? Bilko, the con man . . . Ralph Kramden, the braggart . . . or Archie Bunker, the bigot?[2] Some would argue that *All in the Family* contradicts your view that the big hits always relay solid values.

RODDENBERRY: Not at all. The key phrase is: "heart of gold." None of them contradicts the pattern. Archie Bunker certainly doesn't contradict it. For all of his verbal bigotry, he never does a thing that actually *hurts* anyone.

TINKER: Right. If he actually hurt anyone, the audience would reject him.

RICH: That's right. Nobody ever gets hurt in *All in the Family.* I saw a show recently about a Chicano family who wanted to move in next door. When Archie heard about it, he went crazy. As the story worked out, the Chicanos did not get the house next door—they got a *better* house! If the story hadn't been resolved that way, the show would be out!

EFRON: And Archie would be out?

RODDENBERRY: Exactly!

EFRON: Let's examine this public ethical response a bit more. What about the so-called "relevant" shows—the ones that explicitly professed great concern for people? Most of them failed disastrously. Why?

TINKER: Because the shows you're asking about portray unsolvable problems. People don't want to be reminded of those problems.

RODDENBERRY: I'm not so sure that's the reason. I think people were consciously trying to write "relevant" shows. But you just can't write good stories that way. You have to start with an idea that's very important to you. Then, as it develops, it may—or may not—include "relevant" elements.

MARTIN: That's true. We included a good many of the so-called

2. Sargeant Ernie Bilko, played by Phil Silvers, was the leading character in one of the most successful comedy series of the 1950s. The series began in 1955 as *You'll Never Get Rich* and ended its network run in 1959 as *The Phil Silvers Show.* Bus driver Ralph Kramden is a character created by Jackie Gleason and has appeared since 1951 in various Gleason series. Archie Bunker has been played by Carroll O'Connor since *All in the Family* debuted in January 1971.

relevant isues in our shows—but they were tied in with conflict, and whodunits—and an exciting story. And those shows succeeded.

EFRON: Didn't the relevant shows tend to be antiheroic shows?

MARTIN: I'm not sure. The ones I remember very clearly were *The Storefront Lawyers, The Young Lawyers.* They had heroic people—but they were all involved in very heavy material.

RODDENBERRY: But were they *heroes*? Were the faced with jeopardy? Going around and helping people is not being faced with jeopardy. They *weren't* heroes.

TINKER: No, they weren't heroes. *The Storefront Lawyers,* all those shows had protagonists who were social-worker types. They were all *anti*heroes.

RICH: Right.

TINKER: They were *cheek-turners.* I can't remember a cheek-turner who has ever made it in TV. Even Mary isn't a cheek-turner. Eventually she stands up and says, "I want $50 more a week because the guy who had the job before me got that."

EFRON: Do you think this is true only of TV? Isn't it equally true of movies, plays, novels?

MARTIN: Yes. If you look at the movies, it's *The Poseidon Adventure, The Day of the Jackal, Airport* that [make] the fortunes. Tightly plotted stories in which men overcome great obstacles. In fact, throughout the history of literature, the heroes have never been cheek-turners, they've been battlers. People fighting against great odds, in life-and-death conflicts. Those are the universal themes of all heroic literature.

EFRON: Which raises another question. In view of the universality of such themes, why does the intelligentsia generally call TV plays junk?

TINKER: They are turned off by their profusion. It's incredible that you can tune in at any time and find competently crafted entertainment on the air. They think that just because there's so much of it, it must necessarily be junk.

RODDENBERRY: Oh, you know . . . they say that 90 per cent of TV is junk. But 90 per cent of *everything* is junk; 90 per cent of all novels is junk; 90 per cent of all painting is junk.

MARTIN: I wouldn't settle for that. I'd say that 75 per cent of TV is better than *most* movies that have been made; 75 per cent of TV is better than *most* plays on Broadway; 75 per cent of TV is better than *most* novels. You tune in our shows—they're carefully crafted, they have beginnings, middles and ends, they have plots, they're entertaining.

EFRON: But you'll note that the literary world doesn't bestow its prizes on plot writers.

RODDENBERRY: But the public does. The best-selling authors are always plot writers.

MARTIN: Of course. These are forms that have been important to people since time immemorial. Heroes, plots go back to the tales told in the caves. They're built into civilization.

TINKER: People loved stories then—and they still do.

EFRON: All the more reason to wonder why the plot is disdained by the literati. In fact, every hack on a talk show feels he has the right to insult the successful plot writers.

RODDENBERRY: That's because the hacks *can't* do it.

MARTIN: Oh, what's the difference if they sneer at Jacqueline Susann or at Irving Wallace on talk shows? It jacks up the sneerers' self-esteem. It's unimportant.

RICH: Sure, it's fashionable. It makes them look like critics.

EFRON: It's fashionable—but is it just?

RODDENBERRY: No, it's unjust. Irving Wallace has been hurt. But he's got his head screwed on right. He knows what he is doing. He goes ahead and does his work.

MARTIN: Neil Simon has been hurt too. But I'd rather see his plays than read some plotless, formless novel.

RICH: Basically, this attack is coming from a small, angry group—mainly in New York and from Cambridge, maybe. They're of no importance to those of us who write for the public.

RODDENBERRY: I think this whole attack is typical of New York. New York has historically produced these people. I remember taking a class in writing at Columbia. There were just 30 people there. I was ready to give up after three days. I didn't know what they were talking about! And out of the whole group, I'm the only who ever became a writer!

TINKER: That's not television's New York. Or television's Boston.

The story is *not* dead. The ivory-tower people are irrelevant to the public, and to entertainment TV.

RICH: Completely irrelevant.

EFRON: Then the disdain of the critics, of the poets-in-residence, doesn't bother you?

MARTIN: Poets-in-residence? Do you know what the poets-in-residence actually do in their spare time? They watch TV!

LEMUEL B. SCHOFIELD

Don't Look For the Home-town Touch

The networks provide most of what we see on television, but the basis for our current broadcasting system is generally considered to be service to the local community. Jack Harris, station manager of KPRC-TV (Houston) and 1978 winner of the National Association of Broadcasters' highest achievement award, has said "a station must justify its being in what it does in its local operation."

Local ownership and operation of local stations has been encouraged since the beginning of broadcasting. In 1962 Congress asked for "a commercial television system which will be not only truly competitive on a national scale in all large centers of population, but would permit all communities of appreciable size to have at least one television station as an outlet for local self-expression."

The Federal Communication Commission is required by law to allocate television licenses to provide "a fair, efficient and equitable distribution of . . . service." Thus, the frequency allocation scheme adopted by the FCC emphasizes the importance of local service. The alternative would have been to allocate fewer, clear-channel television stations (that is, a frequency assigned exclusively to one station). These stations would have covered large areas, ensured more people a larger number of stations and saved valuable frequency space for other communications services. However, the Commission placed a higher priority on the concept of a station for each community.

Unfortunately, the opportunity for "local self-expression" is going

This essay first appeared April 14, 1979.

largely unexploited. The average commercial television station broadcasts less than 10 per cent local programming. A 1979 FCC report calculated that network affiliates carried 95 per cent of the prime-time programming offered by their networks and 87 per cent of all network nonprime-time offerings. Norman Lear commented: "Stations are money making machines run by people who play golf all day. They just turn on the network switch, the programs go out, the money comes in and everything is fine. . . ." Station manager Lemuel Schofield gives his explanation of why many stations do little local programming other than local news.

"You know, I'll bet if you folks put on a local country-music show, everybody'd watch."

"Hey! How come you guys never carry any of the city softball-league games on weekends? You'd get a bigger audience than you do with that dumb wrestling show."

"I wonder if your station has ever thought of doing a local talk show. You know, like Johnny Carson or something. You could use home-town talent and everyone would tune in."

Calls like these come into local stations all around the country every day. Some are motivated by simple self-interest. But they all raise the implied question: "Why isn't there more local programming on TV?"

Probably most stations would like to do more local shows. They are, after all, the "fun" of broadcasting.

And some stations in the larger cities do produce some local shows. But why isn't there more local programming done by a "typical" station?

Surely, with perhaps as many as 750,000 people in its viewing area, a medium-sized station should be able to produce a number of shows; even the smaller stations, with fewer than 250,000 viewers, should be anxious to do a few.

But most stations simply don't have the money. The notion that a television license is a license to print dollars is an exaggeration.

There are many stations that lose money every year and more that struggle to break even.[1]

But aren't local stations obligated, under the law, to operate in the "public interest"? Yes. However, the Federal Communications Commission does not set any specific standards for local programming. The FCC requires annual reports from all stations that must state how much local programming was carried in a typical week during the preceding year. If that report shows that less than 5 per cent of all programs was locally produced, the Commission may take a closer look.[2]

But this minimum translates to 54 minutes—less than one hour a day. Most stations exceed this standard with just their local news programs. And, indeed, the commitment to local news programming is one that is taken seriously by most broadcasters.

But a good news operation is costly. People, equipment, cars, film, news services—they all add up to a staggering amount, from many thousands a year for a modest operation to several hundred thousand for larger news departments. So, after budgets are set for the news effort, little is left for other local programs. Besides, news shows are usually profitable, while other local programs rarely are.

But local programming sometimes works well. For example, Wally Dunham, at WCPO-TV in Cincinnati and later at KTEW in Tulsa, Okla., created a program that has been imitated by other

1. The latest FCC official figures, available in March 1980, regarding profits of local television stations were those for 1978. Of the 642 stations—460 VHF and 182 UHF—which reported their earnings, 83 reported losses—36 VHF (7.8 per cent of the total number of stations) and 47 UHF (25.8 per cent). Of these 83 stations, 58 lost $25,000 or less for the year. Of the 559 stations reporting profits, 362 stations—308 VHF and 54 UHF—made profits of $600,000 or more. Only 10 VHF stations and 20 UHF stations reported profits of $50,000 or less.

2. The FCC has internal guidelines for processing renewal applications. One provision of these guidelines is that the applications of television licensees, except UHF independents, who propose to broadcast less than 5 per cent local programming between the hours of 6:00 A.M. and midnight will be referred by the FCC staff to the commissioners for their review. Because the percentage in the guideline is so low and covers an eighteen-hour period, because it does not apply to UHF independents (some of which the Commission fears may not have the financial resources to do local programming) and because the guideline refers to promises made for the upcoming three-year renewal period rather than to actual performance during the past three years, neither the staff nor the commissioners have had to be concerned about applications failing to meet the guideline.

broadcasters. Usually titled *Call the Doctor,* it is produced in cooperation with a local medical society. Each week (or month) a topic is chosen and a panel of physicians selected. Viewers call the studio with questions. Although the panelists do not diagnose or prescribe on the air, the program provides a helpful service. The series has attracted a large audience.

But how about drama? Situation comedy? Variety? There is no way. If a local station were to produce such a program, it would have to be so good that the obvious comparison with network shows wouldn't be ludicrous. And few local broadcasters have the kind of money that is required for that.

Broadcasting magazine estimates that producing one episode of *Mork & Mindy,* for example, costs [$285,000]. No local station can afford that.

Well, some might suggest that the answer is local sports. The program is already there; all the station needs to do is put it on the air.

But for most small—and medium—market stations, the costs of remote telecasts prohibit them, except on rare occasions. Such a station cannot afford to maintain its own color-television unit with cameras, video-tape machines and associated equipment. The unit must be rented. But even the smallest ones lease for about $1200 a day. With more sophisticated gear (slow motion, isolated camera, etc.) the figure moves quickly up into the thousands.

As the total climbs, the desire on the part of the station manager to broadcast the event diminishes. Nevertheless, some are carried, at a financial loss, to enhance the station's local image. But this is an expensive luxury.

Why not do a local talk show? First, there is the painful truth that local talk shows tend to be dull. The host or hostess is rarely a brilliant professional who can interview a myriad of guests discussing a variety of subjects. The availability of interesting people is limited in smaller markets. The majority of those who want to appear have either a worn ax to grind or a product to push. And there is the question of cost.

Woody Fraser, executive producer of *America Alive!,* NBC's canceled attempt at a daytime talk show, said that the network committed more than $240,000 a week to the program. Even *The Mike Douglas Show,* a less ambitious syndicated production, is estimated to cost about $165,000 a week. For some stations, the entire budget for all local programs including news, is less for a full year than the cost of *Douglas* or *America Alive*! for one week.

Many responsible broadcasters do make an effort to serve the young people in their audience with locally produced children's programs. But few of them are any good. Charles W. Larsen, director of programming at WNBC-TV in New York, says: "With some very notable exceptions, local children's-television programs around the country are a poor stepchild of our industry. With small or nonexistent budgets, they are cranked out of the local-station machine solely to meet the children's/instructional quota to the FCC."

Rust Craft Broadcasting Co., owner of several television stations, has developed a program called *News for Little People,* a daily series of five-minute shows directed at the younger viewer. With only a modest budget, this effort has for several years had a sizable following. Unfortunately, this is one of the "notable exceptions."

Then what can a local station do? News and little else? Well, some are still doing live wrestling! Some still do local dance parties that usually look oh, so sad when they play next to *American Bandstand* or *Soul Train.*

But the best the average broadcaster can hope for is the occasional special. It is here that he can draw upon his limited budgets, his restricted facilities, and the overtaxed creative resources of his staff. A Fourth-of-July special produced in cooperation with a local historical society. A program of Christmas music performed by various church choirs or by choruses and glee clubs from an area college. A documentary on a recent event of local interest or on a home-town team that wins a state title.

The special need not have a big budget. Nor does it have to be put together under the same time pressures that accompany a weekly program. Nor does it need to be dull.

But the special will take some dollars. And, because of their inability to compete for mass audiences with the higher-budgeted network and syndicated programs, local shows are not usually a very efficient use of advertising dollars. But they are an expression of a community's interest and they are an excellent way for an advertiser to build his local image.

More and more, leading local businesses—banks, department stores, utilities—are realizing the value of association with local-television specials. Some are even underwriting a portion of the costs.

In Chattanooga, Tenn., a station brought together a local bank and the "Singing Mocs" of the University of Tennessee at Chattanooga. With a relatively small outlay by the bank, the group was able to prerecord the audio portion of the program at a professional studio. The station made a special effort in building sets. The final product was an excellent special that won an award from the Chattanooga Advertising Federation as Best Program of the Year. Without that extra support from the bank, the program would have been just another show.

Good local shows can be done and sometimes are. But given present conditions, they will continue to be rare exceptions to the usual rule.

DAYTIME PROGRAMMING

Although daytime programming attracts a smaller audience than does prime-time programming, the networks traditionally make 50 to 60 per cent of their profits during the hours between 10 A.M. and 4 P.M. Advertisers pay less for daytime advertisements, an average of $18,000 per minute in 1979, but the programs require a much lower budget than do the prime-time shows and the audience is loyal.

Women make up about two-thirds of the daytime audience. According to some CBS research on the subject, during an average week slightly under 50 million women, or 63 per cent of all women in television households, turn on the television in the daytime. The average viewing time for these women is about ten hours a week. The average viewing time per week is even higher for the 25 million women who are considered to be regular viewers.

Because the daytime audience is more homogeneous than the prime-time audience, a narrower range of products is projected to appeal specifically to housewives who, the advertisers hope, have large families and do the bulk of the family shopping. Approximately 90 per cent of all daytime sales pitches are for toiletries, over-the-counter medicines, soaps and cleansers, and food products.

Neither the networks nor the advertisers have shown much inclination to experiment with the content of daytime programming. As in the days of radio, soap operas and game shows constitute the great majority of the programs. The fact that what little experimentation has occurred has generally failed in the ratings suggests that the audience also has little wish to tamper with the status quo.

ELLEN TORGERSON

Heartache, Illness and Crime Do *Pay*

Soap operas have always been and still are the most popular daytime programs. Nine of the ten highest-rated daytime shows in 1978–79 were soaps—the exception was an ABC game show, *Family Feud.* Soaps are very profitable for the networks. NBC's highest-rated soap, the ninety-minute *Another World* was earning a profit of about $3 million per month in early 1980. In that same period NBC was clearing almost $2 million a month from its one-hour soap *Days of Our Lives* and about $1 million per month from the thirty-minute *Doctors.*

Ellen Torgerson discusses the continuing importance of soaps to the networks and to daytime viewers.

Around 11 A.M. every day of the work-week, the serious business of choosing between a $500 imported Italian suit and a similarly priced English tweed comes to a predestined, screeching halt in one exclusive Beverly Hills men's shop. Customers and salespeople alike happily file into a corner, turn on the television—and ritually watch another consuming episode of *The Young and the Restless.*

At a New Year's Eve party, Jack Herzberg, producer of *Days of Our Lives,* not knowing a soul, stands quietly by a group of doctors chatting about diseases and patients. A woman nudges him:

"And what is your specialty, doctor?"

"I'm not a doctor," says Herzberg, properly humble, "I'm a television producer . . . *Days of Our Lives.*"

This essay first appeared July 8, 1978.

One of the doctors overhears, and—eyes pleasurably alight—says, "I must compliment you on the way you handled that *placenta privea* operation a few weeks back."

Even our duly elected President of these United States enjoys a soap opera now and again. He watches *All My Children.* Miss Lillian watches, too.

Nobody is in the closet any more: everybody looks at soap operas—intellectuals, college kids, heads of government, barflies, taxi drivers, members of symphony orchestras, welfare recipients, dental hygienists. . . . They gaze unblinkingly at the intricate vagaries and velleities of some fourteen soaps purveyed Monday through Friday by the three major networks.

Nor have the networks lost their traditional audience of housewives, shut-ins, retirees—and a shifting population of teen-agers. Some 20 million loyalists watch at least two soaps a day, starting late in the morning and going on remorselessly until late in the afternoon. Unquestionably, soap operas—or "daytime programs," as the writers, producers, actors and directors of soaps prefer to call them—are as much a part of indigenous American culture as maize, baseball, Manifest Destiny, jazz and margarine.

Gone is the scornful reaction that soaps are merely lower-middle-class melodrama. Soaps are now widely regarded as a legitimate subject for formal sociological study; academe offers courses in soapers. But the soaps' primary function is to generate steady millions for network coffers—and, indeed, to help support the flighty extravagances of nighttime programming.

Soaps are a network's bread and butter, and internecine warfare among broadcasters for control of the daytime airwaves often rages wildly. In 1975, NBC—reaching for ever more profit in television's wealthiest market—expanded its two top-rated soaps, *Days of Our Lives* and *Another World,* to an hour each, effectively flattening the opposition's game shows and half-hour soaps. CBS waited as long as it could, then did the same thing with an hour-long version of *As the World Turns.* Eventually, daytime viewing may be all hour-long soaps, scrapping with each other for the same lucrative audience.

Many prime-time shows lose money for their networks; they need the daytime profits—increasingly healthy all the time—to finance more expensively produced nighttime series. [In 1978–79] an episode of a [one-hour] show cost around [$350,000] to produce, but brought in revenues of only [$250,000]. [In 1978–79] average hour-long soaps cost a trifling $170,000 for an entire week of five episodes, and the daily advertising yield approached $120,000–$600,000 a week; that's a 250 per cent profit.

Everyone, then, is out to win the devoted watcher who, presumably, will buy all those products alluringly displayed in the commercials on the soaps.

"Advertisers prefer a certain kind of viewer," says Arnold Becker, CBS vice president of national research. "What they want is the person who's doing the buying for a large family." Certainly. Six bags of corn chips purchased makes a sponsor merrier than one bag purchased. Or none. What that means is that the most desirable viewer is under 50 and most probably a woman.

Take *The Young and the Restless.* It is, according to Becker, the highest-rated daytime show CBS has among the 18-to-34-year-old audience; 72 per cent of the show's total audience are adult women, 14 per cent are adult men, 6 per cent are teen-agers and 8 per cent are children under 12. The program is a constant source of delight and money for CBS. In the last week of March and the first week of April [1978], *The Young and the Restless* had a Nielsen rating of 7.9 (about 5,700,000 TV households), making it one of the top soaps on the air, along with *Another World* (8.4), *As the World Turns* (8.4), and *All My Children* (7.8).

The Young and the Restless has been delivering a diurnal supply of gold ever since its debut in 1973, thus freeing its writers and producers to proceed along the sensual and sentimental path they have so successfully created—without much network interference.

"We are *very* interested in the ratings," says John Conboy, the series' executive producer, "but we've never had to tailor our scripts to get them. I don't know what we'd do if we had to. I think it's a very dangerous thing to tamper with stories that *come* from our characters' personalities. It's dangerous to force a story on a character." Conboy once produced *Love Is a Many Splendored Thing,* a soap based on a book and a movie. Storylines and characters radically changed from the originals quickly lost the program its audience, so Conboy knows whereof he speaks.

"Maybe if you do something startling," he says, "you might get a 45 share. But it won't last. My audience for *The Young and the Restless* wouldn't relate to a gang rape in a garage."

On the other hand, *General Hospital,* a respectable but fading soap opera, might take a risk now and then. "If the ratings dip," said one *Hospital* insider, "we might throw in something more stimulating—like a murder." Back in 1963, when *General Hospital* joined the soaper ranks, it was exceedingly popular; then the ratings plummeted. Fred Silverman, then ABC programming chief, took Draconian measures. One beloved character after another was summarily executed. It was suggested to the writers that they get jobs in the auto industry or the teaching profession. Efforts were made to buy stars from other series.

"One actress on another soap was number one in the polls," says the insider. "Of course, it was her *character,* not *her,* but ABC thought if they could get her for *General Hospital,* it would pull up the ratings a few points." ABC did manage to steal away the lady for an exorbitant price. "But it didn't do a damn bit of good; in fact the ratings went down," says the insider with a chuckle.

The audience does have some power in dictating to the sponsors, writers and producers of a soap. Mail is carefully scrutinized. Mass dismay can change the minds of a series' packagers. Everyone remembers that such distress might mean the product advertised won't sell, or—heavens, let's not think of it—that the viewer might flick the dial to a competing soap.

"We check our ratings very closely," says Herzberg, "then we study our subject matter. We did jettison one story—brought it to an end months ahead of time." The story that met an abrupt end was about wife beating. "People just didn't go for it," says Herzberg, "so we brought it to a fast conclusion. After we dropped the story, our ratings went up two points."

Search for Tomorrow tried a story involving a teen center with predominantly young blacks. The predominantly white audience didn't like it. The center was excised from future scripts.

Just what does attract viewers to a particular soap? The desire for entertainment—escapism—the feeling that even people who *should* be happy have problems. Boredom's a factor, too—nothing else to do if you have to be at home; and the sheer sweep of the ongoing high drama also lures viewers. For the younger audiences, it is the combination of relevance and sensuality. The most successful soaps offer franker-than-prime-time discussions of abortion, the Pill, the Vietnam War (*All My Children* dealt with it), breast cancer, child abuse, impotence and frigidity. *The Young and the Restless,* a paradigm for the more recent soaps, pioneered seminude scenes. And enough open-mouth kissing to humidify the atmosphere. As well as some very plain pillow talk between the handsome men and beautiful young women (the older people on that show are not less candid, too).

John Leonard, a TV critic in one of his previous incarnations and now a columinst for the *New York Times,* once said that daytime TV is "like being locked inside the *Reader's Digest* for the rest of your life." If he were looking at daytime programs today, he might want to change that image to *Cosmopolitan.*

JAMES LIPTON

Soap Operas Are for Real

As CBS programming chief Bud Grant has observed, soap operas are "the most durable form of drama we have." Audiences have been intensely loyal to the soaps since they were first broadcast on radio. One theory for their popularity was set forth in a study of soap operas made by Kerta Herzog in the early 1940s. She concluded that soaps are successful because they provide emotional release, they allow momentary escape from real problems and the characters may advise the listener on coping with daily life.

Modern audiences are still loyal to the soaps, many of the same ones that Kerta Herzog studied. A number of radio soap operas were simply transferred to television in the 1950s—*Love of Life, Search for Tomorrow, The Guiding Light, The Edge of Night, As the World Turns*—and they are watched faithfully. Although there has been no major study examining the popularity of the television soap operas, James Lipton suggests some reasons viewers become addicted.

What *is* the soap opera's "secret"? I believe it lies in a single rather surprising word: soap operas are *real.* For some years serials have been dealing with themes that nighttime TV is only beginning to come to.

. . . What [soap characters] do is approximately what the American television viewers do: they are born, they marry, they hope, they worry, they succeed, they fail—they even die when they get sick. And it is in those last two facts—failure and death—that the secret of the soap opera lies.

Excerpts have been taken from this essay, which first appeared February 14, 1970.

When the TV viewer watches *Mission: Impossible,* he can relax; no matter what jeopardy threatens his heroes and heroines, he knows that, one way or another, they'll survive. How does he know? Simple. They're already scheduled for a return next week, same time, same station. . . . Not so in daytime. When our heroes and heroines get sick, they may just die—*and the viewer knows it.* Our dangers aren't nighttime dangers—three-foot hurdles, certain to be surmounted, straw-man villains with round heels. Our cancers really kill, and the childbirth has all the hazards of the real event. If our heroines sip coffee and worry about their children or their love affairs or the fidelity of their husbands, it is because our viewers sip coffee and worry about their children or their love affairs or the fidelity of their husbands. That soap operas are, in large part, domestic drama is undeniable, but we are, in large part, a domestic society.

Soap operas begin where movies fade out. In movies the lovers are united, they marry and walk off into the golden sunset. Television "asks the question" (as its parodists enjoy saying): what happens *after* that happy fadeout? And, since all of us *live* in that world after the fadeout, it just may have pertinence to all our lives.

We worry about our soap-opera heroines because they are as vulnerable to the vagaries of fate as we are; they bleed as readily as we do, bullets fired at point-blank range *don't* miss them, and they *even make mistakes*—big ones, irredeemable ones—unlike most of their cardboard nighttime counterparts. If serial characters are sentimental, it is because they are repelled, like us, by life as it really is; if they are miscreant, it is because they are hungry for something and blocked from it. *In fine,* all I am saying is that if serials seem real, perhaps it is because they *are* real.

As for the criticism that production in daytime TV is ragged compared to nighttime's slick filmed look, remember that soap operas are recorded live on tape, so that the fluffs—and the excitement—of actual, on-the-spot creation are visible, as they were in the Golden Days of live TV and still are on the stage.

[The soap] is not the smoothly homogenized product of Hollywood's film factories, but it isn't amateur theatricals either. The fact is that, in the late 1950s, when Hollywood supplanted New York as the television capital, daytime serials became the last refuge of live

TV drama. In time this fact has become apparent to a number of writers who are tired of writing about horses, holsters and hillbillies. As a result there has been an influx, into this once-scorned field, of writers with first-rate talent and experience. . . .

Like many other writers, I go from one project and one medium to another, but when I feel an itch to write contemporary drama, I find the readiest and most receptive market in that most maligned of all literary fields, the soap opera. Hence this defense—of a dramatic mode that needs less defending than those lordly nighttime programs that no longer have the right to bill themselves as television prime time.

NEIL HICKEY

What Do You Mean It's Only a Game?

Game-show host Monty Hall suggests that a person "can learn more about America by watching one half-hour of *Let's Make a Deal* [his show] than . . . by watching Walter Cronkite for an entire month."

Game shows are an important part of the equation for successful daytime programming. Because of low production costs, an average of $12,000 per program, a game show has even greater potential for profit. In her book *TV Game Shows,* Maxine Faber estimated that a hit game show could earn more than $1 million each week. In 1979, game shows made the networks about $200 million richer in gross advertising revenues and were a bargain for the advertisers—a commercial minute cost about $12,000.

Madeleine David, former head of daytime programming for NBC, attributes the success of game shows to the fact that their formats are compatible with interruptions: "You don't really have to watch them all of the time. People can go out shopping, do chores, change a diaper." Neil Hickey examines the popularity of the television games and offers some thoughts about what makes a game show successful.

In the beginning there was "Break the Bank" and "Chance of a Lifetime" and "Stop the Music" and "Take It or Leave It" and "The $64 Question" and "Dr. IQ" and scores of others—all of them vastly popular ornaments of the great age of network radio. And then, as television transfixed us during the 1950s, the TV game show burst forth from its cocoon. [In 1979 a hard core of] 10 million viewers

This essay first appeared August 10, 1974.

spent an average of [between 1¼ and 1½] hours a day exulting with an endless parade of contestants, experiencing vicariously their thrill of victory and their agony of defeat.[1]

What's behind [the abundance of] televised parlor games? From a TV executive's viewpoint, the answer is simple: game shows are cheap to produce [about $85,000 a week for five daily half-hour shows in 1979–80][2] and enormously profitable. Sponsors eagerly line up for a crack at that key 18-to-49-year-old female homemaker who controls the family purse strings for the purchase of washday miracles, furniture polish, pain killers, convenience foods, denture adhesives, false eyelashes, girdles, deodorants, laxatives, air fresheners, pet food, rug cleaners, diet colas and corn remedies.

While soap operas are considered more valuable to a network in the long run than game shows (they attract a somewhat younger female audience), they also require a year or more to build a following sufficiently loyal to ensure their survival. (Says one network executive: "It takes a spunky programmer to make that kind of commitment.") The pulling power of a game show, on the other hand, is apparent in a matter of weeks, and it can be either junked or renewed with a minimum of fiscal trauma. . . .

As to why audiences like game shows—well, that's more difficult to pinpoint. "A viewer can sit at home, watch a game show and forget his problems because he is involved with the game," says Allen Ludden, longtime host of *Password.* Lin Bolen, NBC's vice president for daytime programming, says that game shows "do not demand a great deal from the players at home. They are entertained and stimulated without a major commitment on their part. A woman can go to the laundry room, come back in five minutes, and go right on watching the game."

Says Mark Goodson of Goodson-Todman, the biggest, richest and oldest suppliers extant (*The Price Is Right, Password Plus* and *Concentration*): "Nobody really knows what it is that makes people

1. The most popular daytime game (e.g., ABC's *Family Feud*) may attract 10 million viewers daily, but some of those viewers watch only that one game show and are not considered part of the hard-core game-show audience.

2. If a "stripped daytime" game show (one that is broadcast Monday through Friday every week) had a nighttime (prime-time access period) version in 1979–80, an extra $35,000–$40,000 per week might have been budgeted; a game show made for prime-time access only had a budget of $60,000–$70,000 for each half hour.

tune in to game shows. Maybe it's the Cinderella ingredient: the fun of watching somebody make it big. One thing I feel sure of: very little of game shows' appeal is based on greed. There may be such a thing as vicarious sex, but I don't think there is vicarious greed. If you were starving to death, would you tune in a TV show to watch somebody eat?"

A different view is held by gamesman Chuck Barris (*The Newlywed Game, The Dating Game, The Parent Game,* et al.), who believes that greed is the powerful magnet that attracts both audiences and contestants to such shows as *Let's Make a Deal, The Price Is Right* and his own *The New Treasure Hunt.* "These shows bring out the worst in human beings, and reduce them to a state that isn't very attractive to see. We make a strong appeal to the greed in them. They agonize, they cry, they hyperventilate. And we *show* all that.

"It doesn't bother *me* that we show it, because I'm hypocritical and greedy enough myself to want to make money out of it," Barris said, perched one day in the Plaza Hotel's Oak Room, sipping a Shirley Temple. "If I felt strongly enough about it—which I don't—I'd take my shows off the air." He added, grinning boyishly: "Somebody recently called me 'The King of Slob Culture'."

What *makes* a good game show, anyway? Is there a secret ingredient that's common to all the successful ones? Says CBS's Bud Grant, vice president of daytime programming: "It's the capacity of the home audience to participate, in one fashion or other, in the game. That's vital." Says Monty Hall, of *Let's Make a Deal*: "Involvement. You've got to involve the audience to the degree that they're testing themselves on the game to see if they can play it. Or perhaps they're involved because they're identifying with one of the contestants, or because they're emotionally involved, like spectators at a sporting event."

Game shows, say the experts, are extraordinarily difficult to dream up. Goodson-Todman gets its ideas, says Mark Goodson, "by agonizing, sweating, free-associating. It takes months of pounding away. You try to come up with a novel concept or one with such a pronounced switch that it seems new."

Only fifty to a hundred people in the whole country have an instinct for this kind of activity, Goodson claims, and "only about twenty-five of those are really any good." His own all-time favorite game show is *To Tell the Truth,* which he calls "a textbook idea of a great game."

Dealers in this entertainment form tend to divvy up game shows into four main categories: The Greed Show (*Let's Make a Deal, The Price Is Right, The Joker's Wild, The New Treasure Hunt*), in which contestants are prompted to parade their lust for big prizes and cash money. Then there's the People Show (*The Newlywed Game, To Tell the Truth, I've Got a Secret, What's My Line?, Tattletale*), which depends on whatever fun can be extracted from human foibles, differences and eccentricities.

The so-called Hard Quiz program (*Jeopardy!, Split-Second*) requires that contestants be knowledgeable, rather than merely zany or good guessers. Finally, there's the Celebrity Show (*Hollywood Squares, Match Game, Celebrity Sweepstakes*), which relies on lots of humorous byplay among supposedly witty celebrities.

In fact, a certain kind of semicelebrity is an important ingredient in many of the game shows currently on the air. Says one major packager: "Where does a glib, ad-libbing actor go to make a living these days? Many actors and actresses are eternally 'between jobs,' and they're only too happy to earn their bread by sitting on a panel and making flip remarks."

But it was the "hard quiz" format that got TV game shows into hot water in the late 1950s, and almost quashed them for good. Cash prizes in the hundreds of thousands of dollars were being handed out on prime-time shows like *Twenty One, The $64,000 Question* and *The $64,000 Challenge*. Disclosures of collusion and "fixing" erupted in the quiz-show scandal that drove all the high-stakes programs off the air amid public outrage over such blatant duplicity. The have never made a comeback in prime time although there have been a few brief efforts to revive them.

Nobody expects the high-stakes, hard-quiz giveaways to be resurrected, but even if they were, there now exist tough safeguards against hanky-panky: it's a federal offense ([$20,000] fine and/or one year in prison) to tamper with a game show. And the networks police themselves to the edge of paranoia. "They're uptight about it all the time," one packager declares. "They hang over our shoulders and drive us nuts. TV audiences have long since forgotton about the quiz-show scandals. The networks will never forget."

Game-show prizes, by the way, are a subject unto themselves.

They come in three classes: 1) smallish prizes valued at a few dollars (packages of food, furniture polish, etc.), for which the manufacturer pays to have the product mentioned and given away on the air; 2) expensive prizes (cars, motor homes, etc.) purchased outright from manufacturers with revenue earned from category 1; and, 3) middle-range prizes procured in dollar-for-dollar trade-offs (no money changes hands—the manufacturer donates the item in exchange for an on-the-air mention).

Two networks—CBS and NBC—have in-house departments specifically set up to solicit and purchase prizes for all the game shows they broadcast. Companies making shows for ABC obtain their own prizes. Prize procurers are called (affectionately, in the trade) "Schlockmeisters."

Yet another intriguing aspect of the game-show phenomenon is that peculiar breed of human being—glib, brisk, incurably affable—called the game-show host, all of whom appear to have been bred for the part. (There are no game-show "hostesses," by the way; the profession continues as an all-male redoubt.)

"Aside from their cheery dispositions and hearty laughs, all game-show hosts have one other important thing in common," says a prominent producer. "They are all rich." [In 1979] the top earners—men like Bob Barker, Peter Marshall, Jack Barry and Gene Rayburn—commanded up to [$10,000] per week, 52 weeks a year (no reruns). And that's for one day's work a week, since most shows tape five programs in one day.[3]

What makes a good game-show host? "The ability to take charge, to run things," says Mark Goodson. "Affability is least important. I can get affable people for 10 cents." There are ten or fifteen really good hosts, he says, and they're getting harder to find because most of the current crop came out of the great days of network radio.

The skills a host needs, Goodson believes, are most closely allied with those of a TV newscaster. "I could take Dan Rather, for example, and turn him into a great game-show host. Don't forget that Walter Cronkite was, in fact, the host of a TV game show back in 1954 called *It's News to Me.*"

The game-show phenomenon appears destined to dominate day-

3. Some game shows have a nighttime version which usually appears on local stations during the prime-time access period. A top game-show host might get another $5000 for each of these shows.

time television in the forseeable future. Professional TV critics almost unanimously pronounce game shows the most primitive and banal form of televised entertainment. Thus, they either ignore them completely (as being beneath criticism) or clobber them with salvos of contumely as "an appalling and cynical use of the public's airwaves."

But the networks are impervious to criticism on this front partly because (as Ed Vane, an ABC programming executive, puts it): "On a ratio of profit to investment, game shows are far and away the most lucrative kind of TV programming." And because the massed brainpower of the television industry has been unsuccessful in devising any other program form (besides soap operas) that can attract viewers in sufficient numbers over the long haul to satisfy advertisers. Thus, the networks have mutually descended to competing at the game-show level during the daytime hours.

"It's a great mystery!" says Bob Stewart, one of the most successful of game-show creators (*The $10,000 Pyramid, Jackpot!* and *Winning Streak*). "Why can't somebody dream up a new format that could attract enough people to survive? It doesn't seem right." Talk shows, variety shows, 90-minute dramas and reruns of old situation comedies have all stumbled in the daytime sweepstakes. As a result, more creative energy is now being ploughed into fabricating new, more piquant TV games than into the search for innovative daytime forms. . . .

PAUL HEMPHILL

Praise the Lord— and Cue the Cameraman

For spiritual uplifting, there is an alternative to church—turn on the television. By March 1980, estimates were that at least 14 million Americans were watching at least one religious program each week. Thirty-five television stations were broadcasting large amounts of religious programming, and this figure was increasing at the rate of almost one station a month. Four religious networks were offering programs via satellite to those and other TV stations and/or to cable television systems throughout the nation.

Along with the growing importance of televised religion, the propriety of on-the-air worship is of increasing concern to the traditional clergy, as expressed by Dean Colin Williams of the Yale Divinity School:

> The breadth of the Gospel is not reflected in the narrow compass of the electronic church of TV. Electronic evangelism allows itself to become constricted by the medium and it becomes a consumer religion of instant gratification. . . . It doesn't help people think. . . . It draws upon people's feelings of disappointment and alienation.

Pat Robertson of the Christian Broadcasting Network defends religious programming:

> To say that the church shouldn't be involved with televsion is utter folly. The needs are the same, the message is the same, but the delivery system can change. . . . It would be folly for the church not to get involved with the most formative force in America. . . . The attention span of the modern audience is terrible. You've got to say what you have to say in five minutes or less. You may not like it but that's the way it is.

This essay first appeared August 12, 1978.

The electronic church leans toward evangelism, and an estimated 50 million people are tied to evangelical or fundamentalist churches or are part of a neo-Pentecostal movement. Twenty religious groups recently financed a Gallup poll which partially explains the mushrooming growth of televised religion. Approximately one-third of those questioned considered themselves born-again Christians. According to George Gallup, Jr., the results of the poll suggest that traditional clergy may not be prepared to "deal with religious experience." A "special ministry" is needed for those "people who are all charged up about their faith."

Television preaching has become big business, and many evangelistic associations engaging in prime-time religion have profits equal to those of numerous multinational corporations. Christians contribute more than $250 million to eight television ministries alone. Among the most important and lucrative of these ministries is the Christian Broadcasting Network, which is described by Paul Hemphill.

It would, at first glance, appear to be a sprightly version of NBC-TV's *The Tonight Show.* The camera work is classy. The set is decorated with potted plants and a walnut desk and comfortable chairs against a fake-skyline background. There is a wildly cheering live audience and an in-house band. The guests for the show include a fast-selling author and a gold-record singer and the wife of a troubled bureaucrat. More than three million people are viewing the show all across America, thanks to an expensive satellite hookup, and it is only 10 A.M. The host wears a pin-striped three-piece suit and a demeanor that is a match for Johnny Carson's. His sidekick, a black man's Ed McMahon, wears a trim Afro and a double-knit leisure suit.

The illusion of another *Tonight Show* is broken the minute Dr. M. G. (Pat) Robertson, the host of the show, opens his mouth. "Praise the Lord," he says. "Thank you, Jesus," says Ben Kinchlow, his straight man. And *The 700 Club* is off and running again. Jeannie C. Riley ("Harper Valley P.T.A.") sings and talks about being "born again." LaBelle Lance, the wife of former budget director

Bert Lance, explains about how nobody seems to understand the banking business and she and Bert wouldn't have made it without the help of the Lord. A woman who has just come out with a book about angels undergoes an in-depth interview about angels.

This is not, obviously, *The Tonight Show*. Buzz-words fly—"Jesus told me . . . With the Lord's help . . . A miracle . . . God and I decided"—and then the host and the co-host at the end are on their knees reading from clipboards and praying. "Praise God," says Robertson. "Here's a case of venereal disease cured by the Lord in Texas. A philandering husband in Indiana has been brought back home. Alcoholism has been stopped in Alabama. . . ." Et cetera. "It is," says a cynical Southern liberal writer, "like a Tupperware Party for Jesus."

But Christian broadcasting—the feverish evangelical type—has gone into a new orbit. It was always with us, going back to the days when a younger Oral Roberts would ask radio listeners to put their arthritic hands atop the radio set as the back-roads evangelists prayed and healed and asked for mailed contributions (". . . this Magic Prayer Cloth, only $4.95, for as long as He makes this offer possible . . ."). And then came television and satellites and cablevision and much simpler ways to take the way of the Lord to the people.

There is an abundance of Christian broadcasters now—the election of Jimmy Carter, a "born-again" Southerner, didn't hurt—and it is probable that they will have a powerful effect on the television networks. "All of us just became concerned about the violence and the general degeneration of morals on network shows," says Pat Robertson of the Christian Broadcasting Network. He wants to see more of Pat Boone and Anita Bryant and "those other wholesome types" on television and less of the "sex and murder and immorality" featured on network shows. Bryant and Boone, along with Charles Colson and converted athletes and "born-again" alcoholics and ex-convicts, are the guests for his show.

"I want to know if John or Peter or Paul," says Marshall Frady, a Southern writer [of] a massive biography of Billy Graham, "would buy a blue shirt and go on television." Maybe yes, maybe no; but scores of modern-day disciples are doing it. Oral Roberts, who doesn't like to talk about the old days when he was accused of hucksterism on radio, televises weekly from his glassy campus in Tulsa, Okla. Rex Humbard does the same, from his Cathedral of Tomorrow in Ohio. Then there is Jim Bakker, a former protegé of Robertson's, whose *PTL Club* out of Charlotte, N.C. (PTL for "Praise the Lord"), is boomed as the nation's fourth-largest purchaser of syndicated air time ("with [140] affiliates").[1] Most of them follow essentially the same format: upbeat gospel music, "prayer counselors" taking calls during the show, visits from "born-again" guests, tales of miracles, conservative commentary, financing coming from the flow of $5 and $10 "gifts" from Out There.

Pat Robertson, a 48-year-old ordained minister, is clearly the leader of this new breed of TV evangelist. Attractive and glib, Robertson "gave my heart to God" in 1956. An energetic man with a peripatetic background (son of a former U.S. senator from Virginia, ex-Golden Gloves boxer, trouble-shooter for W. R. Grace & Co., Marine Corps combat officer, Yale Law School graduate), Robertson in 1959 arrived in Portsmouth, Va., with $70 in his pocket and took over a rundown UHF station when "the Lord told me, 'Buy this station'."[2] So began, with 700 local Christians sending in $10 each month to support it, *The 700 Club.*

Today the Christian Broadcasting Network, which includes *The 700 Club* show, is a huge conglomerate. There is an Earth satellite enabling the show to go anywhere in the world. There is a 142-acre college campus that soon will begin producing evangelists and tomorrow's Christian broadcasters. CBN, looking to become the "fourth network," consists of four television stations and six radio operations.[3] The annual operating budget is around [$60] million. There are nearly 19,000 trained volunteer "counselors" to man switchboards around the world (CBN claims to receive nearly a

1. In addition, CBN was broadcasting to more than 7.5 million cable-TV homes via satellite in the spring of 1980, and its programming was carried on 150 radio stations.

2. Robertson named the UHF station WYAH, making it the first television station ever to be called by God's name (Yahweh). Robertson's was the first TV license application in FCC history for a station that would devote over 50 per cent of its air time to religious programming. The station does not accept any advertising.

3. The four television stations owned by CBN are all UHF. They are located in Atlanta, Dallas, Boston and Portsmouth, Va. Pat Robertson indicated in an August 1979 press conference that God had told him a fourth network is needed as a forum for religion.

million "prayer calls" each year as local phone numbers flash across the screen during *700 Club* broadcasts) and an estimated 41,000 people annually make "professions of faith" over the telephone alone.

And Robertson, who receives nearly 200 requests per year but seldom has the time for personal appearances on other shows and at religious rallies, sees no end to it. He starts preparing for that day's *700 Club* broadcast by 7 A.M., in his modest home in the country outside of Portsmouth, drives in his small Mercury sedan to the CBN studio for the live show at 10 o'clock, then goes to the paneled CBN headquarters in Virginia Beach to spend a working lunch and a frenetic afternoon arranging guests, dealing with finances, drawing broad plans. "When I get to the office, I take off my ministry cap and put on my business cap."

Business or ministry, however, there is always religion in the air at any of the CBN offices in the Norfolk-Portsmouth-Virginia Beach complex. "You don't have to be a Christian to work for us," says a British-born press agent for CBN, noting the daily noon "prayer meetings" in chapels at every office, "but I suspect you'd be miserable if you weren't." He and others spoke of the many cameramen and reporters and other of the 800-odd CBN personnel who "left the rat race" of the networks to go to work in the calmer spiritual atmosphere of CBN. "You don't find any people working here who don't smile all the time and can't go to sleep at night," said one of them.

Robertson [is] ebullient about the future. "The satellite," he said, "is our slingshot against the three Goliaths. The resources and the power of the networks are unbelievable. They can spend $600 million a year or more on programming alone—pilots, canceled programs, talent—and we can't come anywhere near that. We're small, but we can turn faster and adjust just like small ships." His favorite guests on *The 700 Club*, he said, were former black militant Eldridge Cleaver (*Soul on Ice*) and former heavyweight boxing champion George Foreman; and a runner-up was Anita Bryant. ("I felt it was a disservice if I didn't come right out and say that the homosexual life style is a sin because it says so in the Bible.")

People with annual budgets of [$60] million who enjoy "non-profit, religious, nonstock" tax statuses are, of course, watched closely by the government. CBN got into trouble in 1974 when the Securities and Exchange Commission filed a civil suit over failure to disclose a "deteriorating financial condition" to supporters who had made interest-bearing loans. To avoid huge legal fees, CBN agreed to improve its financial disclosure.

CBN's finances remain hazy—as do those of Oral Roberts of Tulsa, Billy Graham of Charlotte, Rex Humbard of Ohio and Jim Bakker of Charlotte[4]—but CBN officials will say that 80 per cent of the [$60] million comes from $10 contributions and the rest from ad revenues over CBN's radio and television outlets. When a little old lady in Dubuque calls in a prayer request and joins *The 700 Club,* she immediately receives a color poster of Jesus and a subscription to the monthly publication *The Flame* and an invitation to send money. "The mainline denominations are jealous, even mad as hell, about how easily CBN can raise money," says a newspaper religion editor in the South, "because it is taking money right out of their collection plates." Robertson, with four kids and a wife, takes an annual salary of about $30,000. Many CBN emplyees give a portion of their salaries back to CBN as a "tithe." The total take of [$60] million is poured back into CBN's operations: radio, television, publications and the $20-million theology-and-communications school at Virginia Beach.[5]

"All of this sounds like a lot of money," says another religion editor in the most fervent Biblical corner of America, "but you have to understand what it means to a widow on welfare in North Carolina when she sits down and writes a check to Pat Robertson, her hero, for $5."

Typical of the CBN-owned stations would be the one in Atlanta, WANX-TV, [which] telecasts *The 700 Club* at 10 A.M. and repeats the show at 9 P.M. A third of each day's programming is of a religious nature; the rest of the day is given over to *Mighty Mouse, Heckle & Jeckle, Deputy Dawg, The Life of Riley, Popeye, Superman, The Brady Bunch, The Rifleman, Star Trek* and the like. WANX is also, says station manager Everett Martin, deeply in-

4. Bakker's *PTL Club* was being investigated by the FCC in 1980 for alleged violations of a federal law that prohibits anyone from seeking funds over the air for one announced purpose and then directing them to another.

5. In March 1980, the total assets of CBN were just over $100 million.

volved in "good works in the community," such as monthly five-hour prayer breakfasts at a motel, which have drawn more than 2000 businessmen. . . .

Arbitron ratings, though, are more objective than the Lord. WANX-TV (Channel 46 in Atlanta) fares poorly. Its rating, based on the percentage of people viewing TV in the metropolitan area, in May [1978] was one out of 25, while WSB-TV (the local NBC station) drew 9 of 25. Arbitron showed the following audiences for comparable time periods: ABC (*Charlie's Angels*), 237,000 homes; CBS (*M*A*S*H*), 174,000 homes; NBC (movie), 308,000 homes; CBN (*The 700 Club*), 8000 homes. Pat Robertson and his people at CBN talk about the dearth of "good wholesome entertainment" on the networks, but the fact is that when WANX of Atlanta shows *The Brady Bunch* at 6 P.M., up against the terrors of the nightly news, *Brady* hits 31,000 homes and the local NBC news goes into 166,000.

"The thing we have to pray for," Robertson says, in responding to those facts, "is the 'tap-root' theory. Our people believe more deeply than others. It means something—it's got to mean something—when you receive 6000 letters every day. The networks may have more viewers, but that mail response is all out of proportion. It tells us that our people *care*. With the Lord's help, we'll make it."

SPORTS

For an advertiser, one of the best ways to reach the American male population is to sponsor a sports telecast. One-fourth of the American man's television viewing time is spent watching sports, the figure for women is 15 per cent.

Sports coverage was an attractive and relatively inexpensive way to fill up a great deal of air time in the early days of television. Then, as the audiences and the number of stations multiplied, investments were made in other types of programming. Sports faded into the background, becoming, for the most part, weekend entertainment. Many sports promoters, afraid that their events had been overexposed and their box-office receipts had suffered because of television, encouraged limited coverage.

By the late 1960s, however, the pendulum had swung back. Sports was again a major programming feature. Sponsors, especially those for such items as beer, razor blades, automobiles, tires, airlines, power tools and insurance firms, had decided that their products needed the male sports enthusiast. Consequently, by the end of that decade, more than 700 hours of sports were telecast each year by the three major networks, and sponsors annually spent well over $200 million for commercials. By 1977, the networks were telecasting ten times as many hours of sports as they had in 1960.

The most recent development in televised sports is a cable network devoted exclusively to sports, twenty-four hours a day—the Entertainment and Sports Programming Network. Financed principally by the Getty Oil Company and headed by Chester Simmons, former head of sports for NBC, ESPN began operations in November 1979 on 625 cable systems serving more than 4.5 million households. The 8760 hours of programming have been divided three ways: 65 per cent for coverage of 18 different NCAA sports (including delayed tapes of NCAA football games), 20 per cent for covering non-NCAA events and 15 per cent planned for non-event sports programs such as news and interview shows.

The creation of a twenty-four-hour sports network (allowing the home viewer to watch sports whenever he or she wishes) and the inclusion of huge television screens in new sports complexes so the spectators can see the event as it is seen by those watching at home (enthusiasts can check replays while at the stadium), are just two recent examples of what sportscaster Frank Gifford observed in 1962: “TV and athletic events are forever tied together.”

DON KOWET

Playing for Blood

The increasing popularity and amount of televised sports should mean greater profits for the networks. Not so. Over the course of a year, the profits from televised sports are lower than those from other types of programming because the costs have spiralled upward. A former vice president of sports at CBS said, "in any other business we'd be arrested for throwing money away."

One key to the inflated costs of telecasting sports events is prestige, and the most prestigious event is the Olympics. In 1960, CBS paid $550,000 for the rights to broadcast that year's Olympics from Rome. The rights to cover the Munich Games in 1972 cost ABC $13.5 million. The 1976 Montreal Olympics cost ABC $25 million. NBC entered the competition to broadcast the Moscow Olympics in 1980 and won the privilege for $87 million, which included the construction of a broadcast center at the site of the Games. The bidding for the summer Olympics of 1984 in Los Angeles has been settled; ABC will pay $225 million, including production and support facilities. None of these totals includes the actual production costs, which have increased significantly over the years.

The networks may recoup their outlays for the Olympic Games and perhaps make a profit through the high advertising rates they are able to charge. But, in many cases, the revenues do not equal the costs. Don Kowet explains why former NBC vice president for sports Carl Lendemann has characterized sports telecasting over the last few years as "a vicious circle of network competition and prestige."

Excerpts have been taken from this two-part essay, which first appeared October 15, October 22, 1977.

With the networks devoting [more than] 1200 hours to TV sports programming annually, it has turned into a contest worthy of the Olympics, World Series and Super Bowl all rolled into one. The goal in this "game" is to score higher ratings than the opponents. As for rules of conduct, there are none . . . except that kicking, gouging, pinching, biting and butting are definitely recommended.

Here is how the game is played:

For years, NBC had been on a losing streak. In fact, by 1975, there was only one really major property NBC had all to itself. Major-league baseball. An then, in that year, ABC ended that exclusive coverage.

On the surface, it seems major-league baseball was merely acting in its best financial interests by letting ABC on board. After all, the deal with ABC and NBC jointly would net baseball $92.8 million for four years, beginning in 1976—$20 million more than NBC had been paying. The fact is, though, only by crying "foul" did NBC manage to salvage any share of the package (the less desirable Saturday-afternoon games, while ABC got the Monday-night prime-time slot), including the right to alternate telecasting of the All-Star, play-off and World Series games with ABC. The "foul" NBC executives were sure they spotted was, in their minds, foul play: John Lazarus, baseball's director of radio and TV then, and architect of the ABC contract, was a former employee of ABC.[1]

Call it skill, call it cunning, call it subversion—by any name, ABC's tactics have paid a handsome dividend: a reputation as the No. 1 network for sports.

"And the fact that we were leaders in sports programming bought time for the rest of the company," says Jim Spence, who started at ABC [in 1960 and] became an assistant to Roone Arledge in 1973. "Sports became something for the network to hang its hat on, while the entertainment end was struggling. Sports gave us not only profits, but prestige."

A network acquires that prestige by obtaining rights to broadcast the "majors"—major-league baseball, NBA basketball, NCAA basketball and football, NFL football, the play-offs and championships

1. New contracts with major-league baseball for the 1980–83 seasons have been signed by NBC and ABC for prices estimated to be double those for coverage from 1976 to 1980.

in these sports, tennis tournaments such as Forest Hills and Wimbledon, golf classics, premier auto races—and, of course, the Olympics. Prestige—but not necessarily profits, since a network may have to pay more for one of these events than it can ever recover in advertising revenues—rises in proportion to ratings and whether or not a property can draw in prime time (like baseball and pro football).

"There are three reasons why the networks allocate such huge portions of their programming budgets to acquiring major sports events," says Herb Gross, second at CBS to sports chief Barry Frank. "First, the viewers like it. Second, the advertisers like it. And because viewers and advertisers like it," he adds, "the affiliates like it. Prestige events in sports cement affiliate loyalities." (For example: for years ABC carried NCAA football at a loss, mainly to please ABC affiliates located in areas that didn't have pro football teams.) . . .

[By 1976, NBC had] decided to make a major effort to obtain exclusive rights to the most prestigious event of all—the 1980 Moscow Olympics. "I think the Olympics established credibility for ABC," says [NBC's Sports chief Al] Rush. (ABC has telecast six of the last eight summer and winter Olympics.) "I think it probably put a little more meaning into their claim that they were the most watched, the leading sports network, around the world."

Rush says NBC pursued the Olympics diligently. His competitors, with the cynicism appropriate to also-rans, allege that NBC won the Olympics [for $87 million] through blind luck. "Hell, says Herb Gross of CBS, "we had the *man.* We had Lothar Bock." Bock is the itinerant German impresario who almost delivered the Olympics to CBS, then did deliver the Games to NBC, after CBS got fed up with the Russians and pulled out of the competition.

"Hell," says Jim Spence of ABC, "the Russians couldn't even remember NBC's letters—they kept referring to them as the NBA, the CBC—anything. Anyway, despite what CBS says, *we* had the man."

"We had someone much bigger than Lothar Bock," says another source at ABC. "I mean, we had *the head of the whole damn country*—Alexei Kosygin himself. He wanted ABC on its past performance. Kosygin was outraged when Ignati Novikov, the head of their Olympic Committee, suddenly announced he had signed the deal with NBC. But it was too late. They would have had to tear up the contract. That would have been too embarrassing. "Even," he adds, "for a Russian." Kosygin's standing in the Russian hierarchy was downgraded shortly thereafter, presumably for other reasons.

[While network programmers disagree as to the extent to which NBC's coverage—152 hours at a total estimated cost of $130 to $140 million—will be profitable,[2] most would agree with Herb Gross of CBS that] "The Olympics will have an effect at NBC. . . . More attention will be paid to sports programming at NBC, and, as NBC becomes more competitive, that will put more pressure on all of us."

The benevolent objective of all this pressurized contention, the network sports chiefs allege, is to bestow the greatest number of sports events upon the largest mass audience. In fact, though, much of TV's sports programming is designed to suit the preferences (and prejudices) of only a sovereign elite. That explains why golf (whose Nielsen ratings have long been abysmal) [accounts for over 10] per cent of all network sports, although a typical golf tournament costs five or six times more to broadcast than the typical baseball or basketball game.[3]

Golf is almost completely devoid of the elements of sports drama: speed, action and one-against-one match-ups. In recent years, the charismatic personalities (Palmer, Nicklaus, Trevino) who gave the game its pizazz in the '60s have been all but supplanted by an army of male-mannequin lookalikes. So why, after Portland's 109-107 sixth-game victory over Philadelphia [in 1977]—good for the NBA championship—did CBS switch hastily to a forgettable pit stop on the pro golf tour called the Kemper Open, while its viewers were clamoring for a peep at the Walton Gang cavorting in the winners' locker room? (So eager was CBS to air that Kemper Open, it had asked the Trail Blazers' management to start the crucial Sunday play-off game at 10 A.M.!)

2. NBC was reportedly hoping to earn a net profit of as much as $30 million from its July 19–August 3, 1980 Olympic telecast. By March 1980, NBC was said to have sold 1210 minutes of advertising for a total of $170 million.

3. In early 1980, the production costs of covering a golf tournament often exceeded $400,000.

The answer is: the average golf fan is way above average when it comes to wealth and a willingness to part with it. The networks serve him up on a silver tee for advertisers able and willing to pay a premium to plug high-priced items such as luxury cars, life insurance, air travel and business machines. So, although bowling, for example, has approximately 44.4 million participants nationally versus golf's 16.6 million, and although telelvised bowling almost always outdraws televised golf, the three networks broadcast about three times more golf than bowling.[4] The message is clear. All sports fans are equal, but some are more equal than others.

What makes a successful sports programmer? . . .

"Personableness" [or] the ability to charm sports executives and sports talent into doing a network's bidding. In the [1976] Olympics, ABC developed close contacts with Dorothy Hamill and Ray Leonard, the one an Olympic figure-skating champion, the other an Olympic boxing champion. Afterward, ABC signed both to contracts. CBS's Barry Frank [made] friends at ABC's 1980 Winter Olympics at Lake Placid, N.Y. Among his most intimate buddies he can now count the entire U.S. ski team, which, from now through the winter of 1981 (except during the Olympics), will slalom and skid only for CBS. Thus, if a U.S. ski hero emerges on ABC during the Olympics, CBS will reap the post-Olympic publicity harvest. Frank—not the bashful type—insists his friends in boxing are even better.

"ABC had the Montreal Olympics, and the stars of that Olympics, as far as America was concerned, were the boxers," he says. "OK, everyone knows that ABC signed Ray Leonard to a contract and that we signed Howard Davis, as well as the Spinks brothers. Few people are aware, however, that we could have signed Leonard, too." CBS, Frank alleges, had the respected fight trainer Gil Clancy look over both Leonard and Davis. "Gil said that Davis had the best potential of all the Olympic champs. He said that Leonard was a

4. In 1979, the *Pro Bowler's Tour,* in its eighteenth season on ABC, went head to head with NBC's *Baseball Game of the Week* and *The Masters Golf Tournament.* Bowling came out on top with an 8.9 rating. Baseball got a 7.4 rating and golf only 6.6. Yet the cost of advertising on a bowling telecast is about one-half that during coverage of a golf tournament.

question mark—he had fragile hands and probably couldn't take a punch. That's why we got Davis—and ABC got Leonard."

A source at ABC denies that CBS could have signed Leonard and suggests only time will tell who got the better fighter. "One thing is sure," he adds, "even if the Howard Davis deal is good for CBS, it's bad for boxing and for the kid himself. They signed him to a long-term contract, at a phenomenal sum—much more than we're paying Leonard, for much longer. So CBS is committed to a long-term buildup. What happens if the kid loses? The money and the promos go out the window. So CBS has to make sure the kid doesn't lose, by showcasing him with handpicked opponents."

"Well," rebuts a source at CBS, "CBS only got involved in signing boxers to contracts because ABC was determined to do it. Initially, we rejected the idea—and ABC knew it. But they were determined. Once they signed their kid, we had to sign ours, just to stay competitive."

NBC didn't sign any boxers to contracts at all. "I think there's a simple reason," Al Rush says quietly. "We're exhibitors. Our function is to televise programs. I don't think we're in the business of being fight promoters. There should be a line," he adds, "between broadcasting events—and confecting them." . . .

When network programmers aren't competing through innovation, they're competing through imitation. ABC develops *Wide World of Sports*; CBS counters with *CBS Sports Spectacular*. *Superstars* (ABC) fathers "Battle of the Network Stars" (ABC), *The Challenge of the Sexes* (CBS) and "Us Against the World" (an NBC show involving teams of celebrities from various countries). CBS devises a program (*The NFL Today*) to serve as an umbrella for its pro football coverage, and NBC responds with a parasol called *Grandstand,* for its NFL coverage.

"The key is," says Chet Simmons, second at NBC to Al Rush, and NBC's long-time chief of sports production, "what can you do that's a bit different from your competition?" Often the answer lies in new technologies.

ABC's *Wide World of Sports* pioneered a host of new engineering techniques, including the first color, stop-action, slow-motion video-tape system in the TV industry. In 1965, it presented telecasts via satellite of the Le Mans 24-hour Grand Prix, the first European sports event ever to be seen live in the U.S. It created an underwater camera to cover swimming and diving events. Its engineers converted a 200-foot industrial crane into a mount for panoramic camera views.

TV cameras themselves have been both refined and miniaturized. "The smaller camera gives us better positioning," says Chet Simmons. "You used to go to an NCAA tournament, and the officials would say, 'You can't put that camera there; it's going to block seven seats.' So now it blocks only two seats."

Aside from slow motion and stop-frames, network production chiefs laud the capabilities of the Arvin Echo. "This machine gives us the ability to isolate, frame-by-frame, up to 300 pictures that we want," says ABC's Chuck Howard. A pitcher's motion, for example, can therefore be examined from 300 different angles.

A world-wide system of orbiting satellites positively revolutionized coverage of the Olympics and, in so doing, enhanced the price tag of that event astronomically. "Let me tell you something else satellite technology has done for us," says NBC's Simmons. "It was on a Sunday morning [in 1976] that we found out O. J. Simpson had signed his contract, after saying he wasn't going to play for the Buffalo Bills any more. We called our station in Burbank. We told them that Simpson had signed. We told them he was leaving right away for Buffalo, and gave them his flight number. They took a minicam and a tape recorder out to the L.A. airport.

"There's a domestic satellite now," Simmons adds. "That interview was put on microwave cable from the airport back to Burbank, then put on the satellite. We had it within 10 minutes. We had it on the air an hour or two after we'd heard that Simpson had signed his contract."

No one knows what technological wizardry the future will bring. But Barry Frank thinks he perceives, if dimly, the shape of future sports programming. "We'll all be into more 'hard' sports," he says. "Auto racing, karate, soccer even. I think the life span of some of the made-for-television events may be limited. . . .

MELVIN DURSLAG

From Barrel Jumpers to Belly-Floppers

Alongside the telecasting of sporting events such as the NFL football games, sports anthologies have recently become a major element of weekend television programming. Here too, many feel the competition for coverage rights is getting out of control. Melvin Durslag reviews the problems faced by the networks while they try to slake the television audience's increasing thirst for sports—any sports.

As European sports coordinator for NBC, Geoff Mason bid for the rights [in 1978] to a Swedish motorcycle race, a few minutes of which were planned for *Sports World.* "The promoter and I agreed that about $2500 would be right," recalls Mason. "The next day, he phoned me. 'I'm embarrassed to tell you this,' he said, 'but ABC walked in and offered me $20,000. What should I do?' I answered, 'Take the kronor and run'."

It occurred to NBC that for $2500 these days, you are lucky to buy Swedish meatballs, let alone Swedish motorcycle racing.

"Example number two," continues Mason. "The promoter of the World Cup track-and-field meet got $200,000 for TV rights at Dusseldorf in 1977. For the next World Cup, in 1979 [at Montreal], we entered into the bidding. We figured it might be worth a half-million, at best, but decided to bite the bullet and go as high as $600,000, feeling we were a cinch. ABC took it home for about a million."

This essay first appeared February 17, 1979.

Somehow, the idea grows with Mason that ABC "is trying to blow the rest of us out of the marketplace." But, of course, little moisture forms in the eyes of NBC competitors, who recall the [$87] million proffered for the Moscow Olympics.

Escalation of bidding in behalf of the weekly sports-anthology shows, however, is cause for serious concern among the networks, which see promoters taking advantage of TV's battle to obtain material, to fatten themselves up. The question also arises about how long anthology programs will be financially advisable if a cap isn't put on gushing costs. And, finally, there are leaders of these sports programs who already are thinking of "creative" events as a substitute for what is being shopped. By "creative" they mean programming they initiate exclusively for television, eliminating the middleman—the promoter.

Launched in 1961, *Wide World of Sports* is generally accepted today as the premier anthology show. For eight months a year it is seen on ABC for 90 minutes on Saturday and Sunday. The other four months it is carried only on Saturday. With careful planning, great expenditure of energy and banknotes, and exhaustive promotion. *Wide World* has gained an acceptance that is the envy of its rivals, who admit candidly they are in a catch-up position.[1]

Beginning modestly, at a time when little competition in this area existed,[2] *Wide World* has changed its concept over the years. "Often," says Jim Spence, senior vice president of ABC Sports, "we did the full 90 minutes on one subject. But now that sports viewers have become more sophisticated, they won't sit still for a 90-minute subject any more, unless it is very special. So we break most shows into three or four segments, which, of course, means greater procurement of material and greater cost."

As the show's success has increased, more effort has been given, according to Spence, to events of international impact. "We aim primarily for big events one step below major spectator games. That would include, for instance, boxing, figure skating, swimming and

1. In 1979, both the Saturday and the Sunday editions of *Wide World* had larger audiences than the combined viewership of the leading anthology shows of the other two networks—*CBS Sports Spectacular* and NBC's *SportsWorld.*

2. ABC's launching of *Wide World of Sports* came at a time when its competitive position in sports was suffering. College football was the only major sport for which ABC had coverage rights and ABC was forced to try something different.

diving, gymnastics, weight lifting. We try to sign as many world championships as possible. Our secondary aim is to fill the gaps with minor events that are visually exciting. Examples would be the cliff divers of Acapulco, surfers in the giant waves of Hawaii, tobogganers at St. Moritz, even barrel jumpers at Grossinger's. No one particularly cares who wins these secondary events, but they are good action."

Don Ohlmeyer, executive producer of NBC Sports, doesn't feel many particularly care who wins the primary events either. A former ABC man, who did considerable work on *Wide World,* Ohlmeyer contends: "There's such a thing as taking yourself too seriously with billings of world this, international that and interplanetary the other thing. To how many viewers do those so-called world championships mean anything? Our philosophy on *SportsWorld* is to produce a lively and imaginative family show that is fun for people who do things to amuse themselves."

SportsWorld, for instance, has signed an extravaganza called the World Belly-flop Championship, an event open to males weighing 250 pounds or more. NBC appreciates this show for two reasons: (a) the price is right (it was bought with a phone call and a token fee) and (b) stage mothers don't shepherd belly-floppers, as they do straight divers.

Then *SportsWorld* also has snatched such biggies as the bar-stool racing championship, blackjack championship, softball on ice and motorcycle racing on ice. And, in Switzerland, it even discovered horse racing on ice. The exacta, presumably, is picking the first two entrants to get frostbite.

When Ohlmeyer confesses that *Wide World*'s budget is roughly twice that of *SportsWorld,* Eddie Einhorn, executive producer of *CBS Sports Spectacular,* grumbles that he should be so lucky. "*Wide World*'s budget is probably triple ours," says Eddie. "But we don't feel we have to spend a ton to be good. We hope to do it with careful buying, clever programming and strong promotion."

It is Einhorn's feeling that the sports direction, production and technical know-how of CBS easily matches that of ABC, but that ABC, up to now, cunningly has outpromoted its rivals. ABC suffocates audiences with house plugs. If, on *Monday Night Football,* the score is 14-10 in the last minute and the team behind is driving suspensefully for the go-ahead touchdown, Howard Cosell is apt to start yammering about Nadia Comaneci, coming up exclusively on ABC. The infuriated fan rises from his chair like a helium balloon. "It irritates the hell out of the viewers," says Einhorn, "but it sells the other shows. If you don't promote in this business, you've got nothing. We aim to promote."

If he weren't selective, Einhorn contends he would have little trouble finding material for *CBS Sports Spectacular*. "We're approached by everyone and his dog," he says. "In fact, a guy tried to sell us a dog frisbee-catching championship. We also have been offered tractor-pulling (by humans), swamp-buggy races, tug-of-war, even jousting. We don't want kooky stuff and we don't want an overload of world championships, either. We want a certain number of wide-interest sports, balanced off by pretty things, like figure skating, and events unconventional but appealing, like the Mr. Universe contest." The subtle distinction between Mr. Universe and tractor-pulling as athletic events has eluded all analysts except Einhorn. . . .

[Between 1978 and 1979, according to] Mike Trager, vice president of programming for NBC, who does most of the domestic buying for *Sports World*, "prices for anthology material have roughly doubled. When you get into a tough bidding competition, which is often, you must be careful not to buy to satisfy your ego. In other words, you don't say to yourself, 'I'm not going to lose to those other so-and-sos if it kills me.' You always can win if you're willing to pay the price."

Trager calls boxing promoters the premier whipsaw artists in televised sports. "They're getting far more for boxing than it's worth," he says, "and the reason seems to be that network people are getting snowed. We don't know enough about boxing and its audience appeal, and the spread is crazy. For divisional title fights, under the heavyweight class, the price can run from $75,000 to $400,000. And what you get for $400,000 may not bring a higher rating than a $75,000 fight. These prices will start to return to earth once we learn more about what we're bidding for."

"But even if boxing prices stabilize, Chet Simmons, head of NBC Sports, has no confidence that other material will stop escalating. "We thought that pro football, too, had reached its ceiling years ago," says Simmons, "and the cost is now wilder than ever. Since we can't be sure what rights fees will climb to in anthology sports, we have to start thinking in terms of control. And, as a safeguard, the answer may be programming that we put together ourselves. *Super Stars,* for instance, has been called 'trash sports' and 'junk sports,' but it's entertaining and it makes money for ABC because its cost can be controlled. All of us are doing OK now with anthology sports, but we won't be if tabs keep growing and sponsors balk."

Certainly Eddie Einhorn isn't repulsed by the idea of networks putting together their own events. "It's simple," he says. "You get a field, or a gym, or a rink, and you line up your performers. Everything on TV doesn't have to be a world title. This is entertainment, and we may have to create to be competitive."

If things reach that stage, you could be looking one day at *Trash Sports Spectacular, Junk Sports World* and *Wide World of In-House Sports.*

DON KOWET

For Better or for Worse?

A few years ago, Notre Dame and the University of Georgia agreed to shift their football game from Saturday, November 9, to Monday, September 9, because they wanted to receive national television coverage. Both schools were criticized; but Bear Bryant, the legendary coach of the University of Alabama, applauded. "We think TV exposure is so important to our program, so important to our university, that we will schedule ourselves to fit the medium. I'll play at midnight if that's what TV wants." In 1979, some National Open Tennis finals were rescheduled to begin after the football game was over at 5:00 P.M. This created inconveniences for the players and audience—not the least of which were the poor lighting conditions at the end of the day.

Sometimes the scheduling for television affects the character of the sports event. Important tournaments sponsored by the Professional Golfers' Association used to require golfers to play 36 holes on the final day. Now the final round is split into two days—Saturday and Sunday—of 18 holes each. This arrangement is more convenient for the networks.

What is the impact of television on American sports and society? Many critics insist it is substantial and negative and that the integrity of some sports has been jeopardized by accommodations made to television. Don Kowet summarizes the debate.

Remember 1949? Forty-two million Americans sweltered in flimsy bleachers, cheering minor-league baseball in 488 stadiums. Hockey

This essay first appeared July 1, 1978.

players didn't do their brawling in arenas shaded by magnolias. NFL quarterbacks didn't model pantyhose.

Then, during the decades that followed, network TV helped to change American sports. The tool the networks used was money: $250 million in 1975; [$400] million [in 1978]; estimates of close to $1 billion [in] 1980.

The question is: in trimming sports events to fit the curve of cathode tubes, have the networks cut off only the fat—or the lean, too?

Consider some of the criticisms we hear about television's impact on sports:

TV's weekend bombardment of viewers with sports will inevitably turn the U.S. into a nation of observers, not doers.

Since the start of the 1970s, critics of network sports have been waiting for participant sports to wither away. In fact, though, TV's impact has been just the reverse. According to Nielsen studies, more Americans are involved actively in sports than ever before.

Golf is a sport that has prospered since the networks "tampered" with it, eliminating match-play to make the length of matches more predictable. Likewise, tennis has benefited from TV exposure, after adding the set-ending tie breaker. Top-flight tennis on TV generated a grass-roots explosion, ignited, say the experts, on that September day in 1973 when Billie Jean King trounced Bobby Riggs.

"Not only was it watched by 37.2 million people," recalls one source at Nielsen, "but it was watched by more women than men. Right away we noticed a big upsurge in the number of people playing tennis, especially women."

Similarly, before TV made a star out of gymnast Olga Korbut, gymnastics had about 100,000 adherents. Now that figure has more than tripled. "Back in '72, before the Munich Olympics," says Don Ohlmeyer, NBC executive producer for sports, "they held important gymnastics meets at high-school gyms, and couldn't sell tickets. Now they hold important meets in Madison Square Garden, and the scalpers stand outside getting their price."

TV selfishly reshapes sports to fit its scheduling requirements.

Critics cite two examples in 1978 alone: at the $250,000 Grand Slam tennis competition in Boca Raton, Fla., a near riot occurred outside the stadium, with angry fans, brandishing their tickets, clamoring to get in. The starting time on their tickets read 1 P.M., but to accommodate the taping requirements of TV, the tennis match had been rescheduled for 12:30 P.M. Now, at 1:15 P.M., with the match well into the second set, the spectators were still being barred, prohibited from reaching their seats till the players switched courts.

A few weeks later, the World Boxing Association (WBA) refused to sanction a scheduled title fight in Oklahoma City between its featherweight champion, Cecilio Lastra, and challenger Sean O'Grady. Without WBA sanction, NBC refused to broadcast the fight. Without the NBC broadcast, there was no fight.

The Super Bowl is telecast at 6 P.M. . . . the basketball season stretches into June. "Remember, though, that we're not the ones always applying the pressure to make changes," cautions one network executive. "Take the decision to play weekday World Series games at night. We weren't very anxious to televise the World Series at night, since it coincides with our big fall entertainment season."

"NBC did not want nighttime television in the 1975 World Series," confirms baseball commissioner Bowie Kuhn. "We did—because you may have a difference in audience of 25 million people from afternoon to night. We're trying to promote baseball to the American public. How are we going to do that by playing these big games on a Wednesday afternoon?"

Even so dogged a critic of the networks as Peter Gruenstein, director of F.A.N.S. (the Ralph Nader-supported citizen's sports lobby) sees no harm in such schedule shifts. "If the NFL wants to play a game at 4 P.M. instead of 1 P.M., or baseball wants to go to nights during the World Series, all so more people can watch on TV, we have no objection. After all, the value of TV is its ability to make sports available to more people. On the other hand," he adds, "when the NFL restructures its whole schedule to give people not more matches but 'better' ones, we think that's wrong. When TV starts controlling events that way, it's acting like a promoter, not just a broadcaster." Beginning [in 1978], the last season's NFL division champions [played] much tougher schedules, and the top teams in any one division [played] more equal schedules. An NFL spokesman admits that "better games for TV" was a consideration in the new arrangement, "but not the only one."

TV peppers sporting contests with contrived timeouts, turning games into glue connecting network commercials.

Truer in sports like basketball and hockey than in sports equipped with natural pauses—boxing's 60-second rest period between rounds, football's pauses to shift offensive and defensive units, baseball's leisurely hiatus between innings.

"Even those few artificial timeouts inserted for commercial purposes are a small price to pay to provide fans with a continuous diet of quality sports," insists ABC's Jim Spence.

Meanwhile, TV has enlivened other "dead time" through the use of videotape replays, some of which are not only entertaining but instructive. "Kids today are much better basketball players than they used to be. TV, not vitamins, should get the credit," says Ray Meyer, coach at De Paul University in Chicago [since 1942] and one of the winningest active coaches in college basketball. "Today, every kid who's interested can watch all the games he wants on TV, with the fine points shown him in slow-motion instant replay."

TV, at the collegiate level, has given a few schools the edge in recruiting.

If TV is producing more proficient high-school athletes, critics contend, it is also ensuring that most of them matriculate at the same handful of universities. "We haven't been on TV even regionally for years," says one losing Big-Ten [football] coach, "but some of the schools we recruit against, like Notre Dame, Nebraska and Ohio State, are on national TV twice or three times a year. National TV is where the good youngsters want to be," he adds, "and they know our school isn't likely to get them there."

On the other hand, network spokesmen point out that about 50 of the NCAA's 140 major-college [football] teams are given some national exposure on ABC each year—and that every team in a conference usually shares the revenues earned by these top TV attractions.

TV bullies sports into altering their rules.

"Who really did instigate all those NFL rules changes in recent years?" asks John Dockery, once a football player for the Steelers and Jets, and now a reporter for New York's WNEW-TV. "Was it the advertisers? Was it the networks, looking for a more marketable product?"

"I can tell you," replies Bob Cochran, former broadcast adviser to the NFL, "that no advertiser, nor any network, has ever had the slightest input into rules changes in the NFL. In every case, the impetus has come from the league itself, in an effort to make the games more exciting."

Currently, the NHL, anxious to get hockey back on network TV, is considering a proposal to drop its traditional three 20-minute periods for four 15-minute periods, with a shorter time between periods. This, they hope, will help keep viewers from wandering away from their sets.

"The networks don't tell you what to do," says one source close to the NHL. "They don't have to. You figure out what's good for them—then do it yourself, or else you don't get that fat network contract."

TV distorts the nature of the games it covers, promoting a "cult of the individual," instead of the team concept.

"TV takes a game like baseball and turns it into a series of one-on-one confrontations between pitcher and batter," says Michael Novak, sports author and philosophy professor, "because it thinks that's more entertaining than the game itself. By ignoring the other eight men on the field, it misses what the game is really about. That's true of other sports, too."

"When the Knicks won their championship in 1970," rebuts Mike Burke, a vice president of Madison Square Garden, "I don't think there was any doubt in anyone's mind that they won because they played better as a team than anyone else. Portland, which won in 1977, did so primarily through good team play, too. I don't think that identifying the parts, the great individual players, means that TV is claiming those parts are greater than the whole."

Rounding out the pros and cons of TV's impact on sports, the plus side of the ledger should include the following:

TV aroused the sleepy hinterlands, transmitting images that conveyed reality as radio never could. ("Not only does it provide big revenue," argues Baltimore Orioles manager Earl Weaver, "but it give people all over the U.S. a chance to see all the great players.") TV created a new appetite for big-league sports, and the major leagues—to nearly everyone's satisfaction—were willing and able (in the jet age) to supply a new diet of big-league franchises. And besides contributing to the expansion of existing leagues, TV helped create entire leagues out of whole cloth (the AFL, the ABA, etc.). It raised pro football to a par in popularity with baseball. It introduced millions to tennis and golf (particularly women). It turned pro sports into a socially acceptable profession, and a desirable one.

On the minus side, though, TV turned most of these 488 minor-league baseball stadiums into supermarkets and parking lots. And TV has legitimized such pseudo-sports as demolition derbies and wrist-wrestling, by presenting them, as one critic puts it, "with all the solemnity of the British Open."

There's no guarantee that the tenuous balance won't tip toward the negative. As the networks' financial commitment grows, so does their clout—and the temptation to use that power to further tailor sports to TV's image. The FCC, for instance, [in 1978 took] punitive measures against CBS, for mispromoting a series of tennis matches as "winner-take-all."[1] . . .

"Unless the networks adopt the necessary safeguards to police themselves," warns NBC's Don Ohlmeyer, "Congress will pass laws. In any case, I think the networks will eventually get out of the area of bidding for, and producing, major sporting events altogether. Just as they do in prime time, they'll rely on outside organizations—the equivalent of Hollywood production companies—to confect, develop and deliver sports programming."

And that might create TV's biggest impact on sports of all.

"So many sports organizations have built their entire budgets around network TV," says ABC's sports (and news) chief Roone Arledge, "that if we ever withdrew the money, the whole structure would collapse." But the networks are extremely unlikely to withdraw the money—not unless the ratings go down. And that will happen only if Americans lose their avid interest in sports.

1. In July 1978, the FCC voted to give CBS's owned and operated station in Los Angeles (KNXT-TV) only a short-term, one-year license renewal, instead of the normal three-year renewal. This was the first time that a network-owned station has been penalized simply because of the timing of its license renewal application. The four tennis matches in question were billed as the "Heavyweight Championship of Tennis" and were all won by Jimmy Connors. But, unknown to the public, all the losers received substantial compensation.

ADVERTISING

"If we consider democracy as a set of institutions which aim to make everything available to everybody, it would not be an overstatement to describe advertising as the characteristic rhetoric of democracy. . . ." When Daniel Boorstin, historian and librarian for the Library of Congress, made this statement, he was not referring specifically to television advertising. However, over half of all national media advertising is for television, and by 1986 television is expected to become the leading local advertising medium, with about $8 million in local ad revenues. According to economist John Kenneth Galbraith, "the industrial system is profoundly dependent upon commercial television and could not exist in its present form without it. . . ."

A pamphlet published by the National Association of Broadcasters refers to advertising as "a key factor in this country's standard of living which is the highest in the world." The broadcast industry claims that advertising permits free television because the advertiser, not the viewer, pays for the programming. Former FCC commissioner Nicholas Johnson, now head of the National Citizens Communication Lobby, disagrees. He claims that television actually costs taxpayers about $15 billion a year: the cost of buying, using and maintaining the television receiver plus the increased costs to the consumer of advertised goods, costs passed on by the advertiser to help defray expenses of television commercials.

There are over two thousand advertisers using television, and more than one-fifth of television air time is devoted to commercials. In 1979, more than $10 billion was spent on television commercials, not including the cost of producing them. That figure is expected to exceed $12 billion in 1980. The Television Bureau of Advertising projects that by 1985 television advertising revenues will be greater than $21 billion and by 1990 will be about $40 billion.

The major share of the revenues goes to the networks, and the hundred largest advertisers normally spend more than half of that amount. In 1979, twelve national advertisers each spent over $100 million in television advertising. Proctor & Gamble, traditionally the biggest spender for television ads, invested $463 million. The eleven other advertisers in order of expenditure were General Foods, American Home Products, General Mills, General Motors, Bristol-Myers, McDonald's, Pepsi Company, Lever Brothers, Coca-Cola Company and Philip Morris.

In recent years, the number of prime-time commercial minutes has increased by 42 per cent, and advertising now occupies nearly eight minutes of every hour. About 60 per cent of that time is devoted to promoting five product categories: toiletries and toilet goods, food products, over-the-counter medicines, automobiles and accessories, and cleaning products. Another five categories comprise approximately 26 per cent: household equipment, confectionary and soft drinks, sporting goods and toys, insurance and pet foods. Most television advertisers especially want to attract adults between the ages of 18 and 49 who live in the 300 largest metropolitan areas. These people buy about 80 per cent of the goods and services purchased in the United States during the course of a year.

Television advertisers in the 1979–80 season were charged anywhere from $25 per minute for a commercial broadcast after 1:00 A.M. on an Ohio station to $200,000 for a 30-second spot during the movie *Jaws* and the 1980 Super Bowl. The important measurement in television advertising is cost per thousand homes, or CPM, and the standard length of a TV ad is now 30-seconds. The CPM for a 30-second prime-time network commercial in the fall of 1980 is expected to average about $4.50. This would be about 9 per cent higher than the figure for the fall of 1979.

The cost of producing commercials in 1979 was also higher than for previous years. Many 60-second commercials cost up to $100,000 to produce, some as much as $400,000. Producing a 30-second spot could cost over $75,000. Most commercials in 1979 ranged from $25,000 to $50,000 to produce.

The cost of commercials can vary greatly depending upon the difficulty and location of filming and the prestige of the talent. Celebrity advertising may have been initiated when Eleanor Roosevelt was paid $43,000 to do a margarine commercial in the 1950s. By

1978, Sir Laurence Olivier received $500,000 a year for Polaroid ads, and talent alone cost the producers of commercials over $100 million.

In 1966, *Newsweek* stated that commercials were "better than the programs they sponsor" and often more expensive. Today, commercials are no longer as arty or creative as they were then, thus one expensive production cost has been eliminated. Advertisers discovered that artistic commercials were too popular. Consumers loved the commercials, but forgot the products. So advertising returned to the hard sell and in 1976 *Newsweek* commented, "the trend today has evolved toward an older, simpler style, with commercials taking their cue from the vindictive charge of 'Ring around the collar' or the Charmin grocer, George Whipple, furtively squeezing a role of toilet paper."

A new development that may become widespread in the 1980s is the time-compressed ad, in which a 30-second commercial can be reduced to 20 seconds by electronically speeding up the sound track. Preliminary experiments suggest that speeded-up versions of commercials are "more interesting," provide higher recall and make people on the screen appear "brisker and more alert." If they are in fact more effective, time-compressed ads could have notable advantages. Networks and local stations could air more commercials and the cost to advertisers would be reduced because less time would be purchased for each ad.

The potential of television advertising was described in 1931 by an advertising executive, Edgar Fox. He noted how improvements in photographic reproduction techniques and color printing processes helped stimulate ads: "The cigar advertiser who appeals to young men can actually demonstrate that cigar smoking will make any young man look like a major executive. . . . A reproduction of a luscious strawberry shortcake [will be] much more effective than creating an appetite by any word-of-mouth description." Because of its ability to illustrate and dramatize the advertiser's message, television would become "the most powerful medium for sales stimulation." Fox's statement seems to have been prophetic. Many believe television is among the most recession proof industries in the country because advertisers will always be reluctant to cut back on their television expenditures for fear of losing their shares of the market.

MARTIN MAYER

Does TV Advertising Make You Buy?

The vice president of advertising service for Bristol-Myers and the man who oversees Clairol advertising, Pete Spengler, stated: "When a woman buys a bottle of shampoo, there's no way to know for certain whether the primary impetus was a TV ad, a magazine ad, the label on the bottle, or something else. She probably doesn't know herself."

The advertiser's first criterion for a television commercial is, "Does it sell?" There is no easy answer to this question. Martin Mayer explores the problems of attempting to measure the effects of television advertising on sales.

For six [and a half] hours every day the television set is on in the home of that mythical personage with the enormous buying power, the Average American Householder. At least [70] minutes of that six [and a half] hours are given over to commercial messages, which means [over 125] separate messages a day; [about 900] a week; more than [46,000] a year. For the privilege of putting such messages before the Average American Householder and his [or her] Friends, advertisers in [1979] paid [over 10] billion dollars.

Did they get their money's worth? Oddly enough, nobody knows. As Charles K. Raymond, former technical director of the Advertising Research Foundation, wrote in the *Harvard Business Review,* "Virtually no large manufacturer knows how much of his profit was

Excerpts have been taken from this essay, which first appeared in two parts, January 8, January 15, 1966.

caused by his advertising."[1] From ratings surveys, market research studies, "recall" interviews and the like, the advertiser can say for sure that a lot of horses have been led to the water. And the incessant disappearance of goods from the stores into the homes means that somebody has been lapping it up. But no one can say for sure that these particular horses have been persuaded to drink.

Some commercials, unquestionably, have moved merchandise. The split head for Anacin, the white knight for Ajax, that genial tiger for [Exxon]—all these presented a new view of a product that was itself virtually unchanged, that was still for sale at the same places for the same prices, and suddenly the "tonnage" zoomed. Only the new commercials could explain the change.

In the present state of the art of research, these what-else-could-it-be? measurements are most advertisers' only way of judging the effectiveness of their commercials. Such tactics work fine when the sales increase is a big one, but usually it isn't. Normally, over the life of a single advertising campaign, there isn't anything left over as a sure thing after the computers have calculated the *possible* benefits to sales from special store promotions, tax cuts, new packaging, the messy divorce of the competitor's regional sales manager, hot spells and the like. So you can't prove anything. Justifying their advertising expenditures to their stockholders, most managements must fall back on something like the remark once made by advertising researcher Paul Gerhold, "If you think your advertising doesn't pay, just stop it for a while and see what happens." . . .

The perfect product for a television commercial is a new beauty aid sold at a rack beside the cash register in the store. The commercial demonstrates the product, suggests you too could look like that by using it, and shows the package—which stays in the mind enough to be remembered when seen while the money is actually in hand. Because nobody who buys beauty aids is really wholly pleased with the way she (or he) looks, there is almost no brand loyalty to fight against. And because hope springs eternal, the new grease has a built-in edge.

The worst product for a television commercial (not counting things like drop-forge machinery which are unlikely to interest the Householder) is probably the one that requires the grasp of an

1. Charles K. Raymond, "Must Advertising Communicate To Sell?," *Harvard Business Review,* September-October 1965, pp. 148–59.

abstract idea followed by a special trip to a place not on your normal daily route. Not many advertisers who have tried television have abandoned it, but the Florists Trans-world Delivery Association is a case in point. Back in 1959, after sponsoring several shows, FTD decided TV couldn't persuade viewers to send flowers by wire, and so bowed out [FTD later went into nonnetwork advertising].

Many television commercials, of course, do not aim to make an immediate sale of a specific product. Even at [$100,000 or more] for a single nighttime commercial minute on a network, an advertiser may feel he gets his money's worth just by building his name.[2] Squibb introduced the electric toothbrush; but when General Electric put out a similar item ("Progress Is Our Most Important Product") it took away much of the business. Such image building can be done in print, too—but the TV commercial intensifies the mood created by print advertising.

Some commercials are aimed as much at the salesman as they are at the consumer. Avon Products, which sells through housewives picking up some commission income in their spare time, advertises in daytime television to give its amateur order takers a model they can follow when they ring the next doorbell. . . .

Sometimes the purpose can be to make a little company seem more prominent in its field. A Midwest fishing-tackle maker, Shakespeare, bought occasional inexpensive minutes on the *Today* show and was delighted at the improvement of its booth positions at sportsman's shows.

Department stores and discount houses use television just the way they use the big "advertised special" in the newspapers—to pull people into the store, where they will buy more than they planned to buy. "People shop at certain stores by habit, and you want to break that habit pattern," Pete Cash [vice chairman of the Television Bureau of Advertising] argues. "Well, the newspaper can't say, 'Now, wait a minute!' But a forcing television commercial can, by its intrusiveness."

"That line about 'I know half the money I spend on advertising is

2. Sometimes the effect of advertising on name-building is immediate and measurable. For example, in 1972, Northwestern Mutual Life Insurance Company spent over one million dollars in advertising during the Munich Olympics. A nationwide poll taken just prior to the opening of the Olympics showed Northwestern thirty-fourth in a ranking of insurance name familiarity scores. Two weeks later, a similar poll ranked Northwestern third.

wasted, but I can never find out which half,'" said Horace Schwerin [a pioneer in testing the effectiveness of television commericals]. "Whoever said it first—whether it was John Wanamaker here or Lord Leverhulme in England—he was way off. An optimist. The fact is, all but about 10 percent of the money spent on television commercials is wasted. The amazing thing is that television pays out, running at an efficiency of 10 percent." . . .

For most advertisers, indeed, the whole question of the effectiveness of commercials reduces to the simple business of audience size. What television offers . . . is [an] enormous audience. The effectiveness of the commercial itself strikes many advertisers (including some of the most experienced and successful) as a number on a roulette wheel: You may hit a winner, but you'd better not count on it. These advertisers measure the effectiveness of their commercials simply in terms of the number of homes they reach divided by the cost of the time—the "CPM," or cost-per-thousand, which is the Rock of Gibraltar of the industry. They make up their budget on the assumption that they want to secure so-and-so many "exposures," assuming a fixed value for each time the commercial actually appears on the home screen. . . .

SALLY BEDELL

Wanna See a TV Preview?

As in the case of pilots for new prime-time series, most new commercials are subjected to testing in order to provide advertisers with an idea of whether or not the commercial will increase the sales of the product. Jonathan Price, author of *The Best Thing on TV: Commercials,* suggests that previewing is undertaken "simply because people like to have the obvious to be confirmed before okaying a $3 million ad strategy."

The two most common ways to try out a new commercial are over-the-air testing in selected markets and theater testing. Sally Bedell describes how commercials are theater tested.

"We have taken the liberty of selecting you for an important role in television and are, herewith, inviting you to participate as a member of a handpicked, special audience at our two-hour session 'Television Preview'. . . ."

The invitation continues in crisp, businesslike language. It is signed by one H. J. Shreeve, Director, Audience Selection Staff. There is nothing required except some time. As an added inducement, $80 worth of prizes will be awarded. Ultimately, the offer tantalizes.

On the appointed night, some fifty people congregate at the Roof Garden atop the Adelphia House in Philadelphia for the evening's entertainment. But first, a bit of work. The participants are asked to volunteer a few vital statistics and to select their preferred brands from several categories of products (dog foods, air fresheners, etc.) that would be offered in "shopping bags" awarded to the winners of a drawing.

This essay first appeared November 26, 1977.

After the drawing, the "television preview manager" (so designated by the tag on his natty three-piece suit) tells everyone that producers and network executives are seeking the opinions of the public before deciding what to put on television. And by the way, he adds, commercials will be included to duplicate the cozy living-room atmosphere and render the preview more realistic. The crowd groans.

The 19-inch screen lights up first with *The Nancy Dussault Show* and then *Two's Company* starring John Amos—both shopworn pilots from earlier TV seasons. A cursory questionnaire about the plot lines and characters follows. Then yet another brand list is distributed for a second drawing. It carries many of the products on the first list. Some have even appeared in the commercials nestled within the pilots (Aha!). One brief McDonald's commercial and two more questionnaires later, the "preview" has ended.

For the participants, the evening ranks on the excitement scale one notch below turtle races. But H. J. Shreeve and the folks at Research Systems Corporation's Audience Selection Staff have extracted what they wanted: a measure of the effectiveness—or ineffectiveness—of several commercials for their clients.

In the advertising industry, such an evening is called a theater test, a captive-audience test or, somewhat ominously, a forced-viewing test. It is one method in an array of testing strategies that advertisers use to assess the impact of their messages before they illuminate the TV screen. With a 30-second prime-time spot going for [as high as $150,000] these days, a TV advertiser needs something tangible to buttress his instincts before laying out his multimillion-dollar ad campaign. Says one executive at a major consumer-products company, "You like to have a warm feeling that what you are trying to communicate is being communicated." Theater-test results weigh heavily when a new commercial campaign is being launched, but they are also used when an established commercial takes a major departure. For example, the TV ads for one leading laundry detergent have routinely used ordinary housewives attesting to the quality of the product. When someone suggested that men be used for the testimonials as well, the ad agency found some husbands who pitched in with the laundry and recorded their comments. The resulting commercial was subjected to theater tests. The "warm feeling" prevailed, and the new line of ads got the go-ahead.

Almost any market-research company can be called on to construct a captive-audience test, but three companies occupy the theater-testing empyrean. They shroud their techniques in the cloak of "security" and "competitive information." Publicity, they feel, might jeopardize their research results.

ASI Market Research, Inc., better known as ASI, boasts the most elaborate facilities: a 400-seat theater in Los Angeles described by an ASI brochure as "decoratively bland to avoid any possible extraneous influence." Most of ASI's testing takes place in the theater. ASI services a roster of more than 100 advertisers, including some of the biggest (Colgate, Bristol-Myers). The company's income from theater testing amounts to an estimated $8 million annually.

McCollum/Spielman & Company in Long Island, N.Y., and Research Systems Corporation of deliberately unobtrusive Evansville, Ind., operate on a slightly smaller scale. Nearly $1 million of RSC income is derived from theater tests for about 40 of the top 100 advertisers. McCollum/Spielman earns several million dollars from the 60 advertisers it serves. In short, theater testing is healthy business.

Neither McCollum/Spielman nor RSC has a permanent facility of the ASI sort. Both companies set up shop at motels or apartment houses in a scattering of cities around the country, according to their research needs. Like a band of Gypsies, their researchers keep shifting from one city to the next. Says Meg Blair, president of Research Systems Corporation, "We move when everybody figures out why we are there."

More than 500,000 people pass through theater tests each year. There can be as many as several thousand participants nationwide on any given day. Except, that is, during Christmas holiday season when tests are suspended because, says Harold Spielman, a president of McCollum/Spielman, "People tend to be in a good, happy frame of mind. They tend not to be critical."

Theater testing has been around since 1946. It was pioneered by Horace Schwerin of the now-defunct Schwerin Research Corporation, which he sold to RSC in 1968. The approach carried out by Schwerin's disciples (all of whom worked for him) may vary slightly from one company to the next, but the basic idea is to entice a preselected group of people to a specified location under the pretense of evaluating new television programs.

The invitations originate, for the most part, with "reverse directories," phone books broken down by location rather than name. The ASI people also track down prospective viewers in shopping malls. Through telephone calls and face-to-face interviews, ASI researchers shape their prospective audiences according to specific demographic characteristics: age, sex, socioeconomic status and television-viewing habits. Whenever someone expresses an interest in attending, the ASI interviewer actually tries to talk him out of it just to test his commitment to attend.

When the list has congealed, nicely engraved invitations are issued. RSC's Meg Blair says, "We put a lot of money into our invitation so it would be objective. We don't want it to overpromise and we don't want it to underpromise. If it's too classy it may promise too much." In the RSC invitation the words "pilot" and "commercial" are artfully omitted. The wording merely informs the recipient that he will see "television material." Flattery figures prominently as well. If the preview material is eventually telecast, the invitation says, "you will be able to feel that you were a member of the team that helped judge and evaluate them for their final release over television networks and stations." Anywhere from 15 to 45 per cent of those invited accept the invitation and appear at the preview, clutching a ticket.

The preview described earlier was a typical theater test run by RSC. The also-ran pilots served as "control" material. RSC always has about ten such duds at the ready. Explains Meg Blair, "If we are testing commercials we have to hold the programs constant. We try to keep them as recent as possible."

In fairness, it should be noted that in some instances the theater testing companies genuinely preview freshly minted pilots. At RSC, pilot testing has grown to nearly 20 per cent of the business. ASI probably devotes just as much time to testing pilots and movies as it does to commercials. However, Jerry Lukeman, president of ASI, admits, "When the networks are not testing, we use as filler material pilots that at the time have been rejected."

Once an audience has been captured for an evening, the theater tester analyzes more responses than a fortuneteller has tea leaves. The persuasiveness of an advertising message emerges when the viewers tick off the lists of brands before and after seeing commercials. A persuasive commercial for brand X presumably persuades a brand Y viewer to switch over to X after absorbing the message. Questionnaires gauge reactions to an advertisement's every element—its spokesman, music, theme and so forth. At ASI, certain viewers are assigned seats with "dial-interest recorders," little knobs that they can turn to indicate their approval or disapproval of what they see on the screen. The resulting responses are tracked continuously on interest "flow charts."

In view of all that activity, one would have to be comatose to ignore the importance of commercials in these "previews." Why, then, construct the ruse of evaluating new programs at all? Explains one advertising-agency executive, "If you tell them you want them to watch commercials, they will become instant experts, and they'll forget the message because they will be concentrating too hard."

Besides avoiding the commercial connoisseur, theater testers may have other reasons for their guise as well. "The aura of television, the idea of sneak preview of possible TV series, is very important," says Marvin Mord, vice president of research at ABC. "People wouldn't come just to look at commercials unless they were paid."

Advertisers and ad agencies alike have been fully aware of the theater-testing technique for years. It is, in their view, utterly defensible. "I don't think it's unethical," says one ad-agency executive. "People enjoy it, and some of them win prizes." Says a former research director for another ad agency, "Nobody is taking anything out of their pockets. Yes, they are being misled slightly, but nobody is irreparably harmed."

Executives at the networks generally line up with Madison Avenue. They all understand the theater testing *modus operandi.* Marvin Mord thinks attending a theater test is "a risk and an experience. It is like going to night court. It's something everyone should do once. I don't think the viewers are cheated or misled."

Naturally theater-testing companies unflinchingly defend their philosophy and approach. Jerry Lukeman says, "The material we show to people is interesting stuff. And besides, they like it. They feel that they are participating in a process. They have an opportunity to say something that has been on their minds a long time." Indeed, Lukeman and other executives in the field point out that 80 to 90 per cent of the audience leaves a theater test feeling satisfied. Even in this entertainment-drenched era, it seems that a free show has an enduring allure.

JOHN MARIANI

Can Advertisers Read—and Control—Our Emotions?

One shortcoming of theater testing or other traditional means of determining the effectiveness of television commercials is the inability of the tester to gauge whether the respondent is giving his or her honest reaction to the ad in question. Further, the conscious reaction might differ from the subconscious reaction to the advertisement. Scientists are conducting physiological testing to try to determine the viewer's *true* response to commercials. John Mariani reviews the methods and the debate associated with this new form of evaluating the effectiveness of a television ad.

It is closer to 1984 than you think. You're sitting in a lounge chair in a laboratory watching [one of your favorite programs]. An electrode is stuck to your head. A wire is sending electrical currents through your fingers. An infrared light is scanning across your pupils. And a highly sensitive microphone is recording every gurgle in your throat.

A commercial comes on the screen: a well-known blonde in a bikini is caressing a bright-red sports car. Suddenly some scientists in white coats come through a door, unstrap all the apparatus, thank you and send you home. One scientist turns to the others and says, "Well *she* doesn't turn him on any more. His sweat glands were not activated. His left brain did not respond to the part about the rack-and-pinion steering, and his eyes were not directed at the manufacturer's logo. And the only sound in his throat was the

This essay first appeared March 31, 1979.

swallow of beer. Gentlemen, this commercial will not sell this automobile, and that blonde is being paid too much. Tell that creative director at the ad agency he's fired."

This situation is more or less fictitious—at least at the moment—for Madison Avenue does not always judge the effectiveness of its commercials quite so scientifically. The traditional method is to create a campaign, have numerous expensive lunches and then ask a lot of people if they'd go out and buy the product after seeing the commercial. This is what is called in advertising, "running it up the flagpole to see who'll salute."

Nevertheless, the laboratory techniques described *are* being used right now by a few scientists who are trying to help some agencies find out if you might be telling the truth about your response to TV commercials. Through a series of physiological tests that measure brain waves, skin arousal, eye movement and voice response, these experimenters may prove that—deep down—you really do like Mr. Whipple.

One of the scientists is Dr. Sidney Weinstein of the NeuroCommunication Research Laboratories in Danbury, Conn. Weinstein, who investigates brain waves, has demonstrated that the left side of the human brain is analytical and reasoning, and more responsive to the message and details of a commercial. The right side is more involved with the appreciation of space, emotions and the mood evoked by such sensory stimuli as colors, romantic sunsets or girls in bikinis. Weinstein believes that some products—like perfume or beer, which are sold on feelings rather than on specifics—should pitch toward the right-brain stimuli. Cars and life insurance, on the other hand are usually sold to the left brain, in a detailed, analytical way.

By attaching a few small electrodes to the scalp of a viewer, Weinstein can measure which half of the brain is being stimulated. In addition, he believes he can tell whether that response is positive or negative by measuring a third brain wave (called the "cortical evoked potential"), which indicates whether or not the viewer is interested enough to buy the product.

Dr. Herbert E. Krugman, General Electric's manager of public-opinion research, agrees with Weinstein. "Much of the response to advertising is right-brain," Krugman says. "And students of media behavior may yet confront the embarrassing fact that television audiences pay close attention, for long periods of time, to stimuli that create no thought and little recall. Why do they do it? What's happening? Perhaps a way has been opened to find out."

Other scientists are trying to find what really gets under our skin while our eyes are on the set. Walt Wesley, a pioneer in the commercial applications of psychogalvanic skin response, tests commercials by running a very low (and unfelt) electric current through a viewer's finger. This measures the activation of the person's sweat glands, which is an indicator of "emotional arousal." Wesley found that what viewers often say about a commercial does not always jibe with their unconscious sweat-gland responses. "We're giving the ad people the strongest motivational impact," says the California-based researcher. "Eighty per cent of our work today is on TV ads, often to gauge what will be effective before money is spent on the actual production of a commercial. I've issued a challenge to my critics to hold a Super Bowl competition in which every copy-testing company belonging to the American Marketing Association tries to measure ad effectiveness as well as my psychogalvanometer. Sales figures will decide the winner." So far, Wesley's competitors have not taken the challenge.

Another scientist who uses psycholgalvanic tests is Dr. Tom Turicchi of the Consumer Behavior Center in Richardson, Texas. Turicchi's methods are almost the same as Wesley's—with one important difference. During the tests, Turicchi asks the viewers to enter a positive or negative reaction on an electronic voting device. He then follows this up with a post-test questionnaire, which he uses to determine specific attitudes toward the product. Though Wesley does some follow-up questioning, he places primary importance on arousal—or lack of it.

Nonetheless, Turicchi's accuracy in predicting successful marketing is high: he is able, he claims, to determine whether any given record will make *Billboard* magazine's Top 20 hit list in advance with 92 per-cent accuracy, and he has helped test the music in the Kentucky Fried Chicken and Dr. Pepper campaigns.

Al Remson of Ardek research in East Norwalk, Conn., has experimented with infrared eye scans that track the rapid movements of the viewer's eye over a television screen. Remson, though, feels that "television is a difficult medium for eye-tracking, because it's so dynamic. There's *so* much movement, and the viewer is not in control of what he sees. All we can try to find out is whether the viewer's eye is on the blonde in the bikini or on the company's name and product. If the eye is well-directed, you may not even need a long commercial or extraneous visuals, because the unconscious eye is attentive to what is important to the viewer."

Jerry Ohlsten, the research director of Cunningham-Walsh Advertising, also has a few thoughts about eye-movement tests. "We've learned," he says, "that people are not passive when they watch. They are selective, if unconsciously so. We used to think that the first three to five seconds of an ad was the setup, so we put lots of effort into that time spot. But now our research shows that people may focus in on one small section of the screen in the first *quarter* of a second, and that their eye movements are not quite so random as we thought."

A still more fascinating methodology is voice response, a field studied at the Consumer Response Corporation in New York. The pitch of one's voice is largely involuntary, says CRC's president, David Schwartz; and as the individual's feelings intensify, the larynx becomes tight and the pitch increases, which is why people's voices tend to get higher when aroused. Schwartz uses a computer to measure this physiological response as he asks questions about what the viewer has just seen on the screen. The viewer's voice, recorded on tape, is then studied for its "hertz levels," which indicate the emotion that lies beneath the verbal response. "Let's say you're just being nice by saying you'll buy my product after seeing the ad," says Schwartz. "But the computer shows a hertz level that indicates you really didn't care emotionally for what you'd just seen. That kind of information is more valuable than what we'd get by simply asking a person about his feelings. Normal market research is fine for comparing two car ads, but when you're talking about a product that has an ambiguous, emotional appeal, voice response is very valuable. The world of advertising as a fly-by-the-seat-of-your-pants operation is dying off. Advertisers need stronger evidence than their own feelings to go on."

Some Madison Avenue marketers, though, feel intimidated by

these kinds of tests, and some creative directors have admitted that the tests could compromise their jobs. But most research directors take a wait-and-see attitude. Max Bonfeld, director of consumer research services for Young & Rubicam, wonders whether the experiments actually measure positive or negative emotional responses at all. "Do these tests actually show how you feel about a commercial?" he asks. "I don't even know how scientific it all is. One of the constructs of scientific experimentation is the ability to repeat the results. I'm not convinced they can.

"To measure sweat or brain waves is not telling us much yet. Years ago there was a brassiere ad in some magazines that many women said was offensive. It showed a woman in various public places wearing a brassiere and no blouse. Well, the product was a great success—because the *idea* appealed to women who had a problem with their breasts. Could these tests measure that? And, most important, do they actually predict sales success? I don't think they do."

Francis Van Bortel, executive vice president in charge of strategy development at McCann-Erickson, is also not yet persuaded. "We've always had an interest in these tests, and they may be of some value. I think Krugman's work on brain waves is interesting, and eye-movement experiments seem to work all right on print ads. But remember, I've got to persuade all the members of an ad agency to go along with the results of these tests. And before they become staples of the industry, there must be a real academic and business shakedown and agreement as to what the tests actually measure."

Another research director at a major agency, who preferred not to be named, admitted: "Sure, some of these tests seem to work. But some of our clients are quite conservative and like to play it safe with marketing. Advertising is a small, small part of marketing, so how can you measure a test's effectiveness unless you can prove that the sales of a product were due specifically to one three-second shot of a girl in a bikini? It's ridiculous, and not very probable."

No one in either the ad agencies or the research labs thinks the tests smack of mind manipulation. In the films *A Clockwork Orange* and *The Parallax View* visual images were used to intimidate, persuade and mold the mind of an unwitting guinea pig. But the idea of millions of Americans, trudging zombielike to the supermarket as they chant "Cocoa Puffs, Cocoa Puffs," is a little farfetched. It seems certain, though, that TV commercials, in the future, will be carefully designed to appeal more to our subconscious minds—once the scientists figure out what it is that really turns us all on.

DAVID CHAGALL

The Child Probers

One popular advertising technique is to use children as a ploy to influence the purchasing decisions of their parents. An advertisement for a Boston TV station in *Broadcasting* magazine told potential advertisers:

> If you're selling, Charlie's Mom is buying. But you've got to sell Charlie first. His allowance is only 50¢ a week, but his buying power is an American phenomenon. He's not only tight with his Mom, but he has a way with his Dad, his Grandma and Aunt Harriet, too.
>
> When Charlie sees something he likes, he usually gets it. Just ask General Mills or McDonald's. . . .
>
> Of course, if you want to sell Charlie, you have to catch him when he's sitting down. Or at least standing still. And that's not easy. Lucky for you, Charlie's into TV.

A recent study by ABC's research department revealed that 65 per cent of all mothers are accompanied by their small children to the supermarket; 34 per cent take their children on *every* food shopping trip. More than half of the mothers surveyed said their children actually selected items to be bought. David Chagall describes how major advertisers are investigating the importance of directing advertising at children.

All across America children are periodically rounded up to serve as guinea pigs in child-research laboratories. Under a shroud of secrecy, youngsters are handed over to highly trained professionals who probe and analyze them in psychological experiments for pay.

This essay first appeared November 8, 1977.

The purpose? To uncover kids' hidden needs—knowledge that is then used to develop television commercials calculated to make children grab for supermarket impulse items or nag parents for sponsor brands.

Children are heavy television watchers. Two- to 5-year-olds typically spend [over 33] hours a week before the TV set, the 6-11 group about [30] hours. Advertisers spend an estimated $400 million a year to beam their messages at little people.

They do this because their research tells them that children make important choices about which brands of toys, candy, cereal and soft drinks the family buys. Less publicized is how strongly the kids also influence decisions on such adult products as vitamins, drugs and gasoline. Young children are hypersensitive to TV commercials, as most parents of nagging offspring already know too well.

The secrecy in this kind of research matches the cloak-and-dagger stuff of international spying. Researchers say the concealment is necessary to keep ahead of their rivals. Marty Miller, director of research at Mattel Toys, says, "I never heard of Procter & Gamble or General Motors saying, 'Here are the test results for our products.' If they did that, all their competitors would be right on their bandwagon. We're all sitting here trying to find secrets to put us one step ahead."

There may be other reasons, too. The uncovering of information used to manipulate human behavior is a sensitive subject in itself. When applied to children, it becomes explosive. One research executive confided, "We have a whole generation who have grown up reacting to commercials and television visuals. Add that to the tons of research done in the '50s and '60s and you understand why TV commercials have never been so effective. Child research is important because if you get them young, you keep them."

Some manufacturers and advertising agencies conduct testing programs of their own. But the more elaborate projects are farmed out to specialized firms, such as The Gene Reilly Group in Connecticut or Gilbert Youth Research in New York. One outfit—Child Reseach Service, Inc., funded by the well-known opinion-research company Yankelovich, Skelly and White—devotes itself exclusively to research on preteen children.

Headquartered in New York City, Child Research has its laboratory across the Hudson River in Rutherford, N.J., a dignified town of 20,000. At 50 Park Avenue in the town's tree-lined main shopping district, Maxine's sells women's apparel. In a four-room suite above the dress shop, the child researchers work in secret. No sign identifies the business. The front door is always kept locked. Though the lab has been here several years, it remains a mystery to its neighbors.

During test times, children arrive in cars early in the afternoon, stay a few hours and get picked up afterward. A child recruiter living nearby gets most of her names from PTA and church groups, scout troops and schools. She keeps detailed file cards on every child, noting ethnic origins, family income and social traits.

When children are provided by a group, the group keeps the fees—usually $1 per child for an hour's work, up to $35 for a full day of scrutiny. The chore of rounding up and driving the youngsters is the responsibility of the sponsoring organization. If children are recruited individually, the family gets the money. When large numbers of children are needed, local grammar schools volunteer their auditoriums and students. Some parents are so eager to push their kids into "show business" that they not only hand them over free but even drive them to and from the testing.

One room of the Child Research lab is equipped as a play and display center where children use experimental products or act out situations. Prodded by child psychologists, they pretend they are on a shopping tour in a simulated supermarket, complete with bulging shelves of brightly packaged goods, and demonstrate how they pester their mothers to buy products.

On the other side of two-way-mirrored wall panels, executives of the research company, the client manufacturer and its ad agency watch and listen, and hidden microphones and video recorders capture the action for later analysis. In an adjacent room, a dozen chairs are placed in a circle and children are urged to discuss their innermost feelings. Conducted by experts in dramatic improvisation, child behavior and marketing, these sessions explore how much and what kinds of influence kids exert on family buying patterns.

Often this research involves products not normally associated with children—items like bottled water or cheese spreads or gasoline. For instance, Texaco research established that most motorists believe all gasoline brands are alike. The company surmised that child nagging power could make a big difference, and so it launched a promotion giving away little fire trucks with fill-ups of fuel. Business improved appreciably.

Child Research uses special projective techniques in working with kids. For instance, they may have children cast secret votes that are whispered to the group leader, so that one child's ideas cannot influence another's. Or the kids are instructed to express an idea in a drawing instead of straining their limited vocabularies to verbalize it. Or they are encouraged to "role-play," pretending to be their mothers, fathers or other children. (When children can hide behind the mask of another personality, researchers find, they reveal more intimate information.)

Several years ago Miles Laboratories approached Child Research with a problem. The company wanted to market a vitamin that would appeal to kids and was considering using a pill shaped like Batman.[1] Child Research Service rounded up some children and put them through a session in which they probed the kids' feelings about a number of popular cartoon characters. Using these findings as a basis, they produced a questionnaire that contained drawings of the cartoon personalities. Then, in more extensive tests, the kids were asked to rate the characters for appeal.

The measuring device used in these tests was the "smiley scale"—a clever pictorial version of adult attitude ratings. This technique shows the familiar moon face with a smiling upturned mouth to indicate "I like that a lot"; a straight-lined mouth means "It's just OK"; and a downturned frown is the child's symbol for "Forget it!" When the questionnaires had been tabulated and analyzed, Child Research discovered that Fred Flintstone and friends had won the popularity contest hands down over Batman and Robin. So Miles

1. The National Association of Broadcasters' TV Code was later amended to prohibit ads for vitamins or drugs to be broadcast during programs designed primarily for children under 12 years of age. This action was taken in response to complaints to the industry and government by various citizen groups, especially the Massachusetts-based Action for Children's Television. The NAB Code now reads: "Appeals involving matters of health which should be determined by physicians should not be directed primarily to children."

switched its cartoon allegiance for their chewable vitamin product, featured the Flintstones—and grabbed a healthy 20 per-cent share of the child-vitamin market.

Many major companies use Child Research Service for their marketing problems, including General Mills for cereals, Libby's Foods for dinners, Burger King for drive-ins and even CBS Television, which wanted to know why one of its children's programs had slipped in the ratings.

Some large companies like Nabisco and Coca-Cola operate their own child-testing programs. One of the more elaborate setups is found inside the Mattel Toys plant in Hawthorne, Cal. On the second floor, there are four playrooms where children work with experimental toys. Behind mirrored wall panels, teams of market researchers, toy designers and sales executives watch every move, while hidden microphones and tape recorders store the reactions.

The toy company also draws on the resources of the academic community. It has arrangements with the University of Southern California, for instance, where faculty psychologists develop sophisticated research techniques based on the latest theories about how children develop, learn and take in information. These Ph.D.s monitor kids' reactions to colors and shapes, experiment with proposed toy ideas and discover which parts of a toy really excite youngsters. The findings are used to produce hard-hitting commercials that move the toys off the shelves.

After its ad agency, Ogilvy & Mather, has filmed some test commercials, Mattel takes over a theater to try them out. Once a month they rent a neighborhood movie house. Buying big display ads in local newspapers, Mattel copywriters promise: "SUPER SHOW SATURDAY! CLOWNS, MAGICIANS, GAMES, GIVEAWAYS, PRIZES, LOTS OF CARTOONS, ONLY 25¢!"

Mattel studies show that middle-class children generally react alike to toys and dolls. They are also the best customers for these products. So the monthly theater test travels from one neighborhood to another, minimizing repeaters and avoiding posh areas like Beverly Hills or depressed sections like Watts.

The ad draws a crowd of about 800 kids, mostly 6 to 11 years old. A magician walks on stage, quiets his audience with a few jokes, gives out door prizes and then asks the kids to fill out a questionnaire. Specially designed for youngsters who do not read well, it consists mostly of photos—trucks and cars for the boys, dolls for girls, four pictures to a page. One picture shows an experimental Mattel product; the others are successful toys being sold by competitors.

"Which toy do you like best on page one?" the magician asks. The children mark their preferences with an X. "How about page two?" After the four-page survey is completed, houselights darken and the show begins—a near-perfect replica of Saturday-morning children's television.

First the kids see two minutes of commercials, then ten minutes of cartoons. Those are followed by another two minutes of commercials. Finally they're shown the main attraction, starring dolphins or other friendly beasts. When the program ends, a clown climbs on stage with some bad news. It seems the first questionnaires have been "lost" by the magician or "ruined" by another clown who spilled grape soda all over them. To qualify for the special drawing, the kids will have to fill out the questionnaire again. By comparing results of the second set of commercials to the first, as well as to "control" commercials whose selling power is already known, Mattel researchers can determine which new commercials are the strongest child persuaders.

Real-estate investor Robert Choate ran into the child laboratories when he invented a supermarket game and sought marketing advice. He talked to research companies on both coasts and came away dismayed at what he learned.

"Industry doesn't want anyone to know about child research," he said. "Everything is secret, proprietary. Studies years old are locked away in sponsor and agency files—information that is used to make children into secret agents of big business in the home. I felt somebody had to do something about it."

What Choate did was to organize the Washington, D.C., based Council on Children, Media and Merchandising. Originally financed out of Choate's pocket, the Council is now funded by grants from the government and the Ford Foundation to collect information and offer testimony to Congress, broadcasters and business.

"These labs make their bucks putting our children under a microscope," Choate points out. "It's immoral because of the secrecy involved. They refuse to share their information with people who want to protect youngsters. We've got to find out what constitutes fair business communications aimed at children."

The secrecy aspect may indeed prove no more ominous than Macy's not telling Gimbels its business. But some observers raise serious questions about the effects of such high-powered research and advertising on the minds of children. Noted pediatrician Dr. Lendon Smith, author of highly regarded books on parenting, objects to young people being made into whiners for advertised products.

"It's a dirty trick to research them this way," he says. "Kids can't stand the pressure, they think anything adults do is OK. That's why they're so vulnerable. For kids under 10, there is no sharp line between fantasy and reality."

Dr. Karl Menninger, co-founder of Topeka's Menninger Clinic, says, "Capitalism has a perfect right to do these things unless damage is done to somebody. Does this injure the children? We should know that. And who is it that permits children to be spied on this way? Those PTA groups and adults who sell or volunteer their children for such experiments can examine their own consciences."

Marty Miller of Mattel not only defends his company's research but claims it actually benefits American children. "Our research is not designed to take advantage of kids but to help us build toys that appeal to them and they can enjoy. That's the top consideration in everything we do, including the commercials we develop for television.

Mel Helitzer, author of an authoritative book called *The Youth Market* and president of Helitzer Advertising, Inc., of New York, feels that critics of child research are really complaining about specific products like sugar-coated cereals. "Children do benefit from research," Helitzer insists. "They end up getting better products at cheaper prices, and mass production is still the name of the game in America. A child's vulnerability means he or she comes to mommy or daddy whining 'Buy me!' The real problem is the inability of many parents to say no. The second and ultimate weapon is for parents to turn off the TV set when it causes problems." . . .

NEWS

James Madison described the significance of news in 1822: "A popular government without popular information, or the means of acquiring it, is but a prologue to a farce or a tragedy; or perhaps both." Over the last three decades, television has become the most popular source of information in the United States. In the spring of 1980, 56.3 million people watched one or more of the three network evening newscasts every weekday, and the Public Broadcasting System's *MacNeil/Lehrer Report* had an audience of four million people. Recent Roper surveys financed by the television industry have concluded that television is not only the primary source of news for two-thirds of all Americans but also the most believable medium.

The dominance of television news was confirmed by *US News and World Report* in its 1979 annual report of 1439 decision makers. Television ranked as the fifth most influential institution in America—behind the White House, large business, the Senate and the Supreme Court: ahead of the federal bureaucracy, the House of Representatives, labor unions, banks, and lobby and pressure groups. A 1978 Lou Harris survey, "Confidence in Institutions," placed television third in influence—behind medicine and higher institutions of learning: ahead of organized religion, the Supreme Court and the military.

Television coverage can in fact influence events. For example, coverage of the civil rights movement hastened passage of the Civil Rights Act of 1964 and the Voting Rights Act of 1968. The United

States' withdrawal from Vietnam was influenced by television coverage which eroded public support for the conflict. Television publicity of the Watergate scandal helped precipitate President Nixon's resignation and the subsequent passage of new legislation. This suffering caused by the famine in Cambodia in 1979 was televised and relief efforts were promptly mobilized.

As in other areas of programming, the networks engage in fierce competition for the biggest news audience, but not, according to network spokesmen, for the profits associated with dominance in the ratings. Former NBC chairman Julian Goodman expressed the public stance toward news coverage: "No news organization really makes money. They are not profit centers. . . . They are responsibilities the networks have to deliver . . . a service to the audience." Actually, the evening news programs are making money for the networks, though they are not as lucrative as other forms of programming.

Most network officials believe that if news leadership does not result directly in big profits, it does result in great prestige which indirectly benefits the network. When ABC began to lead in the ratings for weekly entertainment shows, ABC chairman Leonard Goldenson told his colleagues that "without a first class news operation," ABC would never be the number one network. Consequently, ABC hired 29 on-camera reporters and 20 producers-directors from the other networks, and unveiled its *World News Tonight* during the 1978–79 season. Its average evening news audience increased by 25 per cent or 1.9 million viewers.

By July 1979, ABC was "fully competitive," according to news chief Bill Leonard. Avram Westin, the producer of *World News Tonight,* said that ABC had "scaled the foothills" by tying *NBC Nightly News* in the ratings and "may be ready for Mount Everest," that is, to tackle Walter Cronkite and the 20 million viewers of *CBS Evening News.* In March 1980, ABC began the only regular network late-evening newcast, a 20-minute program at 11:30 P.M. called *ABC News Nightline.*

ABC's competitiveness provoked quick reaction from the other two networks. NBC hired former CBS news president Richard Salant and former Cronkite producer Paul Greenberg to help strengthen its news operation, and a new set and graphics were developed for *NBC Nightly News.* In August 1979, CBS began broadcasting a western edition of the *CBS Evening News* that expands national stories with regional impact and inserts items of special interest to the Pacific area.

The responsibility to deliver the news cost the networks a combined $115 million in 1970 and $207 million in 1977. In 1979, the cost of network news operations was over $300 million. CBS president John Backe estimates that the total 1980 budgets for news will be over one-third of a billion dollars. The critics argue that even though more and more money is being spent on television news operations, the increases in money being spent on other types of programming are greater. Thus, news investment as a percentage of the networks' total revenues has actually decreased in recent years.

Despite the acknowledged importance of television news and the networks' own emphasis on news leadership, the number of news and public-affairs documentaries produced during prime time has dwindled from 121 in 1964 to fewer than 60 in 1979. Don Hewitt, producer of the highly successful CBS public-affairs program *60 Minutes,* believes the public is responsible for the paucity of news and documentaries in prime time. "If there is not more news on the air during [prime-time] hours it's not because television hasn't put its money where its mouth is. It's because the public hasn't put its dials where its mouth is." Hewitt argues that the networks "have made an astronomical financial investment in information programming" and would "like nothing better than to get some of that money back through better public acceptance of a more even split between news and entertainment in prime time." To support his claim, Hewitt points to six CBS documentaries shown in prime time in 1978. Five finished last in the weekly ratings and one finished next to last.

Richard Salant disagrees: "They [the network schedulers] hide them [documentaries]. They put them in the places where they'll do the least damage. You want to see where the competition is going to run the Oscars and you put them in there." Salant contends that if the programs were broadcast regularly, "so people would know they're coming, once a week" and if the documentaries were scheduled with sufficient lead time, "so you can publicize them, advertise them," the news specials and documentaries would get much higher ratings. Those who support Salant's views point to *60 Minutes* as an example. *60 Minutes* was the number one-ranked program in March 1980 and CBS was able to charge advertisers $145,000 for a 30-second commercial.

The 1980s may witness a significant increase in network news and informational programming broadcast during prime-time hours. In fact, CBS founder and chairman William Paley, who has been intimately involved in determining the program schedule of CBS since its inception, suggests that "by 1985 more than half of network programming will be informational." Paley's reason: "There just isn't enough mediocrity to go around in the fiction area." Others who predict expansion of news and informational offerings cite as motivating factors the success of *60 Minutes* and ABC's *20/20*, the recent growth in audience for the nightly news and the escalating cost of entertainment programming. The cost of prime-time entertainment programming increased 40 per cent between 1978 and 1980; also, unlike news and documentaries, entertainment programs cannot be directly controlled by the networks because these programs are purchased from outside sources. Another development which may eventually prove to be an influence on network program decision making in the 1980s is the 24-hour cable news network (CNN) which began operation in June 1980.

News programming is just as important to the local stations as to the networks and has, in fact, been called the *raison d'être* of local stations. Miami TV News director Ralph Renick told colleagues in a keynote address to the Radio Television News Director's Association: "News is the only vestige of creative local programming left. . . . News is the only point adequately differentiating between a good station and a bad station. . . . News is the main identifying watermark of a station." In 1979, approximately 9 per cent of the average television station's programming was local news.

Local news attracts large audiences, sometimes greater than those for network news. A recent study suggests that this is true of local early evening news programs in 14 of the Top-20 markets (rated according to population); in three other Top-20 markets, the size of the local news audience equaled the network news audience. Westinghouse's Group W has estimated that affiliated stations would lose about $75 million in advertising revenues each year if a half-hour local news program were to be replaced by an expanded one-hour news from the network.

Large audiences equal high potential profits. Competition for the local news audience is strong, and stations invest heavily in their news organizations. According to Frank Magid, head of one of the two leading firms hired by stations as news consultants, the average amount spent by stations in the Top-10 television markets in 1979 for news operations was about $2.6 million; the average amount in markets 11–20 was about $1.3 million; and in markets 21–30, the amount varied from somewhere in the "high six figures" to one million dollars. Magid said that even some stations in markets smaller than market 70 spend more than $750,000 each year on news.

Television news on both the local and national levels has been the recipient of a variety of criticisms. Local stations are criticized for the lack of expert reporting. Frank Magid and Phil McHugh, Magid's leading competitor, both discuss the very "apparent" needs for major improvement in the skills of local reporters and for more specialists on such topics as energy and the economy. However, expertise is not yet a major qualification for a local television news reporter. In 1979, KNXT-TV, Los Angeles, the country's second most-watched TV station, which is owned and operated by CBS, chose CBS network sportscaster Brent Musburger as its news anchorman. The management's reason? "He's a real upbeat person."

The print media is the source for most of the strongest criticism of television news. To print journalists, reporting means writing in depth for the newspaper, not spouting brevities to the camera. Newspapermen further insist that television journalism is unduly influenced by businessmen, entertainers and advertisers.

Television journalism is defended by Walter Cronkite who began his career in print journalism. He has drawn some relevant comparisons between electronic journalism and the press. The press criticizes television for interrupting news with commercials, but newspapers continually force readers to chase through pages of advertising in order to finish a story begun on page one. Television news coverage is labeled sensationalism even though newspapers cover the same stories, often with front-page photographs. Cronkite points to the vicious circulation battles between newspapers in the same locality during the earlier days of competition in answer to the criticism that television news is too concerned with competitive ratings. Television news is accused of presenting bland interviews; these often appear in the next day's paper. Newspapermen decry the rigid time limits imposed by television news broadcasting. However, the number of columns in a newspaper is determined by the amount of advertising obtained, not by the news of the day. Furthermore, newspaper owners are inspired by the same motives as are station owners—profits. Despite these comments, Cronkite believes it important that people read newspapers and has expressed concern about the decline in newspaper readership.

Television news is accused of placing too much emphasis on show business values, concentrating on recording action rather than probing for its significance, overemphasizing firstness or fastness, preferring conflict or violence, using quantity and expense as the criteria for excellence. Critics insist that television news is fragmentary and has little continuity. Television news is accused of preoccupation with gadgetry and profit. Television newscasters are said to be meek in the face of industry censorship and succumb too easily to outside pressures.

One of the most constant criticisms heaped on television news is the charge of superficiality, particularly at the network level; the number of words in a half-hour network newscast equals about two-thirds of those on the front page of a standard newspaper. David Brinkley maintains that although the network newscasts are brief, they are not superficial: "There's a difference."

Walter Cronkite acknowledges that network newscasts "are a front-page service," but he adds that the television news audience is introduced to the people and places making news in a way that is not possible in any other medium. The public evidently agrees. As Public Broadcasting's news anchorman Robert MacNeil has expressed it: "TV has created a nation of news junkies who tune in every night to get their fix on the world."

The Hottest TV News Controversies

In November 1969, then Vice President Spiro Agnew attacked the network news executives as "a tiny enclosed fraternity" who talk constantly to one another to reinforce shared viewpoints. Avram Westin, then the executive producer of ABC's evening newscast, was quick to react: "I'll be damned if I'll compare notes with anyone. My job is to beat the hell out of the other networks." Westin had reportedly not even met his counterparts at CBS and NBC prior to Agnew's speech.

In late 1978, *TV Guide* brought together the presidents of the three network news divisions for an informal discussion about television journalism and network news operations. The interviewees were Richard Salant of CBS, Les Crystal of NBC and Roone Arledge of ABC. A few months after the interview, Salant was retired at age 65 from CBS. He then surprised industry observers by joining NBC as vice chairman and overseer of NBC News.

TVG: You three gentlemen, taken together, constitute the single most influential force in the country, in the dissemination of news, and probably in the formation of public opinion as well. You play a unique role in the way the country learns about itself. I wonder how heavily or how lightly this responsibility rests upon you and if you ever agonize about the news judgments that you are called upon to make.

Excerpts have been taken from this essay, which first appeared January 13, 1979.

SALANT: I question your premise. I always read that we are terribly influential. And I think we have to behave as though that's true. But if you look at the literature, it's questionable. The old saw of the communications sociologists is that mass media are instruments of reinforcement rather than conversion. And the masser the medium—and we're the massest—the more that's true. So I put a pin in the premise. But I think we have to go ahead as though we *have* this enormous influence. There is all sorts of evidence that we don't.

Having said that—yeah, the responsibility is awesome, and I think all of us, at all three shops, do an awful lot of introspection and agonizing over what we do, why we do it, whether there isn't a better way.

CRYSTAL: I agree with all of what Dick said. I think there are a whole lot of forces in this country that shape public opinion and influence public opinion, and we probably don't know which ones are the more influential.

The burden weighs heavily, but not in the sense that you come to work each day with this terrible thing on your shoulders. It isn't that kind of burden, because I think the decisions we make on a daily basis, which we agonize over, are not the sort that suddenly change the whole country around. The real problem and difficulty with all this is the cumulative effect of anything that we do. It's over a period of time that we have to look at what we are doing and how well we are doing it and what general effect that is having.

ARLEDGE: Well, obviously I agree with both Dick and Les. First of all, let me say that I think we spend more time, and I am sure they do too, checking, double-checking, assuring accuracy, because of this responsibility and because of the fact that, unlike many other organizations, whether we have the power or don't have the power, we have to operate on the assumption that we may have this power that everybody talks about, and therefore we really do have to be more careful than almost any other news organizations.

But there are two different levels. One is the level of deciding how to cover something, and whether or not we subtly characterize the event in a certain way, and that influences people. I agree with Dick on that. I don't think we do it, but if we did, I don't think we would have that much influence on people.

Where we have great influence is when people *use* our medium. If a President of the United States decides to walk down Pennsylvania Avenue[1] instead of riding in an armored car, we are in a sense innocent victims of his usage of our medium. And I think in that regard it has incredible power, just the pure transmission of actual events. And I think the same is true of what Les said. Vietnam, and particularly civil-rights demonstrations: what we did or didn't do about them had less impact than our merely showing them. To that degree, we have awesome power, and I think we understandably spend an awful lot of time seeing that that power is used correctly. . . .

TVG: How much interplay is there among you?

CRYSTAL: This interview is the extent of the interplay. *(Laughter)*

SALANT: As a matter of fact, if the lawyers knew that all three of us were sitting here, they'd probably stop us. There is no interplay. We obviously watch what the others do, just as we read the major newspapers. But there is almost no conversation. Not because we don't love each other, but because we don't have time.

CRYSTAL: We're too competitive, as well, to want to do much consultation.

TVG: You do watch each other's evening news programs rather faithfully though, do you not?

SALANT: Yeah, absolutely. And with trepidation.

TVG: Why do you watch them, and why with trepidation?

SALANT: We run a free competitive enterprise. We know damn well that we're not infallible and our judgments are not always correct and we want to see how the other guy is doing to see whether we can't learn something.

ARLEDGE: It's a perfectly normal thing. It's like you reading other magazines. . . .

TVG: Are you interested or uninterested in the ratings of your news shows and documentaries? What is the emphasis on ratings within the news divisions?

SALANT: Less than it is in the entertainment division. *(Laughter)*

ARLEDGE: I find myself uninterested on occasional weeks.

1. President Jimmy Carter decided to stroll down Pennsylvania Avenue during the Inauguration Parade in January 1977.

SALANT: I'm uninterested when they're low and fascinated when they're high. *(Laughter)*

TVG: But how does the need to get higher ratings affect your decision making about what sort of news programs you're going to put on the air?

ARLEDGE: I think it's an archaic system we have. To start with, I don't believe the Nielsen ratings can accurately determine how many people watch programs. It is, however, the guideline of our business, for better or for worse. And therefore attention has to be paid to this, because all of us have the problem of paying for a news organization. It costs hundreds and hundreds and hundreds of thousands of dollars everytime a Pope dies, or whatever. The costs are tremendous. It's supported by advertisers, and Nielsen figures are the ones that are used. It is worse yet that news organizations have to be measured by the same standard that entertainment programs are measured by.

I have never met anyone in television who is as fascinated with Nielsen ratings as the print press is. We are constantly being accused of always thinking of nothing but ratings. And yet everytime I try to talk to a newspaper or magazine writer about improving quality or providing a better service, I cannot get the conversation off Nielsen ratings. Most local stations live and die by the Nielsen ratings of their local news, which has become one of their biggest profit centers. I think it's a very dangerous trend. I don't know of anything I can do to stop it. But I think the idea that network news programs should constantly be compared by Nielsen ratings is dangerous.

CRYSTAL: I would subscribe to very much of what you said. The implication of the question, I think, is that what we put on the air and how we put it on the air depends on ratings. It would be nice if we didn't have the ratings. But the economy of our industry is tied to how many people watch, and it is a very difficult thing to live with. I think we have successfully resisted the general pressures to create programs or make changes in programs because of ratings considerations.

SALANT: Yes, that's the key.

CRYSTAL: We are constantly looking at ways to make the programs more interesting. And you look for the widest possible circulation, never letting it get distorted. I think it would be nice, because of the responsibility we have, if somehow in our fantasy land, as Roone said, the news programs and documentaries were not asked to compete in the same way that the entertainment programs are. And I think there is an implicit willingness to do that to a certain degree, anyhow. There is a commitment to do the news programs because it's necessary and important to do them. The preoccupation is of great concern.

I find it not helpful, in terms of the general consciousness, to read about ratings in television and radio columns the same way that I read baseball standings on the sports pages. The preoccupation of the media press is to seize on some evidence of the altering of news and public-affairs programs for the ratings, and the distortion of those programs for the ratings. But we have resisted, with support from our management, the ratings' being a decisive factor in what we do in our programs internally, and I think we will be able to resist it externally.

TVG: Internally, who puts the pressure on you?

CRYSTAL: Would you like a list of names? *(Laughter)*

TVG: It would be helpful.

CRYSTAL: It's the general atmosphere, no one specifically.

ARLEDGE: You have no idea of the generalized pressure. We're in an era now where the stock of companies rises and falls on Nielsen ratings. Competitive factors militate against networks' living up to their responsibilities. It's a major step for a network to preempt a prime-time entertainment program to do a news program, because the results are going to be that your ratings for the week or for that night are going to be lower. And huge things rise and fall on this.

SALANT: What my colleagues are saying is exactly right, but I think that on the network level, at least, ratings don't affect news judgments and news content. At the broader level that Roone is speaking about, it is absolutely true that ratings have a very large effect. If our ratings for documentaries or news specials were anywhere in the neighborhood of the entertainment ratings, you'd see us occupying a great deal more of the prime-time schedule than we do.

ARLEDGE: I think one of the things that we're saying here is that all of us are constantly fighting, in the noncombative sense, and sometimes the combative sense, for air time for news. But the people who are resisting this are not necessarily villains.

TVG: What people, Roone?

ARLEDGE: Entertainment people at the networks.

SALANT: This goes to an impossible demand that is made on us by a great many critics. For better or for worse, and I think it's obviously better when you look at the alternatives, the American system of broadcasting is a system of free, competitive enterprise. And yet there seems to be a demand made on television that it should behave as though it weren't. Well, it just can't. Our bosses have an obligation different from our obligation. Our obligation is to try to get as much time as we can when we think it's warranted and damn the consequences. They must look at the fact that they're in a business. And that has to color their decisions. And so when Roone says there are no heroes and villains, I couldn't agree with him more. That's exactly right. And if you don't like the free, competitive enterprise system for broadcasting, then say so, and we'll go on and examine whether a government-controlled system or something else is better. I happen to think not.

TVG: In a speech, Dick Salant said that a basic issue has emerged in TV news (and in print journalism, as well) over whether a news organization's main role is to tell its audience what it *ought* to know to be well-informed citizens, or merely what it's interested in hearing about. Why is that a basic issue?

SALANT: That's the definition of what news is about. What is journalistic responsibility? And I don't think there is any disagreement among the three of us here. Local stations in some places, yes. But I see no signs among the three commercial networks that there is any disagreement that our primary emphasis should be, *has* to be, on what people ought to know, rather than what people want to hear. . . .

CRYSTAL: One of our biggest responsibilities is to convey to people information that is not inherently interesting but that is important to their lives. And what is more interesting to any kind of audience, be it readers or viewers or listeners, than those things which affect their lives? So that's where suddenly the business of significance, of importance, of what people ought to know starts to bridge over into interest as well. And the two *are* mixed, and there *is* a balancing act. Why does the local newspaper lead on a given morning or afternoon with the water-main break that has an entire neighborhood flooded out, whereas a significant Supreme Court decision that was made that day is on page 2? Why is this? Well, their lives are affected and they're more interested.

TVG: In the evening news programs for which each of you is responsible, only about 22 minutes of actual news is conveyed each night. Is it possible for you to give the viewer what he needs to know in 22 minutes?

SALANT: No.

CRYSTAL: Some of it, not enough of it.

TVG: So what can you do about it? More stories of shorter length? Or perhaps you might devote the whole 22 minutes to a single, important story?

SALANT: No, you really can't do that, in general, because the world, with all its complexity and the increasing flow of news from all over—much of which can well affect the whole nature of our society in this country—makes it impossible to ignore everything else for the sake of one story.

The only answer that I have ever been able to find is to expand the time for our news.[2] And that gets into a very difficult problem. Where are you going to get that extra half hour? You either have to take it from the stations or you have to take it from the entertainment schedule. Both are adamant, and for the time being there's no way to resolve it.

TVG: Are you all in agreement that there *ought* to be more time for the evening news?

ARLEDGE: Absolutely. It's a shame that [in 1976] when network news was about to go to a longer form, NBC was the network that sabotaged it. I don't think Les played any part in that decision. When Barbara Walters was coming to ABC, her contract absolutely guaranteed that the evening news was going to be longer than a half-hour form. It was the moment in history for a breakthrough. However artificially arrived at, the moment had come where it could happen. But shortly before ABC was to meet with its affiliates' board of governors, NBC announced that under no circumstances were they going to go to an hour. That gave all the ammunition that was

2. It was Richard Salant who in 1963 convinced CBS to expand its evening news from 15 minutes to 30 minutes. One week after CBS's first 30-minute newscast, NBC expanded its evening news to a half hour.

needed to our affiliates. That moment having been lost, it appears to me more and more difficult ever to recover it, because stations are learning how much money they can make from local news. And they are very successful, by and large, at programming local news. I think, except for major events, local stations would prefer that the networks be almost like a wire service. Not that they don't have pride in carrying news programs, but they'd much rather carry their own. And their own are locally oriented.

TVG: Since each of your networks owns five stations in the nation's largest cities, why don't you create an hour-long network news program for *them*? No one could stop your doing that, and you'd reach a very substantial percentage of the national viewing audience.[3]

SALANT: It would be somewhat frustrating to pour all our blood, sweat and tears—*that's* an original phrase—into an hour news, which really ought to be great, and have it cleared by five stations, five stations out of 200. That's your first problem.

The second point is, where would they put it? Where would we demand that they put it? Because on local stations local news *is* important. They have a franchise. And I hesitate to demand that they cut down on their local news. I think this logjam is going to be broken one day, but we haven't found the way. You have the Prime-Time Access Rule which bars us from the 7:30 time period. Perhaps the answer is a network news from 8 to 9.

CRYSTAL: I'm hoping that someday someone will come up with the formula that will allow us to have an hour of network news, whether it comes from 7 to 8 or from 8 to 9. I don't know—I wasn't involved—whether NBC truly sabotaged it at the critical moment. I am sure Roone feels that way. Whether our silence at that time would have made the difference in terms of ABC's decision—I am sure that Roone believes it would.

ARLEDGE: I was not head of news at the time, and if sabotage is the wrong word, then I—

3. CBS's five owned and operated stations (WCBS-TV in New York, WBBM-TV in Chicago, KMOX-TV in St. Louis, KNXT-TV in Los Angeles and WCAV-TV in Philadelphia) can be viewed in almost one-quarter of the nation's 76,300,000 television homes. The potential combined audience of the ABC and NBC owned and operated stations is slightly smaller, but both include the nation's three largest markets—New York, Los Angeles and Chicago.

SALANT: But historically you're quite right. We came closer at that time, we were just a few feet away from it, and then everything fell apart. . . .

TVG: Are there any subjects that television is not very good at covering?

SALANT: Yes. The world of abstract ideas. There are some subjects that need a book or a long magazine article, and it's futile to try them on television. Actually there are relatively few such subjects. A good producer can bring most things alive. There are some things that are so difficult and so complex that you've got to have the luxury of print, where if you don't understand one sentence or one paragraph you can go back and read it. Well, we don't give the viewer or the listener that kind of luxury. We can't. Print gives the consumer the luxury of picking and choosing. We don't. There are some things that we simply can't deliver because of the nature of our medium, even though we would like to.

TVG: Does anybody disagree with that?

ARLEDGE: The amount of air time that's available to the three television-network news departments creates some problems. We don't have an awful lot of outlets for specialized information. The biggest tragedy every night is the stories that are left out of the evening-news broadcast. . . .

TVG: Networks occasionally are accused of staging news within your news programs and documentaries. Would you state your policy on that?

CRYSTAL: Opposed to it.

SALANT: Our written standards flatly forbid that. It's something that we have to be particularly careful of in broadcast news because we are so surrounded by entertainment and staging. It's perfectly legitimate there, *but* we have to draw a very sharp line. I suppose it may happen from time to time by an overenthusiastic person in the field. You try to catch it, and when you do, out it goes.

ARLEDGE: We have very rigid standards in that regard. I suspect they are very similar to the other two networks. There is no circumstance that I can imagine, unless we want to simulate something and identify it as such, where that would be permissible under our standard. . . .

TVG: Many independent documentary producers are irked by a network policy that effectively excludes them from access to your air time. Will you state the reasons for that policy?

SALANT: I'll take that on. Our policy, in general, is that we will not take outside-produced news or documentaries from people who haven't established a track record as journalists. All others we will take, which seems to be, really, a perfectly justified position. We might find ourselves in the position of taking documentaries from people with axes to grind who are propagandists or showmen, but not journalists. We'll take anything from somebody who is a real journalist.

CRYSTAL: There's a very rigid editorial process in reaching the final production of a documentary program. And we have to have access to all the information, to all the raw material, in order to be responsible for a program. That's why it's important for us to do our own.

SALANT: You have no real protection against [news] staging, which *is* an abomination, when you don't know who did what to whom. And there *have* been clear examples of outside productions that have gotten on the air where, because you didn't know what questions to ask, staging was involved. . . .

TVG: We appreciate your having taken this time to chat with us. Is there any question that you are genuinely relieved we haven't asked you? And what is it?

SALANT: My question is that—since I'm retiring from CBS News on April 30, [1979]—I would like to appeal to Les and Roone for a job.

DAVID BRINKLEY

A Question for Television Newsmen: Does Anyone Care?

The criteria for what constitutes news on television are based on tradition in other media and on what the newsmen think the public ought to know. CBS network president Gene Jankowski stated that "the big challenge of the networks is to package information that the public ought to have in ways that would make them want to watch it." David Brinkley discusses what television news should and should not be.

Television is a mature and serious news medium, and it is time we who work in it had our own standards of news judgment, instead of those handed down to us from the newspapers.

It is time to do things our own way, to meet the needs of our audiences and the strengths and the weaknesses of the medium we work in.

Why should we develop our own standards? Those we inherited are pretty good. They've served the newspapers well for a long time, and the public is used to them.

And, if it is news in a newspaper, is it not also news on radio and television? No.

No, it is not, and for a basic reason we all know but tend to forget. The basic reason we are different is that in a newspaper you can skip around, read what is interesting to you, and ignore the rest. While on a news broadcast you have to take it as it comes, in order.

This essay first appeared March 19, 1977.

A newspaper can print items most of its readers don't care about, because those who don't care about them can skip them, and go on to something else. We can't.

So, what does that mean? In my opinion, it means we should not put a story on the air unless we believe it is interesting to at least 10 per cent of the audience. Preferably more. But at least 10 per cent.

For example, one night we put on the *NBC Nightly News* a two-minute story about the Lebanese civil war. There was a little military skirmish on the front line, and we ran two minutes on it with great confidence and assurance that this was important news.

But was it? That night I spent a little time thinking about it. Why did we put that on the air? Who, in this country, really cared about it?

Who really cared about it? Lebanese living in the U.S.? Even if they do, they're a tiny fraction of one per cent of our population. Americans who have business or other interests in Lebanon? How many can that be? A fraction of one per cent? Foreign-policy specialists, government and private? How many can that be? A fraction of one per cent?

Ordinary working Americans like the rest of us? A fraction of one per cent? That is not enough.

The Middle East is of great interest to Americans, but Lebanon is peripheral to the area we're concerned about. It has very little effect on the lives, hopes, problems, needs, fears or future security of Americans sitting at home looking at television. In my judgment, 99.9 per cent of them did not give a damn.

What I concluded in thinking about it that night was that practically nobody was interested in our story from Lebanon and that the two minutes we devoted to it were an utter waste of effort, money and air time.

So why did we put it on? Because nobody stopped to ask all these questions. Because the decision was made by habit, by rote, unthinkingly. Wars are always news, aren't they?

Well, no, they aren't. It depends on who's fighting whom and what they're fighting about and what the consequences are likely to be.

We couldn't even use the excuse that the story was easy to get. It wasn't. It was hard, dangerous work for a correspondent and a camera crew and it was sent to the U.S. by satellite, which is expensive.

And in the end, after all the work, danger, time and money, who really wanted to see it? In my opinion, almost nobody.

But even so, we do that kind of thing frequently, if not every day.

Because we continue—in radio and television—making news judgments by habit, by rote and formula developed over the years by the newspapers and inherited by us.

This is not to be critical of the newspapers. I enjoy reading them, have worked on them and may sometime do so again. The good ones do their job very well.

But their structure and format are so totally different from ours that very few of their rules and habits are relevant to broadcasting. We follow them, nevertheless. We really ought to stop it.

The Lebanon story is only one example. We could all think of many more.

If news is something worth knowing that we did not know already—as it is—then the appropriate test is: Worth knowing to whom? And to how many? The right question to ask is: Who really cares about this? Does anyone care and should anyone care?

It's a question we often forget to ask ourselves. If we did, and built our programs accordingly, we'd have bigger audiences, better served . . . which is supposed to be our job.

Obviously, applying this little test would not eliminate foreign news and shouldn't. It would not eliminate any particular kind of news. It would not eliminate news our viewers are not informed about but which they would find interesting if we did inform them.

But it would eliminate a lot of stuff, like the Lebanon story, that we put on without really thinking about it because it sort of looks like news, or sounds like it, even though when you get down to it, it is not.

Of course, there are days, as we all know, when material of any kind is scarce, and we have to use what we can get, including some we know is not great, but air time is air time and it has to be filled.

On those days we all just do the best we can.

But on the days when we have a choice, I don't want to see a news program filled with jokes and laughs and light stories about children and cats and dogs and the reporters elbowing each other in the ribs and laughing it up. We have more than enough of that.

I do not suggest more light or frivolous news, or more laughs.

What I do suggest is that the news judgments the newspapers and wire services have developed over the generations may be fine for them, but not for us. We should stop using their habits and practices and develop our own.

We should not bore the audience any more than necessary.

ERIC LEVIN

Anatomy of a Newscast

The translation of a news event into a piece for the evening network news is a complex procedure. Once the decision to include the story is made, the producers, technicians and reporters have the combined responsibility to present the story within the split-second timing of television. Eric Levin describes the putting together of one night's edition of *NBC Nightly News.*

When Tom Brokaw entered the NBC booth in the White House press room on a Wednesday morning [in the fall of 1975], he had been assigned to a story that had only a marginal chance of getting on the air.

Mayors from fourteen large cities were coming to Washington to ask President Ford to alter his stance against federal aid to New York City. The informed speculation, however, was that Mr. Ford would simply restate his earlier objections, so Brokaw sat by his telephone and, leafing through the morning papers, prepared to dig for other stories.

At about the same time, a large, cluttered room in New York was coming to life—the headquarters of the *NBC Nightly News.* Harry Griggs, an associate producer, flipped on the lights. The news day had started.

It was 9:15 A.M. For Griggs, the first order of business was to set up a conference call to get an idea of what stories NBC News' regional bureaus would file that day. The Washington bureau reported first: Brokaw would be covering the mayors, but would keep his eyes peeled for other White House doings, Irving R. Levine would cover AFL-CIO president George Meany, who was scheduled to give

This essay first appeared February 26, 1976.

Congress his criticisms of the government's policy on layoffs. Carl Stern would report on the General Accounting Office's audit of the FBI. Ford Rowan would continue his coverage of the Senate committee hearings on domestic spying by the CIA.

The other bureaus followed. Atlanta expected to file a report on hurricane damage. Chicago and Cleveland were working on stories for future broadcast. In California, the Burbank bureau was hoping to file a report on the controversy over aerosol sprays and the ozone layer. The Northeast bureau (in New York) was working on a teachers' strike in Delaware and a Broadway musicians' strike. Most of the bureaus had other stories awaiting developments.

By 10:10, Les Crystal, the executive producer, had come in, as had John Chancellor, producer Joe Angotti (assigned to news specials), and most of the other editors and staff. At the daily briefing for top executives of NBC News, Bud Lewis, director of NBC News Poll, gave the results of an NBC poll on the capture of Patty Hearst that had been broadcast that morning on the *Today* show. It was decided to include the results in the *Nightly News*.

In theory, the number of stories available for the evening broadcast was infinite, but more realistically, there were about 80 candidates, counting stories already assigned, scheduled events (meetings, etc.), updates of continuing stories, and feature or overview stories already completed and waiting "on the shelf." Of the roughly 80 possibilities, about 25 held the editors' attention. The overriding reality each day is that a half-hour newscast can accommodate only 14 to 20 reports.

Meanwhile, Brokaw—and every other reporter at the White House—knew that this was President Ford's first full day in Washington after Sara Jane Moore's assassination attempt in San Francisco. Unanswered questions hung in the air: Why hadn't the Secret Service detained Mrs. Moore after she threatened to "test" the security system? Would Mr. Ford demand a review of Secret Service procedures? Would he travel less?

For the moment, there wasn't much Brokaw could do but wait. Checking out another story, he placed a call to an Administration source he knew to be in line for an important promotion. A secretary promised to have the man return the call.

At 10:40, Herb Dudnick, the Washington producer, relayed a major development to New York. Senator Frank Church, chairman of the Senate Intelligence Committee, had just revealed the that CIA had opened some of President Nixon's mail without his knowledge. The committee's hearing now became a story of major importance.

At 11:35 came the daily briefing by Ron Nessen, President Ford's press secretary. From it, the skeleton of a story had emerged: Nessen said the Secret Service had told Mr. Ford not to go into the crowd outside the St. Francis Hotel, where Sara Jane Moore was standing, and he hinted that Mr. Ford would continue to travel, but would not "press the flesh" so often. Brokaw called his office and it was decided that he should concentrate on the security story and let someone else handle the mayors' meeting with the President.

In New York, the day's second conference call to the bureaus had just been held. Burbank said it would probably file a report on the gun collector who had sold the pistol to Sara Jane Moore. The Northeast bureau said its two strike stories would probably not be ready until the following day.

In most respects, the day was unfolding typically, but it was unusual because there were no pressing reports due from overseas bureaus. A report on conditions in Saigon was being edited four floors above the *Nightly News* office, and three background stories were being edited in London and Vienna. But all could be held a day or more without losing news value.

At the same time, in Washington, Brokaw's phone rang. It was his Administration source, who told Brokaw he hadn't decided if he would accept the offered promotion. It meant Brokaw would have to sit on the story a few days longer.

At about 12:15, the *Nightly News* staff assembled in Les Crystal's office for the day's first major meeting, the Rundown Meeting. "It looks like Washington is going to be very heavy again today," Crystal told the staff. "I don't see any way around it. There are four or five stories possible. Obviously, 'the mail,' 'the FBI,' 'Ford,' 'the mayors'. . . ." There was a general nod of assent.

With Crystal generally leading the meeting—and John Chancellor, Angotti and news editor Gilbert Millstein commenting frequently—the staff discussed the day's stories and ideas for future reports. At 1 P.M., some of the staff went to lunch while others pulled up chairs for their daily poker game.

In the White House press booth, meanwhile, Brokaw listened on the phone, as a source—an aide to Mayor Joseph Alioto of San Francisco—read from a report on the city police department's role in the Sara Jane Moore affair. "I wish I could have gotten some of this yesterday," Brokaw muttered.

At 1:30, Brokaw pulled on a jacket and Irish tweed hat and went out for a sandwich. "Sometimes lunch is like this," he said. "Sometimes it's a big expense-account thing. Sometimes it's no lunch at all."

At 2:10, Angotti in New York and Herb Dudnick in Washington made story decisions over the phone. The CIA mail-opening got another boost, as did the audit of the FBI. Coverage of George Meany's appearance on Capitol Hill was scrapped—he had expressed his views earlier. The mayor's story would be a 30-second film spot, with Irving R. Levine covering.

At 2:40, Brokaw struck pay dirt, finally contacting a source in the Secret Service. The agent confirmed that the Secret Service had told Mr. Ford not to step into the crowd outside the hotel. He also said that in the kind of half-hour interview the Secret Service had with Mrs. Moore it is impossible to determine if someone is really a threat, and that there are so many "kooks" around, it would take 15,000 agents to screen them all. At last, Brokaw had some exclusive quotes for his story.

Brokaw was still hoping to get through to an Administration source to find out if Mr. Ford was critically examining the Secret Service's performance. Barring success there, he would have to wait until 5 P.M.—when the President was scheduled to address leaders of the American Chamber of Commerce. Perhaps Mr. Ford would use that occasion to make a statement about the Secret Service.

Around this time, another element became important to Brokaw: it had been raining heavily all day, so he would not be able to film his report on the White House lawn. He would have to file from the Washington bureau, several miles away, and that would take extra time.

At 3:15—only a few hours before air time—a meeting was held in Les Crystal's office. The bureaus had phoned in the anticipated lengths of the film stories they would be submitting. Now the staff's job was to choose and position the stories, and allot time for introductions, closes and the items John Chancellor would read himself.

Some decisions required almost no discussion, such as giving Brokaw the relatively modest 90 seconds requested for his Ford security story. But there was a clash over an NBC poll on reactions to the attempts on Mr. Ford's life. One question asked if respondents thought the assassinations and attempted assassinations of recent years were the work of individuals or conspiracies. The results were 46 per cent for individuals, 41 per cent for conspiracies, and 13 per cent undecided.

"I think it's an invalid question, asked in an emotionally charged atmosphere," objected Chancellor. "There's not a shred of evidence that any of these people were connected. You go out and ask a lot of simple people, 'Do you think Chicken Little was right?' and you're gonna get 41 per cent for Chicken Little."

Eventually, it was decided to use only one poll question, on whether the President should avoid crowds in the future (45 per cent yes, 47 per cent no, 8 per cent undecided).

Bambi Tascarella, the production associate, added up the story lengths and announced how close the total was to the target of 22½ minutes—the length of the newscast less commercials and station breaks. There were 55 seconds to spare "That ain't so bad," said Crystal. The extra seconds would be helpful if any stories ran long.

In the newsroom, the staff began to divide the writing chores: introductions, closes, and stories to be read by Chancellor. Chancellor and Gilbert Millstein usually divide the writing more or less equally, with Chancellor getting first choice of material and generally choosing to write the top of the show.

At 3:30, Brokaw wound a piece of paper into his typewriter—and hammered out "nightly . . . Brokaw . . ." and the date at the top. He stopped to check his notes. Irving R. Levine popped into the booth to say that New York had decided to reduce the mayors story to a 30-second film clip with narration by Chancellor. Brokaw typed out a paragraph of his Ford security story and read it back to himself softly, timing it on his wristwatch. By 4 P.M., Brokaw had a rough draft ready.

Back in New York, the tempo was accelerating rapidly. Chancellor and Millstein read each other's copy, which then went to Angotti and Crystal for checking and then to the production assistants, who would hold it until air time. In the editing room, stories filed by the bureaus were being worked on. Color slides and artwork, which would be displayed behind Chancellor during the newscast, were being checked and set in order.

With five minutes to go before Mr. Ford's 5 P.M. speech, a sudden commotion brought Brokaw to the door of the NBC booth. Reporters returning from a reception for women stockbrokers were bubbling about a chance remark by Mrs. Ford. Under questioning from CBS's Phil Jones, the First Lady had said she hoped the President would keep traveling but "just stay away from the people." NBC had not covered the reception, thinking it wouldn't prove newsworthy—and in itself, it didn't. But Mrs. Ford's statement fitted naturally into the day's developments, and Brokaw would have to work it into his piece. He hung up and hurried upstairs to hear the President's address.

In New York, the phones jangled as bureaus called in the scripts for their film reports. Washington called to say the film of the mayors was stuck in the processing machine and might not be ready; 15 minutes later they called back—it was ready.

Brokaw was listening to the President speak when he felt a tap on his shoulder. A messenger told him something that went like this: "Your office says the rain has traffic jammed up all over the city. They want you to get the hell back right now or you'll never make air."

At 5:55—35 minutes to air time—Burbank transmitted the report on the ozone controversy, and it was recorded in New York on video tape. The sound was out of synchronization with the picture, a problem the technicians would have to hurry to correct. At 6:05 the report on hurricane damage was fed from Mobile, Ala.

At 6:15—15 minutes to air time—Angotti totaled up the latest story length and barked, "We're a minute over." He decided to drop the film of the mayors and settle for a brief mention of the story by Chancellor. At 6:20, the piece on the gun collector who sold the pistol to Sara Jane Moore was filed from San Francisco. Five minutes later, the editors checked the adjustment in the sync of the ozone story. Better; not perfect, but it would have to do. At 6:25, Chancellor pulled on his sports jacket and left for the studio, two floors below. To save time, it was decided that the Washinton stories would be transmitted live.

It was now 6:30. Floor manager Fred Lights gave the signal, and Chancellor opened the newscast with his customary "Good evening." In ten minutes, he would reach the cue for Brokaw's live report.

In Washington, Brokaw had reached the NBC bureau only 40 minutes earlier—and was still rewriting his story when the newscast began. Finishing it quickly, he hurried to the studio. He had hardly taken his seat when the cameraman gave the signal for him to begin to read his report. It was 6:40.

Five minutes later, in New York, Angotti realized the show was running late. He began barking orders to cut small news items from the roster. After Angotti slashed four stories, Bambi Tascarella, who was keeping track of the time, breathed a sigh of relief.

"We're OK," she said. "We're fine."

Minutes later, after the filmed report on the ozone controversy, the camera returned to Chancellor, who looked up and said, "And good night for NBC News."

About 40 per cent of NBC's affiliated stations carry the network news live at 6:30. The rest carry the news on a video-tape "feed," so even as the live telecast was running, engineers were recording it and eliminating minor errors. They worked quickly, because the taped feed would begin as soon as the live telecast ended—at exactly 7 P.M.

The tape was ready and rolled on time; the news was repeated. By a little past 7:30, the newsroom was empty.

EDWIN DIAMOND

Sunday Punch

David Brinkley has joked: "Cronkite and I have been on [television] longer than anyone or anything, even including *Lassie.* And on *Lassie,* they changed dogs." Although Brinkley may be correct regarding the "anyone," the oldest continuous run for news programs belongs to *Meet the Press* which began in 1947.

Sunday-morning television programming traditionally includes news interview programs, such as *Meet the Press,* geared to appeal to the "intellectual ghetto." Edwin Diamond evaluates these programs and their contributions to network news coverage.

Sunday mornings across the United States, the television set becomes a kind of time machine. It is the dawn of an old era, the hour of the Sunday interview programs—*Meet the Press* on NBC, *Face the Nation* (CBS) and *Issues and Answers* (ABC). A serious-faced news maker—typically a government official—fields questions from an unsmiling panel of journalists.

There is no "happy talk" banter; there are no dazzling visuals or switches; no expert video-tape editing to help the interviewer gain the upper hand on the interviewee. The programs are *live.* A can of hair spray would last the season for this whole untelegenic crew. The year could be 1947, when *Meet the Press* started; or 1954, when the first guest faced the nation; or 1960, the birth of *Issues and Answers.*

It is square, serious, talking-heads television, and the networks do just about everything to hide these quaint news fixtures, as if they were dusty old pieces of furniture, not fit for company to see and best relegated to the basement that is Sunday-morning television.

Excerpts have been taken from this essay, which first appeared October 14, 1978.

After looking at these "old-fashioned" programs over a period of time, however, I've concluded that the policies of ABC, CBS and NBC are shortsighted. While the Sunday interview programs have many faults, they deserve more care, more thought and more display. If the networks would spend just a few dollars on a little refurbishing, the payoffs could be highly satisfying for TV viewers.

Most critics, I know, have little use for *Meet/Face/Issues.* The usual criticism goes something like this: the programs are little more than public-relations outlets for politicians with some line to push; the networks provide a Sunday platform for the same people who dominate the news the other six days, and in exchange get a free guest for a low-budget production.

About the only positive result is that the shows sometimes produce a fresh headline for the Sunday-evening news or the Monday-morning newspapers, but since Sunday is a slow news day anyway, even nonnews developments will command some air time and ink.

True, the Sunday interview programs too often do fill slow news days with predictable guests speaking guarded officialese. They are old-fashioned: the programs haven't changed much in thirty years. Even the model is creaky—a 1950s courtroom drama, with the journalist-prosecutor trying to get the guest-witness to say something incriminating (or something newsy). The technique is fine, except that in practice the moderator cannot perform like a judge—sharpening questions, cutting off windy obfuscations, directing the witness to answer directly on pain of a contempt citation.

Yet, on occasion, the Sunday interview programs can offer real news from living, breathing guests with something to say. Producers of all three shows scramble hard each week to line up an "exclusive" with the news maker of the moment. "It can be quite competitive," notes William Small, a former CBS news vice president. On the other hand many "news makers" seek out the shows to advance themselves, or let their staff do the actual lobbying. . . .

Because the Sunday interview shows are so resolutely devoted to politics and to Washington, they tend to be best in election years, when public interest in national affairs is highest. During the 1976 primaries and general campaign, some of us in the News Study Group at MIT examined the Sunday interview programs from the point of view of what the voters can learn from them.

In national campaigns, voters ordinarily "see" the various candidates in two formats. One is the constricted form of the network evening news programs, where 45 or 60 seconds of a candidate's speech or appearance may be presented under the control of the program's producers. The other is the even more constricted form of the political commercial, where the images are controlled and edited by the candidate's media managers.

Neither form is very high in information content. When we looked at the candidates' appearances on the Sunday interview shows, however, we found relatively rich information for the voters. With all their faults, the Sunday interview programs nevertheless permitted unscripted communication between the candidates and their interviewers—and, by extension, with the audience as well. The candidates, in their answers, talked to the voters without the intervention of editors. There was enough time for some of the character of the candidates to come through. The voters saw the "real" candidates, or at least the candidate free of the artful constructions of the commercial spot. Until the Ford-Carter debates, the Sunday interview shows served as the principal means for most voters to observe the Presidential candidates in live, direct, uncontrolled appearances.

The Sunday interview programs get their aura of seriousness not just from the status of the guests, but also from the demeanor of the panelists. The print orientation of most of these panelists gives the Sunday interview programs their distinct—and valued—air of objectivity. Paula Cassidy of our News Study Group videotaped and analyzed all of the Sunday programs from June 1 to August 1 [1978]. She found the interviewers' style more substantive than the slicker efforts of such television news magazine shows as CBS's *60 Minutes* and ABC's *20/20*. "By their nature," she concluded, "the Sunday panel shows are deliberately muted. They lack the stagecraft of *60 Minutes'* exposé style or the *20/20* attempts to reduce everything to a shorthand. The audience itself has to do more work; questions are unencumbered by the interviewer's personality or the program format. The questions tend to find their targets. These print refugees don't smile; but they ask detailed questions, and the best of them press for detailed answers."

It would be pleasant to report that the Sunday programs with their earnest reporters putting serious questions to settled authorities, have attracted a large, loyal and growing following. They haven't. If the style of these programs hasn't changed over the last two decades, then neither have their audiences. *Face the Nation,* for example, earned ratings of 3.7 in 1966 (the first year it became sponsored); the ratings figure [in 1977] was 3.1 (meaning about 4 million people watched the program [in 1966], perhaps 3.5 million [in 1977]). The figures for *Meet the Press* and *Issues and Answers* show the same long-term trend.

Network news people understandably try to look on the bright side of these figures. "We reach the movers and shakers," says Bill Small. The general viewer is thought to be uninterested. Actually, government officials, commentators and opinion leaders aren't watching television Sunday mornings either. Much like the rest of us, they tend to (1) sleep late Sunday morning, or (2) go to church, or (3) head out of the house to concentrate on their backhands rather than the issue of the moment. A young journalist friend of mine, and would-be mover and shaker, lives in Portland Ore., where the Sunday interview programs go on at about 9 A.M.—without him. "Maybe I'd get up to see [Soviet President Leonid] Brezhnev," he says, "but no one else."

Worse still, when the guest is anyone less than a Brezhnev, viewers are hard put to know who is going to be on the air. Since guests may not be decided upon until the Friday before a Sunday show, the listings in *TV Guide* and most local newspapers cannot carry their names. The obvious solution would be to promote the guest during station breaks on the network during Friday- and Saturday-night prime time. But television promos cost time that could be, and is, used to promote other, more profitable, network fare.

Because the audience for serious politics has been judged to be small, the networks schedule their interview shows at a time that practically ensures a small audience, and then keeps it a big secret in case someone should try to find the programs.

The networks claim that they are happy with the low-key, low-profile, low-audience image of the Sunday interview programs. I asked a CBS executive why he didn't fight to break *Face the Nation* out of the Sunday-morning ghetto into a better time period, say, early Sunday night after *60 Minutes.* "I'm not unhappy where it is now," he replied. "If I could get more Sunday-night time for news, I'd have other priorities—news specials or documentaries." . . .

The Sunday interview programs have been undeservedly assigned to a small, barely tolerated place in the network schedules. Yet, while other news programs flail around looking for the right format and purpose, the Sunday shows *know* what they are and what they are trying to do. Sure, the information can be superficial. But the programs possess that precious special strength of the live, unscripted television interview—the promise of revealing the character of the guests. Too often, perhaps, the programs don't deliver on that promise. Too often, perhaps, they aren't tough enough on those guests, certified official fog banks who obscure rather than illuminate. But when the shows do what they do best—capture and display a Khrushchev or the ERA debaters or a Begin—the moments shine through, and make it worthwhile to give up tennis or a lazy morning to watch.

JOHN BIRT

There Is a Bias in Television Journalism

The editing of news for television, the decision to present certain news items rather than others, infers an almost inescapable bias in television news. Reuven Frank, former president of NBC News, has acknowledged the existence of a more conscious bias: "Television is a medium for transmitting experience. It has never covered a national budget and it never will. . . . We don't consciously put things on no one will watch."

John Birt suggests that this attitude helps contribute to TV's overemphasis on story versus issue journalism.

There is a bias in television journalism. It is not against any particular party or point of view—it is a bias against understanding. To understand where this bias comes from, it is useful to classify the different types of journalism practiced on television. There are three main categories: news, feature and issue journalism. The categories are determined by the extent to which an item is put into a larger context.

Take, for example, the case of a particular battle during the fighting in Vietnam. A journalist's first job is to explain to his audience the immediate circumstances: where the battle took place, the number of casualties and so on. From this he can widen the coverage to set the battle into the context of the military strategies of both sides; and thus show how those strategies are faring.

He could widen the context still further by relating the military strategies to the political circumstances of both sides. This would

This essay first appeared August 9, 1975.

necessarily involve an understanding of the real (and not just the apparent) thinking and behavior of the protagonists in Hanoi, Saigon, Peking, Moscow and Washington.

The problem for television journalists and producers is to decide in how wide or how narrow a context to set each item or program. I believe that too little emphasis placed on this concept, by those responsible for producing television news, has contributed to the bias against understanding. We can see how things go wrong if we examine the different forms of television journalism one by one.

Television news programs cover a large number of stories, often more than twenty items in a span of about half an hour. As a result, the focus in any one story is extremely narrow. But unfortunately, the most important stories of the moment—for example, stories about the economy or oil or the Mideast—suffer from such a narrow treatment.

Economic problems manifest themselves in a wide variety of symptoms: deteriorating balance of payments, a sinking dollar, rising unemployment, accelerating inflation and so on. The news, devoting two minutes on successive nights to the latest unemployment figures or the state of the stock market, with no time to put the story in context, gives the viewer no sense of how any of these problems relate to each other. It is likely to leave him [or her] confused and uneasy.

Feature journalism tends to concentrate on one aspect or one instance of a major problem rather than on that problem as a whole. Feature journalists will, for example, make a film about a particular instance of famine rather than about the world food problem. They expose the dangers of particular nuclear reactors rather than examine what the government's energy policy is or could be.

Feature journalists working on news programs and on current affairs programs like *60 Minutes* perform a valuable job in seeking out society's specific sores. But television feature journalism continually suffers because producers and reporters do not take the trouble to think their ideas through. If they did, they might discover the tenuousness of the link between, say, one unemployed man and the real causes of unemployment; or between one refugee and the causes of a war. Consequently an unilluminating, though possibly diverting, program is made.

The constant emphasis placed on society's sores by television feature journalists, with little or no attempt to seek out the root causes may even be dangerous. It may contribute to the alienation felt by the victims of society's inadequacies and imperfections. They can be forgiven for sharing in the assumption apparently made by many feature journalists that a sore easily highlighted should be a sore easily [healed].

Bad feature journalism encourages the victims (and most of us are victims of something or other) not to relate their problems to those of society as a whole, and to conceal from themselves how often one man's grievance is another man's right.

Issue journalism aims to go beyond the context provided by the feature journalist and to look at such subjects as the related components of our economic problems or what our foreign policy should be. Trying to come to grips with the often bewildering complexity of modern problems such as these is a formidable task, even without trying to put the result on television; and the failure rate is high. The realities one is seeking are abstract—macroeconomic mechanisms, political philosophies, international strategies—and cannot be directly televised like a battle zone or a demonstration.

This kind of journalism has many hazards. Attempting to answer a question like "What are the causes of inflation?" is intellectually very taxing and issue journalists in television often lack the knowledge to settle on the right framework for asking such a question. For example, they may focus on wage control in such a way as to imply that it is the only possible cure for inflation. If the other variables and constraints on the economy are not explained, the complex causes of inflation will not be understood. And, moreover, politically dangerous myths will be created. . . .

The journalistic tool almost always chosen for dealing with issues, especially abstract issues, is the studio discussion. Rarely has a technique been so abused.

A hawk and a dove quarreling over Vietnam, or two economists discussing inflation, or Israeli and Arab sympathizers exchanging rhetoric about the Palestinians will not succeed in 30 minutes in communicating anything other than confusion. These discussions are generally set up to examine disagreements, rather than areas of agreement; and they place an unnaturally high premium on the resourcefulness under pressure of the participants. They encourage interviewees to abandon any attempt to discuss issues in a fresh and sophisticated manner. They scarcely ever promote understanding of complicated problems and are little more than an entertaining way of feeding the viewers' already existing prejudices.

But even when that small proportion of issue journalism that does not rely on studio discussion finally gets on the air, it faces a further obstacle. It runs the risk of being boring. A well-made report on a famine, or even on one starving family in Appalachia, will be more watchable than a report on the world food problem. A program on living conditions in Watts or Harlem will be more diverting than a report on housing policy.

The main consequence of this is that television journalists prefer story journalism to issue journalism. It's easier to do and it's more fun. As a result, there are very few issue-oriented programs. And, worse, most of them are scheduled at very poor hours, far less favorably than the news and feature stories that issue journalism seeks to put into context.

I believe that the various forms and techniques of television journalism—news programs, feature reports, the presentation and discussion of issues—can all too easily conspire together to create a bias against the audience's understanding of the society in which it lives. And there is a danger that the pressure brought to bear on politicians by the incoherent highlighting of society's sores by television will lead politicians (ever aware of the ballot box) to deal merely with symptoms of crisis rather than taking a longer time to search out fundamental causes and dealing with them.

There is an even greater danger awaiting politicians if they surmount this hurdle and succeed in searching out the basic causes of our problems. They may be inhibited from taking the necessary action because of the outrage they fear it would provoke. This age-old problem of democracy is aggravated because the media in their present forms instinctively fasten onto the snags and drawbacks in any proposed new policy. Television normally communicates these more effectively than the policy as a whole or, indeed, than the overall problem to be solved.

We should redesign television news programs so that they devote much more time than they presently do to the main stories of the day; and so that these stories are put into the fullest possible context in the time available. Feature programs must be organized so that they are more aware of the need to find a relevant focus. There should be more programs that deal with issues. News editors should rely less on bombs, strikes, demonstrations and the other staples of our television diet.

Whether immature mass media give rise to immature political institutions, or vice versa, I do not know. I suspect, though, that the politicians would behave differently if the mass media behaved differently.

If the emphasis of the mass media were to change; if, on television, we were to stop packaging the great issues of our time into two-minute gobbets of news; if, in place of engendering a bias against understanding, we were instead to put events into perspective; if we were constantly to analyze the great issues of our time; if, in short, we were radically and unrecognizably to change the present type and mix of our news and current-affairs programs, then perhaps we would see our political institutions maturing too.

Our present coverage of events and issues seems to me to be born of the age of the plow. If the center of the debate (and there is a debate) does not move from the wings to the center of the stage, then we will soon be in trouble.

RICHARD TOWNLEY

The News Merchants

Local news accounts for from one-third to one-half of the total profits for most television stations. Many stations are hiring news consultants whose tasks are to analyze the news program and help the station determine what actions will increase its local news audience and its advertising revenues.

Walter Cronkite has called news consultants "idiots." Former NBC chairman Julian Goodman has said that consultants have "harmed the news business" because they "want to slice news up like sausages and deliver it as though it were from a delicatessen." Harold Baker, past president of the Radio Television News Directors Association, considers news consultants the "number one enemy" of local television stations' news directors.

Richard Townley discusses the methods of the news consultants, their impact on local television news and the controversy surrounding them.

They call him Billy Blue Collar. He never went to college, has never been on an airplane, has never seen a copy of the *New York Times*. He rarely reads anything, in fact. And for the most part he ignores television news. Yet, in an official policy memo at KFMB-TV in San Diego, and in a growing number of other TV newsrooms across the Nation, he is the accepted stereotype of the average television news viewer. And his tastes and preferences are having a profound influence on the kinds of news programs you are watching on television.

Excerpts have been taken from this two-part essay, which first appeared March 9, March 16, 1974.

In cities from Philadelphia to Oakland broadcasters are designing news programs to attract Billy Blue Collar and other audience prototypes discovered through motivational research and sophisticated surveys. And what the viewer often ends up with is a slick, breezy news show, dispensing glib headlines, socko action films and orchestrated "spontaneity"—newscasts, as one critic says, "for people who can't stand television news."

Their creators operate on the premise that news programs—like everything else on TV—can be merchandised, packaged to appeal to the "massest" mass audience. After all, they reason, broadcasters are licensed to give the public what it wants. But a good many TV newsmen see the rapid spread of action-oriented "happy-talk" formats as a menace—a danger to TV news' integrity, a hindrance to public understanding of complex issues and a threat to many newsmen's jobs.

In any controversy involving high stakes, emotion and tradition, the truth probably lies between the extremes. And in the midground between the TV newsman and the often hazy, indistinct audience he serves is a new breed of social scientist. One that not only tells broadcasters what their audience wants, but also how to give it to them.

They label themselves "media consultants," but in the trade they're often called "shows doctors" or, less kindly, "hucksters." Of the handful of consulting firms in the news field, two companies dominate.

Frank N. Magid Associates of Marion, Iowa, is a multimillion-dollar research outfit headed by a one-time University of Iowa professor. Magid's consultant division has clients in about [sixty] cities. His [130]-person staff of "action-oriented, commercially aware" pragmatists handles everything from audience polling to overseeing a station's newscasts.

McHugh and Hoffman, Inc., the oldest of the consulting companies, operates out of McLean, Va. Its staff of "[seven] guys and four girls" consults with stations in about [forty] cities, farming out the audience surveys to other companies.

Magid and McHugh and Hoffman have sharp differences in methods and philosophy. But they, and the other consultants, share some common beliefs.

1. *Local news is important.* It's good insurance against the government's taking away a station's license. And it can quite often be an important source of local commercial revenue.

2. *To attract viewers, you've got to know what they like.* And the way to find out is through personal interviews with a statistical cross section of the entire local TV audience (400 interviews is the average).

3. *Research is worthless unless it's properly interpreted.* And since interpretation is a specialized science, the broadcaster can't do it alone.

4. Even if the broadcaster understands his audience's preferences, *he may not have the know-how to translate this information into a highly rated news program.*

Like any good salesman, the consultant doesn't present a problem unless he can offer a solution. "If you want to find out more about getting to be Number One or about staying there, please call us. . . ," says an M and H ad. . . .

The consultants, of course, claim that their recommendations are tailor-made for each client, suited to the individual makeup of each local audience. But in moments of candor they will admit that there are very few truly original ideas around, and in a tightly knit industry like television there's a lot of copying of successful formulas. The consultant merely collects successful ideas in an organized way, suggesting features and gimmicks that seem to be transferable from one city to another.

The decision to accept or reject the ideas falls, usually, on the news director. And the experience of two prominent Magid clients illustrates the divergent reactions found among affected newsmen.

Ralph Renick of station WTVJ in Miami has consistently opposed his consultants, calling their influence "extremely dangerous" to the news profession. He accuses consultants of becoming absentee news czars. "They dictate who should be on the air, how the news should be presented, and load up the newscast with show biz."

He agrees with another news director's view that consultants offer only ". . . a cynical gimmick formula designed to fool the audience into thinking it is watching news."

By contrast, Mel Kampmann of WPVI-TV in Philadelphia thinks consultants offer journalists a "major tool" with which to wage a competitive strategy. And he's got results to back his view.

WPVI was a third-ranked station in news audience until 1969. That year Magid did a survey of Philadelphia's TV audience. And, says Kampmann, "Using what the public said it liked and disliked about this market, we then used this input to formulate what became *Action News* and turned this station around to No. 1 in one year's time."

Philadelphia TV has never been the same. The competing stations became revolving doors for general managers and news directors, with rapid staff turnovers and lots of head-rolling. Following what has become a familiar path in other markets, one of the Magid victims—KYW-TV—hired McHugh and Hoffman to help wage the competitive battle.

Action News is fast-moving; its people young, dynamic, informal; its graphics vibrant. It has flash. It has *Action.* One news producer glumly calls its genre the "dazzle 'em with footwork" school of news.

Kampmann sees no journalistic contradiction: "Our station has used a consultant and we have also won many journalistic awards. So they do work hand in hand."

But as the consultants' impact has spread, the inevitable result is a news philosophy like the one circulated at KFMB-TV in San Diego, a Magid client: "Unlike earlier concepts of 'what is news' which defined the product as 'what people *should* know,' *Action News* is defined as 'what people *want* to know.' Note the difference. Don't ignore it. Repeatedly, across the country, stations which have ignored this shift in concept have been destroyed by aggressive broadcasters."

Frank Magid denies that this represents his philosophy. But it bears a striking resemblance to remarks his chief consultant, Leigh Stowell, made at a gathering of broadcast educators: "The country is filled with stations that have . . . gone down in absolute flames to a station that comes on with a contemporary style of presentation."

Magid and his counterpart, Phil McHugh, also deny a Cro Magnon view of the average TV viewer, as represented by good old Billy Blue Collar. But one West Coast newsman reports: "When I suggested that a part of our job is to educate as well as entertain, the consultant remarked, 'Show me a news director who wants to educate somebody and I'll show you a station in third place'."

Again, Leigh Stowell: "Anybody who is practicing journalism on a day-in, day-out basis that doesn't believe that his product has to very interesting from a visual standpoint is in the wrong business. To *succeed,* that is."

The repetition of certain words becomes obvious: succeed . . . product . . . interesting. And a visually interesting, successful product is what a Magid client strives for. Again, that KFMB-TV staff memo, in part: "Put action into your film. Don't stand when you can be moving. . . . Get the first film on the air :15 after the open. . . . No film should run longer than 90 seconds."

The *Action News* formula promises staffers: "You'll become the most important people in San Diego because you know everything that's happening." For that reason, the news staff is told, "We must always *appear* to be on top of every story."

If, as the consultants say, there is no magic formula for success, there is at least striking similarity in the recommendations reported by news directors who work with consultants. In 14 out of 17 news departments surveyed, a consultant recommended replacement of one or more on-air personalities. At some stations entire staffs of anchorpeople, sports and weather reporters have been cleaned out practically overnight. . . .

The premium, in this unending pirating, trading and buying, is on people who match the formula: warm, likable, "human" people who like their fellow newsmen and love their work.

Another common denominator of all consultant recommendations seems to be shorter news stories, and more of them. Ninety seconds seems to be standard, 18 to 20 stories per half-hour program the sought-after goal, except in the slow-talking South, where the recommended average is 10.

Promotion of the news product is heavily emphasized. (Sell, sell, sell.)

And talking-head stories (people who are merely *saying* things, not *doing* things) are to be avoided. As one disenchanted Midwest news director puts it: "Talking heads are garbage and a story runs 1:30 for World War III."

Which exasperates Magid: "For heaven's sake, if the President were shot, is there anyone who could say that this organization would ever suggest that that be treated in 90 seconds?" But he does believe that more stories are better. "When you are putting more into your news shows, you're being fairer with the viewing public."

Still, if a program crams in 20 stories instead of the usual 10, something's got to give. Especially since more time now is taken with chatty interplay and feature material. A California news director worries that his consultant's influence has "subtly caused us to change the coverage of some important stories." Where he once sent a reporter to spend the morning covering city council, that's no longer done because of the demands of a high story count. Besides, official meetings are mostly talking heads. The restrictions, he confesses, "make it difficult to cover stories about ideas which just do not have visual possibilities." . . .

[As the] consulting firms broaden their influence, the reactions from TV news directors and broadcast journalists sometimes reach a high emotional pitch. At gatherings of TV newsmen, the question is being asked with frequency: "Is a small group of social scientists and audience analysts beginning to dominate the whole of television news?"

The consultants find the furor puzzling and irritating. Magid's goals for his clients seem harmless enough. He wants the viewer to be able to "tune out the news at its conclusion and say, 'Gee, that was the best half hour that I watched tonight'." After all, says Leigh Stowell, what's good for the client is good for the consultants.

"There's a report card that comes out, you know," he says, referring to ratings, "and that's how we're graded, frankly. If a station succeeds, we succeed." But, the danger, says one broadcast journalist, lies in "the potential of forgetting who is working for whom."

Dave Wright, a Greensboro, N.C., news director, brings the conflict into focus: "The journalist seeks clarity and truth. The consultant seeks watchers of the journalist's product." Reconciling this conflict falls into the hands of station owners and general managers like one described by Stowell: "The owner sat behind his desk and said, 'We're going to do everything you say for us to do—everything! And if we aren't Number One in a year, it's going to be your fannies'."

The consultants deny that they want any such turnkey control over news departments. And they are sensitive to implications that they have anything to say about the *content* of news programs. "One thing we don't do, not only for obvious ethical reasons, but also for blatant legal reasons, is we never make advice on the content of the newscast," says Stowell. At bottom, vows Magid, consultants are only interested in "the manner in which it's packaged," which statement denies the arguments of broadcasters who contend, "Everything we do—sets, format, talent, visuals, story selection, pacing, style, etc.—represents a journalistic judgment."

But if consultants deny they want to "control" news operations, they admit they expect "cooperation" from their clients. "We feel," says Magid, "if our advice is taken, they will gain a larger share of the audience." But, he says with a shrug, "That's still up to them."

However, [with the high costs of] consulting fees [and surveys], the odds are strong that the station management is not going to simply file the consultant's report away as useful information. The commitment to cooperate, says Stowell, is usually "made before they're going to shell out that kind of money." . . .

Beneath the emotion and defensiveness surrounding the consultant invasion lie some very real questions that broadcasters, newsmen, consultants and the viewing public should seriously consider:

- Are consultants eroding the independence of local news programmers?
- Are they merely, as some news directors charge, providing station managements with "cop-outs" to cover their own inadequate commitment to responsible news programming?
- Are local news directors allowing the drive for ratings and management approval to overcome common sense?

The consultants have called into question some of the very basic premises held by journalists: Who decides what is news? What rights does the television audience have in this decision making? And is it possible to alter the "packaging" of news programs, making them more palatable to the consumer, without also altering their meaning and thrust?

Some newsmen believe that the influence of consulting firms will pass when more news directors become capable of deciphering audience data themselves, when all the gimmicks, formulas and formats have become shopworn and tiresome. Meanwhile, unchecked influence by people who are essentially nonjournalists poses a very real threat to [the] medium.

Perhaps the view of one big-city news director offers the best hope for the future. He observes, "One group stubbornly wants everything we do to be based on how much audience it will get;

another group of hard noses bases every decision on importance rather than interest. I think we need a greater discipline—people who want to do important and legitimate stories so well and in such an interesting manner that they also build audience. That is the only way we will maintain our integrity and serve a mass audience, and make money at the same time."

The problem is, he concludes, "I don't think there are enough of those people, among either consultants or news directors or general managers."

The person who has the largest stake in the outcome is the television news viewer. Most people who flip the dial to their favorite local news program are probably unaware that they have anything at all to say about the way that program is presented. And that belief has led to much of the dismay and frustration evident in the mounting criticism of news programming. But the sophisticated audience-sampling techniques of the consultants are making the viewer's opinions felt with mounting force. The result may be a true reflection of the audience's distaste for "bad news," producing a drift toward entertaining but shallow news programming.

The real danger is that every station in the country will wind up with a program aimed at the lowest common denominator of its audience, a perhaps uneducated, unread, untraveled cartoon figure, [who] may determine how this struggle for control of television news will ultimately turn out.

NEIL HICKEY

Is Television Doing Its Investigative Reporting Job?

Investigative reporting has never been a major staple of most television news operations, even thought the technical capabilities of television are such that large amounts of information can be conveyed in very short periods of time. CBS's Robert Pierpoint thinks there are two reasons. First, there is the "very real problem of getting a picture of a story that is complex and mainly intellectual, or mainly requires private talking on the telephone with people who don't want to be seen and don't want to be quoted." The second and "real reason" is that "the name of the game in show business is to get your picture on the tube." Television is show business, according to Pierpoint, and reporters who spend hours tracking down stories and making phone calls are not as visible to the viewers as are their colleagues.

Former Pulitzer Prize-winning television columnist Ron Power, author of *The Newscasters,* claims that "in very few cases [is] there a sense of mission about the TV newscasts; a sense of continuity in the life of the city (or 'market') covered; a palpable willingness to perform the vigorous, adversary, check-on-government intervening role that American journalism has traditionally performed." Broadcasters feel differently. Eric Ober, news director of WBBM-TV, Chicago, told *Broadcasting* magazine in the summer of 1979 that investigative journalism "used to be a luxury or a rarity; now it's required." However, McHugh and Hoffman chairman Philip McHugh commented that "a lot of stations are talking about [investigative journalism] more than doing it." Neil Hickey reviews the state of the art.

Excerpts have been taken from this two-part essay, which first appeared April 2, April 9, 1977.

"Investigative reporting is the sacred cow of journalism in our time," says ABC newsman Brit Hume. American journalists are off on a muckraking binge the like of which hasn't been seen since the century's first decade, when writers like Ida Tarbell, Lincoln Steffens and Upton Sinclair were bending to their task of rooting out malfeasance and malpractice in government and big business.

America is in "the age of the great exaltation of the investigative reporter," said the *New York Times*'s ace investigator, Seymour Hersh, in accepting the Drew Pearson Foundation award for uncovering CIA meddling in Chile. The search for scandal in high places "has become almost obsessive since Watergate," says *Newsweek.* Journalism schools are crowded with students avid for their own crack at stories like the Pentagon Papers, My Lai, sex in Congress, and consumer fraud.

By far the biggest part of this muckraking glut is showing up in newspapers, magazines and books. Television, for whatever reasons (and some of them are valid, say the medium's defenders), is far off the pace in uncovering official villainy. "The state of investigative reporting on television is pitiful," says a network staff producer. "Everybody pays it lip service but practically nothing ever appears on the air. I defy you to name more than a handful of true investigative reports in the whole 30-year history of television."

"Our job is to comfort the afflicted and afflict the comfortable," says Steve Bauman, an investigative newsman at New York's WNEW. "The trouble is, television doesn't do enough of either."

Many local stations, some observers claim, are more involved in undercover reporting than the networks are. In Des Moines, for example, station WHO-TV filmed decoys exchanging food stamps illegally in a four-part series that resulted in federal scrutiny of food-stamp abuse. New York's WABC-TV mounted an elaborate and prolonged exposé of a state school for the mentally retarded called Willowbrook, causing public outcry and offical redress. Elsewhere, stations have hammered away at petty fraud, collusion and conflict of interest among county and municipal office holders.

But even at the local level, there's less muckraking than meets the eye. "Very few stations are really participating in true investigative reporting," says Gene Strul, news director of WCKT in Miami, which has won Peabody Awards two years in a row for investigative reporting. "Stations set up investigative units with the best of intentions and then, for whatever reasons, they fall into disuse. The investigative reporting that does get done receives a lot of promotion, which misleads people into believing it's far more extensive on television than it really is."

Some network newsmen argue hotly that TV has been as bold and as active as any other medium in producing tough exposés—CBS's "The Selling of the Pentagon," for example; NBC's "Pensions: The Broken Promise"; and ABC's "Fire!" They submit that series like *60 Minutes, ABC News Closeup* and NBC's *Weekend* are doing creative and original reporting on behind-the-scenes stories; that hard-hitting mini-documentaries (e.g., NBC's five-parter on the Teamsters' union, and CBS's three-part study of the Russian wheat deal) have appeared on network nightly news programs from time to time; and that network television, overall, is the possessor of an impressive tradition of robust documentaries going back to "Harvest of Shame" (Edward R. Murrow's 1960 study of migrant workers), "Who Killed Lake Erie?" "The Banks and the Poor" (on public television), "Biography of a Bookie Joint," "The Business of Heroin" and others.

But it's clear that the actual volume of investigative reports on television—week by week—is minuscule in view of the legendary resources, riches and far-flung news-gathering potential of TV journalism; in view also of the fertile plain that stretches before any energetic reporter looking for misdeeds—government, the courts, the military, big business, big labor, the professions.

Critics detect a subtle, pervasive self-censorship at work, growing out of network television's genetic relationship to three important constituencies: the U.S. government, the affiliated stations and advertisers.

It's the government, the argument goes, that is the benevolent landlord that allows television to graze in such green pastures and produce such brawny profits. And while TV's chieftains may be craven, they are not stupid. They are sensitive to the weapons the government can bring into play against them should an exposé touch the wrong nerves.

The powerful affiliates, for their part, are presumptively more conservative, both temperamentally and politically, than network newsmen and are thus uncomfortable with tough, antiestablishment journalism. So influential indeed are the affiliates that their collective disfavor caused the networks to junk their enthusiastic plans for an expansion of the evening news programs to one hour—a move that could have paved the way for more frequent investigative reports.

TV advertisers—many of them multinational corporations and conglomerates—are imagined by critics to take a dim view of reportage that cavils about price-fixing, collusion with regulatory agencies and influence-peddling in the U.S. Congress and abroad. . . .

There's a whole laundry list of reasons—invoked regularly by TV people and outside observers alike—why the television medium is *not* fully competitive in the muckraking game:

- TV needs pictures, but investigative stories often tend to be encyclopedic and nonvisual affairs with a "talking head" spouting hard-to-follow facts in front of a few incomprehensible graphs and charts.
- An important TV exposé might take six to twelve months of research and undercover legwork, then fail to produce a "smoking pistol" or an airtight case. It could then be junked as too risky or too inconclusive to be put on the air.
- TV, unlike the print media, has an obligation under the Fairness Doctrine [see pp. 337–48] to provide opposing views when treating matters of public importance, or when engaging in anything that might be broadly construed as a "personal attack." As a result, tough, investigative stories sometimes get "balanced out of existence" and lose their bite. . . .
- A decent investigative story on the nightly news programs needs four or five minutes (out of 22) to lay out the facts with any clarity or completeness. That's more than networks are willing to commit except for exceptional stories.
- TV has nagging logistical problems that almost defeat the best efforts of undercover reporters. Says documentarist Peter Davis ("The Selling of the Pentagon," "Hearts and Minds"): "If Woodward and Bernstein had shown up at their rendezvous with Deep Throat lugging a camera, lights and sound equipment, the whole Watergate exposé might never have happened. People who want to remain anonymous simply are not going to have their pictures taken, even in disguise."

Underlying all such rationales, of course, lurks the guiding principle that inspirits (or dispirits) the entire television medium: ratings. "There simply is no great appetite for this kind of programming," says a TV executive. "People get bored to tears with corruption stories unless they relate either to the White House or to some sex bomb in a Congressman's office." . . .

The suspicion persists among TV theorists that, no matter how much muckraking the medium does or how well it does it, television simply is not a hospitable place for this kind of fare. TV viewers are used to the steady drip-drip-drip of game shows, situation comedies, melodramas and variety shows that require little but semiattentive passivity. The intrusion of a sober and accusatory documentary, requiring one's full attention, is too jarring to be effective—or so the argument goes.

Says ABC's Brit Hume, once an aide to Jack Anderson: "An investigative report requires that the viewer concentrate on what he's being told. It's usually complicated stuff, and sophisticated in the sense that it involves judgments about what should and shouldn't be. But TV makes you lazy mentally. It may be in the nature of the medium. We are not used to thinking while watching TV—so we won't and don't." . . .

In sum, the whole practice of investigative reporting on television is so expensive, risky, time-consuming, potentially litigious, speculative and unmarketable that it's a wonder *any* ever gets on the medium. Futhermore, nobody ever got in trouble with the FCC for *not* exposing scandal, so why should a station or network walk willingly into that Sargasso Sea? . . .

JOE SALTZMAN

It's Live—and It's Terrifying

Television news is charged with the overuse of sensationalism. Morley Safer of *60 Minutes* feels that sensationalism is inherent in television "because you're not talking about it, you're showing it. The magic of the stuff coming through the tube *is* sensational." New developments in the equipment used by television journalists pose the danger that news coverage may include even more sensationalism and become more superficial. Joe Saltzman elaborates.

BOB SIMMONS, *television reporter:* It's a bad time to talk to you I know, but just tell me what you have seen here . . . (*Gunfire*). . . .

LOS ANGELES POLICE SERGEANT: You've got as close as I have.

(*Loud gunshot. Sound of a bullet ricocheting next to the camera.*)

SIMMONS: Look out there. That's bad. That's bad. Get back, guys. (*Confusion, many voices.*) We just took, we just took a ricochet or direct. I don't know which.

BILL DEIZ, *television reporter:* We just got missed by a bullet. Ooh, that's as close as I ever want to get.

SIMMONS: It went through the house right beside us here. I can see a hole in the screen, I believe.

(*Noise, more gunfire.*)

SIMMONS: Let's see if we couldn't still get this picture, but from a little better location, huh?

DEIZ: I don't know if it's a good idea to interview someone right now.

(*Burst of gunfire fills the air.*)

This essay first appeared March 15, 1975.

Millions of Americans were watching as KNXT in Los Angeles sent out its live coverage of the shoot-out between police and members of the Symbionese Liberation Army (SLA) [in 1975]. Homes throughout the country picked up the TV images instantly: a South Central Los Angeles neighborhood turned into a battlefield around a yellow stucco house on 54th Street, ringed by about 400 police and FBI men.

In the San Francisco suburb of Hillsborough, 350 miles north, the family of 20-year-old publishing heiress Patricia Campbell Hearst watched the live coverage. Her parents, her two sisters and a small cluster of friends looked to see if their Patty—kidnapped and apparently radicalized by the SLA—was inside a house now being riddled by bullets and set afire in front of their startled eyes.

In San Diego, 100 miles to the south, Steven Weed, Patty's 26-year-old financé, also watched and waited. So did other relatives and friends of SLA members—perhaps even Patty Hearst herself. In Pennsylvania, the father of William Wolfe, one of the six incinerated in the shoot-out, couldn't believe what he saw. In Indiana, Mrs. Betty Bunnell, the mother of SLA member William Harris, wondered aloud if her son were inside the inferno. Later, she would ask her son to give himself up, saying: "After watching the hell that was turned loose in Los Angeles, I just don't want Billy to end like that." In Illinois, Frederick W. Schwartz, father of Harris's wife, Emily, would say much the same thing.

And in Los Angeles, the KNXT news director (Bill Eames), his top assistant (Al Greenstein) and the newsroom staff were also watching, as astounded as everyone else at what they were witnessing. "The Real-Time, live picture of the SLA shoot-out excited even as it horrified all of us," says Eames. "We congratulated ourselves on the exclusive coverage and, for a brief moment, were almost swept away by the 'Gee whiz, look what we're doing' aspect of it."

Nothing in television news is more exciting or more terrifying to the electronic journalist today than what they're calling "Real-Time" coverage.

Real-Time is giving video and audio information to the audience as it is happening. It is reducing to zero the gap between the time of an event and the telling about the event.

It is nothing new. Radio does it all the time. And for decades on television we have had Real-Time television coverage of planned events—political conventions, space shots, sporting events, parades. But now, almost anything can be broadcast live and immediately, using new portable cameras and smaller, lighter backup equipment. For television stations all over the country, such "minicam" equipment is the latest plaything, and Real-Time coverage is the newest game in town.

Eames explains why Real-Time coverage is so exciting:

"Small children are locked into television in a way adults seldom understand because they believe what they are seeing is going on at the same time. They are caught up in it. It is real to them.

"Real-Time coverage does this for the adult. It is happening right now—no film, no video tape, no delays, no editing. There is always dramatic tension in any live report because anything might happen." In Real-Time, what the viewer gets is the drama of the moment, the anticipation of not knowing what is going to happen next.

The SLA shoot-out is a good case in point. Until the fiery climax, the video information in two hours was limited and unchanging. For the most part, the viewer looked down an alley at the side of a house. But no one was bored. There were the continuing sounds of gunfire, the fine audio reports and, above all, the uncertainty, the anticipation.

But in exchange for this raw excitement and drama, the broadcast journalist trades a lot. In Real-Time coverage the problems of doing a good job of reporting are so difficult that many electronic journalists, including Eames and Greenstein, are privately concerned.

First, there is the danger of giving the viewer misinformation and rumor.

"In a running account of a story, there will always be misinformation no matter how hard the reporter works," says Greenstein. "Errors are understandable, but I'm afraid not excusable. The fact that it is a live report, a running story, doesn't relieve you of the responsibility of being accurate, no matter how hard it is to live up to that responsibility."

During the SLA shoot-out, many rumors were reported, often directly from police and FBI sources. One rumor was that Patty

Hearst was inside the house. Reporters Simmons and Deiz kept qualifying the report, but since it had come from an FBI source, it had to be reported.

Eames is philosophical about this kind of problem, pointing out it has existed as long as news has been reported. He says news operations always run the risk of giving out misinformation, but in Real-Time the risk is greater.

"The farther away you get from an event, the better your information. You get far enough away from the event and you have history. We always try to check out the bits of information we get, but in a Real-Time situation, there is no time. So you do the best you can. It is, and has always been, our responsibility to correct misinformation as quickly and as accurately as we can."

Real-Time coverage puts an incredible burden on the field reporter. . . . There is no time to evaluate a situation, to make a report fair, to edit out anything. Even with a seven-second tape delay, it is far more difficult to exercise good news judgment in a Real-Time situation. But, Greenstein says, the responsibility is still there: "The public isn't demanding live coverage. We're saying this event is something you should see. If we show something offensive, we can't say, 'Sorry it's live.' So you have the same responsibility, but the job is so much tougher." . . .

There is the danger of being "used," of creating a news story simply by covering an event live.

[One] example occurred in front of live television cameras in Los Angeles when a man holding several persons hostage inside a bar used the live coverage to try to negotiate his safe passage through police lines. Public officials arrived because, all of a sudden, their total constituency was informed of the event. If the incident had occurred before a film or tape camera, it is unlikely that any official would have bothered to show up, but the presence of the live cameras escalated a garden-variety type of story into something much larger.

There is the danger of newsmen overreacting, overplaying and exaggerating a story, giving the event too much prominence and air time.

After KNXT scored its exclusive coverage of the SLA shootout—a "once-in-a-lifetime achievement," say local news officials—it was no secret that competitive newsmen were angry. Their pride was hurt. One was heard to say, "Next time I'll be there first no matter what."

The temptation for a field reporter to overreact during a fast-breaking news situation has always been a real one; in a Real-Time situation, when there is no second-guessing, the danger is even greater.

The impact of this kind of judgment is immense. [In July 1974] Randolph Hearst and his wife heard a live audio report that their daughter was holed up in a North Hollywood, Cal., house surrounded by police. It looked like the SLA shoot-out all over again. They immediately flew to Los Angeles. During the flight, they were told it was a false alarm.

There is the danger of being simplistic and one-dimensional in the reporting of complex events.

Real-Time coverage is, by its very nature, one-dimensional. It is superficial: a reporter describing what both he and the viewer are seeing. The more complex the story, the more danger there is of doing a superficial job of reporting.

A picket line is a good example. On video tape or film, the reporter would talk to those on the line, would interview union leaders, a union family at home, management officials, public officials, show an empty plant and develop a polished story that covers all angles. In Real-Time coverage, the reporter goes to the demonstration and reports on it, doing it all ad-lib over one static picture from one location.

"Real-Time coverage must be the beginning, not the end of our reporting effort," Eames says. "Real-Time, live coverage does not help thorough, in-depth reporting and, clearly, it does not excuse us from doing it."

In the end, the real danger of more and more Real-Time coverage is that it will become a substitute for other forms of reporting. If that happens, the fear among many journalists is that television's coverage of the world in which we live will become even more superficial than it is now.

JOHN WEISMAN

When Hostages' Lives Are at Stake

In November 1979, the United States Embassy in Iran was attacked by Iranian revolutionaries, and approximately sixty people were taken hostage. The situation was covered extensively by television. On December 1, *Time* reported that "with the near total breakdown of communications between the U.S. and Iranian governments, news organizations—especially the television networks—have become conduits for semi-official exchanges, reluctant publicists for Iran, and a valuable source of information for the U.S. government."

The Iranian crisis illustrates the sensitive nature of the relationship between the news media on the one hand and the hostages and their captors on the other. John Weisman describes the responsibilities, burdens and dangers of live television coverage when hostages are taken.

Hostages. That word makes law-enforcement officials very nervous these days. But there is another word, too. One that makes cops, FBI men and security people equally jittery. And *that* word is television. "Combine the two in the wrong way," says a U.S. Department of Justice official, "and you could have real trouble on your hands."

In [recent] years, the United States has experienced scores of hostage-taking incidents. Most, fortunately, have been resolved without loss of life. But during the tense hours of waiting and negotiating, the greatest disagreement, antagonism and conflict often have

This essay first appeared August 26, 1978.

been not between hostage takers and the police, but between the cops and the news media—especially TV.

So far as anyone can tell, no hostage has yet been killed because of something a broadcaster put on the air. Some TV newsmen call that skill. "But it is just damn luck," says a former Los Angeles police chief, Edward M. Davis. Others in law enforcement agree with him. So do dozens of former hostages, many of whom feel that broadcast coverage of their own situations had actually put their lives in jeopardy.

What some in law enforcement call a textbook example of the kinds of mistakes broadcasters can make took place in Washington, D.C., in March 1977. There, twelve Hanafi Muslims occupied three buildings for 39 hours. More than 140 hostages were captured in the siege. Eight in the District Building, two blocks from the White House; eleven in the city's Islamic Center, right in the heart of Embassy Row; and 123 at the national headquarters of B'nai B'rith.

It was, one reporter said at the time, a story made for television. But in the scramble for news, and the competition for scoops, the broadcast media made mistakes. Enough of them, in fact, to cause 70 per cent of the listeners in a subsequent radio poll to say that media coverage might have threatened the lives of the hostages. Broadcast coverage was given an even more dismal rating by the Hanafis' hostages themselves. Virtually all thought that the media had had no regard for their lives at one time or another.

What mistakes were made by broadcast journalists during the Hanafi siege?

- During an on-the-air interview, Hamaas Abdul Khaalis, leader of the Hanafis, was asked by one broadcast journalist whether or not he felt that he could trust the police negotiators.
- A radio reporter mistakenly referred to the Hanafis as "Black Muslims." Word came back to the station that unless an on-air apology was made, several hostages would be decapitated. (The apology was made.)
- Another broadcaster, during an interview with Khaalis, asked whether or not the Hanafi leader had "set any deadlines yet." Fortunately, Khaalis overlooked the question.
- A minicam unit started setting up in a building just across from the eighth-floor area Khaalis occupied. One of the terrorists spotted

it. According to Hank Siegel, a hostage at the B'nai B'rith site, the Hanafi said, "Oh, great—television. We'll hang a couple of old men out the window by their ankles. Let 'em take pictures of that!"

▪ Hostage Alan Grip recalls a broadcast reporting that a fire ladder was being erected outside the District Building and police were going up the ladder. "The reporter implied—although he didn't say it directly—that they were about to rush the room where we were being kept. One of the gunmen just went crazy. He screamed, 'You tell those police to take the ladder away or we're gonna start blowing people away'."

Dr. Frank Ochberg, a psychiatrist at the National Institute of Mental Health, serves as a consultant to the FBI on terrorism and hostage taking. "The problem," he says, "is that you're pitting newsmen's First Amendment rights against the managing of life-and-death situations. What you've got is an almost impossible situation. And the hostages are caught right in the middle of it all."

Despite a history of mutual mistrust, there are some places in which the police and the news media have come to an understanding. New York City is one of them. The NYPD formed a hostage-negotiating unit shortly after the 1972 Munich Olympics. It was headed by Dr. Harvey Schlossberg, a career police officer who until his retirement ran the NYPD's Department of Psychological Services; and Capt. Frank Bolz, a 22-year veteran working out of police headquarters. Both Schlossberg and Bolz characterize their relations with the media as good; a sentiment echoed by a number of New York's TV reporters. But they learned to deal with the media through mistakes.

"I remember our first hostage-negotiating job," says Schlossberg. "The John & Al Sporting Goods store in Brooklyn. Four terrorists holding 14 hostages. Our first mistake was we wanted a news blackout. So we told the press, 'You can't have nothing.' That made 'em good and mad.

"Then we shut off the electric power in the area, so cameramen couldn't use their lights. So the TV stations sent portable generators down to the site, and the next thing you know the criminals were in the dark and the cops were all lit up nice and bright."

Schlossberg's negotiating team managed to rescue the hostages and persuade the terrorists to surrender without a shot being fired.

But during the after-siege critique that is part of the NYPD negotiating team's routine, most of the police officers' questions revolved around the media. "We had spent so much time arguing with the media," says Schlossberg. "We knew that neither party was malicious. I decided that it was just a question of misunderstanding."

The NYPD decided to remedy the situation. Bolz and Schlossberg started to include reporters in the same training sessions used by NYPD hostage negotiators (more than seventy-five reporters have gone through the program so far). "We try to take away the mystique," says Bolz. "If they understand what we do, we think they'll honor our requests."

Why are on-air interviews with hostage takers such a sore point with law-enforcement officers? One reason, says Bolz, is that "reporters don't know if the question they're asking will set the terrorist off.

"Sometimes," adds Bolz, "reporters are just stupid. A Canadian reporter once called in to a hostage taker. The perpetrator told him he wanted to trade the hostages for narcotics. So the reporter says, 'Don't be stupid—if you give up all your hostages, you won't have anything to deal with'."

Another reason law-enforcement people dislike detailed coverage is that it tends to harden the position on both sides. Dr. Robert Shellow, who was the principal social scientist for the National Advisory Commission on Social Disorders, puts it this way: "The more the situation becomes public, the more it loses fluidity. It's like labor negotiations or politics. The President and the Congress can argue in private and make progress—each side giving, each taking. But once the press reports where each stands, the positions are set in stone. The same dynamic holds for hostage situations."

"The telephone is a two-edged sword," says Bill Small, senior vice president of CBS News. "Sometimes, I think, it's therapeutic for the terrorist to talk, to tell his story. On the other hand, it's very possible for a reporter to infuriate the terrorist by asking the wrong question."

CBS, the first network to issue written guidelines to its news staff regarding hostage situations, does not rule out making phone calls to terrorists. But, the guidelines continue, "CBS News representatives should endeavor to contact experts dealing with the hostage situation to determine whether they have any guidance on such questions as phraseology to be avoided [or] what kind of questions or reports might tend to exacerbate the situation."

One hostage, who asked to go unidentified, suggests that the networks are not so much at fault in their reports as local TV stations, which tend to send less experienced reporters out to cover hostage situations. The point is echoed by Murray Schwartz, president of Merv Griffin Productions, who was a hostage of Palestinian terrorists at Entebbe. Schwartz adds: "There may also be too much concern on the press's part about the holders, and not enough about the hostages."

NBC has written guidelines for its staff, according to NBC News president Lester Crystal. ABC does not have any, however. Neither do most local stations—the first, usually, to send reporters onto the scene. Indeed, many local stations do not *want* guidelines. James Snyder, news director of WDIV-TV, Detroit, who directed coverage of the Hanafis when he worked in Washington, says, "I'll be happy to sit down and write a whole set on what to do the next time somebody named Khaalis takes over three buildings within two miles of the White House. But I'm not so sure that I can write them to cover every terrorist act that comes up."

Harvey Schlossberg disagrees. Sure, he says, there are several different forms of hostage taking. "But all of these situations can be reduced to some pretty basic psychological dynamics," says Schlossberg. "What we're doing is talking about people who consider themselves losers. But instead of lying on the floor and kicking their feet or holding their breath, they do something powerful—they take hostages. It's a way for them to manipulate the world. You might say that hostage-taking is a problem-solving device for one with an inadequate personality.

"Now I'm *not* talking about censorship in any way," Schlossberg insists. "But reporters have got to know that they're part of the dynamics too. These hostage-takers go from obscurity to world power in two minutes just by holding a gun to somebody's head. So you've got to be careful about how much media coverage you give them. Not enough and they're liable to do something outrageous. Too much and they become insatiable."

It would make many law-enforcement officials happy to see the press formulate guidelines that would rule out such elements of hostage coverage as telephone calls to the criminals, broadcasts describing police tactics, live reports and interviews with the hostage taker's family.

Many reporters, however, feel that the public's right to know is absolute. "No one is out to jeopardize a hostage's life if the police say that putting this or that on the air will do that," says WDVM-TV (Washington) reporter Susan King. "But we must let the community know what is going on. What I report may turn out for good, or it may turn out for evil. Either way, I have no choice: I have to report, and let the editors make the choice about whether to use it or not."

While most former hostages disagree with King, one who does not is Charles Fenyvesi. Fenyvesi, the editor of the *National Jewish Monthly,* was captured by Hamaas Khaalis at the B'nai B'rith building. And despite his harrowing experience, Fenyvesi insists that, as a reporter, he would feel obligated to call up a terrorist in the course of covering a hostage situation.

"Sure, there are dangers in calling in. But it's also a way to allow the hostage-taker to let off steam. I remember Khaalis coming in and telling us, 'The whole world is watching me; the whole world is calling me!' It was his moment of glory. Instead of killing us, that became his high point."

Is there any answer to the problem of covering hostage takers? The most frequently heard one is training. But former hostage Fenyvesi adds some cautionary words: "Face it—as reporters, we all thrive on crisis. But somewhere along the line, reporters have got to be told that their primary assignment is to protect life. The media have got to take *life* over *scoop*.

"I can tell you, as a former hostage, that no one has really redefined the assignment of covering hostage situations in that way, yet. I just hope that they—that *we* do it, and soon."

AUDIENCE

A lot of people watch a lot of television; the numbers increase every year. In fact, when not sleeping or working, the average American is probably sitting in front of the television set. Some professional observers have raised the possibility that by the next century we will be watching television even more than we sleep or work, what with the shorter work week, the energy crisis and so forth.

A hardcover book is a best seller if it reaches anywhere from 100,000 to 500,000 homes, and a best-selling paperback may sell one to two million copies. The New York *Daily News* and the *Wall Street Journal,* with the largest circulations in the United States, each sell about two million copies daily. A highly successful movie may draw six million patrons. *TV Guide* sells approximately twenty million copies a week, making it the best-selling magazine. For a television program, however, twenty million viewers may not be a large enough audience to keep the program on the air.

According to the A. C. Nielsen Company estimates, there were 76,300,000 television households in the United States in January 1980. This represents 97.8 per cent of all households in the 48 contiguous states, and more than four of every five of these homes have at least one color set. Approximately half of the television households have two or more sets, even though the average size of the television household declined from 3.23 to 2.75 persons during the 1970s.

Of course, merely owning the television set is not the same as turning it on. However, the Nielsen statistics indicate that people watched more television during *each month* of 1979 than ever before. For the year, at least one of the family television sets was turned on for an average of 6 hours, 28 minutes a day, every day. In February 1980, daily household viewing was the highest in television history—7 hours, 22 minutes a day.

The number of people watching television varies according to the viewer's sex and age, the season and time of day, the day of the week, and the size and makeup of the household. These variables are of considerable importance to the networks and their advertisers, who like to know as much as possible about who is watching television when.

The average individual (not the household) watched television for 4 hours, 6 minutes a day during April 1980. The Nielsen Company has categorized the television audience according to age and sex. Women who are 55 years old and over represented 12 per cent of the potential viewing audience; this group watched the most television that month, an average of 37 hours, 19 minutes a week. Men aged 55 and over, who watched 35 hours, 32 minutes a week, ranked second. Next in line were women aged 25 to 54, followed by women aged 18 to 24 and children between two and five years old. Men aged 25 to 54 watched less television than the previous groups, as did teen-agers. Men aged 18 to 24 watched the least television in April 1980, an average of 21 hours, 12 minutes a week.

Most people tend to watch more television in the winter than in the summer. In January 1979, for example, the average television household had a set on for about 7 hours, 20 minutes a day; in July, the figure was 5 hours, 46 minutes. Except for children between two and five years old, the largest number of households watch television during the prime-time hours (8:00 to 11:00 P.M.). Approximately one-third of all viewing occurs during prime time and, at 9:00 P.M. on a winter's night, about two-thirds of all television households will have at least one set turned on. During the summer months, this figure normally falls to under 50 per cent. Over the course of a year, about 55 per cent of television households or 98 million people will have a set turned on at 9:00 P.M.

Although prime time has the biggest audience, viewing levels vary significantly during the day. On a typical day, the audience size increases steadily from 7:00 to 10:00 A.M., then begins to level off. By noon just over 20 per cent of television households have a set on. During the afternoon, more sets are turned on, and by 6:00 P.M. 35 to 40 per cent of the households are watching at least one set.

To attract the most viewers, a program probably should be scheduled for prime time on a Sunday evening and, of course, in the winter. Sunday and Monday are the biggest prime-time viewing nights. The evenings that attract the smallest audiences are Thursday and Friday. In 1979, Thursday night's audience was the smallest, usually about 84 million people, 21 million fewer than those watching on a typical Sunday night.

The amount of television viewing is significantly affected by the size and makeup of the household, in a predictable way. A larger household watches more television; a household with children watches more television. The figures for April 1980 were as follows: Households with five or more people had at least one set on for an average of 64 hours, 26 minutes a week; with three to four persons, 53 hours, 35 minutes; with one or two persons, 37 hours, 12 minutes. Households with children under age 18 had a set on for an average of 56 hours, 56 minutes a week; adult-only households watched 39 hours, 3 minutes. The average amount of time that all households had at least one set on was 46 hours, 27 minutes a week during April 1980. The family's income does not seem to affect the amount of television watching in the household. There was very little variation between watching by families with incomes over $20,000 and that by families with smaller incomes.

As in most commercial endeavors, the television industry depends heavily on information provided by market-research organizations—specifically, the Nielsen ratings—to determine actual viewing habits. The importance of the ratings to the industry is illustrated by a statement made in an official publication of the Broadcast Rating Council, formed by broadcasters and advertisers to monitor standards of performance of the broadcast ratings services:

> Ratings largely determine what programs live or die, where advertisers place commercials, what rates will be charged, the market value of broadcast stations, which network is in the ascendancy, and the career fate of broadcast

executives. When evaluating industry stocks, Wall Street analysts watch ratings trends more closely than earnings statements because profits follow ratings.

According to some experts, an extra rating point can, over the course of a season, mean up to an extra $75 million to the network, but the cost of programs remains relatively constant—whether or not those programs are hits.

The ratings services also provide audience demographics, which are of extreme importance to the advertiser and, therefore, to the network programmer. Even a program that ranks high in total audience is subject to cancellation if it is not attracting the desired type of viewer. For example, CBS cancelled the seventh-rated *Red Skelton Show* after its nineteenth season. The reason: CBS wanted a younger and more urban audience. The same network later scrapped the long-running and successful *Petticoat Junction, Green Acres* and the *Beverly Hillbillies* because these programs were not delivering the type of audience desired.

The Nielsen weekly program ratings are compiled for the networks, not for local commercial stations, primarily because they are not willing to pay the cost. Local stations depend on periodic comprehensive ratings provided by Nielsen and the other major rating service, American Research Bureau. Each service distributes about 100,000 diaries in every television market in the country during the four months of the year deemed typical of the seasons: February, May, three weeks in July, and November. These months are called sweep periods.

The sweep periods, especially February and November, are crucial to the local station because its advertising rates are based on the size of its audience when the surveys are conducted. Naturally, stations attempt to obtain the best and most popular programming during the sweeps. Network affiliates, especially, put tremendous pressure on the networks in order to obtain the most powerful blockbusters during these times. The pressure is effective; each network spent an estimated $60 million or so for prime-time programming during the November 1979 sweep.

The sweeps are in general disfavor with both the networks and the creative community. Former CBS president Robert Wood refers to "the goddamn sweeps" as "artificial and destructive"; they "contribute to the general feeling of paranoia" which pervades much of television scheduling. Former NBC chairman Julian Goodman refers to the sweeps as "controlled insanity" because of the "killing competition" that takes place between the networks during those periods. From the point of view of the creative community, the sweeps are devastating: many of the best programs are placed in direct competition as a result of the networks' response to their affiliates' needs.

In 1979, the Hollywood Caucus for Producers, Writers and Directors told its members, the American Association of Advertising Agencies, and the National Association of Broadcasters that they should "end the ridiculous idea of sweeps." The Caucus indicated it would "oppose sweeps and . . . do everything possible to minimize their impact," including the insertion of clauses in future contracts with the networks that would specify that telefilms (made-for-TV movies), mini-series and specials not be delivered during sweep periods.

One way to eliminate the sweeps would be to initiate continuous audience measurement on the local level for at least most of the year. The networks expressed increased interest in this concept in the spring of 1979, but the local stations were less than enthusiastic. Continuous audience measurement would cost 10 to 15 million dollars more—a CBS estimate—than the 25 million-dollar price tag for the sweeps, the bulk of which is paid by the local stations. Many stations feel that if longer rating periods are desired, the advertisers should foot the bill with the networks chipping in. Another problem from the local station's point of view has to do with the way advertising rates are fixed. Station owners fear that advertising agencies could use selective data from a time period not previously known by the station to attack the accuracy of the station's claimed rating. The total samples used in the longer rating periods would also be smaller than those used in the quarterly sweeps.

The attitude of local stations notwithstanding, CBS president James Rosenfield predicts that audience ratings of local stations for about 47 weeks of the year will soon be available, because "the need is so acute and universally accepted." The cost of extending ratings to local stations for most of the year would be a small percentage of the revenues of the industry. Rosenfield notes that the increased costs would be minor compared to the current costs of forcing major programming efforts to compete for the rating advantage during one of the sweep periods.

Few would deny that ratings, even in the present forms of sweeps for the local stations and continuous audience measurement for the network programs, are very important to the well-being of the broadcast industry. However, even many broadcasters feel the industry puts too much emphasis on ratings. ABC president Fred Pierce states the case:

> The focus, unfortunately, is always on the ratings battle and on what are the top ten shows. I mean, it's like a crime if you're not in the top ten these days, which is mindboggling. You can have a show that reaches 14 million or 15 million households, and it may be ranked in the top forty. Somehow or other, it's written up as a potential miss, which is something I find rather extraordinary.

Producer Norman Lear insists that "it is because of the fanatic drive for ratings and profits that we see no ballet on American commercial television. We see no art. There is very little drama of historical significance and no science to speak of. Most shockingly, there is little opportunity to groom television's Eugene O'Neills, Arthur Millers, and Tennessee Williamses." FCC Chairman Charles Ferris suggests innovative program ideas are "sacrificed on the altar of the ratings competition. We have asked for inspiration and we have reached the moral equivalent of the *Gong Show.*" Ferris drew another, more ominous conclusion: "The potentially chilling effect of government regulation is more than matched in practice by the chilling effect of the Nielsen ratings."

In defense of the industry's reliance on ratings, Vincent Wasilewski, president of the National Association of Broadcasters, argues that the ratings are a form of voting: people are able to vote for their program choice and the program with the most votes stays on the air. CBS research director Jay Eliasberg does admit, however, that the so-called voting is not totally democratic; "some people are more equal than others." Because 80 per cent of all goods and services in the United States are purchased in the 100 largest metropolitan areas by adults between the ages of 18 and 49, the advertisers and networks tend to pay the most attention to these people's preferences.

The founder and board chairman of CBS, William Paley, points out that "ratings are necessary because the economic well-being of each network is dependent on them." He does acknowledge that inflationary costs and revenues, as well as increased financial stakes associated with television programming, have meant that "the shows which contribute to the total ratings picture have become more important today than they ever have been." One network executive considers the real problem with the industry's dependence on the ratings is not in the concept of rating programs but rather in what the ratings do not tell the networks:

> None of us ever talks to a real person about watching television. Each morning they pass across our desks as numbers—ratings. It's totally impersonal in the worst sense of the word. We know nothing about why people watch or what they'd like to see. We only know what percentage of them chose which of three things they were offered at nine o'clock last night. So we talk to each other, look at the numbers, imitate and choose things for our own reasons. It's out of control.

A solution may lie in the use of qualitative ratings. In late 1977, General Foods gave the National Citizens Committee for Broadcasting, a public-interest group now headed by Ralph Nader and former FCC Commissioner Nicholas Johnson, a grant to conduct pilot studies for qualitative ratings. A study of 200 adults in the Washington, D.C., area revealed some significant differences between a show's quantitative and qualitative ratings. Public television's *I Claudius* ranked first in terms of perceived quality and engaging, enriching and enlightening entertainment; but it ranked only 46th in the quantitative ratings. *Happy Days* ranked third in numbers of viewers, but the same sample using a qualitative scale put the show in 27th place.

Although the concept of qualitative ratings does not meet with universal agreement within the industry, former NAB board chairman Donald Thurston believes a quality measurement, or a "Q-factor," would serve both the public and broadcasting. Thurston argues: "If a show came in with good but not great ratings, but the

Q-factor showed that it left viewers with wonderful feelings, it might have a chance to stay on the air." Many others, however, feel that qualitative ratings would complicate the buying and selling of commercial time. Advertisers could point to low qualitative ratings in attempts to lower the price for commercials in a particular program, despite the show's having a high Nielsen ranking. Under the current system, networks and stations can continue to maintain that "if the public watches us they like our programs."

The Nielsen Company readily admits that its ratings do not measure program quality. In one of its publications it states: "As far as we're concerned, there is no such thing as a TV rating. . . . The word 'rating' is a misnomer, becauser it implies a measurement of program quality—and this we never do. NEVER." Misnomer or not, ratings, in whatever form they may evolve, will continue to have tremendous impact on what Americans receive on their television sets for some time to come.

ARTHUR C. NIELSEN, JR.
THEODORE BERLAND

Nielsen Defends His Ratings

Television ratings are based on random samples—a technique used extensively by poll takers, social scientists and the government. A. C. Nielsen, with Theodore Berland, details how his company compiles its ratings, and discusses their value to the public and the industry when used in the proper manner.

Did you ever watch someone start on a bowl of soup? He stirs the liquid, lifts the spoon to his lips and sips. He has just tasted a sample and rated it; whether he adds salt or not depends on that random spoonful.

You'll notice that he never denounces the spoon when there is too little salt.

Not so in TV ratings—despite the fact that rating techniques employ some of the most advanced statistical methods known, and some of the most sophisticated electronics.

Ratings are today's TV scapegoat: Shows with low ratings blame the raters; those who think television quality can and should be elevated blame the raters; and some owners of magazines and newspapers which lose advertising revenue to television attack the raters.

As the nation's most listened-to rating, the Nielsen Television Index (NTI) often is the target of these attacks. After years of patience, I'd like to rise to its defense.

First, be sure you clearly separate *ratings* from *programming.* While one may affect the other, they are not the same. Ratings are

This essay first appeared November 7, 1964. The Nielsen Company uses the same methods for determining the ratings that it employed in 1964. Program titles and figures have been brought up to date.

television's batting averages—they indicate how many people programs are hitting. They are not critical measures of any program's intrinsic merit.

They observe, with objectivity and impartiality, the relative appeal of a given program by measuring how many households are tuned to it. Blaming the ratings when you don't like a popular program is like blaming the soup spoon.

Those who would castigate commercial television, incidentally, should remember that it is wholly supported by advertising revenues. Advertising can be effective only if it reaches people. That is why sponsors want programs that attract the largest audiences containing the kinds of people who might buy their products. Whether we like it or not, weighty cultural, educational or artistic shows seldom attract large audiences.

A show's rating is an estimate of how many families watch it. Nielsen ratings estimate how many households have their TV sets tuned to which network shows.

We keep tab by connecting automatic recorders (Audimeters) to a cross section of the nation's TV sets. These Audimeters are placed out of sight—in closets, basements, etc.—and by electronic "photographs" on film, record minute-by-minute whether the sets are on or off, and to what channel they are tuned. This record is kept 24 hours a day, week in and week out. . . .

If there were Audimeters in every American home wired to a giant central computer, we could know instantly how many American households were tuned to what at any moment. Unfortunately, there is no computer large enough to do this job—and even if there were, it would cost too much to get the ratings by this method. More practical and far less expensive is the method we use which gathers information from a scientifically selected *sample* of homes.

How a sample of homes (we use about [1200]) can properly reflect the actions and tastes of [76,300,000] homes is completely mysterious to many people. Yet sampling is a basic part of our lives.

There's the man sipping soup; the doctor diagnosing your illness after laboratory examination of a few drops of blood; your gas-station attendant judging crankcase dirt by the bit of oil on the dipstick.

Sampling systems such as these are a basic tool used in many types of research. Sampling is a branch of higher mathematics and is a well-developed science. For example, by far the largest division of our company is the Nielsen Retail Index. This division estimates consumer sales for manufacturing clients of consumer products in [23] countries.

These manufacturers eventually get some idea of how their products are doing by totaling up their factory sales. But they have to gear current production to current retail sales—which can differ from factory sales because of changes in retail and wholesale inventories. In addition, they need to compare their own sales progress against their competitors'. The Nielsen Retail Index obtains measurements of product sales, brand by brand, by actually auditing *samples* of supermarkets and corner stores.

Total sales of individual products in all stores are then estimated from these data. When known factory shipments of these products over long periods of time are compared with Nielsen's consumer sales estimates, they compare very closely.

Perhaps the best-known evidence that sampling is practical is found in political polling, where a sample of voters is questioned. Polls, however, face a much more difficult task because they are measuring *opinions* and *future action,* rather than precise matters such as whether a TV set is on or off, or how many packages of a given brand have been sold in a particular store. Despite these difficulties, predictions of nationally known political poll takers, [are usually] within a few per cent of the actual Presidential vote.

Unfortunately, there are no such figures as factory shipments or final election results with which to check the accuracy of television ratings. But our television rating sample is selected by the same general principles as are the retail store samples we use. We very accurately measure the sales of thousands of such products as soap, beverages, foods and drugs so it is reasonable to assume that the TV ratings are similarly accurate.

We're all used to seeing such vital statistics as the U.S. cost-of-living index or total unemployed. These statistics were all obtained from samples. Like TV ratings they are estimates—and are not *precisely* accurate. It is impossible to know exactly what the *true* cost of living is or the *exact* number of people who are unemployed. Yet these government estimates based upon samples are very useful and are accurate enough for the intended use.

How accurate are the Nielsen television ratings?

Let's take a program with a rating of 30—perhaps of your favorites, like [*60 Minutes*]. When our report says that the show has a rating of 30 we mean that our best estimate is that 30 per cent of all homes with TV sets are tuned to the show. Now that's an estimate based on our sample, of course. The truth could be higher or lower. Statistical mathematics tell us that 19 times out of 20 such a rating obtained from a perfect probability sample will be off by less than 3 points—here between 27 and 33 per cent.

The ratings could, of course, be made even more accurate by using a larger sample. But to cut the error in half—say, from 3 points on a 30 rating to 1½ points—would mean not just doubling the sample size, but increasing it *fourfold.* This in turn would make the ratings cost nearly four times as much. While we would have no objection to increasing our prices 300 per cent, we strongly doubt that our customers would approve![1]

"Sampling errors" are inherent in ratings, cost-of-living figures and other statistical estimates. There are also other types of errors. But they are small and in all probability wouldn't change the rating user's decision about a particular program.

For example, some people say that just because a TV set is on does not mean anyone is watching it. This is true. All of us may leave our sets on now and again when we aren't viewing. But we have made thousands of phone calls to homes to find out how often this happens. On the average only about one set in a hundred is on with no one viewing it. This can't affect significantly the accuracy of our rating.

Another criticism our ratings sometimes get from nonstatisticians is that each Audimeter home represents approximately [63,600] homes. Repeated often is the story of an Arkansas woman who disliked Jack Paar's remarks about a situation in Mississippi and turned him off every time his face appeared. Because her set was

1. Each of the three networks pay the Nielsen Company from $1.5 million to $2 million a year for the existing service. Nielsen has several hundred other subscribers to the national ratings who pay far less than that amount.

metered, the story goes, she felt she had special power in getting him off the air.

First, such criticism ignores the fact that many other viewers may also have been offended by Paar. Second, while this woman statistically did stand for many other viewers, she did not specifically represent them. [At the time] she was just one individual viewer in [what was then] a sample of 1100 households containing over 3500 viewers. Since her action represented only one individual out of 3500 she could have very little effect on the rating, because the rating is based upon what the 3500 people do—not just one, or even a handful.

Separately, she represented no one. To understand this point, consider the picture on your TV screen. Look closely and you will see it is a series of lines—actually 525 in number. Looked at together, these lines form an image of what the camera sees; but any one line is by itself meaningless.

Unlike the line you might pick out on your TV screen, homes that have Audimeters are not selected haphazardly. They are part of the sample of the population systematically selected according to methods devised by top statisticians, both in and out of the Nielsen Company, using data from the U.S. Housing Census.

Every housing unit in the country is assigned to a small census area, technically known as an enumeration district. [In delineating these census areas Nielsen uses 620 sample counties to represent the 3110 counties in the 48 contiguous states.] A computer picks the houses to be used in our sample from these districts in such a way that every house in the country has an equal chance of being selected. The computer selects say, every tenth house on a street but does not supply the addresses. Hence, a special force of Nielsen men must go out and get the street addresses of every house chosen. This is how the Nielsen "Master Sample" is developed.

But, the job still is not complete. Our regular field men then travel to these computer-selected homes and ask to install our Audimeter. The families are paid for this cooperation. [In 1975 Nielsen was paying $25 for the privilege of installing the Audimeter, one-half of any television repair bills and $1 per set per month. Nielsen has had some difficulties in getting blacks and other minorities to permit the Audimeter into their homes. Viewers may remain a part of the Nielsen sample for a maximum of five years, but Nielsen claims that there is a 45 per cent turnover in the sample each year due to death, divorces, people moving to new households and people who no longer wish to participate.] Most households accept; alternates are selected for those who don't.

Thus the sample, in many ways, reflects the actions of the millions of viewers. One check, for instance, showed that 26 per cent of the sample families [owned] Chevrolets and 2 percent [owned] Cadillacs. National license registrations [for the same year showed] that 25 per cent of American families [owned] Chevrolets, and 2 per cent [owned] Cadillacs.

In other words, our TV ratings are reasonable estimates of the public's viewing habits. They are not represented to be the *exact* number of homes tuning in a given program. They are, however, very useful in indicating to broadcasters how certain shows are doing—in relation to other shows and over certain periods of time to show trends in viewing. Our customers tell us that the accuracy is about right for their purposes.

We can never know *exactly* how many eyes are on [any particular program] or *exactly* how many sets are tuned to [that program] at any minute. But ratings such as NTI give the best approximations there are.

TV ratings are a tool designed for a specific job. With their limitations kept firmly in mind, their users get from them valuable and highly useful information otherwise unavailable. Just as you do when you sample a bowl of soup. So, if a sponsor decides that his offering needs more salt, don't blame the spoon!

And most important to the viewing audience, ratings are the democratic way of counting the vote in terms of number of homes watching. It's the broadcaster's way of "giving the lady what she wants."

DAVID CHAGALL

Can You Believe the Ratings?

Former CBS News president Fred Friendly has criticized the ratings: "Independent specialists in the field of sampling are convinced that the television industry whose revenues total . . . [more than $10 billion] a year and [which] spends so little on audience research as to afford only a survey of the Nielsen proportions, is in the position of gauging space-age tolerances with the kind of dipstick used to measure the amount of gas in a Model T." David Chagall examines the level of accuracy of the Nielsen methodology.

In Dunedin, Fla., a town of 20,000 near the Gulf of Mexico, there is a small computer with giant responsibilities. Each day it sends out telephonic signals to automatic printers all over the country, robots typing out reports that finally determine what will be available on television for you and me and every other American.

The computer is owned by the Media Research Division, A. C. Nielsen Company—the same people who from the first years of television broadcasting have been giving us "The Ratings."

The Nielsen organization is the biggest marketing research firm on Earth, earning [over] a third of a billion dollars a year. Operating in [twenty-three] countries, it makes most of its money checking supermarket and drugstore shelves to find out how well certain products, brands and sizes are selling.

Another big chunk of its business comes from handling supermarket cents-off coupons. The company employs 13,000 people and

Excerpts have been taken from this essay, which first appeared in two parts, June 24, July 1, 1978.

is a name feared and respected in the business world. Its closest U.S. competitor in marketing research, the SAMI company grosses less than 15 per cent of Nielsen's annual income.

Television ratings are a small part of Nielsen's activities, though an important small part. Travis Whitlow, the company's press-relations officer, explains that "ratings may account for only 11 per cent of our earnings, but they're responsible for 99 per cent of our fame."

Ratings act as judge and jury for all network shows, deciding which ones stay on the air and which are canceled. Ratings are the basis for celebration and mourning, hirings, firings and the risking of billions of advertising dollars every year. Now, after almost thirty years of grudging acceptance, many people in the television industry are taking a harder look at those Nielsen numbers. . . .

During any biweekly rating period, not all [of the approximately 1200] Nielsen families are counted. Some have agreed to allow the hardware into their homes but have not yet been visited by a [representative] and connected up. Others are lost because of malfunctions in the telephone lines or the Nielsen meter. Nielsen has no way of knowing if these homes are watching TV. Thus, on a typical ratings day Nielsen [reports] viewing information from about 993 homes. Included are sets that burn out or go dark because of power failures, families out for the evening or even away on vacation—all are counted as "no viewing" for that day.

A ratings number is the percentage of those homes tuned to the same show. For example, if *Welcome Back, Kotter* scores a "20 rating" for the week, that means 20 per cent of the sample homes had that show tuned in for at least six minutes. Nielsen then assumes the same proportion of all American TV households are watching that show, and reports in its ratings book that an estimated 15 million homes are tuned in. The company records other such numbers, higher and lower, for every show on the air. It also reports what percentage of homes watching TV are tuned to [that] show. This number is called "share of audience."

. . . A Top-10 ad agency may pay $300,000 a year for the Nielsen service. Networks pay more, other users less. In return for their money, subscribers get a series of reports filled with rows of numbers—Nielsen estimates of TV-show popularity. . . .

"Clients and agencies both take the numbers very seriously," confided a media buyer from a Top-10 agency. "We must buy to gross-rating-point goals. We tell our clients the number of weekly gross rating points we bought, how much we spent, the number of target-audience bodies we'll deliver and the cost-per-thousand for those bodies. The client wants to know how many people he's reaching with his TV money, and ratings are all we have to go on.

"Agencies are forced to live and die with the Nielsen numbers. If something doesn't deliver the way it's supposed to, we have to tell our clients why. So we prepare a report that mumbles something about there being an inconsistency from one survey to the next."

To help support the thinking behind their buys of television time, ad agencies also subscribe to Arbitron, the only other TV rater. Arbitron—a subsidiary of Control Data Corporation—offers little difference from the product Nielsen sells for local TV markets.

Both services use virtually identical diary studies to rate local viewing. Viewers are asked to keep a record of what each member of the family watches. Arbitron offers a meter service that duplicates Nielsen readings in New York and Los Angeles. The Nielsen and Arbitron formats, age breaks, day parts and other reporting procedures mirror one another. The two companies' local-market figures occasionally agree, but, despite their nearly identical research and sampling methods, users report a frequent difference of several rating points between the two, with the disagreement sometimes reaching 25 per cent. . . .

Leonard Goldberg, partner in Spelling/Goldberg Productions, which turns out the highly successful *Charlie's Angels,* insists he is a realist who accepts the Nielsen ratings as the final word. "When you enter television, you enter the ratings game," he says. "If you get high Nielsen ratings, you stay on the air. If you don't, you go off. You can try to change the rules, but I don't know many games where the rules have changed over the past 25 years. Within limits, Nielsen is accurate."

Other producers are not so sure. Grant Tinker of MTM Enterprises is unique, having worked under the ratings system in all three industry capacities. He has been a top ad-agency executive, then a programming vice president at NBC and is now an independent producer selling shows to networks. Despite his many years in the business, Tinker admits he knows next to nothing about how reliable the Nielsen ratings are.

"I just know what I've always read," he explained. "Since the networks have giant research departments who say, 'Let's use it,' I've always assumed they have value. But I'm skeptical like everybody else. There's an awful lot of opportunity for error.

"People in our business react in an obvious way to ratings. If your shows are rating well, Nielsen is terrific. If they're not, you're more likely to qualify your answers.

"I've spent 30 years of my life in television," Tinker observed. "And all those years I've been vitally affected by the Nielsen numbers. Quality shows go down the tubes because Nielsen says nobody is watching. I hate to think I've been living a lie all those years."

In fact, it is quite possible that Tinker's canceled *Betty White Show* may have died unjustly with many millions more Americans watching it than were credited. This sad possibility exists because of the laws of sampling that rule the whole marketing-research industry, including the Nielsen ratings.

Whenever a research firm sets up a panel of [about 1200] homes from a total of [over 76] million and uses 993 of them to measure TV viewing for everyone else, mathematical laws limit the accuracy of such measurements. One of these laws is called *sampling error.*

Suppose you take a coin and flip it 100 times. Probability theory suggests you'll end up with 50 heads and 50 tails. But when you actually take a penny and toss it, you will probably show something different than a 50/50 count. That is because of sampling error, which operates every time you test only a small part of anything. By tossing that coin 1000 to 100,000 times, you will find yourself getting ever closer to that perfect 50/50 split. . . .

The best way to get a true count of anything is to go out and count *everything.* That's what the U.S. Census tries to do every ten years. Yet David L. Kaplan, who heads the population count, reports that a small error still takes place because people move, refuse to talk to census takers and so on. During the last head count in 1970, the miss rate was 2.5 per cent—over five million Americans who got left out.

Sampling theory says the fewer homes we count, the more chance for error. For an average of 993 homes reporting, Nielsen tells users the sampling error is plus-or-minus 1.3 points at a rating of 20. That means a 20-rated show like *Welcome Back, Kotter* might have as few as 18.7 per cent or as many as 21.3 per cent of all American homes watching.

But standard statistical procedure would say that the real error is double that: plus-or-minus 2.6 points. Nielsen statisticians minimize the extent of their sampling error behind a mathematical technicality called *level of confidence.* When Nielsen reports its ratings to users, somewhere in the report they say their numbers "are true two out of three times." That is called the "68 per-cent confidence level" by researchers and it means the numbers are wrong one-third of the time. . . . Statisticians agree that using a 68 per-cent level of confidence means that you have to double the calculated sampling error in order to increase the confidence level to 95 per cent.

Dr. James H. Myers is a noted professor of marketing at the University of Southern California and a research consultant to corporate giants like Sears, Carnation and *The Los Angeles Times.* The author of two respected textbooks on marketing research, Dr. Myers was asked for his view of the Nielsen numbers. "I've never seen any reputable firm using such a low level of confidence," he said. "If I were advising any business firm using their data, I would tell them caveat emptor—let the buyer beware."

When I visited Nielsen's Northbrook headquarters outside Chicago, I asked their head of statistical research, Ed Schillmoeller, why they used such a low level of confidence. "Many firms use 68 per cent," he replied. "For all reports from the Census Bureau, it's 68 per cent. The reason we use the 68 per-cent level is that it makes it very convenient for a user."

Schillmoeller feels that for the money spent on the service, users get a fairly accurate reading. "Say somebody makes a wrong decision based on a faulty estimate because of sampling error. How much more money are they willing to pay for improving the reliability? Sure, there are inaccuracies involved, but overall we think we're pretty accurate."

When I returned home, I contacted a dozen top research companies to ask about their use of the 68 per-cent level. Not a single one ever used it. My last call was to Charlie Jones, chief of statistics at Census Bureau headquarters in Washington, D.C.

"In our work we always use the 95 per-cent level," Jones said. "The only time someone might want to use the 68 per-cent level is when a guy wanted just a general idea about something and then only when it's not a very important application. It's not something I'd use to come to any conclusions about U.S. population."

By applying the research-industry 95 per-cent confidence standard to the Nielsen ratings, the sampling error jumps to plus-or-minus 2.6 points—a total fluctuation of over 5 rating points. During any ratings week, that big a variation makes a shambles of the Nielsen rankings.

Nielsen's Travis Whitlow admitted this might be the case for a single week's ratings. "But when you take repeated measurements of the same people many times, that lowers the error. I'll send you the formula we use for reducing that error. Over a full season it fades away to almost nothing."

A week later I got a printed sheet in the mail titled: "Statistical Interpretations and Related." It included a special formula used by Nielsen statisticians to lower their published sampling error through many measurements of the same people. The formula succeeded in reducing the error from 2.6 points to 1.8 points over a 13-week period. Along with the formula came the Top-40 rankings for [the fall 1977 season].

The chart [below] shows what Nielsen's formula for reducing sampling error does to the ratings.

The chart shows how *The Six Million Dollar Man* in 19th place could really be as high as *On Our Own* in 9th place. It might also be no better than *NBC Saturday Night Movie* in 34th place. Of course, it might also be true that *Six Million Dollar Man* really is No. 19.

The Betty White Show, canceled because of poor ratings, is ranked in a tie for 31st position in the 13-week totals. But sampling error alone says that *White* may really have been watched by more people than *Six Million Dollar Man* in 19th place. It could also rank somewhere below No. 40 or anywhere between. Of course, every show on the list has its own high and low points because of the range of sampling error involved. What we are seeing here is a frame frozen to show the effects of sampling error on the popularity rankings.

NIELSEN AVERAGE RATINGS

(*Top 40 regular shows, Sept. 11 through Dec. 10, 1977*)

Rank	Program	Average Rating
1	Laverne & Shirley	31.6
2	Happy Days	31.0
3	Three's Company	26.5
4	Charlie's Angels	25.8
5	All in the Family	25.4
6	Alice	23.8
7	60 Minutes	23.7
8	NBC Monday Movie	23.0
9	On Our Own	22.2
10	Little House on Prairie	22.1
11	ABC Sunday Movie	21.6
12	Eight Is Enough	21.5
12	Rhoda	21.5
12	Soap	21.5
15	Monday Night Football	21.2
16	M*A*S*H	21.1
17	One Day at a Time	21.0
18	Barney Miller	20.9
19	Six Million Dollar Man	20.4
20	The Love Boat	20.3
20	What's Happening!!	20.3
20	Barnaby Jones	20.3
20	Welcome Back, Kotter	20.3
24	The Big Event	20.1
25	Donny & Marie	19.8
26	Family	19.5
27	ABC Friday Movie	19.4
28	Hawaii Five-O	19.3
29	Baretta	19.1
30	Starsky & Hutch	18.9
31	CBS Sunday Movie	18.7
31	Carter Country	18.7
31	The Betty White Show	18.7
34	NBC Saturday Movie	18.6
35	The Waltons	18.3
36	CBS Wednesday Movie	18.1
37	Good Times	17.9
38	World of Disney	17.7
38	Tabitha	17.7
40	Maude	17.6

You can work out the error range for any show on the list near the 20-point level. Just add 1.8 points to find its high mark and subtract 1.8 points for its low limit. For shows near a 30 rating, you must add and subtract 1.7 points. This imprecision comes from one simple fact—the Nielsen ratings typically count only 993 homes.

The most widespread complaint heard from critics of the Nielsen ratings is that the Nielsen sample is out of balance. According to some marketing professionals, the Nielsen families do not truly represent all segments of American society.

The research director for a Top-10 ad agency feels comfortable only when he uses the ratings as "a big, broad cut of what Middle America is watching.

"If you're after the real top-money groups, the Nielsen numbers are not accurate," he explains. "It's weak at the low end, too, because the rich and the poor are not well reflected in their sample. That usually doesn't bother us too much because we generally go after the big middle mass. If we want the top groups, we buy into FM radio.

"When it's Middle America we want, the odds are that a show with a 20 rating has a somewhat bigger audience than one with a 15. The odds may be small, but they lean a little bit that way. It's a crapshoot.

"Ratings are inflated because any family that allows a meter in the house has an interest in the medium that someone who refuses does not have. I would not let them put a meter and a telephone hookup in my house even though I have plenty of *professional* interest in television."

The ratings are not simply a matter of counting how many homes are viewing television. To answer the question "Who is watching?" for their advertiser and broadcaster customers, Nielsen persuades [3200] families nationally to accept a logbook or diary.[1] They are instructed to write in all television watching for everybody in the family for a full week at a time. About 1600 homes mail back usable completed diaries. After considerable editing, these are added up

1. During sweep periods in February, May, July and November, about 100,000 diaries are distributed to families throughout the country and each local television market is measured.

and published as regular reports purporting to show how many men, women and children in different age groups watch each show on the air.

Ken Struman, president of Walker and Struman Research in Los Angeles, uses many forms of the diary approach in his work for major gasoline, auto and snack-food companies. Struman seriously challenges the diary's use for TV ratings.

"People change their behavior when they know they're being watched," he points out. "Anything socially questionable or inconsistent with the image they want to project tends to be omitted. We see this a lot in our magazine studies where people report they are readers of very sophisticated magazines. The truth is they really read material that is a few notches down the scale.

"These Nielsen diaries supposedly tell us who in the house is watching each show—children, males, people 34-55 or whatever. Now I've tried keeping diaries myself and it is a very tedious assignment. If you just do it for something as simple as every piece of food you eat in a day, you see how hard it is. You have to discipline yourself in a very unnatural way. When applied to all television programs for everyone in a house, I question its legitimacy."

Despite the problems involved with using diaries to discover who is watching, no one has yet come up with a better way to get that information. Nielsen reports about half the people they ask to keep a diary say no. According to Dr. James Myers of USC, that large a group of people who refuse to cooperate plays havoc with the accuracy of the numbers.

"This is probably a bigger source of error than their sampling error," Dr. Myers explains. "Who is being left out? One thing we know is that higher-income people tend not to do this sort of thing. Then how do high-income people who agree to take part differ from those who won't? One underlying feeling may be liberalism versus conservatism. Liberals tend to be more receptive to trials of this kind while conservatives are not. They don't have the same sensitivity for new things.

"When you get as high as 50 per cent saying no, you have some real selection going on. When you must pay people to cooperate, even bigger differences are operating. How that relates to television viewing is a very big and very unanswered question. As a social scientist, I would not be satisfied with less than 80 to 90 per cent of the homes originally contacted. . . .

For the past twenty years it has been common knowledge in the broadcast industry that minority groups, particularly poorer black and Hispanic families, are shortchanged by the Nielsen counts. Nielsen itself admits to "lighter sampling" among these groups.

For example, they claim that 9 per cent of the national ratings panel is black. Census figures show a national population figure of 10.5 per cent blacks, which means the Nielsen panel has 14 per cent fewer black families than it should have for a balanced sample. For the Los Angeles overnight ratings, black homes account for 7 per cent of the total. Census reports say the true population is 11 per cent. So Nielsen, is undercounting blacks in Los Angeles by 36 per cent.

Nielsen allots 4 per cent of its panel to Spanish-speaking families. But census figures say the true number is 5.3 per cent. Again, Nielsen is undercounting, this time by 25 per cent.

One big reason for this minority-group weakness is the reported hostility white field representatives meet when they knock on a door in the ghetto or barrio. There is instant suspicion. If the rep can't win the family's confidence in the first few seconds, he never gets a chance to complete his sales spiel, let alone sign anyone up for a meter.[2]

It is harder to find black and Hispanic families who will agree to fill out diaries. The high level of literacy it demands, plus the tedious chore of keeping constant records of every family member's TV-watching the moment it takes place, limits cooperation to the better-educated, middle-class black and Hispanic homes whose viewing patterns tend to match the white, middle-class audiences. Since Spanish-speaking families in certain markets cannot handle the English language well, they are often eliminated from taking part, but Nielsen has recently begun to distribute Spanish-language diaries.

2. In order to increase the number of black and Hispanic households in its sample, Nielsen sometimes gives extra amounts of compensation to blacks and Hispanics who allow the Audimeter into their homes.

WGPR-TV in Detroit [was the first] black owned and operated station in the country. Its vice president and programming chief, George E. White, sees the Nielsen ratings as an insurmountable barrier keeping his station from its rightful share of advertising dollars.

"We cover a 15-county area with our signal," White complained. "But the ratings say we have only 30,000 viewers. And half this entire community is black! So the ad agencies look at those numbers and say they don't justify any buys on our station.

"Nielsen's sample doesn't really get into the black neighborhoods. We know we have hundreds of thousands watching just from the letters, calls and promotions we do. Blacks are vastly underrepresented in the ratings not only in Detroit, but in major cities all over this country."

Bill Stiles is a top executive for SIN, the Spanish television network that comprises fifteen stations in big markets like New York, Chicago, Los Angeles, San Francisco and Miami. Stiles is not only convinced the ratings grossly undercount Hispanic viewers; he offers the research to prove it.

"The ratings are designed to measure Middle America," he points out. "They don't measure the rich or poor very well. When you apply this system to the Spanish market, you measure only the upper part—people who are extremely bilingual and come from Anglicized homes.

"We hired Pulse [a market research firm] to do studies for us where they use bilingual interviewers to knock on doors. Their studies show three times the numbers for our programs than the regular ratings. The problem with Nielsen and Arbitron is that they are not set up to deal with the Spanish community. Even in their regular surveys with middle-class Anglos, they get only half the people to cooperate. In Spanish neighborhoods, it goes down to just 15 per cent—and those who participate are more Anglicized. Remember, we're talking about a population mass of 11 million Spanish-speaking people." . . .

Another group Nielsen admits undercounting are people who live alone. Nearly half of them are older people over 65. In 1977, lone households accounted for 23 per cent of all U.S. homes, but only 17 per cent of the Nielsen panel. This means that about a fourth of all people living alone [were] not being represented.

Some TV viewers are never rated at all. NBC has always argued that the *Today* show's audience is underestimated because so many of the nation's TV sets are watched in places like hotels, hospitals, bars, prisons, clubs, old-people's homes, summer homes, military bases and barracks. The largest unmeasured viewing takes place in college dormitories. Such audiences account for more than five million unmeasured TV sets.

Adding up the missing blacks, Hispanics, old people, college students, rich people, poor people, soldiers and other neglected segments, it amounts to almost ten million American households that appear to be ignored by the ratings. Nielsen now has a pilot project in the works designed to count some of the missing people.

After the 1963 Congressional hearings on the ratings uncovered serious weaknesses in the Nielsen operation, there were murmurs of government intervention. Nine months later a private group called the Broadcast Rating Council was formed. With a board of twelve members, mostly from the networks with a smattering of advertising people, the Council proclaims by its certificate of accreditation that all is well with the way ratings are put together.

To ease doubts in the minds of Nielsen and Arbitron users, it sends accountants from the firms of Ernst & Ernst and Touche Ross & Co. to check out how sample homes are picked, approached and persuaded to cooperate. They write a confidential report, after which the ratings service gets its seal of approval. No research experts go with the accountants when they do their checking, and no one outside the BRC can ever peek at those reports.

Lately there has been grumbling from behind the closed doors of advertising suites. *Media Decisions,* a trade magazine, did a survey of media-research people at the biggest agencies and found most of them unhappy with the secrecy of the ratings procedures.

"There's no reason why the advertising community must take the word of the BRC that broadcast-measurement reports have been found up to snuff," complained Pat Murray of Young & Rubicam. "Maybe if we had a first-hand look at how the Nielsen numbers are arrived at, we wouldn't now be questioning prime-time viewing levels."

When I visited Nielsen ratings boss Jim Lyons at his Northbrook, Ill., office, I asked him what he would do to improve the ratings if he had twice as much money to work with.

"We might increase the sample size and improve the meter itself," he said. "We're now working on a meter that would not need wires attached to the sets. Then I think people would be more willing to say, 'Yes, you can come in and monitor us'." . . .

HARRY SKORNIA

Don't Give the Public What It Wants

Quantitiy, or popularity, versus quality is the central theme of much mass media criticism, particularly that of television. Former NBC chairman Julian Goodman summarized the point of view held by many broadcasters that television provides "the kind of program service the public wants. . . . The evidence is in the fantastic growth of television homes and the hours people spend watching television."

Ralph Nader criticizes this argument, suggesting that justifying broadcasters' existence in this fashion puts them on a level with those who operate "porno shows." Even NBC's own former news president Reuven Frank believes that giving the public what it wants is a poor defense, "the drug pusher's argument." Harry Skornia supports Nader and Frank.

Do you go to a lecture to hear what a man wants to say about a subject? Or do you go to have him tell you what you want to hear?

Does an atomic scientist change his subject from fission to his latest trip through the Alps because it would be more entertaining and he has excellent slides available?

Ratings are based on the assumption that stations should broadcast What the Public Wants. This premise should be examined.

Years ago journalists were criticized for providing too little news about nuclear fallout. Editors explained that before press coverage of this problem could be increased, the public must demand it.

The chicken-and-the-egg relationship in such a statement is obvious. From what, if not from news, is the public to know that such information is available?

This essay first appeared September 18, 1965.

Or how is the public to know that fallout is or was reaching dangerous levels, and therefore should be considered news?

The market for news items—like that for products—can be either created or not created.

Years ago speakers, artists and writers had things to say. The available media—print, podium and radio—dictated only the subject's form. Now the communicator asks the public: What do you want said? The dangers of carrying the What-the-Public-Wants practice to an extreme are obvious.

But this is only a small part of the problem. The slogan "Give the public what it wants" implies, first, that the public *knows* what it wants. Second, it implies that the public is an *it* instead of a *they*. Third, it implies that there is a clear and accurate way for wants to be transmitted to the decision makers.

Alan Thomas has said that people play three roles in relation to TV—as Audience, as Market and as Public.

As Audience, people are a series of unconnected homes or individuals. Because they are so unconnected and isolated from each other, they cannot set standards—which is what [CBS president] Frank Stanton and others say they do. The Audience exists only from moment to moment. The Audience's vote is expressed by ratings. And the ratings count *sets* rather than *people* or likes and dislikes in general.

As Market, the people become buying units—economic rather than human entities. Market success is measured by sales and profits; i.e., dollars. Market, too, is temporary. It is created by advertising.

As Public, people exist in thier capacity as *citizens*. People who may vote *for* a program as Audience (through ratings) may, as Public (citizens), vote *against* the same program if they find the sponsor dishonest. As a part of the Public, a man may even support stricter government regulation to correct indecencies, dishonesty, rigging, deceit, excessive violence or any other objectionable content in the very programs he voted *for* as Audience (by tuning in) and may even have voted for as Market (by buying the product).

The role of Public makes the citizen ask himself what is the *responsible* thing to do, rather than merely what is it that he *likes* or *wants*. This role is the only continuing and rational one of the three.

Only in the role of Public do the people operate as a nation. Only in this role have they an accurate mechanism for voting—the ballot box. The Public has voted for the creation of regulatory agencies by voting for congressmen who wrote legislation to create these agencies. As Audience or Market, people may want lewd programs, or dope; as Public, or citizens, however, they will ask for limitations on both.

So the behavior of citizens as Audience is likely to be quite different from their behavior as citizens, when they are asked for a considered and responsible decision for the good of their country, their children and the general welfare.

The Public regulates. The Audience watches programs and laughs at regulation violations. And the Market buys. Only in their role as the Public do the people recognize their *duties* and *needs* as well as their *wants* in the perspective which democracy requires.

To quote ratings, then, is not to quote the Public—it is only to quote the Audience—it means (1) quoting appetite instead of hunger, (2) want instead of need, (3) irresponsibility instead of responsibility, (4) short-term instead of long-term, (5) irrationality instead of rationality.

Yet Audience (ratings) is the constituency which the broadcast industry so often quotes in support of its programming.

Newton Minow [as FCC chairman] told the industry that his personal random survey of children showed that most of them preferred candy to spinach, movies to Sunday School, and soap operas and game shows to school. There is nothing wrong, he said with giving children some of the things they want—but we pass laws requiring attendance at school—which is clearly in violation of children's freedom. The fact that democracy is based on laws indicates that you simply cannot let children or anybody else do whatever they want.

Even for adults, *want* is not a sound standard for determining value. *Hunger* and *appetite* are not the same. Traffic laws and the controls placed on certain drugs are examples of the rules needed in all areas of life.

The give-the-public-what-it-wants philosophy fails to take into account that the satisfaction of *needs* is more likely to ensure survival of individuals as well as of democracy than the satisfaction of *wants*. People do not necessrily *want* what they *need.* Needs are objective, and they represent requirements; they are relatively lasting. Wants, on the other hand, are subjective. They are irrational and can be created by all kinds of irresponsible temptations and lures.

Something a man *needs* is something it is harmful for him not to have. What he *wants* may actually be harmful.

PAUL L. KLEIN

Why You Watch What You Watch When You Watch

When broadcasters argue that television gives the public what it wants, they are assuming that the public and the audience are the same. Not so, according to *New York Times* television columnist Les Brown. He points out that the distinction between the two terms is important because the ratings reflect only the preferences of the actual audience, not those of the public. Furthermore, at least half of the potential audience—the public—will not usually be watching at a given time.

For those people who do watch, however, television can become habit forming as Les Brown has indicated: "a predictable number of people will be watching each hour of the night" regardless of what is on the air. Paul Klein, former NBC research chief, has characterized the typical television viewer as "a kid with candy [who] eats and eats" and "does not want to think." Klein gives his explanation of the viewing habits of the television addict.

It is about time that you all stop lying to each other and face up to your problems: you love television and you view too much.

I used to be the guy in charge of the ratings at NBC, and my waking hours were filled with people either complaining about how inaccurate the ratings were or, without my asking them, volunteering that they "never watch TV, because the programs stink, particularly this season."

Let's look at the facts, because only by examining the nature of the disease can we cure it, or at least make peace with it.

Excerpts have been taken from this essay, which first appeared July 24, 1971.

The Census Bureau tells us that [97.8] per cent of U.S. homes have a television set (and [about one-half] of those have two or more sets, with the number of homes and sets growing each day). The Census Bureau also shows that TV penetration is highest among the more affluent and better-educated segment of the population. In fact, 99 per cent of the homes with [$15,000-$20,000] annual income have at least one TV set—the majority of them have more than one—and most of them have a color set. And also we all know how they complain about the programs and how they say they never watch the stuff.

The truth is that you buy extra sets, color sets, and even pay a monthly charge for CATV to view television. Yet when you view an evening's worth of TV you are full of complaints about what you have viewed. But the next night you're right back there, hoping against hope for satisfying content, never really learning from experience, and another night is shot. Instead of turning the set off and doing something else, you persist in exercising the medium.

With more TV sets and clearer, more colorful pictures on those sets, you are tuned to TV *more* this year than last and last year more than the previous year, etc.

The fact is that you view TV regardless of its content. Because of the nature of the limited spectrum (only a few channels in each city) and the economic need of the networks to attract an audience large enough to attain advertising dollars which will cover the cost of production of the TV program, pay the station carrying the program and also make a profit, you are viewing programs which by necessity must appeal to the rich and poor, smart and stupid, tall and short, wild and tame, together. Therefore, you are in the vast majority of cases viewing something that is not to your taste. From the time you bought a set to now, you have viewed thousands of programs which were not to your taste. The result is the hiding of, and lying about, all that viewing. Because of the hiding and lying, you are guilty. The guilt is expressed in the feeling that "I should have been reading instead of viewing."

It is of course much more difficult to read than to view, even for people making [$15,000-$20,000] a year. Reading requires a process called *decoding*, which causes a slowdown in the information taken in by the user. TV viewing is very simple to do—kids do it better than adults because they are unencumbered by guilt—and the amount of information derived from an hour's viewing is infinitely more than is derived from an hour's reading.

But print has been around for a long time and it has attracted people who have learned to express themselves in this medium, so the printed content, on the whole, is superior to the TV content. Still, most of us prefer television.

Despite the lack of quality content, the visual medium is so compelling that it attracts the vast majority of adults each day to a progression of shows that most of these people would ignore in printed form.

The process of viewing works like this: A family has just finished dinner and one member says, "Let's see what's on TV tonight." The set gets turned on or *TV Guide* gets pulled out. If it's *TV Guide,* then the list of programs (most of which are repeats) is so unappealing that each member of the family says to himself that he remembers when *TV Guide* made an awful error in its program listings back in 1967 and maybe it has happened again.

The set is turned on whether a good program is listed or not at that time. Chances are over 100 to one that there is nothing on that meets this or any family's taste at that moment. But the medium meets their taste.

The viewer(s) then slowly turns the channel selector, grumbling at each image he sees on the channel. Perhaps he'll go around the dial two or three times before settling on one channel whose program is *least objectionable.*

"Well, let's watch this," someone in the family says. "There's nothing better on." So they watch. No one thinks of jogging a couple of laps around the block or getting out the old Parcheesi board. They watch whatever is least objectionable.

The programmers for the networks have argued that this is a "most satisfying" choice—not LOP (least objectionable program). But if it were, then why would everybody be complaining and lying about TV viewing? I don't deny that in some rare time periods, "least objectionable" is actually most satisfying, but the bulk of the time people are viewing programs they don't particularly consider good and *that* is why the medium is so powerful and rich. . . .

We view content we dislike, content that is frivolous, unsatisfying, unrewarding. We state that what we want from TV is more important content—like public affairs. Well, when public affairs is on, we really want to see it, we really should see it, but it's too objectionable compared to the entertainment programs opposite it. . . .

It is very rare that viewing in any time period is lower than normal. It is very difficult to either raise or lower the "sets-in-use" in a time period, indicating once and for all that viewing has little to do with content. When *Bridge on the River Kwai* was on (first time), sets-in-use rose five points—and when *Laugh-In* was a national phenomenon sets-in-use were up somewhat. But [when the number one-rated *Marcus*] *Welby* was preempted for a public-affairs-type program . . . on a [night] when public-affairs shows were on [the other two networks], more people saw public affairs than had seen that kind of beloved program since [the same thing] happened many years ago in the same time period. All three networks enjoyed greater viewing in the *forced* viewing situation—you either watched public affairs or you did not watch [any network programs]—than they would have had each program been opposite entertainment.

All three of the programs were repeated later and they got very small audiences. Apparently no one felt so bad about missing the two he didn't see that he searched them out when they were repeated. . . .

People love TV. They love the ease of viewing and the ease of distribution; video pictures delivered right to the home. Somebody's going to figure out how to give this medium more satisfying content as we head toward a completely visual culture.

ARNOLD TOYNBEE

Television: The Lion That Squeaks

As the amount of leisure time has increased, so has television viewing. According to a 1960 Gallup poll, 28 per cent of the people questioned indicated that their favorite leisure activity was watching television. In 1979 the corresponding figure had risen to 46 per cent. Arnold Toynbee offers insights into why contemporary society, with its increasing leisure time, is turning more and more to an indiscriminate use of television as a pastime.

Television is not the only one of our marvelous modern means of communication that is being largely wasted on frivolities. The same sad tale is told by the headlines and advertisements in the evening newspapers—and not only in the evening ones—all over the world.

There is a contrast here, and a misfit, that is striking and painful: On the one hand a technology that is a *chef d'oeuvre* of intellectual creative power and ingenuity; on the other hand a prostitution of this product of mature human genius to serve childish tastes.

A pessimist, looking into the future, might predict that this really shocking combination of incongruous means and ends will condition mankind into becoming a race of technician-morons—creatures that will be lower than our prehuman ancestors in terms of truly human values.

What causes this disconcerting trend? Can it be arrested, reversed?

One thing, for certain, is *not* the cause. It is not the inventors' fault that their inventions are being so deplorably misused. The

This essay first appeared December 4, 1965.

apparatus with which our inventive geniuses have endowed us is neutral. It could be used, just as easily and effectively, for the highest purposes as it is being used for the lowest purposes today. If this potent new instrument is being so largely misused at present, the fault lies not with the human inventors of these mechanical genies; it lies with their human users.

Which set of users is chiefly to blame? The viewers of television or the commercial purveyors of it, who stand between the viewers and the inventors? They share the blame, I should say. If the viewers were to stop viewing such inferior stuff, then sheer commercial self-interest would push the purveyors into giving their customers something better.

Conversely, if the purveyors did give the customers something better, they would be educating the public to raise the standard of its demand.

Insofar as the viewers' present abysmally low standard is low by the viewers' own choice, and not because this standard has been imposed on them by the purveyors, what is it that accounts for the viewers' childishness? I think there are several causes on which one can put one's finger.

One cause of present-day childishness in grown-up people is the change in the character of the work by which an ever-increasing proportion of the world's population has come to be earning its living since the beginning of the Industrial Revolution. The mechanization of the world's work has been lightening mankind's physical labor, but this at the price of imposing on the factory worker a psychological curse from which the pre-industrial farmer was free. This curse is the curse of boredom.

The farmer's work on an unmechanized farm of the traditional kind is laborious. He must work from dawn to dark, year in and year out; his cows, sheep and fowls require as constant attention as human infants.

But, by the same token, a farmer's life is never dull. A human mother does not easily get bored with her grueling job of bringing up her children, and the farmer does not get bored—in the sense of time on his hands—with his livestock and crops.

On the other hand, how can the factory worker's life *not* be dull? The "means of production" that he is tending are machines processing "raw materials"—a poor exchange, in psychological terms, for his farmer-grandfather's fields and pastures and crops and cows. The factory worker's relation to the machinery is impersonal.

If the wheels are to be made to pay, they must be kept turning 24 hours in the day, so the machine tender works on a shift; the machine is not his own, in the sense in which the farmer's cow and crop are his.

The factory is not only kept in operation all round the clock, it is insulated from the elements. A thermostat automatically keeps it at whatever temperature the technician chooses; and rain and hail can batter on the factory roof without any effect on the work that is going on under the roof's shelter. The control of the environment inside the factory walls makes the output regular and predictable, but it consequently makes the job of producing the output dull.

The factory worker will be able to hand over to the next shift, and to leave the building, the moment his stint of work is completed. He may come out physically fresh; but he is likely to find himself psychologically jaded. What he craves for, in his off-time, is recreation; and, of course, he is tempted to choose the kind of recreation that makes the lowest spiritual demand on him.

The middle-class office worker is also making the same choice, without having the same excuse. In his case, perhaps, the cause is not so much boredom as it is anxiety. His higher education has made him more acutely aware of problems—political, social, moral and spiritual—that are baffling him. His flight from these cares to soap-box opera is a case of escapism.

Moreover, the incentives to seek frivolous distractions are growing in strength. The problems that create anxiety become more menacing, and daily work becomes more boring as automation's pace accelerates.

Working hours are continually becoming shorter and leisure hours correspondingly longer; and here we have a second cause of the public's present choice of forms of recreation that are frivolous and childish.

For the mass of mankind—for everyone except a tiny privileged minority—leisure was, until within living memory, a blessing, or curse, of which they had had hardly any experience. Abundant leisure has now suddenly descended on them while they are still psychologically unprepared for coping with it.

This social revolution (it amounts to that) has been sudden because the pace of technological advance has become so fast. People are still unprepared for it because the pace of psychological change has always been slower than the pace of technological change—and the pace of psychological change cannot be speeded up, to match, by any ingenious mechanical inventions.

In the fable, the tortoise won its race against the hare—but turn the live hare into an electric hare, and what chance is left to the tortoise for keeping pace with that?

When human beings are given leisure, they misuse it unless and until they have educated themselves to do better than that. I have mentioned the tiny privileged minority that enjoyed a monopoly of leisure in the premechanical age. By the eighteenth century, this minority has already had about five thousand years for learning how to use its leisure for social, cultural and spiritual purposes.

But what is that privileged eighteenth-century minority's record? It flattered itself that it was an elite. Yet, for one Voltaire, Franklin, Rousseau, Jefferson or Wesley, there were thousands who misspent their leisure on hunting, gambling and philandering.

The frivolities on which the majority is now largely wasting its recently acquired leisure have, on the whole, less vice in them than the leisured eighteenth-century minority's frivolous pursuits had. That, however, is a small mercy to be thankful for. The misspending of leisure, even on comparatively innocent frivolities, will lead to social, cultural and moral regression if it continues unchecked.

In our attitude toward this evil, we cannot afford to be indulgent or complacent. We have to get the viewer of television to raise his sights. How far does this depend on him, and how far does it depend on the policy of the commercial organization that purveys to him those silly programs to which the viewer is now giving an appallingly high proportion of his viewing time?

Here, I am afraid, we are caught in a vicious circle. The purveyor of television, like other tradesmen, is primarily concerned to sell his wares as profitably for himself as he can; and this consideration governs his policy. Shall he try to raise his viewers' standards by giving them programs that will be rather higher than the level of their average present demand as estimated by the purveying firm's customer-research department?

The purveyor shrinks from venturing on this public-spirited experiment. He shrinks because he fears that, if he did raise the standard even one inch above the average level of demand, there might be a mass flight from television.

The purveyor therefore allows himself a margin of safety. He sets the level of his wares below the average level of demand, not above it, and this poor-spirited policy gives him greater freedom of play; for his researchers tell him that he can depress the level of his wares at least 12 inches below the average level of demand before his low-brow customers will give up television in disgust because they are finding it too banal to please even them.

Can this vicious circle be broken? No doubt there is some hope to be found in the spread of higher education. In this sphere, television is already beginning to be used for constructive purposes. But it is only in our time that higher education has become accessible to the majority, and the first generation of children who receive it have to come to it without the help of any cultural background in their homes. It is only in the second or third generation that the effects of higher education in school and college begin to become cumulative by creating a fund of culture in the home to give the high school and university student's education an initial boost and a perpetual encouragement.

Will this hoped-for effect of the spread of higher education be enough to produce an improvement in the quality of the average demand of television viewers? We are relying here on education in the formal sense, and this may be capable of producing a change for the better in taste.

But will just educating the head be enough? The head cannot run far in advance of the heart; and, for bringing about a change of heart, something more than an improvement in formal education is required. A spiritual revolution is needed; and here, I think, we are touching the heart of the matter. We are putting our finger on what is wrong, not just with present-day television, but with present-day Western life. In present-day Ethiopia there [was] no television [in the mid-1960s], but for centuries there have been viewers there.

What they come to view—sometimes walking many miles over the mountains—is the pictures of the Bible story on the walls of their churches.

Our own medieval ancestors, too, were viewers of that kind. In our time, we have lost the lofty vision and the serious purpose with which our forefathers used to be inspired by their ancestral religions. This inspiration has now been lost by many people who still attend church and temple and mosque. How is this vital inspiration to be regained? The future of television, and of everything else, will depend on our answer.

BARRY COLE MAL OETTINGER

Can an Angry Viewer Get Any Action Out of the FCC?

Television viewers can do more than to simply react by turning their sets on or off, passively accepting the Nielsen ratings as a measure of their wishes. Viewers can write letters: to the stations, to the networks and to the Federal Communications Commission.

FCC chairman Charles Ferris has said that he has "a strong feeling that every citizen that writes to the Commission should get an answer. But we're overwhelmed by the letters." Barry Cole and Mal Oettinger discuss what the FCC does with the thousands of letters it receives every year.

People sometimes feel strongly enough about what they see on television to complain about it. That, one might suppose, can be considered a tribute to the power of the medium. And if it is, broadcasting [is being] honored by record [numbers] of complaints to the Federal Communications Commission. How many other people [feel] like complaining but [fail] to write can only be a matter of speculation.

But there is no doubt that some viewers are unhappy—and thousands of them [have been] furious about programs they [haven't] even seen. Before *Soap* went on the air [in 1977], the FCC was deluged with letters asking—demanding—that the agency somehow scrub the show on the launching pad. What TV watchers perceived as a decline in morality was the main source of their discontent. And in indignant postcards and thoughtful letters, viewers begged the

This essay first appeared April 1, 1978.

FCC to curb several other programs they believed corrupted youth and weakened the moral fiber of the family.

Even the White House was involved, forwarding to the Commission 2082 copies of the following complaint. "Dear Mr. President," it read. "I wish to express my concern over all the illicit sex, homosexuality, violence, drinking, swearing and blasphemous statements against the Bible, Jesus Christ and the New Birth on television. Will you and our Congress please put pressure on the networks to stop this blatant godlessness that is so undermining our beloved Nation?" . . .

"Every [complaint letter] gets read," says William B. Ray, the veteran chief of the FCC's Complaints & Compliance Division. "But in 99.95 per cent of the cases, there's simply nothing the agency can do. Some people consider the phrase 'son of a bitch' obscene and expect us to prosecute a risqué skit. I don't think people realize they are asking a few bureaucrats in Washington to censor thousands of stations."

Viewer complaints fall into three general categories. The largest, perhaps 70 per cent of the total, concerns matters of taste and morals, allegations of un-American or Communist propaganda, and suspicions of news bias. If the FCC pursued each of these complaints, the shades of John Peter Zenger, Thomas Jefferson and H. L. Mencken would rise to assault the agency's citadel. And on a more practical level, the courts would reverse the FCC's rulings—because the Communications Act forbids censorship. Anyone with complaints in this category, FCC officials agree, would do better to take them up with the station than with the government.

A second category of complaints reflects viewers' irritation with broadcast practices that the FCC's policies cover in a narrow or hazy fashion. The Commission usually does little about such complaints, for a Catch-22 reason: the complainant must cite specific rule violations—but the FCC has few firm rules governing programming performance. A viewer, for example, who complains of too many commercials must cite the number aired per clock hour. Then the FCC may ask its field bureau to check on whether the station properly logged (or recorded) that many spots. If not, the station may be fined for violating FCC logging rules. But if the station's logs are in order, nothing usually happens—because the FCC has no rule limiting the number of commercials that may be aired.

Citizen groups have often complained that the FCC moves swiftly and efficiently to punish stations that violate business regulations, while ignoring violations that irritate viewers. Ray explains that most complaints about business practices come from competitors or advertisers, who can often provide solid proof to back up assertions of a specific FCC rule violation.

The third category of complaints raises legitimate questions about a television station's service to the public, making allegations that, if true, could warrant Commission action under current rules. In dealing with these complaints—a relatively small percentage of those received—the agency has been hampered by lack of manpower in the Complaints & Compliance Division, or by a lack of interest on the part of commissioners. When the division was established in 1960, in the wake of quiz-show fixing and payola scandals, FCC chairman Frederick Ford envisioned a unit with as many as twenty-five field investigators who would audit programming as well as technical violations. But appropriations for personnel have always been limited, and periodically a charade is played out in Commission meetings. A commissioner charges the division with failing to handle a complaint, and a staff member responds—accurately—that the division is understaffed and overworked. There the matter lies. In an internal memorandum in 1970, William Ray informed the commissioners that only 5 per cent of the complaints that *should* be investigated are. Even now the division has just [forty-eight] employees, and only [ten] of them are investigators. Yet the volume of correspondence has increased more than ninefold since 1962.

The FCC answers most viewers' complaints with one or another form letter. If the complaint is forwarded by a member of Congress or the White House staff, a personalized reply is sent. "But the information is exactly the same," says Arthur Ginsburg, deputy chief of the Division. At the other extreme of attention, complaints that are part of a letter-writing campaign generally go unanswered. "We don't have the manpower to answer campaigns that generate 20,000 to 30,000 pieces of mail," Ginsburg says. Petitions, by the way, are counted as a single complaint, no matter how many people sign them.

When the FCC decides a complaint may have merit, it sends a copy to the TV station involved and a form letter to the complainant, saying that "the Commission will take whatever action is deemed appropriate." The complainant probably will hear nothing more about it. "It would be unfair to the stations," says Ray, "to announce investigations if the facts do not support any action." He relies on local newspapers to inform the public about whatever punitive actions are taken.

Can a single complaint from a lone individual really make a difference? Indeed it can. In 1967, John F. Banzhaf III, fresh out of law school, complained to the FCC that a New York TV station was violating the Fairness Doctrine—by simply running cigarette commercials that showed the pleasures of smoking and not the adverse consequences. Banzhaf, now a law professor at George Washington University, composed his complaint aboard a cruise ship, as a member of the crew. "My only legal references were a book on admiralty law and an FCC pamphlet," he says. But that was enough. Banzhaf's complaint led the Commission to rule that stations running cigarette commercials would be obliged to run countercommercials warning of health hazards of smoking, too. Eventually, all cigarette commercials were banned by Congress, and the FCC spent years explaining to complainants that the cigarette case was unique and did not necessarily apply to oil commercials or phosphate-based detergent ads.

Banzhaf believes it still may do some good to complain to the FCC—"if you know enough to file an effective and hard-hitting complaint." But the rarity of his experience is underlined by the fact that the FCC received some 4300 Fairness Doctrine complaints in a two-year period. In only nineteen of them did the decisions go against the stations.

At times FCC personnel can do no more than sympathize with complainants' plights. A minister, for instance, asked the FCC to reprimand a station for broadcasting the names of accident victims before the family was notified (they saw the newscast). A woman protested a gum commercial depicting a lifeguard chewing gum while attempting to rescue a swimmer: two children had drowned in her town while chewing gum and swimming at the same time. Another viewer complained because network commercials for the racy *79 Park Avenue* were placed in the middle of a children's program, *The Wonderful World of Disney*.

But commercials draw a light response, [and many] complaints about ads on television [concern] allegations of bad taste. The agency refers charges of false and misleading advertising by national companies to the Federal Trade Commission. Ray's staff investigates those about misleading local commercials, most of which involve faith healers or used-car dealers. But the FCC will usually take action only if a guarantee made to viewers was not honored. "And most of them are too slick to do that," observes Ray.

For years the FCC virtually ignored complaints about loud commercials. Then, in a 1975 FCC meeting, a commissioner asked if the agency had any firm rule prohibiting loud commercials. Ray replied that no rule existed because the FCC had concluded there was no objective way of judging how loud is too loud. Robert E. Lee, a commissioner for more than twenty years, remarked: "We once said, 'If you wake up during a program, the commercial is too loud.' Years ago, there was going to be a machine to measure loud commercials. But it didn't work." Chairman Richard Wiley came up with a solution: the Commission would resurrect a public notice issued ten years earlier, in 1965, reminding broadcasters that they have "an affirmative obligation to see that objectionably loud commercials are not broadcast." No method of enforcement has yet been devised.

Ray's office has sent numerous examples of complaints to the seven commissioners, who have tended to regard them simply as "information items" and have seldom inquired what was done about them.

Complaints, however, are not always that passive. Sometimes viewers harboring a major grievance against a station go beyond writing informal complaints, and [in recent] years commissioners have been meeting with disgruntled public groups. Many of them are representatives of ethnic minorities who charge discrimination in station employment, unfair stereotypes in programming, or a lack of programs directed to their segments of the community. Anyone who believes a station has been so unresponsive to public needs that it should lose its license can file a petition to deny license renewal and ask for a formal hearing.

FCC cannot ignore such a petition. However, the agency has chosen to sit strictly as a judge, with the burden of proof falling heavily on the complainant. Not being geared to investigate the charges on its own, the Commission weighs the specific allegations against the station's replies, and then decides if a formal hearing is necessary. If the complaint is well founded, the station may choose to "settle out of court," by signing an agreement specifying programming it will run, employment practices it will follow, or oversights it will correct.

In most cases, viewers will find it more effective to complain directly to station management than to the FCC. But the agency stands in the background, a court of last resort able to supply legal fortification in serious cases.

Some viewers turn up in Ray's office to press their cases in person. One man appeared a few years ago with wet brow and glistening eyes to report that television was reading his mind and that programs were constantly discussing his personal problems. "They're stealing my mind," he said. Ray listened carefully to the man and then suggested, "Why don't you take this to the FBI?" "I did," the man replied. "And they sent me here."

MARTIN MAYER

The Challengers

The Communications Act of 1934 stressed the importance of local stations to serve individual communities, and in a manual explaining its policies and procedures the FCC states: "Establishing and maintaining quality broadcasting services in a community is . . . a matter in which members of the community have a vital concern and in which they can and should play a prominent role."

As was indicated in the previous essay, citizens who are unhappy with the local station's responses to their concerns can ask the FCC to enforce the ultimate punishment for the station; they can file a petition to deny the station's license renewal. Martin Mayer discusses the use and success of such petitions.

Though there hasn't been much evidence of it on the screen, the broadcasting industry [since 1966] has lived through a series of earthquakes that has left many of its leaders trembling with fear that their world is coming to an end. The very foundation of their business, the license to use the airwaves, has been shaken by the federal courts and, to a lesser extent, the Federal Communications Commission, which have opened the doors for anyone who lives within range of a station's signal to challenge the station's right to continue in operation.

Given the temper of the times, this invitation was sure to be taken up by all sorts of people, and it has been. . . . Petitions have been brought by blacks, Chicanos, American Indians, Chinese-Americans, women's libbers, conservationists, individual crusaders, extor-

These excerpts are taken from two parts of a three-part essay and first appeared February 3, February 17, 1973.

tionists. Most petitioners accuse the stations of discriminating against minority groups in employment, and charge bias or neglect in programs.

There are earnest advocates of simple causes. One has brought petitions against stations that refuse to carry countercommercials to fight the sale of Chevron gasoline with F-310.

There are crooks. One went around to all the television stations in a fairly large Midwestern city, proposing that for $1000 a month (from each) he could guarantee against a petition from any black group. There are more imaginative crooks, like the group that suggested to another TV station that it could avoid a challenge to its license by being the angel for a season of plays it wanted to present.

There are even clowns. When the San Francisco licenses were up for renewal in 1971, the San Francisco *Bay Guardian,* that city's semiunderground paper, gave its front page to a feature entitled "How to Terrorize Your Local Broadcaster for Fun and Profit."

But there are also—and this is a point the broadcasters often omit from the discussion—people who are honestly and unselfishly seeking better television service for their communities, and have grabbed for a legal weapon because in fact they have no other way to make the local broadcasters take them seriously. . . .

Under the Federal Communications Act, every three years a [broadcaster] must come back to the Federal Communications Commission and get [its] license renewed.

For years the FCC treated these applications for license renewals the way a state motor-vehicle bureau treats renewals of drivers' licenses. A person who uses his car in bank robberies or gets convicted of drunk driving is denied a license renewal; a person who used his broadcasting license to swindle advertisers or corrupt the audience could be denied his renewal. But it almost never happened. Licensees of broadcasting channels began to behave as though they did own the air. Channels were bought and sold for twenty times what the physical equipment was worth, because the person who bought the station also bought a license he could reasonably consider permanent. Increasingly, big national companies became the owners of what were supposed to be local stations.

Meanwhile, in another part of the forest, the civil-rights movement was changing the face of America but not the face of television. In the South, especially, some broadcasters were giving the movement and its leaders a very hard time, portraying them as Communists, criminals and sex perverts. Some of the ministers involved in Martin Luther King's Southern Christian Leadership Conference had been ordained in the United Church of Christ. They took their complaints about what the broadcasters were doing to them to the director of the Office of Communications of that church. He is the Rev. Everett Parker, a rather small man with diminishing sandy hair and a quizzical grin, who mixes cynicism and earnestness in a highly personal combination.

Parker, a product of the Divinity School of the University of Chicago, had gone to Washington to work for the New Deal immediately after graduation in the 1930s. His first job was in the press department of the Works Progress Administration. "My father," he calls, "was a rich businessman and didn't approve; when his friends would ask what I was doing, he'd say I was on relief."

Experiences in government had given Parker no very high opinion of federal agencies. He thought the best pressure point the church would have in fighting unfairness by Southern broadcasters was the industry itself. Parker set up a network of churchmen, students and civil-rights workers around the South to monitor the performance of local broadcasting stations, and took his evidence of race prejudice to LeRoy Collins, the former governor of Florida who was then head of the National Association of Broadcasters. Parker asked the NAB to issue a policy statement calling for all members to give blacks a fair shake in programs and in employment practices.

"Collins was friendly but noncommittal," Parker recalls. "It's an interesting fact that all the troubles the broadcasters have with their license renewals came about because the directors of the NAB were such reactionaries. If they'd given us our statement, we probably wouldn't have gone further." Frustrated at the NAB's failure to issue any statement on guidelines, Parker and the lawyers who worked for the church went looking for some way to compel Southern broadcasters to behave. They decided the only pressure point they had was the license-renewal system, and they helped residents of Jackson, Miss., file a "petition to deny" renewal of the license of WLBT-TV, which the Martin Luther King group considered the worst station in the country.

The FCC threw out the petition on the grounds that the citizen's group lacked "standing"—they had no *financial* interest in the operations of the station. Only people whose business interests were affected, the Commission ruled, had the right to intervene in a license renewal proceeding. Parker and his lawyer, Earle K. ("Dick") Moore, an erect but casual Wall Street aristocrat, took an appeal to the Circuit Court of Appeals for the District of Columbia, which ordered the FCC to hold hearings on the petition. The viewers' stake in how a broadcaster conducted himself, the court ruled, was at least as great as any advertiser's stake.[1]

At the hearings, Parker's group produced convincing evidence of misbehavior in WLBT's news broadcasts, and of failure to carry national public-affairs programs that presented favorable comment on the civil-rights movement. The Commission still refused to bite the bullet. Accepting the licensee's claim that he was now a reformed character, the Commission renewed his license anyway. Again, Parker and Moore went to the Court of Appeals, and in his last opinion before President Nixon appointed him Chief Justice, Judge Warren Burger ordered the FCC to find a new licensee for WLBT.[2]

[Only one other] petition to deny has cost a television station a renewal (though several still are pending).[3] The most effective challenges have come in situations where owners were trying to sell their stations to others. The FCC must approve all transfers of licenses, and anyone in the station's coverage area can object to the transfer, which will delay the sale until the objection is dismissed—not just by the Commission, but by the courts on appeal. Meanwhile, of course, economic conditions may change, and the stations may become more valuable or less valuable than they were on the day when one

1. *Office of Communication of the United Church of Christ* v. *Federal Communications Commission,* 359 F.2d 994 (D.C. CIR. 1966).

2. *Office of Communication of the United Church of Christ* v. *Federal Communications Commission,* 425 F.2d 543 (D.C. CIR. 1969).

3. The one other successful petition was filed by a group of Alabama citizens against the eight TV stations operated by the Alabama Educational Television Commission (AETC). The FCC found "a compelling inference that AETC followed racially discriminatory policy in its overall programming practices" and denied renewal of all eight stations. But because the AETC had mended its ways following the filing of the petition, the FCC permitted the stations to remain broadcasting while AETC filed applications for new licenses. As of March 1980 these applications either were granted or were still pending.

person agreed to sell and another buy. At best, all the terms have to be renegotiated; at worst, the deal falls through. . . .

[Although] groups that have filed petitions to deny license renewals do not have as much leverage available as groups which are actually blocking a sale, [their common] threat, at bottom, is that they [may be able to] force the station into an FCC hearing process immensely expensive for the defendants. Howard Monderer, NBC's general attorney in Washington, says that the network would have to budget [over] half a milion dollars to oppose at hearings a petition to deny renewal for any of the network's five owned stations. If that kind of money can [definitely] be saved by promising to hire a few people and air a few programs, many station ownerships will be tempted to go along whether or not they are convinced that the petitioners can make a case. . . .

There is no doubt that many of the challenging groups are evanescent and trivial, and some are worse. Lawrence Rogers of Taft Broadcasting told a meeting [of broadcasters] that a year after his Cincinnati station was challenged "many of the members of the coalition had either left town or gone to jail." Another executive complains that when he sent a letter to the group that challenged his station it was returned addressee unknown, and when he made a phone call he was told the phone had been disconnected.

Some of the complaints made in petitions to deny are almost funny. In Philadelphia, a petition by a group called Concern Communicators cited as proof of discrimination the station's standard form letter replying to an employment application: "Your letter and resume regarding employment with our station have been reviewed. While we have no positions available at the present time for someone of your qualifications, we will retain your resume in our files for consideration in the event of a future opening." The station was accused of bigotry because it sent this letter to black as well as white applicants.

And some "demands" are a little extreme. "The stations," [citizen activist Marcus Garvey] Wilcher says in San Francisco, "must undertake to teach the white middle-class community that controls this society, teach them about racism and how much it costs them. They must tell the 18-year-old, if your mother and father move to the suburbs to get away from blacks, vote for Richard Nixon and his Southern strategy or for Ronald Reagan who uses racism, it means you're going to fight in another Vietnam and get killed. We've asked the FCC to come out and investigate the entire media. We made charges; they wrote and said, give us some data on your changes. Well, data's hard to get. . . ."

[On the other hand, three New York network flagship stations thought enough of the validity of the grievances of] a petitioning group from New Jersey [to sign agreements with the group in return for pledges not to file petitions to deny]. The group complained that New Jersey's chunk of the coverage area of the New York stations (New Jersey houses more than a quarter of those tuned to New York stations) was getting little or no attention on the local news and demanded that the New York stations establish New Jersey bureaus. (The stations agreed to hire correspondents, but not to establish bureaus.) And the mostly Chicano group that blocked [a] McGraw-Hill purchase [of five stations] stuck on an issue of law in which none of them had any stake at all. [An] FCC guideline [then in existence forbade] a single company to buy more than two VHF channels in the top fifty markets. The [policy did] not effect existing ownerships, and [permitted] exceptions on a showing of "compelling public interest." Even after McGraw-Hill had made what everyone admitted was an unexpectedly generous offer in the areas of employment and programming, the Chicanos insisted that there was no "compelling public interest" behind McGraw-Hill's acquisition of three licenses in the top fifty markets, and forced the elimination of one of the stations in the package.

"We are very sensitive," says Dick Moore, who represented the Chicano groups as part of his work for the United Church of Christ, "to the criticism that this is a rip-off, just a way to get some jobs for minorities. We take the position that when issues are raised they must be dealt with, not used as a lever for extortion. In the McGraw-Hill case, these Chicanos were defending the whole society. They were very proud to take that role."

Everett Parker added, "You bet they were. They had made the Government do its job. That's the whole purpose of our work—to make the Government do its job."

EFFECTS

Given the size of its audience and the amount of time viewers spend in front of the television set, there can be no escaping the conclusion that TV's effects on American society are profound. This is especially true of the approximately 120 million Americans born since 1948 who have never known a world without television.

Television historian and critic Jeff Greenfield places television with the automobile as one of the two "transforming devices of American life." In *Television: The First Fifty Years,* he defines how Americans use television:

> With the single exception of the workplace, television is the dominant force in American life today. It is our marketplace, our political forum, our playground, and our school; it is our theater, our recreation, our link to reality, and our escape from it. It is the device through which our assumptions are reflected and a means of assaulting those assumptions. It is the single binding thread of this country, the one experience that touches young and old, rich and poor, learned and illiterate.

Educator Robert Hutchins has stated, "television has more impact on Americans than all our educational and religious institutions," and author David Halberstam goes one step further. Television is "in both overt and subliminal ways, more important and dominant in our lives than newspapers, radio, church, and often, in the rootless America of the seventies, more important than family and more influential and powerful than government itself." A possibly more immediate assessment of television's effects was expressed by a reviewer for the *Hollywood Reporter*: television is "the most easily available sleeping pill without a prescription."

That television affects society is agreed upon most emphatically, but whether those effects are beneficial or harmful is a matter for debate. On the one hand, critics extol the importance of television and its potential for improving the quality of life; on the other hand, they blame television for everything from ruining the eating habits of children to changing the entire American system of values. A 1979 Roper poll (financed by the television industry) conducted a survey of 3001 married couples which showed that the leading cause of matrimonial disputes was disagreement about which television show to watch.

According FCC chairman Charles Ferris, the effects of television on institutions such as the school and the family has become a national issue, like other issues concerning national environment and health. In *Television and Society,* Harry Skornia, former president of the National Association of Educational Broadcasters (NAEB), accused television of the ultimate crime: "Farfetched as it may seem, historians of the future may conclude that never before was there a period during which control of the thinking of a nation was exercised in a more totalitarian manner, or by a smaller group, than it is now by television and radio."

Television is not without defense. Some commentators insist that the influence television has exerted is at the worst inconclusive, that in fact television has had a positive influence on society. Defenders point to the rise of consumerism, the increased interest in the arts, the decline of racial prejudice and the drive for equal treatment of the sexes as some examples of the effects television has had on our society. According to former vice president of CBS Dick Jencks, "beyond its value as pure entertainment it [television] is really our only remaining mass medium, providing a common cultural base and a sense of national community for everyone." President of the National Association of Broadcasters (NAB) Vincent Wasilewski points out that television "broadly serves the tastes and needs of the whole population."

> For the past sixty years broadcasting has been the greatest entertainment media in the world . . . the greatest news media in the world . . . the greatest information media in the world . . . in fact, the standard of the world.

He disagrees with Skornia's statement, claiming that television is "probably the most democratic of our institutions."

The number of research studies conducted on virtually all aspects of the relationship between television and human behavior is staggering—more than 2300 items, according to George Comstock, author of *Television and Its Viewers: What Social Science Sees.* In a speech to the International Industrial Television Association, Comstock concluded:

> There is no general statement that summarizes the scientific literature on television and human behavior, but if forced to make one, perhaps it should be that television's effects are many, typically minimal in magnitude, but sometimes major in social importance.

In 1938, E. B. White stated in *Harpers,* "I believe television is going to be the test of the modern world. . . . We shall stand or fall by television—of that I am quite sure." Since this statement was made, the influence of television on the growth, or lack of it, of the American society has been a favorite topic of social scientists, media critics, scholars, bureaucrats, laborers and dinner guests. Gene F. Jankowski, president of the CBS Broadcasting Group, summed it all up in a speech before the International Radio and Television Society on March 19, 1979:

> To the many who criticize television, I submit that whenever the golden age of television was, is, or will be, one thing is certain. All the talk, criticism, concern and controversy that surrounds our industry today is taking place because of the important role that television plays every day for more than 200 million Americans.

LEE LOEVINGER

"There Need Be No Apology, No Lament"

"Perhaps with television, more than with other popular arts, there has been confusion as to purpose and definition. No one seems to know just what the medium is. . . ." This opinion about television was expressed by Professor Horace Newcomb, who edited *Television: The Critical View,* and is seconded by Lee Loevinger. Loevinger examines two basic issues concerning television's impact on society: "What is television actually doing?" and "What should it be doing?"

. . . Most critics are so anxious to tell us what they think television should be that they neglect to examine what it actually is.

A fairly comprehensive review of what has been written shows five general theories of broadcasting:

First was the hobby theory. When we were winding wire coils on old cereal boxes, making condensers (capacitors) out of tinfoil and waxed paper, using "crystals" and "cat whiskers," and listening on earphones, the real joy of radio was getting the most distant stations. A boy in St. Paul, Minn., thrilled to hear KDKA simply because it was in Pittsburgh. After World War II, much of the interest in television was the novelty of getting a picture in your own home. In those days people enjoyed manipulation of the device as much as programs, and broadcasting was more a hobby than a means of mass communication. Radio is still a hobby for more than a quarter-million licensed amateurs; but most of us have long since become more interested in programs.

This essay first appeared April 6, 1968.

When broadcasting declined as a hobby, it grew as a news medium. In the early 1930s newspaper publishers tried to prevent broadcasting of news. A separate radio news service was established, but finally publishers conceded the rights of broadcasters, and news wire services were offered to radio stations. Public reliance on broadcasting has grown since then until now [surveys indicate] more people look to television as a primary news source than to newspapers. This has led numerous observers to the view that the journalistic function is the principal and proper role of broadcasting.

Others see the journalistic theory as emphasizing mere news reporting too much, while neglecting social influence. They point to the vast audience of broadcasting, larger than any other medium in history both in numbers and percentage of population, and claim this offers a chance for great social influence. Since social problems are now so urgent, this leads to the conclusion that broadcasting is, or should be, an instrument of social reform. This view sees television as a means of doing quickly and easily what home, school, church and state have been struggling to do slowly and painfully for years. A similar view is official in some countries, especially Communist ones, which subject broadcasting to strict government control because of its supposed social and political influence.

Recently some philosophers and scientists have rejected the journalistic and social-reform theories in an effort to discover what broadcasting actually is, rather than starting with their own ideas of what it ought to be. The best-known of these is Marshall McLuhan, a Canadian professor who has become the Billy Rose, or perhaps the P. T. Barnum, of the academic world.

McLuhan's thesis and slogan is, "The medium is the message." This means that each medium changes the environment or creates a new environment, and consequences of this change are more significant than the messages carried. McLuhan regards all media as extensions of human senses, and points to effects of such sense-extensions through printing, radio and television. McLuhan says mass media created "the public," and argues that this fact is more important than any particular message.

William Stephenson, a social scientist at the University of Missouri, has suggested "the play theory of mass communications," based on novel, technical and ingenious methods of investigating and measuring attitudes. Stephenson says play is activity that is self-sufficient and pursued for the pleasure in it, while work involves effort undertaken for some ulterior purpose, such as production of goods, ideas or profit.

Mass communication is engaged in for pleasure, not for information or improvement. For example, people look first in the newspaper to read about events they have been involved in and already know about, as a football game they have seen. This shows they read newspapers not for information but as play. The "fill," the ordinary content, of mass communications is neither debasing nor escapism, but a buffer against anxieties and tensions of modern conditions. Culture and national character are formed by songs, gossip, sports, dances, competition and other forms of communications pleasure. The role of mass communication is to maximize communications pleasure and individual freedom in a world of increasing social controls.

Each of these theories has some useful and accurate observations, but none is wholly adequate to explain obvious facts about television and radio. These are:

First, that broadcasting, especially television, is the most popular communications medium in history. It is the first truly mass medium reaching all classes and groups in society.

Second, American-type broadcasting has universal appeal. Even such typically American programs as Westerns are popular throughout the world, as is American popular music. Public demand has forced even government-operated broadcasting systems to present such programming.

Third, broadcasting is increasingly performing the journalistic function of news reporting for a growing segment of the public, while literacy and prosperity are increasing.

Fourth, television arouses strong emotional reactions in both critics and public. Strangely, those who say they dislike television seem to be as regular in their watching and passionate in their views as those who like it.

Fifth, television is largely disdained by intellectuals, both genuine and would-be. Some publications do not consider it respectable to write about televsion without disparaging it.

Sixth, broadcasting has become more a part of ordinary life than any other means of communication, except possibly talking. It is clearly a component of our common culture.

Testing the five theories we have described against these facts requires a more detailed analysis than is possible here, but such analysis shows that each is consistent with some, but not all of the facts. The difficulty is that each theory has focused on one or a few aspects rather than the whole complex picture. We can better understand broadcasting in modern society if we regard it as an electronic mirror that reflects a vague or ambiguous image. As society is complex and many-faceted, broadcasting reflects a variety of images. These are never precisely focused and completely clear.

Society is reflected in the media mainly as an organized group or groups. But the audience watches as individuals. Looking at a blurred or vague image, different individuals see different things. This is because everyone engages in some projection, a common psychological process which consists of attributing our own attitudes, ideas or feelings to perceptions we get from the environment. . . .

All of us interpret observations according to our attitudes. To a child, *Alice in Wonderland* and *Gulliver's Travels* are stories of adventure; to an adult they are charming and fanciful allegories. Similarly, television programs mean different things to different people, and mean different things to one person at different times, depending upon attitude and mood.

Regarding television as an ambiguous mirror reflecting a slightly blurred image of society in which each viewer sees, by projection, his own vision of society and self, explains the observable facts. Television is popular because, as a reflection of society, it is responsive and adapted to mass attitudes and tastes. It increasingly performs the journalistic function because it is immediate, personal and comprehensive. Television is often better than personal observation as it can go further, faster and see more, yet conveys a sense of personal presence and participation.

There is emotional reaction to television because by projection each person sees some of his ego in his perception, so he reacts as though statements about television were about himself—which they are so far as they involve his impression of television.

A simple test shows how projection involves ego and emotion.

Hide and watch people passing a mirror. Almost no one can resist looking at his own image, and few fail to show some reaction. Or try taking pictures and showing them to the subject. People love to see pictures of themselves but never say they are flattered.

The intellectuals are alienated by television because they want to see images of themselves, as they think they are, and instead they see images of the common man and the mass of society. But television is an element of our culture because it shows things of common and universal interest. National culture is not found in museums or formed by graduate schools or universities. It is composed of common habits and patterns of living of people in daily activities, and of the common interest in entertainment, sports, news and even advertising. The "fill" or ordinary run of material in everyday broadcasting is a more important part of common culture than the occasional artistic triumph or esthetic masterpiece. Whether or not anyone thinks this is the way things should be, observation shows that this is the way things are. The "reflective-projective theory" which regards television as an ambiguous mirror in which each viewer sees an image of both society and self is simply descriptive of known facts.

This view does suggest the role television is best adapted to serve. One of our most pressing needs today is to strengthen our common culture and sense of national unity and purpose. The only media that reach enough people or touch people intimately enough to achieve this are radio and television. Whether television lifts us to esthetic or intellectual heights or elevates our artistic standards is less important than whether it helps us achieve a common culture and sense of national unity and purpose.

It is more likely to do this by responding day after day to the wants and tastes of the million-strong masses than by straining for approval of scornful intellectuals. There need be no apology and should be no lament for a broadcasting industry that provides the mass of people with programs they watch and enjoy daily. Disdainful talk about television seeking "the lowest common denominator" misses the important point. Culture is not arithmetic, and the cultural denominator of popular programs may be the highest, not the lowest, that is truly common. The important point is television does achieve a *common* denominator in society.

If there were less programming it might be of better quality. But the character of life depends upon everyday experience more than upon great infrequent ceremonial occasions. Amiability at the breakfast table is more important to a happy marriage than design of the wedding gown.

As television lets us share daily a common reflection of society and helps us see a similar vision of our relationship to society, it builds a common culture to unite our country. This now appears to be its natural function and highest ideal. It is enough.

LOUIS KRONENBERGER

Uncivilized and Uncivilizing

The effect of television on modern culture, both intellectually and artistically, is of major concern to some critics, particularly because it has become a major tool for disseminating mass culture in America. Social historian Dwight Macdonald theorized that "there is a Gresham's Law in cultural as well as monetary circulation: bad stuff drives out the good, since it is more easily understood and enjoyed."

Macdonald characterizes mass culture as "solely and directly an article of mass consumption, like chewing gum . . . fabricated by technicians hired by business . . . with audiences passive consumers, their participation limited to the choice of buying or not buying." He believes that mass culture is a severe threat to "High Culture" because of "its sheer pervasiveness, its brutal, overwhelming quantity."

Louis Kronenberger argues that television—the "supreme cultural opportunity"—has had a brutalizing effect on our entire culture.

. . . [Television is not just a great new force in modern] life, it virtually *is* modern life. What, one might ask, doesn't it do? It gives us—be we rich, poor, snowbound, bedridden or slow-witted—the time, the weather, the small news, big news, spot news: now in spoken headlines, now in pictured narrative, now at the very scene of the crime or the coronation itself. It plays, sings, whistles and dances for us; takes us to movies and theaters, concerts and operas, prize fights and ball games, ski jumps and tennis tournaments. It delivers babies, probes adolescents, psychoanalyzes adults. It dramatizes floods, fires, earthquakes; takes you to the top of an alp or the

This essay first appeared February 26, 1966.

bottom of an ocean or whirling through space; lets you see a tiger killed or a tiger kill. It becomes a hustings or a house of worship; guesses your age, your weight, your job, your secret; guides you through prisons, orphan asylums, lunatic asylums; introduces you to Presidents, kings, emirs, sultans; lets you see a Winston Churchill buried or a Lee Oswald shot. It teaches you French, rope-dancing, bird calls and first aid; provides debates and seminars and symposiums, quizzes and contests; and it tells you jokes, gags, wheezes, wisecracks, jokes and jokes.

Television is thus a truly stupendous addition to American life—our supreme cultural opportunity. Nothing approaches it, either in the abundance, variety and immediacy of its offerings, or the vastness, heterogeneity and attendance record of its audiences. It offers a mammoth handout of news, fun, art, sport, information; or of free refrigerators, cars, cruises, honeymoons, second honeymoons—all yours just for turning a knob, writing a letter, answering a phone.

Not too unnaturally, along with the handout there goes a sales talk. For this colossal addition of ours to American life, this supreme cultural opportunity, is also a tremendous segment of American business and our supreme cultural commodity. And not too surprisingly, what with Business paying the piper, Business calls—or cuts short, or calls off—the tune. And since television is Big Business operating with the help of Bigger Business, the two together constitute a form of Biggest Business—a fact we must face, since it makes any other fact about TV and its effect upon our civilization ultimately subsidiary and expendable.

It also tends to make any fresh insights and observations about the effect of TV on our civilization hard to come by. Before *we* can have any really new thoughts, TV must itself give proof of really new thinking; before we can find anything notably different to say, television must provide something notably different to say it about. To be sure, there are constantly new craft gadgets, seasonal fashions, technological wrinkles—and there is color television with its greater audience pleasure and fiercer network rivalry. But though these are things that add considerably to our conversation, they add very little to our culture. In providing so vast a menu, television has also—barring lavish Christmas puddings and special treats—pretty much standardized the food, the preparation of it and the after-dinner speeches as well.

A fair amount on the menu is unexceptionable; and a good deal more has given [many millions of] people harmless enjoyment. A certain amount of TV is clearly good; a certain further amount—notably in space-age matters—is both good and unprecedented. But *not* very much else is good, and much beyond that is truly dreadful. Moreover, beyond what television has done, good *or* bad, there is the matter of just how television has done it. The particular nature of what is bad in what TV does, the particular nature of what is bad in the way it does it, indicate what seems to me the *outstanding* effect of TV upon our civilization—which is that it has made it less civilized. There is a decided exception to this, namely educational television; but educational television, for all the charity and technical help it receives from commercial broadcasting, exists in a condition of virtual poverty, which not only underlines the uncivilized effect elsewhere, it argues no very civilizing *intentions*.

Let us gauge the effect in various ways. The *programs* themselves are predominantly geared to mediocre tastes and mass reactions—and geared, it would seem, in the hope that neither tastes nor reactions will improve. This doesn't just mean the proportion of sport to art on TV, or of broad comedy to adult humor; it means, even more, the proportion of trite formula to honest experiment, of glib comment to grown-up thinking. Further, the subject matter of countless programs—sex, gossip, violence, material success, cash itself—is uncivilized and uncivilizing both.

Take the most notorious example. The *technical* crime of the big-money quizzes was their being rigged; the technical immorality, that the networks could hardly not know it. But what was really degrading, indecent, uncivilizing was that, rigged or not, the quizzes pandered to the venality of a whole nation, had multitudes glued to their televisions not at all for the fun of the game, but for the size of the stakes. Knowledge had become the grossest, the most *un*cultural, of commodities. (One can't help wondering whether, if tomorrow playing Russian roulette for huge stakes on TV was declared legal, it too wouldn't become the rage, with wildly mounting remuneration.)

Again, what is more uncivilizing, in fact brutalizing, than all the violence that is offered on TV for sensational and not sociological reasons? What could be less civilized than the endless cheap gags and gossipy wisecracks; what less civilized than TV's flagrant invasion of privacy—not just in terms of outright gossip, but in the way of candid "discussion," or psychiatric "discovery," or photographs of the sick, the unhappy, the doomed? And when the networks do attempt a civilized subject (such as Michelangelo) all too often the treatment makes civilized people squirm.

The *presentation* of the programs is worse, and far more uniform. Whatever the pros and cons for commercial television generally, there can be no argument about how uncivilized, how rife with crudities, timidities, imbecilities, sponsored programs tend to be. The stop-watch technique alone must make a sensitive viewer stop watching. "Men," as Tyrone Guthrie has put it, "stand chalk-white . . . on guard in the studio, charged with the single responsibility of seeing that *Othello* or Beethoven's *Eroica* does not run one-tenth of a second over, or under." If the esthetic distortions resulting from this are often appalling, the grotesque and vulgar intrusions and interpolations—the commericals—are worse. There are, to be sure, exceptions; but for the most part the blatancy of the programs' commercialized approach conveys the impression of a cash register in the drawing room, and even right next to a deathbed.

As with programs and presentation, so with *procedure*. The "ratings" system, which computes not merit but mass popularity, which queries not those best qualified to judge but those most apt to judge routinely, is more than uncivilized: It is anticivilized. It turns any illiterate into a critic; an entrepreneur into a craven; a defeated contestant into a criminal (punishable by instant banishment). For profits-seeker and pleasure-seeker alike, there might be point to conducting polls with a view to correcting faults; but here improved quality is no more the issue than intrinsic quality.

Moreover, the general off-screen *atmosphere* of TV proclaims the lack of accident in how uncivilized the thing as a whole is. Everywhere cutthroat tensions seem mated with back-stabbing tactics. The higher levels of the three great networks suggest a luxury-class Reign of Terror, where the people who live in glass doghouses and the limelighted shake-ups and feuds make TV's administrative life the gossip column's darling. TV doesn't even *wash* its dirty linen in public; it merely waves it. Perhaps the one sure news edge that the press still enjoys over television is the doings and misdoings, the firings and backfirings, of television itself. But though the power side of TV is always agitated and shifting, its money side is solid and stationary. In this, the Great Networks are splendidly assisted by the Great Advertising Agencies and the Great Artists' Representatives, so that the alluring daughters and nieces of art—Language and Laughter, Melody and Declamation and Dancing—are constantly bedded and wedded to the paunchy sons and nephews of Mammon. The general effect is often about as civilized as gluttony.

There is, finally, the cultural *irresponsibility* involved in all this. In an empire so vast as television's, in a network hierarchy so unfixed and collapsible, we must look to the very top for the policies that govern it and for the direction it takes. And there we find men known only for their immense wealth and their business power. Whatever their private enjoyments or hobbies, these are not men publicly identified with high culture; indeed, they have made everything in television that *is* so identified, everything that bespeaks artistic experiment, genuine enlightenment, pretty much shift for itself. Where important cultural events are not news already, these men seem to show small interest in making them so.

As for educational television, for these men it seems enough to give it a pat on the back and gestures of financial aid. Thus educational television remains a kind of sop that under the present system will never become a sufficient offset. Nor does it constitute a sufficient offset to the bill of complaint raised in this article.

Without at all belittling TV's virtues, its triumphs of news coverage, its operas and concerts, its ability to inform or stimulate or amuse, its serviceability to the many millions of people who use it as a food and not a drug, the glaring fact remains that TV has consistently either imposed uncivilized elements on American life, or aggravated and intensified those it found there. It has helped destroy respect for privacy, it has helped foster a more rackety publicity. There has been nothing too elegant for it to coarsen, too artistic for it to vulgarize, too sacred for it to profane.

MARTIN MALONEY

The (Awful) *Effects of Television* (on Everybody)

Over the years since television has become the dominant communications medium, it has collected the blame for almost every problem from which society suffers. Before television, movies and radio were considered prime culprits. The printing press probably received similar criticism.

James Kraft of the National Endowment for the Humanities suggests that television be put into perspective: "I think we tend to judge TV from a point in time, and this can be misleading. TV is not now what it was or what it will be; nor are we. . . . Today we see TV quite differently than, let us say, a child of three will eventually grow up to conceive of it. What we see as a weakness now might be ignored by that child as not even an issue." Martin Maloney also calls for some perspective in evaluating the impact of television on our society.

I guess I am just an old middle-of-the-roader at heart. On the one hand, I don't think I want to be an Oscar Mayer wiener, so everyone will be in love with me. On the other, or left, hand, I don't want to be a television mogul either. Oh, I know about their Countess Mara neckties and four-hour lunches with guinea hen under plastic and 75-to-1 martinis, and their Gotham hatcheries full of [attractive] script girls and secretaries, but—well, I just don't want to be one.

The reason is that, sooner or later, to every television executive comes that moment of truth when he must justify the credit cards which have provided him with the above-named luxuries. He must

Excerpts have been taken from this essay, which first appeared March 25, 1967.

emerge from his mink-lined foxhole and make a public statement, usually a pretty innocuous one, to the effect that there are worse things in this world than television, such as cancer and the napalm bomb. Then, according to time-honored ritual, he is clobbered with a barrage of charges and specifications so horrifying, all-encompassing and unprovable that the late Judge Jeffreys, the Hanging Judge, would have blushed to introduce them during the Bloody Assizes.

The charges inevitably have to do with the doleful effects of television on . . . oh, teen-age motorcycle buffs, redheaded divorcées under 35, Lithuanian numismatists in the middle-income bracket—you name it. The business of figuring out the horrid effects of TV is only one of the lesser American industries; there are few people who actually make a living at it. It is, however, a sort of addiction among intellectuals (an intellectual, in this context, is anyone who owns a typewriter and uses it for any purpose save writing personal letters). And the result is that the unfortunate TV titan, who is manifestly to blame for the medium as well as the message, is in pretty much the same position as was Mr. Sherlock Holmes at that point in his career when Col. Sebastian Moran was gunning for him with Von Herder's air rifle. All he has to do is let his shadow fall across the window blind, and zap!—he's ducking an expanding revolver bullet.

Practically speaking, for the panting and harried vice president, there is no escape. No matter what he says or does, it always turns out that he has very nearly wrecked the Republic. . . .

The practice of relating all the ills of society, from mass murder to the seven-year itch, to whatever medium of public communication happens to be prominent at the time is by no means new. True, I haven't been able to locate any statements by eminent divines, circa 1500, on the subject "Is Movable Type Corrupting Our Youth?"—but I'm sure they were made, and may still survive, hidden somewhere in the junk heap of history. As a matter of fact, some such statements—left atop the junk heap of recent history—do survive; they have to do with one or other of the more antiquated media, such as movies. I cull the following testimony from a 1929 study—an alleged statement from a reformatory inmate on how he got there:

"Once I saw a movie, me and another guy. It was about a man who robbed a house. . . . He got in dat house and stole dis big roll [money]. Me and dis guy, we said, 'Dat's easy, we kin do dat.' So we lef' de show before it was over and here was a man's auto, an open car, parked. We went thu dis car. . . ."[1] But enough.

At least the recent testaments to the responsibility of TV for juvenile experiments in mopery, assault and glue-sniffing, do not come couched in this sort of Happy Hooligan dialect. It's a small mercy, but a welcome one.

I do think that one of the happiest statements on the "effects" of a mass medium is also one of the earliest. Back in the days before the market crash, Herbert Hoover, then regnant in Washington, summoned to him a platoon of scholars and bade them survey recent social trends in the United States. When the survey was completed in 1932, one of the items noted was—well, guess!—"social effects of the radio." Now, in 1929, American radio broadcasting was about eight years old, and network radio hadn't quite reached its third anniversary. There were also no very good methods for establishing the effect of radio on anything. All the same, these good, gray scholars came up with a list of exactly 150 "effects," some of them quite charming. For instance, No. 7: "Illiterates find a new world opened to them"; or No. 20: "Revival of old songs, at least for a time"; No. 65: "Discouragement, it is said, of preachers of lesser abilities."[2]

Of course, sooner or later the critic of mass-media critics has to face his own moment of truth: the question, "Suppose they're right?" My personal opinion, which is worth about $1.35 per cubic mile on the international market, is that nobody knows for sure. I haven't looked at all of the studies of mass-media effects on everybody, but the ones I have looked at make me somewhat dubious of the claims of the more swinging critics.

Take, for instance, the celebrated "War of the Worlds" radio program which created a panic in the Eastern United States in October 1938. Here was a classic case of cause and effect. Whodunit? Orson Welles. What did he do? A scary radio show. What resulted? Panic. Yet when a covey of social scientists headed by

1. Alice Miller Mitchell, *Children and Movies* (Chicago: University of Chicago Press, 1929), p. 142.

2. *Recent Social Trends in the United States* (New York: McGraw-Hill Book Company, 1933), Vol. I, pp. 153–56.

Hadley Cantril investigated the phenomenon, what did they find? Among other things, they found that a good many of the people who had been scared to death were deeply religious citizens, who somehow missed Welles's interplanetary fantasy altogether and thought that the end of the world had come. So if we don't want panic, maybe we should eliminate religion—or at least, the hard-core gospel, the sort of thing that makes people nervous? . . .

I don't want anyone to get the impression from the foregoing that some of my best friends are TV vice presidents. Excoriate them for spending millions on entertainments less entertaining than the annual St. Polycarp's Pageant at Simeon T. Garfunkel High School, if you will; pepper them with rock salt for their arrogance in supposing that their audiences are a clutch of faceless sub-morons, and I am with you. But if you really wonder why people beat children, or take heroin, or bomb civilians or pollute the air they themselves must breathe . . . well, may heaven bless you, and I hope that you find a scapegoat a little more convincing than [a television executive].

DANIEL J. BOORSTIN

The Road to Diplopia

Critic and historian Eric Barnouw once said of television, that it was: "In living color more real than life, the swirling dots [on the television screen] represent the world . . . they have become the environment and the context of our lives."

According to Daniel Boorstin, "television watching has become an addiction comparable only to life itself." The question is, how deeply has this addiction affected the American personality?

It was Karl Marx who observed that all historic events occur twice: once as tragedy and again as comedy. The television screen has given a similarly puzzling duality to our American experience. Every event worth noticing now occurs twice: once out here and again on screen. It is not always easy to say which is the tragedy and which the comedy. A new duality, a new ambiguity, has entered our lives. Which is more real, which is the authentic experience—what happens in our neighborhood, in our office, in our shop, on our farm, or what happens on the television screen?

We know, of course, that what happens on television is usually better planned, more dramatic. What we see there can be reinforced by precise repetition, by rerun, which is never quite the case in the experience out here. Which is more interesting? Millions of Americans give their answer by sitting placidly before the tube when they might be participants in the stream that was once reality out here.

It is not only the multiplication of experience, then, but this new ambiguity of experience that must begin to overwhelm and to puzzle and to trouble us. Our personal (off-screen) experience is to a

This essay first appeared October 14, 1978.

considerable extent in our control. Our TV experience, while within a narrow range of our selection, is emphatically not in our control. In America today, television is the authenticating experience. The television experience is what makes an issue live, what makes a politician into a statesman, what makes (or unmakes) a President, what makes an event catastrophic, what makes a question controversial, what makes a far-off conflict momentous and what makes a neighborhood event significant. In the United States today it is hard to imagine a movie star, a politician, a sportsman or any other national figure who is not more familiar to us on the television screen than anywhere else.

If we are to grasp the significance of broadcasting in human history (which simply means, of course, in our generation) we must modernize our vocabulary. The old distinctions between transportation and communication will no longer serve. The very word "communication"—which the dictionary defines as "the exchange of thoughts, messages or the like, as by speech, signals or writing"—will no longer serve. That notion did well enough for the Age of Publishing and almost well enough for the first stage of our Age of Broadcasting, which was the era of radio. The main purpose of a receiving set back then was still essentially "communication"—to bring messages, to make known or to impart. But not now, not in the television era.

For the first time our technology brings us a universally accessible *experience* that actually competes with all the rest of our experience. A new kind of competition for what we once called reality. With a new power to pose a question mark beside all happenings that do not occur in this new version, on the tube.

If we want to improve our experience, then, we have a double task. We must not only improve the real texture of our lives out here. We must also improve the new reality of television experience. And these two versions of experience—on the tube and off the tube—are independent variables.

What are the national consequences of this diplopia, this "disorder of vision that causes objects to appear double"?

The first was described long before television by the great Spanish satirist Miguel de Cervantes in his *Don Quixote.* The trouble with Quixote was simply that (instead of going hunting or managing his farms) he read so many romances that he finally could not disentangle them from his real life. He made a spectacle of himself by dressing up like a knight and going out to fight imaginary enemies. In his mind commonplace objects acquired the most fearful or most romantic forms. His nag Rosinante became a handsome thoroughbred, the ramshackle inn where he stayed became a castle. And when he saw a field with thirty whirling windmills, he thought they were giants waving their menacing arms at him. He was an amiable and decent man, but he suffered from a seventeenth-century form of diplopia. The pathological duality of *his* experience was induced by too much printed matter.

Now that we are overwhelmed by the experiences on our TV screens, what will save us from our own twentieth-century kind of Quixotry? We, too, go for the alarming, the grandiose and the utopian: for a pollution-free world, where every woman's husband is a paragon, and every man's car a limousine. We, too, find it hard to distinguish the grand from the trivial. Now wonderfully vivid new menaces—of teeth that are not sexually seductive, of laundry that is less than snow white—provide us our own myriad household windmills to tilt at.

The second effect of diplopia is more serious. It expresses itself in an overshadowing mood of helplessness. We are tempted to become spectators, not only of what is on the tube, but of all experience. We see so much, every day on the screen, of catastrophes that we can do nothing about—floods, fires, terrorists attacks, kidnappings, starvation and corruption—that we make these the very prototypes of experience. A world to be looked at, to be entertained by (or alarmed or shocked by). But not a world to act in. When all the world's catastrophes are so conveniently corralled into our living rooms, we can share, or at least be solaced by, the spectacle of the whole world's helplessness. No wonder we feel so frustrated, so out of control!

Still, a free society is rooted in the feeling that everybody can make a difference, not only at the ballot box and in the marketplace, but somehow every day. Our plural society needs and welcomes many views of reality. And our oldest problem is how to preserve a decent society where ideas conflict but people do not. Our newest problem, from our new diplopia, is how to hold on to our sense of reality. How can we enjoy the benefits of doubled vision, of a wonderfully multiplied and extended experience, without losing our grasp on the solid world out here where we live, and which we will master only without delusion.

NEIL HICKEY EDITH EFRON

Does TV Violence Affect Our Society?

"If a picture is worth a thousand words, how much more is that picture worth when it is live and constant?" asked Senator Claiborne Pell, chairman of the Senate Subcommitte on Education. The amount of time people watch television, the belief that commercials can motivate people and the much discussed "qualitative" impact of television, in Senator Pell's view, support the notion that "there must be some connection between violence in television and violence in society."

Pell emphasizes that the collection of "scientific proof" that televised violence causes violence in society is hampered by the fact that "we are not dealing with chemical equations or physical properties; we are dealing with the minds of people, particularly of the young, something that we know relatively little about." Neil Hickey and Edith Efron disagree about whether sufficient proof has been assembled to support the conviction that television violence does have a causal relationship with violence in society.

Yes: Neil Hickey

The jury is in. After hundreds of formal scientific studies and decades of contentious debate, reasonable men are obliged to agree that televised violence does indeed have harmful effects on human character and attitudes, and that something ought to be done about it.

". . . There comes a time when the data are sufficient to justify action," said the U.S. Surgeon General as long ago as 1972, deliver-

Excerpts have been taken from this essay, which first appeared June 14, 1975.

ing to Congress one of the most exhaustive ($1 million, three-year) research projects ever undertaken by social scientists. "The overwhelming consensus [is] that televised violence does have an adverse effect on certain members of society." The evidence was "sufficient to warrant appropriate and immediate remedial action," said the nation's chief health officer, and he added: "These conclusions are based on solid scientific data and not on the opinion of one or another scientist."

In the years since that ringing and unequivocal declaration, TV watchers have been treated to uncounted thousands of brutal homicides, rapes, robberies, fist fights, muggings, maimings and all-out mayhem. TV networks continue their reliance on violence as a staple of their action-adventure series and regularly air theatrical movies like *Bonnie and Clyde, The Godfather* and *In Cold Blood.* In addition, local stations daily offer old gangster, Western and war films, reruns of rampageous prime-time melodramas, and old cartoons now considered too violent for network use.

Thus, it is virtually impossible for Americans, of any age, to avoid the depiction of violence on their TV screens. (One scientist estimates that by the age of 15 the average child will have witnessed 13,400 televised killings.) Also, many local stations have adopted "tabloid" news formats in which they compete for ratings by emphasizing homicides, riots and catastrophes.

As a result, the whole angry debate about blood-and-guts TV continues, as private citizens complain to Congress and the FCC, and those bodies in turn demand that the TV industry rid itself of gratuitous violence. . . .

Meanwhile, violent crime has been increasing at six to ten times the rate of population growth in the United States. (Obviously, nobody blames all of that on television.) Our homicide rate is roughly ten times that of the Scandinavian countries; more murders are committed yearly in Manhattan than in the entire United Kingdom. . . .

Proof that levels of TV violence have remained unacceptably high—even after the Surgeon General's report, and subsequent supportive studies—is easily at hand. In the [1978-79] viewing period, for example, violence occurred in [84.7] per cent of all TV programs and in [86] per cent of adult prime-time [(8-11 P.M. ET) dramatic programming], according to the most recent Violence Profile, published in [1979] by Dean George Gerbner and Professor Larry Gross of the Annenberg School of Communications at the University of Pennsylvania. . . .

The Gerbner and Gross study and, perhaps even more important, their experiments indicate that heavy TV watchers tend to overestimate the danger of physical violence in real life. (Such unreasonable fear was found most acute among young watchers, and, in particular, among young women. Significantly, women are frequently portrayed as "victims" in televised mayhem.)

Yet another study (by University of Utah researchers) appears to prove that children who are heavy TV watchers can become "habituated or 'desensitized' to violence" in the real world. Normal emotional responses to human suffering become blunted, the researchers conclude, and this desensitization may easily cause "not only major increases in our society of acts of personal aggression but also a growing attitude of indifference and nonconcern for the victims" of real-life violence.

Dr. Robert M. Liebert, a psychologist at the State University of New York (and a principal investigator for the Surgeon General's report) says unequivocally:

"The more violence and aggression a youngster sees on television, regardless of his age, sex or social background, the more aggressive he is likely to be in his own attitudes and behavior. The effects are not limited to youngsters who are in some way abnormal, but rather were found for large numbers of perfectly normal American children." That conclusion arises from analysis of more than fifty studies covering the behavior of 10,000 children between the ages 3 and 19.

Liebert added that one significant study showed that "it was not a boy's home life, not his school performance, not his family background, but the amount of TV violence he viewed at age 9 which was the single most important determinant of how aggressive he was ten years later, at age 19." . . .

As long ago as 1954, Senator Estes Kefauver was demanding hard answers to questions about televised violence. He never got them. In 1961, Senator Thomas Dodd heard [Congressional] testimony that TV's utilization of violence had remained (as one observer put it) "both rampant and opportunistic." (One independent producer told of being asked to "inject an 'adequate' diet of violence into scripts."

A network official told another program supplier: "I like the idea of sadism.") Dodd held follow-up hearings in 1964.

Following the 1968 assassinations of Senator Robert F. Kennedy and the Rev. Martin Luther King, as well as bitter rioting on campuses and at political conventions, President Lyndon Johnson established the National Commission on the Causes and Prevention of Violence (headed by Dr. Milton Eisenhower), to undertake a "penetrating search into our national life" in the attempt to get at the roots of our seeming lawlessness.

The Commission, while pointing out that TV is not the sole culprit, concluded that "Violence on television encourages violent forms of behavior, and fosters moral and social values about violence in daily life which are unacceptable in a civilized society . . . it is a matter for grave concern that at a time when the value and the influence of traditional institutions . . . are in question, television is emphasizing violent, antisocial styles of life."

The Commission further complained that, despite repeated promises over the previous fifteen years, the TV industry had failed to reduce violence levels and failed also to conduct research into the effects of televised violence.

An incredible 94.3 per cent of cartoon shows contained violent episodes in 1967 (according to data developed for the Commission by Dean George Gerbner), in 1968 there were 23.5 violent episodes per hour in cartoons. That same year, 81.6 per cent of all prime-time entertainment shows contained violence. Said the Commission: "If television is compared to a meal, programming containing violence clearly is the main course. . . ."

Enter Senator Pastore. In 1969, he set in motion the Surgeon General's investigation, which produced the toughest and best-documented indictment yet on televised violence. During hearings on the completed report in 1972, Senator Pastore labored to cut through scientific jargon and elicit unequivocal testimony on the report's root meaning. He ultimately succeeded.

PASTORE: You, Dr. [Jesse] Steinfeld, as the chief health officer of the United States of America, have said, "There comes a time when the data are sufficient to justify action. That time has come." Is that your unequivocal opinion?

STEINFELD: Yes, sir.

Political scientist Ithiel de Sola Pool, a member of the Surgeon General's Advisory Committee, voiced the consensus: "Twelve scientists of widely different views unanimously agreed that scientific evidence indicates that the viewing of violence by young people causes them to behave more aggressively."

Even network representatives on the Advisory Committee, under dogged questioning by Pastore, confessed their general agreement with the findings. CBS's Dr. Joseph Klapper, for example, admitted that "there are certainly indications of a causal relationship" between TV violence and aggression by children. And NBC's Dr. Thomas Coffin agreed that the time had come for some remedial action.

Even so, a number of network operatives and partisans chose to misinterpret the report in the mischievous hope of blunting its effect. A few network spokesmen, emphasizing its cautious tone (normal for such social-science documents), insisted to friendly journalists that the report was inconclusive and largely meaningless. Similarly, a few ideologues focused their own disagreement on the conviction (unrelated to TV violence's effects or the lack thereof) that government has no business even studying the content of TV programs. That pincers movement was short-lived and unsuccessful. The report easily outlived its critics.

In the heightened glare of public attention, the networks then took a long, hard look at the violence quotient of their programs and did, in fact, significantly reduce the senseless mayhem on Saturday-morning cartoon shows. (Those deposed, violence-ridden cartoons are, nonetheless, seen every afternoon on hundreds of local TV stations.) Less successful, however, was the industry's effort to reduce violence in its prime-time series and movies.

Or, at least, the effort didn't satisfy Congress, which [in 1974] demanded of the FCC some concrete proposals on how to mitigate, once and for all, the wearisome problem. FCC Chairman Richard Wiley summoned the network chieftains to Washington, and after several powwows there emerged the Family Viewing Time concept: a nightly no man's land (7–9 P.M. ET) sanitized of violent and sexy incidents and guaranteed "OK" for the whole family to watch. The plan also provided for "advisories" to warn viewers (both during and after the "family hour") of material that might be harmful or offensive.

While Chairman Wiley called the concept a "landmark" and Senator Pastore said it was "a wonderful idea," hardly anybody, privately, considered it anything but a gentlemen's agreement between Congress, the FCC, the networks and the NAB to take the heat off all of them. . . .

Framers of the scheme conveniently chose to overlook data proving that televised violence can have deleterious effects on adults as well as children; and that kids by the millions are glued to their television sets at *all* hours of the day, not just between 7 and 9. Thus, the "family hour" is perceived by most experts as a subtle carte blanche for "business as usual," or, as one writer put it, "gore as before."

Others take it as final proof that self-regulation of the TV industry can't work; that networks will always place self-interest above the public interest when profits are jeopardized. As Robert Liebert put it: "A significant conflict of interest has existed between people concerned about children and people concerned about profit." So far, that conflict remains unresolved.

Traditionally, TV people have invoked the First Amendment at the mere hint of any government meddling with their right to air violent programs. Lately, however, that argument has been challenged by a growing body of media theorists and civil libertarians who—weary of the television industry's chronic inability to police itself—are saying, in effect, "Bunk!" Says Liebert: "It is a pseudo-issue for broadcasters to claim that they have a right, by reason of constitutional guarantees of freedom of speech, to give kids any sort of junk they want to on the argument that if the broadcaster isn't free and unmonitored, then democracy will be endangered. That isn't so. There is no precedent whatever for believing that adults' freedoms are endangered because a society enforces policies that are necessary for the welfare of its youth."

No society can be indifferent to the ways its citizens publicly entertain themselves, argues Professor Irving Kristol of New York University. Bearbaiting and cockfighting were prohibited by law, not so much out of compassion for the animals, he points out, but mostly because such spectacles "debased and brutalized" the audiences who flocked to see them. That prohibition (among many others) has been counted an acceptable, formal limitation upon people's constitutional rights.

The case for controls in the area of television is debated in a book called *Where Do You Draw the Line? An Exploration into Media Violence, Pornography, and Censorship* (edited by Victor B. Cline, Brigham Young University Press). "The battle for civil liberties should not be fought on the backs of children," writes psychiatrist Fredric Wertham. The argument that protecting children from harmful media exposure is an infringement of civil liberties "has no historical foundation," he says.

"It has never happened in the history of the world that regulations to protect children—be they with regard to child labor, food, drink, arms, sex, publications, entertainment or plastic toys—have played any role whatsoever in the abridgment of political or civil liberties for adults." . . .

[With the Family Viewing hour], the specter of censorship wafts into view like an unwelcome visitor. It's a solution nobody claims to want, but it may become less unthinkable in the current atmosphere of dismay over televised violence and the industry's stewardship of the public's airwaves. [More discussion of censorship of televised violence may be found in Censorship and Control]

No: Edith Efron

. . . It is a tiresome fact that crime antedates network television—Cain and Abel being the archsymbolic case in point. One of the earliest remnants of man lies in state with clear evidence that a primitive ax had been buried in his skull. Bluebeard, Jack the Ripper and Lizzie Borden have acquired a certain renown as small-scale free-lance murderers. As for torture and murder on a grand scale, Attila the Hun, the Inquisition and, in our own century, Stalin, Hitler and Mao cannot be surpassed. And, to my certain knowledge, none of these was inspired by television.

It's another tiresome fact that every new technological development in the history of human communications has always brought the "sex and violence" ministry out of its lairs to cry out dolorous warnings about the threat to public morality. It is never the ministry's morality that is in the slightest danger—only that of the great unwashed. As any history of censorship will tell you, this claque has carried on with an identical frenzy in every era, uttering identical warnings about: the printing press, the nickelodeon, the silent movies, the talkies, comic books, radio and TV. Rarely has it carried on about communications forms primarily enjoyed by the upper classes—such as books or the theater.

There is only one reason today to pay the slightest attention to this claque, and that is: it is now brandishing "scientific" studies at us which allegedly "prove" that the sight of TV "violence" can indeed "cause" real-life violence. And, to complicate matters, a batch of journalists has fallen for these claims, a group of politicians and HEW bureaucrats see glory in endorsing them, a coalition of what *Variety* calls "liberal intelligentsia" and "the blue-collar class" ("Archie Bunker and the professor") has climbed on the bandwagon, and what should have been dismissed as unscientific trash is fast acquiring the luminous aura of revealed "truth"—a "truth" that can lead directly to government censorship.

So there is nothing for it but to argue the case against trash posturing as science. In one article, the analysis must necessarily be restricted to the essentials. . . .

The first thing you should know is that the "TV violence" controversy is merely one of the typically ugly quarrels raging in the social-science community. To understand why, you need merely remember that the social sciences are not true sciences. Although sociology and psychology use statistical measurements, what they choose to measure and what their measurements mean once they've got them are always open to question, generating acute and frequently vicious controversies, particularly as they affect public policy.

The "TV violence" issue has become just such a controversy. Intimidation is in the air, and we are principally hearing the voices of one aggressive pressure group—the group that holds TV as "proven" guilty. Psychologist Ruth Hartley, who has subjected many of the "TV violence" studies to scathing analysis, told me, speaking of her colleagues: "You can't imagine what they do to you if you dare to say that TV *doesn't* hurt children."

You get a full sense of the gutter level of the debate when you know that former FCC Commissioner Nicholas Johnson [once] denounced all network programming executives as "evil men" and "child molesters." Few today, however scornful they may be of the "violence" studies, care to subject themselves to such invective. Ironically, the networks have themselves silenced some of the most brilliant men in the field by the simple act of hiring them to do research. "We are all routinely called prostitutes now, unless we play along," one of them said to me.

All this is sufficient reason to approach the "violence" controversy with immense skepticism and, above all, to use one's own judgment.

Now, with this as background—what about the "violence" studies —in particular the batch of twenty-three different research projects and experiments conducted for the Surgeon General? What do they actually prove? The hardheaded answer is: nothing. And the fastest way to tell you why is to quote from the Report to the Surgeon General itself, written by a jury of twelve social scientists who evaluated this body of research. The jury was, and remains, torn into bitterly hostile factions, which is what makes any statements all have signed quite significant. They all agree that the very problem of analyzing TV's "impact" on viewers is almost unsolvable by its very nature, and they cite a list of reasons. The language is a bit heavy, but plow through it:

- The authors tell us that "the complexities of developmental processes in childhood and adolescence and the variations from one individual to another make it difficult to predict the effects" of any single stimulus, let alone the tremendous barrage of stimuli coming from TV.
- They tell us that "each person in the audience perceives and . . . interprets the stimuli through his [or her] own patterns of ideas, values and responses," thus that generalizations about all people or all children cannot be made.
- They tell us that "the impact of television viewing can only be fully understood when we know something about a young person's own nature, family, neighborhood, school and other major influences in his [or her] life."
- They tell us: "It is difficult to design studies which isolate the effects of television content from these other variables. As a result, generalizing from laboratory experiments, surveys, or short-term studies to the long-term, real-time world can be risky."
- And they tell us: "Understanding the relationship between research results and free-ranging human behavior has been a persis-

tent difficulty in attempts to apply scientific findings to the problems of daily life."

To translate this into ordinary English, it says: We don't know very much, yet, about how people work. . . . Every child and adult in America is different. . . . TV content is complex and is perceived differently by every individual. . . . TV is just one of innumerable influences in any individual's life. . . . We don't know how to test its effects. . . . And when we try to do so, we usually don't understand our own findings.

It should be obvious that even *one* of these objections is enough to kill the whole kit and caboodle of such studies. And *all* of them, taken together, make the project a lost cause. In fact, the jury says as much. They all confess that "it would be easy and scientifically justifiable to abandon the search for real-world causal relationships with the declaration, 'nondemonstrable'."

But TV "violence" researchers are stouthearted types, and the fact that they know something to be rationally impossible doesn't stop them from trying to do it. Even the networks, in their desperate desire to prove to bullying congressmen that they are concerned about America's children, rush in where angels would fear to tread. And all that happens, of course, is that the impossible becomes more impossible yet, because if you can't "demonstrate" something by rational means . . . well, you resort to irrational means! And there are so many irrational aspects to these studies that it is puzzling to know which ones to isolate in a single article. A few illustrations will have to do.

One pertains to the ostensibly dry and dusty realm of definitions. As the Surgeon General's jury—again, all of them—put it: "For scientific investigation, terms must be defined precisely and unambiguously." Well, the definitions in this group of studies would make Funk and Wagnalls weep. "Violence" in these studies means such things as: physical attack . . . self-defense . . . the destruction of property . . . racist stereotypes . . . and playing football! "Aggression" is even more startling. It means everything that "violence" means, plus: "antisocial conduct," a concept that covers everything from small-fry belligerence at the sand pile to mass murder . . . *and the energetic pursuit of any goal, whether pro- or anti-social, creative or destructive!*

Here's the effect of using words so wildly: By such standards, a TV comedy featuring a stereotyped Aunt Jemima mother, with a pushy two-year-old who's always first at the jam pot, and an ambitious, hard-working son who is putting himself through college by playing football, can now be classed as an extremely "violent" film! And among "aggressive" characters, we can now lump: Hitler, cooking millions in ovens . . . Solzhenitsyn, defying a succession of Soviet dictators to write *The Gulag Archipelago* . . . Martin Luther King, leading a nonviolent demonstration to gain voting rights for blacks . . . Helen Reddy, self-assertively belting out "I Am Woman" . . . and Snoopy, trying to shoot down The Red Baron!

So what common phenomenon, what common misbehavior are all these studies investigating? None. Taken as a group, they are resplendently meaningless. And the failure to make moral differentiations between the "violence" of attack and the "violence" of self-defense, between creative self-assertion and murder, is stupefying.

With this kind of conceptual and moral chaos lying concealed at the very base of the project, what kind of "findings" did it produce? They were chaotic and weirdly contradictory: Some testees become more "aggressive" after seeing TV "violence." The majority of testees do not. Some testees become more cooperative and "prosocial" afterwards. Some testees become more "aggressive" after watching comedies and erotic material, than after watching "violent" material. And so forth. The jury—again, all of them—concluded politely from all of this that you can produce either "antisocial" or "prosocial" responses, depending on "the opportunities offered in the experiment." Which is a scholar's way of saying you can manufacture any results you like.

Now, sensible people, facing this kind of intellectual nonsense, will simply put on their hats, go home, and settle down to a jolly evening with [action-adventure shows on TV]. But if your colleagues have just blown one million dollars in tax money, if a U.S. senator demands an accounting, and if you have private or professional reasons for not walking out, you can do one of two things: You can say, loudly, "A causal connection between TV violence and crime has been proved" and then hastily admit that there's a chaotic situation here. Or you can say, loudly, "This is a hopelessly chaotic situation" and then hastily add that some sort of tenuous connection may have been shown.

That's what the Surgeon General's jury said. After describing the chaotic "findings" with such words as "tentative and limited," "not wholly consistent or conclusive," etc., their bottomline conclusion read: "We have noted in the studies at hand a modest association between viewing of violence and aggression, among at least some children, and we have noted some data which are consonant with the interpretation that violence-viewing produces the aggression; this evidence is not conclusive however, and some of the data are also consonant with other interpretations."

What does *that* mean? Nothing. A cartoon in the *American Psychological Association Monitor* for March 1972 satirized the report with a caption reading; "Our studies show conclusively that TV does not cause violence—except when it does."

As far as I can tell, after spending almost a full year of my professional life reading such studies and discussing them with social scientists, there are only two "links" between the watching of TV and crime—*real* crime, as defined by the law—and both warrant close inspection, mainly for what they tell you about the "violence" researchers.

The first "link" lies in a batch of surveys, done both in America and in England, showing that delinquent-type adolescents watch much more TV, and TV "violence," than their stabler nondelinquent peers. Similarly, studies of prison populations indicate unusually heavy watching of TV, and of TV "violence." This "proves," according to some researchers, that the sight of TV "violence" causes crime.

Only it doesn't. Other Anglo-American studies also show, with great consistency, that the group in society that does the heaviest watching of TV "violence" shows is the group that is least intelligent, least educated, poorest, *and most unstable.* But this is precisely the group that has always been the chief reservoir of violent crime, and it was so well *before* the invention of TV, and of televised cops-and-robbers shows.

Further: other Anglo-American studies show with great consistency that normal adolescents not only watch less TV and less TV violence than delinquents, but start getting bored by the set at age

10, if unusually bright, and at age 12, if they're normally intelligent. This, postulates Britain's Hilde Himmelweit, indicates that for stable youngsters, living itself is a more satisfying experience than watching television. Which again suggests that the dividing issue is that of emotional stability, not televised cops-and-robbers. . . .

It is perfectly obvious, when you put these facts together, that only one generalization is possible: that acutely disturbed, anxious and unstable people, whether black or white, criminal or not, are watching more TV, and more TV good-vs.-evil plays, as an escape from the misery of their lives. That is a "link" if you like—but it's not a "causal" link. TV isn't *creating* criminals; criminals, along with the wider unstable population, are *using* TV for their own psychological purposes.

The second "link" is the deranged person who sees a violent act on the air and copies it. And this, to some TV "violence" researchers, along with the most ignorant of the censorious groups, "proves" that TV "causes" crime. Does it? We certainly know that from time to time some sick being sees depictions of crimes in the news, the movies and on TV, and then reenacts them. We know that a scattering of disturbed, often politically alienated people, have imitated kidnappings, bombings, skyjackings and terrorist acts reported in the news. We know that a deranged 15-year-old girl led a gang rape of a 9-year-old girl with a bottle, after seeing a similar scene in an NBC film. We know that when a report of suicide is covered on the front page of the newspapers, a rash of suicides—violence directed at *self*—occurs. This kind of thing happens. It will happen again. People do walk among us who can blow sky high at any moment. But they are statistically rare, and the diverse media of communication are not the "cause" of their dangerous psychic instability. Libraries full of studies of the genesis of crime all over the world attest to the fact that the roots of such psychic instability lie deeply buried in their past.

The plain fact is that TV films, like news or movies, cannot turn otherwise normal people or children into predators or self-destroyers overnight, let alone in ten minutes or two seconds. What's more, the "violence" researchers know this perfectly well. They *claim* that the reason they don't set up experiments to study TV's direct capacity to make people commit crimes is that such experiments would be unethical. That, they say, is why they are obliged to study the alleged substitute, "aggression." But this is plain poppycock.

For many years now, "violence" researchers have been calmly playing miles of "violent" film to hundreds, possibly thousands, of adults and children, and never has one violent crime been committed by a soul, adult or child, after "exposure" to these allegedly dangerous "stimuli." *What's more, the TV researchers never expected this to happen. That is the secret premise of all their studies. TV researchers know perfectly well that in the real world TV "violence" just simply does not do what they charge it with doing.*

Since, for years, no one bothered to pay the slightest attention to researchers as they warned us against what we all *knew* to be untrue, they have invented a mysterious explanation that we cannot check simply by looking around us. They've come up with the scary concept of "cumulative" effects—i.e., that we are all sitting around, year after year, subconsciously storing up violent "stimuli" that are gradually making us "insensitive" to crime and can culminate by "causing" even *normal* people to act criminally. And, of course, they've already come up with studies "proving" a growing insensitivity.

Well, I can't read the subconscious processes of [over] 200,000,000 people. But I can read ratings, I can read sales figures, I can read salary lists and profit reports. And they tell me a strangely different story about possible "cumulative" effects.

What they tell me is this: that the success of the cops-and-robbers shows, like that of all the good-vs.-evil shows on the air, is exclusively a function of the *continuing heroes*. It is the heroes, the pure-hearted men with the dedicated, courageous, indomitable characters, who generate the ratings; whom the people, old and young, tune in faithfully to see every week; and to whom they are loyal year after year.

By contrast, it is not the discontinuous villains who pull in the ratings. These are not the drawing cards, nor do they command the high salaries. They are eminently forgettable props whose sole function is to serve as foils for the heroic virtues.

It is precisely because the heroes are absolutely reliable emotional magnets that the networks schedule so many heroic series. Network TV's economic existence, and an enormous number of its technical calculations, are totally based on the certain, *proved* knowledge that the overwhelming majority of the U.S. public and its kids is fixated on the simple, continuous vision of good, just men. To a striking degree, network TV's profits flourish in the loam of hero worship.

To ignore this *proved* evidence that the overwhelming majority of viewers identify emotionally with the good, and have so identified "cumulatively" for decades—while concocting unprovable scare stories about the collective unconscious and its alleged "cumulative" absorption of evil—is about as intellectually nasty a phenomenon as I know. If, indeed, the "cumulative" watching of evil is turning us all, gradually, into depraved beings, then the "cumulative" watching of good must be turning us all, gradually, into saints! You cannot have one without the other. That is, unless you are prepared to demonstrate that evil is something like cholesterol—something that slowly accumulates and clogs the system while good is something like spinach, easily digested and quickly excreted.

This scare story about "cumulative" effects in normal people is all that stands between the "violence" researchers and a good, gusty laugh from the American public, that would blow them all away into the dustbin where they belong—the archaic dustbin from which censors of the entertainment of "the people" have always sprung. Our contemporary censors are not one whit more rational than their predecessors throughout the ages. Just inconceivably more devious.

NEIL HICKEY EDITH EFRON

Our Greatest Natural Resource—Our Children

8/23/58

At any given moment the typical American child will always have spent more of his or her lifetime watching television than being in a classroom. The average preschool child watches television almost thirty-three hours a week; for school age children under twelve the figure is more than twenty-nine hours. Over the past twenty-three years, the time children under 12 spend in front of the TV screen has increased by more than a full hour per day; present figures are double those for time spent listening to radio before television was available. Children under five watch television an average of 23.5 hours a week.

Approximately half of the more than 2300 experiments and surveys since the mid-1960s about television relative to behavior have been conducted with children and adolescents. This sizable number of studies is an indicator of society's concern about the potential vulnerability of children to actions portrayed on television programs. Neil Hickey and Edith Efron summarize some of the findings concerning television's effects on children.

For some children under some conditions, some television is harmful. For other children under the same conditions, or for the same children under other conditions, it may be beneficial. For most children, under most conditions, most television is probably neither particularly harmful nor particularly beneficial.

That famous quotation from the 1961 study by Schramm, Lyle and Parker (*Television in the Lives of Our Children*) encapsulates all that we know—some say all that we will ever know—about the effects of television upon children.

Excerpts have been taken from this essay, which first appeared November 29, 1969.

And what, indeed, does it tell us?

Very little, obviously. Human beings, including children, are simply too complex, and the influences upon them too diverse, to allow any more precise conclusions about how a single factor in our lives—in this case television—alters our thinking and our behavior.

"Learning theory" . . . is in a seriously primitive state. Dr. Eleanor Maccoby [a noted psychologist at Stanford University] has stated "We are nowhere near figuring out how to explore these learning issues yet. We hardly even know what questions to ask. I'm not sure we would even have the technical means to answer the right questions, once we figure out what they are."

All of which is not to say that we know *nothing* about television in relation to children. A tiny residue of certain knowledge settles at the bottom of the great murky vat which contains all the studies, experiments, polls, graphs, essays and sudden hunches about children vis-à-vis the little box called television. For example:

- At about the age of 2, a child takes his first serious look at the home TV set. By the time he's 3 he has some favorite programs, knows how to ask for them, and is spending about an hour a day watching them. Around the time he leaves grade school, he is watching more than four hours a day.
- A child's earliest preferences are, predictably, for the animated cartoon shows with their fast action and broad comedy; for puppets, live animals, live story-telling and singalongs. Surprising, quickly, however, the child develops a taste for so-called "adult" programs, and even in early grade-school years he is viewing many more adult programs than children's programs—[largely], of course, because there are a lot more of them available to him.
- The most potent single influence upon what a child watches on television is what his parents watch. The children of highly educated parents watch television less than other children, just as their parents use television less frequently than parents with modest educations. In homes where parents take the trouble to offer attractive alternatives to TV, the children watch less TV.
- In early grade school, [however,] brighter children tend to do *more* TV watching—just as they do *more* of everything else, including reading, movie going, radio listening, the playing of musical instruments, and so forth. But by the time the intelligent child is in

the 10–13 age bracket, a major shift in habit occurs: he departs the ranks of heavy viewers and devotes more of himself to other kinds of activities. Less intelligent children remain enthusiastic viewers for longer.

▪ A child who watches "too much" television usually is suffering some emotional distress which is causing him to retreat into TV watching. It's not that he's fascinated with the programs. He's unhappy—consciously or not—with his home life, his school life, or his relations with his friends.

▪ The quality of most network TV designed specifically for children is limited by the networks' competitive desire to attract maximum audiences for advertisers—usually the makers of toys and breakfast foods.

Such truths, scarce though they may be, can lead perceptive and concerned parents to some conclusions of their own about how television can best relate to their family life. For example, many child experts have pointed out that parents who tune in spontaneously to TV's discussion programs, concerts, documentaries and drama specials invariably induce similar tastes and appetites in their children—especially when the program becomes a jumping-off point for a simple discussion at home of what it all meant.

For example, a family watching a TV version of *Death of a Salesman* might be led to ask their children how they felt about Willie Loman's kind of traveling life, whether they thought the two sons acted properly toward their parents, and if the mother reminded them of their own.

In such ways, tiny ideational seeds are planted in the child's mind that will grow blossoms later on. At certain ages, children benefit from such small probes and questions which pique them. Answers will come aplenty in time. The prior problem, however, is: What are the right questions? . . .

"There's a socialization process that goes on," says Dr. Edward L. Palmer, research director of the Children's Television Workshop. "Children come to like what their parents impart value to. In subtle ways, parents wield great influence on what their children watch."

Example is by far the best persuader. It is hard, claims [Professor Wilbur] Schramm, to make a river rise above its source. If public affairs, ethics, science, nature and other such topics are not discussed in the home, "is the child easily convinced that they are important enough to view on television?"

This crucial influence of parents and their life styles upon offspring's habits—including TV-usage patterns—can scarcely be overestimated. . . . Insensitive parents, rather than attracting their children into real-life pursuits, can drive them into TV watching as a refuge. Dr. Lawrence Zelic Freedman, of the Center of Advanced Study in the Behavioral Sciences, has written: "When televiewing is, in fact, excessive . . . it is reasonable to assume that the behavior is symptomatic of intolerable stress in [the child's] environment—whether conflicts in the home, frustrations at school, or among his peers—or of brewing anxiety or emotional instability within him."

Schramm puts it a slightly different way: no child is likely to be harmed very much by television if he has warm and secure social relationships and has no serious psychological troubles. . . .

Most children in their early years benefit intellectually from television—in vocabulary-building, in absorbing a general set of cultural values, in stocking their minds with concepts and facts which otherwise they wouldn't have learned that early. "I suspect that TV informs and instructs in its own way as much as colleges do," says Dr. Palmer. "TV has a greater educational influence than all the formal establishments devoted to education. *So for a parent to say, 'I don't let my child watch television' is to relegate him to cultural deprivation."*

Palmer surmises that TV "just must have a lot to do" with a child's acquisition of simple, basic knowledge about his country and his world; the fact that there are such things as Presidents and policemen and soldiers and that they perform certain functions. As children approach adolescence, however, the brighter ones decide spontaneously that TV has taught them all it can, and turn to books, magazines, records, movies and social activities. The less bright children tend to remain heavy users of TV.

Part of this decline in usage by brighter children seems attributable to the high content of fantasy—instead of reality—in children's TV. The more imaginative child, as he grows older, is hungrier for information than for pure entertainment. Child psychologists have suggested that a medium so potent in the transmission of information—about nature, science, ethics—is derelict when it opts instead for the wispy, fragile world of fantasy, whether live or animated. . . .

In addition, it is a fact that most adults—including television programmers—chronically underestimate how much a child can absorb and understand. One psychologist told us that he believed *any* principle could be taught to *any* child, as long as it was translated into terms familiar to the child.

Says Dr. [Leon] Eisenberg [chief of psychiatry at Massachusetts General Hospital]: "Children often are simply not treated seriously enough. I don't mean that first-graders should be reading *War and Peace*. But some of the truths about life contained in *War and Peace* certainly *can* be taught to children."

Children's programs are afraid to talk about death, [notes] Eisenberg, but many children already have been privy to the deaths of relatives and friends. "They'll have confused ideas [about it] unless we bring some clarity to the subject," he says.

But all such altruistic concerns are simply not the principal preoccupation—nor can they be—of TV programmers in the American system of commercial television: the networking structure which places the advertiser's interests first and the audience's second. "What has held back children's television . . . is the commercial interests of the broadcasters," says Dr. Gerald Lesser, Bigelow professor of education and developmental psychology at Harvard University's Graduate School of Education.

"I have faith in kids. I'm not saying that the programs produced for children have terrible, harmful consequences. But it's meaningless junk that can be put on for little expense and makes a lot of money. The quality of most of it is abysmally bad. Not enough thought has gone into it. Commercial exploitation has produced an endless, grubby bag of cartoons."

Lesser and a number of other psychologists we talked to, lament this fixation by children's programmers with "winning the ratings battle." As long ago as 1961, Schramm and his colleagues were concerned about it, and all the same factors are still operative today:

> We sympathize with television broadcasters for the competitive pressure of the sponsor system. . . . Because of this competition, the networks also are forced to be tough-minded about program ratings—for example, even to discard some lower-rating and higher-quality programs because they influence the rating of programs next to them. It is necessary to maximize the drawing power of the schedule at the cost of experimentation with "quality." This undoubtedly represents a severe problem to commercial

broadcasters. We consider that it also represented a shortsighted attitude which may produce immediate profits, but will ultimately result in harm to both sponsor and broadcaster.

Occasional specials sprinkled into the children's TV schedule mitigate this condition somewhat, but not sufficiently to satisfy most child experts, who feel that the networks produce quality specials almost against their better judgment and only to keep the critics at bay.

"Children's television gets by on good intentions," Lesser says. "They'll frequently take a classic children's book and destroy it. But those programs are rarely subjected to critical analysis in the press, and the networks automatically get a high mark just for effort. But if we ever get beyond this stage of applauding them for merely being well-intentioned, then we can make progress."

He thinks that television has never truly captured the imaginations of children, nor moved them, as much as a handful of authors—Lewis Carroll, E. B. White and illustrator Maurice Sendak, among others—whose special genius has been in touching the minds of children. And that's due partly to the fact that writing TV programs for children has never been the highly prestigious undertaking that would attract the best creative minds.

But what *should* children's television be? That is the pertinent question since (1) children watch so much television and (2) about two-thirds of intellectual development occurs before a child even starts his formal education (according to University of Chicago psychologist Benjamin Bloom).

What kinds of programs *would* satisfy the social scientists and psychologists and educators who are unhappy about the current state of "kidvid" in the United States? We asked that question of a dozen or more specialists and discovered a surprising consistency in their recommendations.

Principally, they favor "reality" as opposed to "fantasy"—stories and essays and mini-documentaries about the real world, meticulously produced with young people in mind. Eisenberg, for example, would like to see programs with "role models" for children to pattern themselves after. "Let them see what doctors do, and what astronauts, writers and poets do. That way they can form career ambitions."

Nobody says that slapstick should be eliminated from children's TV schedules. In small doses, it's a pleasing and helpful satire of all the silliness that goes on in the adult world, and children understand it as such. Similarly, children are quick to perceive the essential foolishness of an adult who is "talking down" to them in patronizing fashion.

But television's chief task ought to be to create a variety of options, a "cafeteria" (in the words of one psychologist) of program types so that children would have at least the *chance* of browsing among reasonable alternatives and picking the best. "Right now, we have no decent range of options," says Dr. Lesser. "There are a few good programs like [*Mister Rogers*] and *Captain Kangaroo,* and after that it's mostly cartoons and things like *Romper Room* and *Bozo the Clown,* which are purely exploitive."

Dr. Sheldon White, professor of psychology at Harvard's Graduate School of Education, says it would be most beneficial to "put before children organized essays on the life around them," with special attention to the needs of children who prefer more serious TV fare. Networks should give at least as much thought, he believes, to what will be good for the children as to what will be good for the ratings. "They have found out that fast slapstick will draw the maximum audiences. Maybe all attempts to break the mold will meet with defeat."

The value of the medium to children is to show them places and events they otherwise wouldn't see, since children, obviously, don't have the chance to get around very much. *The ultimate accomplishment—according to TV Guide's sampling of experts—is to catch the child's imagination by showing him the world, what its possibilities are, how people get along in it, how they interract with each other, and what his place in it might be.* This can be done either through fiction or fact.

TV can also provide the child with information of "folk heroes"—such as Thomas Jefferson, Charles Lindbergh, Daniel Webster, Jonas Salk, Mark Twain, the astronauts, among thousands of others—whose achievements might spur the child to study these lives further, and perhaps even say to himself, "Maybe *I* could do something like that." At the moment such a question forms itself in the mind of a child, television has performed a true and lasting service to the nation's health and future.

Such goals require a cadre of creative people in the ranks of TV programmers—writers, producers and directors, as well as sociologists and psychologists—which has not materialized thus far in the life of television in America: creators in sufficient numbers and of sufficient dedication to employ the medium of television to its highest potential in speaking to children. . . .

ARTHUR SCHLESINGER, JR.

Politics and Television

Television has brought about the most radical change in political communication in the history of the United States, according to Robert MacNeil, news co-anchorman for PBS: "No other medium has brought the idea of an informed electorate so close to reality, yet poses so serious a threat of reducing our politics to triviality."

Arthur Schlesinger, Jr., Pulitzer Prize-winning historian, appraised the effects of television on American politics for *TV Guide* in 1966. Since then he has added new thoughts on the political influence of television in the form of an addendum and has updated his earlier article through correspondence with the editor.

The time has come for a preliminary assessment of the impact of television on our politics. More and more Americans, it appears, are forming their impression of the world on the basis of the things they see on the [television] screen. . . . This widening influence of television over American life raises the question how TV is affecting the basic character of our political system and whether it is strengthening or weakening the workings of our democracy.

Some observers, for example, claim that television is producing a more alert and better-informed electorate; others that it is reducing our politics to a mixture of high-pressure salesmanship and beauty contests. The assessment is bound to be preliminary because the evidence is inadequate, contradictory and inconclusive. . . .

Television touches politics in a number of ways. For purposes of convenience, one may perhaps distinguish four types of coverage: 1. news programs, 2. pseudo-news programs, 3. interpretation and 4. party programs. It may be well to discuss each category and then attempt a general appraisal.

This essay first appeared October 22, 1966.

News. Probably the greatest influence in shaping political judgment is still the reality of events themselves. A depression, a war, a debate over national policy, constitutional rights protected or denied, economic securities enlarged or imperiled, bills passed or defeated: Such facts remain the great determinants of political opinion. And it is in communicating these facts that television has had its most impressive success.

A notable example was the coverage of the hearings on Vietnam before the Senate Foreign Relations Committee. I have no doubt that future historians will conclude that these hearings opened a new phase in the Vietnam debate. Before the hearings, most people had suppressed any disquietude they may have felt over the deepening national involvement in Vietnam on the assumption that the President had more information and no doubt knew best. But the hearings had the clear effect, for better or worse, of legitimatizing dissent. If eminent generals, diplomats and senators were unhappy about our actions in Vietnam, then the ordinary citizen felt free to indulge in his own doubts. And the hearings not only opened up debate over Vietnam; they also ended the taboo which had so long prevented discussion of American relations with Communist China. Would these hearings have had the same effect had they not been on television? I think plainly not—and all the more credit therefore to the NBC network which carried them in full.

Television, through the vivid reporting of actual events, can thus incite new thoughts and emotions in the electorate. It also has the effect in many cases of heightening the sense of popular participation in public matters: Thus the McCarthy-Army hearings undoubtedly made many viewers feel, as they had not before, that the Wisconsin Senator was a threat not just to other people but to themselves. When sustained over a long time, this increased sense of popular participation can alter somewhat the workings of political institutions. It seems already, for example, to have reshaped so basic a device in our politics as the Presidential nominating convention.

For most of our history, the convention was a relatively closed powwow for professional politicians, who got chummily together, discussed their candidates, made their deals and presented the results to a passive public. People might have exclaimed, "Who is James K. Polk?" when they heard (via telegraph) the outcome of the

Democratic Convention of 1884; but they did not feel indignant over the fact that the name of the nominee meant so little to them.

Television has changed all that. The dark-horse candidate, emerging unknown out of smoke-filled rooms for nomination on the 46th ballot, is probably a thing of the past. The [TV] screen has made the public an active partner. The feedback is too quick and intense to encourage any convention to risk ditching the favorite of the national audience in favor of a crony of the party professionals. In addition, television has had the happy effect of making conventions shorter. It is safe to assume that the nation will never again have to endure 103 ballots, as it did during the Democratic Convention of 1924.

Conventions, of course, with their inherent drama and suspense, are particularly well adapted to the inquisitive camera. But even television's day-by-day reporting of politics has undoubtedly given the electorate a larger knowledge of public personalities and a greater acquaintance with public issues. News coverage, I think, represents television's best contribution to democratic responsibility.

Pseudo-News. By "pseudo-news"—a subclassification of Daniel Boorstin's general category of "pseudo-event"—I mean the creation of news on the initiative of the medium. Perhaps the term is unnecessarily invidious; for often the news thus elicited is entirely legitimate. Lawrence Spivak's *Meet the Press* and its various imitators, for example, have greatly advanced public enlightenment through the years by their interrogations of national figures. . . .

My feeling is that organized shows in a press-conference format serve a useful purpose but that television interviews designed to lure or trap people into sensational statements they would not otherwise make can be dispensed with. It is necessary to add, though, that television did not invent this technique; it is another bad habit it picked up from the press.

Interpretation. Editorialization on television has taken the form of thoughtful personal comment (Howard K. Smith, Eric Sevareid) or of editorials by local stations. Neither form has thus far had very striking results. I do not know whether television has an inhibiting effect on comment; but certainly no television commentator has spoken with the pungency or authority of Elmer Davis on radio, and men like Smith and Sevareid often look more constrained on the screen than they used to sound over the loudspeaker.

In the past, networks have attempted panel discussions. This is still done a good deal locally and on [public] television. Unquestionably these programs have improved the level of political discussion, in part because they permit the suggestion of subtleties and complexities in public problems. But, possibly for this reason, such programs do not seem to have been pursued very diligently by the networks.

What television has done most successfully in the field of interpretation is the analytical documentary—the kind of thing that [Edward] Murrow and [Fred] Friendly used to do for CBS, the *NBC White Papers,* the Bell & Howell shows. At their best, such programs have dealt with problems at a reasonable level of complexity and have been a highly effective form of public education.

Party Programs. By this I mean time purchased by political parties and leaders, or otherwise made available to them. This, I would say, has been the area of television's most conspicuous failure; and the trouble here begins with the nature of the medium itself. For the effect of television has been to cheapen political discourse, steadily reducing its length, its substance and its rationality.

[Seventy-five] years ago an audience which traveled many miles to hear William Jennings Bryan or Robert M. La Follette hold forth on railroad regulation or tariff would have felt cheated if the oration lasted less than a couple of hours. The coming of radio set in motion the shrinkage of the political speech, first to 45 minutes, then to half an hour. Then came television. I can recall the insistence of the TV men in Adlai Stevenson's headquarters in 1956 that half an hour was far too long; unless it were a national crisis, 15 minutes, they said, represented the outer limit of the attention span of an American audience.

Now the 15-minute speech is itself almost a thing of the past. The most sinister statistic in political telecasting is the one which records the ominous rise of the spot announcement. [Most] of the money spent by candidates on television in recent general elections has gone for spots; the proportion of funds invested in program time has been steadily declining.

This development can only have the worst possible effect in

degrading the level and character of our political discourse. If it continues, the result will be the vulgarization of issues, the exaltation of the immediately ingratiating personality and, in general, an orgy of electronic demagoguery. You cannot merchandise political candidates like soap and hope to preserve a rational democracy.

While this drift to spot announcements is in great part the preference of the candidates themselves, the industry cannot be held wholly guiltless, for it would much rather sell spots than program time. Both the candidates and the industry, however, prefer to blame the condition on the audience, which, both claim, will simply not sit still for thoughtful disquisitions on public policy. No doubt a large part of the mass audience could not care less about an intelligent discussion of issues. But there remain a substantial number of viewers, even if less than a majority, who do care. Does not television have an obligation to this important minority, too, as well as to the service of democracy in general?

The ultimate answer to this question lies in the movement which must some day come toward the diversification of the viewing public; UHF and pay-TV will no doubt make it easier for the medium to reach specialized audiences. In the meantime, one wonders whether more free time should not be made available to candidates, especially in Presidential elections. If democracy depends on rational communication, if television is now the dominant communications medium and if television licenses are granted, according to the Communications Act with a view to the "public interest, convenience and necessity," then it would seem that one of the richest industries in the country might make systematic provision for free time for public debate, at least during Presidential elections.

I recognize that informally the industry has done a considerable amount of this. But I wonder whether it is doing enough to discharge the obligations which come with its highly profitable licenses. Is it not really pretty important to give the electorate a chance to hear a man who wants to be President, even if this outrages people who would prefer to see *The Beverly Hillbillies*? In addition to lowering the level of the party debate, television may give an initial advantage to the poised, photogenic, otherdirected, manipulable candidate.

The rush of professional actors into politics is an obvious consequence of the television age. One shudders a little to think what would have happened, for example, to the Adamses or Jackson or Lincoln if television had existed in the early years of the republic. On the other hand, television is a relatively unsparing medium; it consumes material voraciously, in politics as well as in comedy and drama; and while it may lend itself to slick first impressions, it probably is not hospitable to sustained phoniness and fakery. In the long run, I think, genuine qualities—intelligence, integrity, humor, firmness of purpose—will win out over calculated effects. The Kennedy-Nixon debates of 1960 was a case in point.

Addendum

The Balance Sheet. Where do we end up? It seems clear that recent changes in the means of communication—above all, the rise of television and of public opinion polls—have hastened the decay of the traditional political structure. For a century, a series of institutions—the political machine, the trade union, the farm organization, the ethnic federation—have mediated between the politician and the voter, passing back and forth between them and representing each to the other. But, with the advent of television, the voter increasingly bases his judgment not on what his party boss or labor or farm or ethnic leader tells him but on what Walter Cronkite or [John Chancellor] shows him.

One result has been to sap the strength of the traditional mediating institutions and to begin the liquidation of the traditional brokers of American politics. Another has been to increase the sense of individual powerlessness, since the broker can no longer serve as the voter's channel to government. The citizen can't argue with the image on the TV screen, and all he has is the vague hope that he might some week be selected to register his views with George Gallup or Louis Harris. The rise of television will soon leave politicians to stand face to face with a diffused, frustrated and irritable public opinion. This is bound to have significant consequences for the political process.

Beyond all this, I have no doubt that Mr. [Marshall] McLuhan is right in contending that the electronic revolution will affect our modes of perceiving experience in ways and with consequences that we can at this time only dimly foresee.

MICHAEL RYAN

View from the Losing Side

Television coverage of national political campaigns is extensive and has become big business. In 1980, each network expects to spend $30 to $35 million on the Presidential campaign; the national conventions were expected to cost the networks, together, about $40 million. Theodore White, chronicler of Presidential campaigns in his series of books, *The Making of the President,* has said: "our thinking is so strongly shaped by television it terrifies me."

Two unsuccessful Presidential candidates, Arizona Senator Barry Goldwater (who lost to Lyndon Johnson in 1964) and South Dakota Senator George McGovern (who lost to Richard Nixon in 1972) are interviewed by Michael Ryan about the impact of television on the national nominating conventions and on the voter's perceptions of the Presidential candidates and their campaigns.

RYAN: What would you say was the effect that television had on your campaigns?

MCGOVERN: I thought television was essential to my winning the nomination in 1972. I was a comparatively unknown candidate. First, I had to establish a grass-roots organization. Once that was in place, then it became important for the voters to know who I was. That was done through a combination of public-service television—when I was interviewed on the *Today* show, *Issues and Answers, Face the Nation* and so on—plus paid television human-interest spots. I think the combination was rather effective.

Where I think television did us in was in the general election, where I was exposed to television under rather unflattering circumstances. I don't think that there was any plot or anything of that

This essay first appeared June 12, 1976.

sort. But I would be out on the hustings somewhere with my hair blowing in the wind—what little hair I have—and there'd be a bad lighting situation at maybe 10 o'clock at night, with the cameras off at a 45-degree angle from me and ten feet below me, and I'd be trying to hammer home some point. What came across to the viewer, I think, was a picture of some kind of a desperate, frantic candidate, out there trying to awaken the nation to something it didn't want to be awakened to.

Nixon was much wiser in the way he used television. He was seldom exposed except under ideal lighting conditions. He was calm, had on a clean shirt, fresh shave, and was shown responding to two or three thoughtful questions. The contrast was pathetic, and devastating to me.

GOLDWATER: My situation was different from George's. I was very well known in the party. Getting the nomination was never any worry, so television didn't play any really big part. I was up against an incumbent, though, and if I had been elected I would have been the third President in about two and a half years.

In television, I don't think there was any organized effort to get me; there wasn't any organized effort to help me, either. For example, I'm a gun collector. I make guns. But I was pictured as a dangerous one to have his finger near the red button. I remember one television show opened up with the door knocker on my apartment, which is an old brass six-shooter. At another interview, in my home in Phoenix, in my library—which is probably the biggest private library on Arizona and Northern Mexico in existence—I had one book titled *The Six-Gun.* That was the only book they centered on in the whole place.

RYAN: Would you agree that the American people get most of their ideas of a President's personality and effectiveness from his television appearances?

GOLDWATER: I would agree with that. When the President wants to make a point, I don't care who the President is, he goes on national television; you get a lot of reaction to that. If he just makes a decision at the White House and it's reported, the reaction is less than mediocre.

RYAN: Does television make the incumbent unbeatable?

GOLDWATER: He can do himself a lot of good. I don't like to

rehearse, but if you go over your cue cards three or four times, and you have people who know lighting, who know camera angles, you've got a decided advantage.

MCGOVERN: I'd agree with that. I think television is a great tool in the hands of an incumbent. The White House is just an enormous advantage. There's an aura of glory and grandeur about it and the television camera can pick that up. The big seal and the Oval Room—these are very impressive to a lot of Americans. They don't want the Presidency assailed by anybody.

RYAN: Both of you ran campaigns with a very strong emphasis on issues. Can TV adequately convey issues?

GOLDWATER: Well, if it were up to what the candidate himself says, and not what the interpretation by the commentators says, I would say yes, that the candidate could have a very decided effect. But when you have a commentator or two on each network or each radio station, immediately after you have said what you wanted to say, telling the public what you *really* said, I think they may destroy a lot of the good that you might do.

MCGOVERN: Let me register one beef from my own campaign. There were times when we would have a great rally where local leaders would tell us, "This is the biggest crowd we've ever seen at Cleveland Airport!" Or: "This is the biggest crowd we've ever had at Post Office Square in Boston!" I would turn on the television set later to see the enormous throng, and, well, there *would* be a 15-second spot of me addressing this crowd. Then, under some kind of curious interpretation of the equal-time rule, since Nixon was not campaigning, they would pick up some guy along the fence who would say, "I think McGovern stinks."

And this would be the way the program would end—or "McGovern said this, but a disgruntled former Democrat interviewed by our roving reporter said this." And then they had some jerk get up and say that I was too radical for him or that I couldn't make up my mind on the issues. What the viewer was left with was a final negative image. It happened repeatedly during the campaign.

GOLDWATER: Those are the little things that can happen when a television reporter is not friendly with your views. I remember in Memphis, I think, we had the biggest turnout they'd ever had in history, and the television reporter said it was a "moderate-sized crowd." I think there were 225,000. I had the same thing in Atlanta, and just as George said, they'd wander around until they found somebody who said, "That Goldwater's an S.O.B." I once said that if I believed all I heard on television and radio that was said about me, I would have voted against the S.O.B. myself.

RYAN: Senator McGovern, it was said that you made poor use of television at the 1972 convention.

MCGOVERN: That's a fair criticism. It was an unstructured and uncontrolled convention situation. It's ridiculous to have the nominee give his acceptance speech at 3 o'clock in the morning. The trouble is that we had been the outsiders and challengers so long that when we actually won the nomination, we weren't prepared for victory. I should have simply got hold of [then chairman of the Democratic National Committee] Larry O'Brien and said, "Look, I want that acceptance speech on the air no later than 10 o'clock; that's it."

RYAN: Has TV changed conventions?

GOLDWATER: Oh Lord, yes. You know the tube's always up there looking. I guess 1952 was the first big year of television, but it's at the point now where everybody is absolutely perfect. They're in their seats; you rarely see anybody drunk. You might see some people sleeping, which you do, and that might be the effect of drink, but today conventions are very tame affairs. Before, you might have had an argument, there might be a fist fight, always obviously people drinking, having a good time. Today, it's serious business.

MCGOVERN: Going back to my criticism of our own timing of the acceptance speech: outside of that, while it is fair to say that we showed a lot of things on prime time that perhaps aroused some anxieties, frankly that '72 Democratic convention was an honest, straightforward expression of what people were thinking. I think some of that came across.

RYAN: Does the convention work more smoothly because television is there?

GOLDWATER: I think so. You now have the advantage that you didn't have a few years ago of a highly portable camera. This lets you get around to caucuses where you couldn't get before. It lets you look in sometimes on the meetings that are being held, talking about

Vice Presidential candidates, talking about this or that. I'd just as soon stay home and watch the convention as be there.

MCGOVERN: The truth of the matter is, you sometimes have to turn on a television set to find out what the hell is going on. With eight or ten trained reporters covering every aspect of not only the convention hall but the key headquarters of the various candidates, they're feeding into that control room more coverage to the television viewer than any one of the delegates is going to get sitting there on the floor. They've got those cameras in the key hotels where the major candidates are, and they're following various activities that you can't see from the convention floor. I found repeatedly at conventions that when I really wanted to get an update on exactly where we were at, I had to go to my room and turn on the television set.

RYAN: Do you find the quality of broadcast journalism as good as print?

GOLDWATER: That's a very interesting question. After my campaign, I asked men I knew, like Harry Reasoner, Walter Cronkite and others, and they made a very good answer. They said, "Look, no matter how we may feel about you, whether we like you or don't like you, we can't hide that fact from our eyes or our tone of voice." In that effect, I think they do show discrimination, but I think it's natural. I think they try to do the best job. If I have any criticism of average coverage, it's that there are not enough men who've ever been in the political game, who know what they're talking about. They don't know what a candidate goes through 18 hours a day. I made 16 speeches one day—that was my record—from Lubbock, Texas, to the Gulf of Mexico. You're so tired, you even get to the point where you wonder, "Good Lord, what did I just say?"

MCGOVERN: That's one of the constant problems in campaigning—the fatigue factor. As I think back on it, I see that most of the mistakes that I made were made when I was tired. I think that's true of most candidates, and that's going to come across more in the visual medium than in the written media.

I'd say this, though: I've seen more bias and personal vendettas from syndicated columnists, who supposedly have a chance to think these things over, than I have from television commentators. I think the television commentators are under the restraint of knowing that they are publicly licensed and that they are supposed to be objective. The syndicated columnists somehow think they have a license to say anything they damn please. Once they have it in for you, even though you may not understand the bias of it, they can make life miserable for you. I've had two or three of them whom I would gladly dump over the nearest cliff if I had the power to do it. . . .

CENSORSHIP AND CONTROL

The desire to limit or alter the content of communications that reach large numbers of people for the so-called benefit of society has, of course, always existed along with society itself. Socrates in *Plato's Republic* argued for censorship: "Then shall we simply allow our children to listen to any stories that anyone happens to make up, and so receive into their minds ideas often the very opposite of those we shall think they ought to have when they grow up?" Censorship has been decried equally as vehemently. When the British Parliament, in 1643, proposed that all books should be licensed by the government, John Milton, in his *Areopagitica,* respectfully and strongly disagreed. He argued that any suppression of books was nothing less than the "execution" of "the breath of reason itself."

In the United States, television is unquestionably the most controlled and highly censored of all the mass media. Television is subject to control by the government: the Congress, the Federal Communications Commission, the Federal Trade Commission, the Anti-Trust Division of the Justice Department, the Food and Drug Administration and, ultimately, the courts. Formal and informal control is also exerted from within over what is shown on television: by individual stations and their staffs, by the National Association of Broadcasters Code Authority, by the Program Practices divisions of the networks, by sponsors, by advertisers and by the individual writers and artists. Finally, pressure groups, audience feedback, ratings and television critics exercise control over programming—not enough in the opinion of some of the critics. The amount of censorship present in the television industry has led Alan Alda of *M*A*S*H* to articulate a warning:

> Now, you may not think that censoring a few jokes infringes on anyone's freedom of speech, but as frivolous as it seems, a joke is an expression of thought. If a joke can be censored today, then a political cartoon can be censored tomorrow and the next day a political speech. It does violence to the Constitution.

The concept that broadcasting ought to be under some control by the government originated with the broadcasters themselves. During the 1920s, when the uncontrolled use of radio frequencies created havoc for broadcasters and listeners alike, the broadcasters appealed to the government for regulation of the use of the frequency spectrum. The result was the passage of the Radio Act of 1927 and the Communications Act of 1934. Incorporated into the acts were several basic concepts which distinguish broadcasting from the other mass media. These concepts have been recognized by the courts as valid justification for some federal regulation of radio and television.

First, when broadcasting was being developed, the number of channels available for stations was limited, whereas anyone theoretically could establish a newspaper, magazine or film company. This being the case, it was felt that broadcast stations should be licensed, partly for fair distribution of channels and partly to protect the public from misbehavior by stations not operating in a totally competitive marketplace. In conjunction with the licensing scheme, broadcasters were excluded from some of the First Amendment guarantees enjoyed by the other media.

This thinking still prevails, even though the times have changed. There are now more television frequencies available through the development of cable and UHF. Radio and television stations now outnumber daily newspapers; indeed, in our present economic system, starting a daily newspaper can often be more expensive than establishing a new television station. Nowadays, opportunities for monopoly or misbehavior are more favorable for newspapers because there are more single-newspaper cities than there are single-station cities. Nevertheless, the Supreme Court has thus far seen no reason to change its mind: "Scarcity is not entirely a thing of the past. . . . While there are substantially more individuals who want to broadcast than there are frequencies to allocate, it is idle to posit an unabridgeable First Amendment right to broadcast comparable to the right of every individual to speak, write or publish."

Second, the existence of broadcasting stations that had full control over a particular frequency posed a potential threat to the First Amendment guarantees to the public's right to hear and know—to have access to information and to be exposed to varying points of view. Thus, reasoned Congress, social power must be used to ensure an uninhibited marketplace of ideas. The Supreme Court agreed, calling the protection of the public's First Amendment rights "paramount" in importance.

Third, broadcasters use public property, the airwaves, and should be subject to special control by representatives of the public—that is, Congress and its regulatory agencies. Although magazines, for example, do need mailing permits to distribute their products, the government does not license them and does not review their performances at periodic intervals. However, in the case of broadcasting, the government not only has the right but also the duty to license and regulate stations in "the public interest, convenience and necessity." In a landmark decision in June 1969, in which the Supreme Court unanimously upheld the Fairness Doctrine (the Fairness Doctrine is discussed on pp. 337–48), it was stated: "A license permits broadcasting, but the licensee has no constitutional right to be the one who holds the license."

Fourth and fifth reasons for government regulation of broadcasting were articulated by another Supreme Court decision, handed down in 1978, involving the question of FCC jurisdiction over the broadcasting of "patently offensive, indecent material presented over the airwaves." The Court concluded that the broadcast media have "established a uniquely pervasive presence in the lives of all Americans." The Court also emphasized that "broadcasting is uniquely accessible to children, even those too young to read." The Court acknowledged broadcasters had some First Amendment rights, but "in the privacy of the home . . . the individual's right to be let alone plainly outweighs the First Amendment rights of an intruder."

The FCC was created by the Communications Act to license the broadcast stations and to police the communications industry. The Supreme Court has suggested that the history of the Communications Act and the activities of the FCC "reflect a continuing search for means to achieve reasonable regulation compatible with the First Amendment rights of the public and the licensee." The Court has referred to "a delicately balanced system of regulation intended to serve the interests of all concerned." From the point of view of the FCC, its job is to ensure "the preservation of a free competitive broadcasting system on the one hand, and the reasonable restriction of that freedom inherent in the public interest standard provided in the Communications Act, on the other."

The courts recognize that this is a difficult position, which the Commission itself has described as "walking a tightrope between saying too much and saying too little." Consequently, the courts, believing that FCC actions are "necessarily dynamic," attempt to enhance the Commission's flexibility by affording "great weight" to its experience. In general, the Commission has been upheld in those few instances when it has limited the activities of broadcasters, but the courts have been reluctant to force the Commission to take restrictive action. For example, when the FCC, instead of adopting rules to require a specific number of children's programs, issued a policy statement urging broadcasters to make "a meaningful effort" to provide adequate programming for children, the court sanctioned the decision. It suggested that the Commission might well have the authority to adopt such rules but "did not act arbitrarily or otherwise abuse its broad discretion" in declining to do so.

The Commission's decision regarding children's television programming is typical of its stance toward the regulation of all television programming. In *Reluctant Regulators: The FCC and the Broadcast Audience,* Barry Cole and Mal Oettinger summarized:

> The commissioners are not eager to stick their necks out on tough problems. Part of this reluctance is understandable; the commissioners prefer to persuade broadcasters to take action in the form of self-regulation rather than to impose rules and regulations. If the commissioners take the latter course, they know they can be overruled by Congress or the courts. Furthermore, commissioners recognize that the [issues are] complex, with valid points on each side, and that reaching a fair compromise is not easy.

When the hour of decision arrives, in most cases, the language upon which the commissioners agree will be open to varying interpretations. The guidelines are certain to be full of loopholes—some placed there intentionally as a result of compromise. This may not be simply pusillanimity on their part; it may be an attempt to give themselves and future commissioners what they consider to be desirable flexibility.

Some remarks made by William Ray, who was the long-time chief of the FCC Complaints & Compliance Division, demonstrate the Commission's method of "walking a tightrope." At a meeting of broadcasters, Ray responded to complaints about FCC statements that all stations were expected to program an unspecified amount of nonentertainment programs: "As long as you are in broadcasting . . . you are going to have some regulation by the government. If you want an industry without regulation, I suggest you open a peanut stand." At another meeting later the same day, Ray heard public complaints about the programming of various local stations. To these people he responded that things would be a good deal worse if the bureaucrats in Washington began to decide what goes on the air.

The government and more specifically the FCC cannot, of course, directly regulate program content. To receive a broadcast license or license renewal, the station makes promises to adhere to certain standards of station operation that the FCC feels are in keeping with the notion that broadcast stations are public trustees of public airwaves. The Commission does have the power to punish a wayward station, through fines, short-term (that is, less than the normal three-year) license renewal or, as a last resort, removal of its license.

For stations who lag behind in fulfilling their responsibilities, the FCC has traditionally used a technique referred to as the raised eyebrow—an oblique way of implying that should improvements not be forthcoming, some action might have to be considered. To accomplish this, the FCC employs policy statements, policy guidelines, speeches by commissioners and meetings between representatives of the FCC and broadcasters. Thus, the FCC reminds broadcasters of their "non-entertainment programming obligations," of the need for "a reasonable proportion of local programs as part of a well-balanced program service" and of the importance of keeping the promises made in the renewal applications.

Hard and fast rules, however, have been avoided by the Commission. There are no fixed percentage requirements for any type of programming. In reviewing the adequacy of the amount of the licensee's nonentertainment and local programming, the FCC makes clear that "we will, of course, limit our inquiry to a determination of its reasonableness." With regard to what stations have promised, the Commission stresses that licensees are not required "to adhere inflexibly in their day-to-day station operation" to promises made in the previous renewal application for "we have long recognized the licensee's discretionary and permissible adjustment of programming and other aspects of station operation to meet changing needs and circumstances." The FCC has yet to take a television license away for a shortage of local or nonentertainment programming or for promise versus performance discrepancies.

As for the number of commercials that may be broadcast, the FCC again has no rules. There are guidelines which, according to former Commission chairman Richard Wiley, "for all practical purposes . . . constitute a rule." The Commission's guidelines are slightly more lenient than those governing commercials in the NAB Code of Good Practices. In the early 1960s, the Commission proposed to adopt as its own rules the NAB limits, but the NAB lobbied Congress and the Commission was told by a 317-47 vote on a resolution in the House of Representatives to avoid passing strict rules limiting the amount of commercials. The matter was dropped.

Congress and more specifically the Communications Subcommittees of the House and Senate oversee the FCC's activities. Although representatives and senators are, of course, sensitive to the desires of their constituents, local broadcasters also have a great deal of influence. It is the local broadcasters who control to a large extent the amount of public exposure members of Congress receive, particularly between elections when broadcasters are not obliged to give equal time to all major political candidates. Thus, the broadcasters usually receive a warm reception in Congressional deliberations and can often influence Congress to discourage the FCC whenever the Commission gets a little too active for the industry's taste. There are times, however, when Congress's attitude toward the broadcast industry is more affected by the constituents than by the broadcasters. When enough concerned citizens complain to their representatives, Congress does react. Often the reaction takes the form of instructing the FCC to "do something" to improve the situation.

In response to a barrage of complaints about children's programming, Rhode Island Senator John Pastore, who was the chairman of the Senate Communications Subcommittee in 1974, told FCC chairman Wiley of a good way to deal with the situation:

> It strikes me that from time to time you could sit down informally with the heads of these networks to review the whole matter as to their responsibility . . . make them recognize they are participants, and they are citizens. Make them recognize their obligations. . . . Without twisting anyone's arm these people should be called from time to time to discuss their responsibility, and if you do not want to do it, I will.

Jawboning between the FCC and the broadcasters is encouraged by Congress, although some feel that Congress is actually passing the buck. Actor Carroll O'Connor (who portrays Archie Bunker) was highly critical of Congressional activities in the controversy about the effects of televised violence: "instead of taking [the] responsibility of going back to their constituents and explaining the way this country should run, and explaining the freedom that we should have, Congressmen find it much easier just to put pressure on the FCC, and the FCC turns around and puts the pressure on the networks."

Pressure for changing program content also comes from sponsors. In the early days of television, one advertiser sponsored an entire show and often was involved in the creation of the program. Theoretically, the sponsor had the right to determine "taste and policy" not "program creativity," but it was not uncommon for sponsors to dictate what appeared on the program. One cigarette company insisted that all heroes and no villains smoke. The Ford Motor Company deleted the New York skyline in order to avoid showing the Chrysler building. The American Gas Association deleted any mention of gas ovens in a *Playhouse 90* version of *Judgment at Nuremberg.* General Mills handed down an edict to the creators of *Tales of the Texas Rangers:*

> There will be no material for or against sharply drawn national or regional controversial issues. There will be nothing slurring any given type of occupation. There will be no ridicule of manners or fashions that may be pecu-

liarly sectional. . . . There will be no material that may give offense either directly or by inference to any organized minority group, lodge or other organization, institution, residents of any state or section of the country, or a commercial organization of any sort. . . .

The Association of National Advertisers defended such practices by noting that the sponsor, who paid for the show, had a right to pass judgment on what his money bought. CBS supported this view: "The advertiser may object to a program or an element thereof, if he believes it is detrimental to his product or good will."

Times have changed: television productions and advertising time are too expensive for advertisers to become involved with a whole program or series—except in rare instances. Now the sponsors' power is limited to choosing the shows in which they wish to place their ads. Today the advertising agency typically receives guidelines from the sponsor, indicating which types of programs are acceptable and which are not, and the agency purchases commercial time accordingly.

Although some types of entertainment programming are unacceptable to some advertisers, they do not commonly refuse to sponsor news shows. Leonard Matthews, president of the American Association of Advertising Agencies, suggested to Association members in 1979 that this too may change. "Until now advertisers—even the biggest—have made remarkably few attempts to influence editorial content in the media, but to expect private companies to go on supporting a medium that is attacking them is like taking up a collection for money among the Christians to buy more lions." *TV/Radio Age* publisher Sol Paul attacked Matthews for his "veiled threat of economic reprisal" and "incitement." Paul warned that "although the First Amendment forbids Government influence over editorial content, it does not interdict an economic boycott by an advertiser. Indeed, there could have been no advertisers' meddling in the time of our Founding Fathers: There was, of course, almost no advertising, and the press received its revenues from readers."

Advertisers are quite naturally very sensitive to the public—the consumers—and public pressure can be very effective as a means of influencing sponsors to withdraw commercials. The Southern Baptist Convention developed a distaste for *Soap* and, according to the Convention, persuaded seven advertisers to abandon their plans to sponsor the show. When the series started on ABC in the fall of 1977, Convention pressure caused, or helped to cause, twenty of ABC's affiliates—most in Southern states—to refuse the series and another fifteen to agree to carry it only on a delayed basis, usually after 11:00 P.M. ABC supposedly lost one million dollars from the experience. The series became successful, but some of its creative people claimed the content was significantly "toned down."

The Parent-Teacher Association compiles an annual list of what are, in its opinion, television's poorest shows. These shows are "selected for a variety of reasons, including offensively portrayed sexuality and violence, stereotyping of women and minorities and general lack of program quality and entertainment." Chosen on the basis of nationwide monitoring by 6000 PTA members, the "winners" (that is, the poorest shows) for the fall of 1979 were *A Man Called Sloane, Best of Saturday Night Live, Vegas, Detective School* and *Charlie's Angels.* The PTA also publishes lists of the "most violent" shows and the "poorest in overall quality" shows, which included *Three's Company, The Ropers, Soap, The Misadventures of Sheriff Lobo* and *The Dukes of Hazzard.* Some recipients of the PTA's "poorest advertisers" label for 1979 were Timex, GTE, Coca-Cola, Seven-Up, Toyota and American Motors. To give advertisers and program producers some positive encouragement, the PTA also lists "distinguished advertisers" and "top quality" shows. In 1979, some "distinguished advertisers" were Hallmark, Polaroid and Quaker Oats; and the "top quality" shows were *Little House on the Prairie, 60 Minutes, The Wonderful World of Disney, Family, The Waltons* and *Eight Is Enough.*

Whether or not pressure applied by the public on the advertisers will, in fact, benefit society is open to question. American Civil Liberties Union executive director Aryeh Neier thinks "it is reprehensible that groups should try to pressure television, through its advertisers, not to deal in controversial material." The *New York Times* responded in an editorial: "What serious alternative is there for those who feel their beliefs are being assaulted, their values mocked? . . . The reality is . . . that the medium responds mainly to the demands of the marketplace. . . . Thus when organizations opposed to violence . . . distribute lists of sponsors of the most objectionable programs, they are behaving in accord with the mores of the medium." The chairman of the ACLU then wrote the *Times,* insisting that although "citizens have a right to pressure advertisers," such pressure has a "pernicious effect" and "represents an attempt by one group of citizens to deny another group of citizens the right to see or hear what they want."

Advertisers are not alone in benefiting from the tender attentions of citizens and pressure groups. The public is encouraged—sometimes even by the broadcasters—to enlighten the networks and the stations as well. A Charlotte, N.C., station owner put editorials on the air urging viewers to send the station letters complaining about programs that "offend your sense of decency and taste." Viewers were told their comments, "re-inforced by others, will be promptly relayed to the networks. . . . Eventually, they must be convinced that Americans want wholesome entertainment not profanity and vile language."

Public activism to affect change in television programming receives endorsement from the FCC. Former FCC commissioner Benjamin Hooks (now executive director of the NAACP) told a public meeting in Chicago: "Black folk raised hell for 35 years and others are just going to have to do the same." Also, the Commission has a hands-off attitude toward most agreements between stations and citizens about program practices. However, the FCC would frown on any agreement in which the licensee officially delegated to any outsider the station's responsibility for its programming or in which the station officially adopted a decision which could not be reversed even if the licensee later believed it was against the public interest.

After a series has appeared on the network affiliates and has been made available to independent stations, local groups can on occasion exercise direct control over programming. Having received complaints about excessive violence, a Los Angeles independent station asked the local PTA to help edit reruns of *Starsky & Hutch,* which had been on the PTA's hit list. The station manager explained: "we're trying to give them an opportunity to do something other than complain." The PTA edited out such scenes as a prostitute's customer pulling up his pants, and the segment's hero being forced to have a heroin injection. Networks do not permit their affiliates to edit network programming. These stations can merely accept or reject the offering in its entirety, or choose to delay the broadcast. The local affiliate who anticipates problems may sometimes precede the program with an announcement concerning the program's content.

Any censorship that occurs on network programming is done by the networks themselves. Geoffrey Cowan states in his book, *See No Evil: The Backstage Battle Over Sex and Violence in Television:*

> With the exception of news and public affairs programming, the networks produce relatively few shows on their own, but they effectively control the essential elements of everything they broadcast: from programming concept to the choice of writers, directors and actors, to the script, and the final print. Having the power to control and distribute programming, the networks, particularly when acting in concert with the NAB, also have the power to censor.

Each network has a Program Practices department which is responsible for the fitness of network entertainment offerings. ABC's Susan Futterman describes the Program Practices people as the "internal consciences" of the networks. She admits her decisions—most of which relate to children's programs—interfere with the creative process, but her concern is television's "responsibility to the public." She feels it is better for the networks to do their own policing: "Change works better out of pressure than regulation."

The networks differ on which programs are suitable and which are not. For example, according to press reports, an animated series, *Speedy Gonzalez,* was turned down by ABC and CBS but accepted by NBC. "Everybody has an opinion," according to Raymond Dewey, who reviews children's programs for NBC's Program Practices department, "and when you're dealing with something as subjective as this [fitness for television], everybody's [opinion] is valid." Paul Bogrow, a Harvard Ph.D. in psychology, supervises the content of children's programs at CBS. He points out that concepts of suitability for children change with the times. The old *Popeye* cartoons which were very popular in the earlier years of television would not be approved by him today. Bogrow states that for today's audience the cartoon would have been not only too violent, but also that Popeye's perpetually helpless girlfriend, Olive, would have been out of keeping with today's perception of women. CBS has a new

Popeye cartoon series in which, according to Bogrow, Olive is a three-dimensional character.

Futterman, Dewey and Bogrow all feel their primary responsibility is to pay particular attention to the depiction of dangerous acts a child might be tempted to imitate, such as gratuitous violence and sexual and racial stereotyping. This concern has led to such actions as lowering the voice pitch of a black female character, making an Indian character more articulate and vetoing a cartoon about a girl who was unable to get along with her friends until she fixed up her hair and dressed like a "southern belle." All three networks try to avoid showing weapons on Saturday-morning children's shows. Futterman, who used to work with the citizen's group, Action for Children's Television, prohibits pie-in-the-face comedy and such scenes as one showing a character push a boulder off a cliff so that it lands on another person. ABC also has "positive goals" for its programs designed for 2-to-16-year-olds, including the need to "present pro-social values from which the child will benefit."

The depiction of sex and violence has caused the most problems and controversy in reviewing network program content. Although there is not very much portrayal of actual sexual activity, Larry Gelbert, who created *M*A*S*H*, points out that the concern over too much sex on television has resulted in "inevitable offshoots—pregnancy, abortion, vasectomy. These areas are out." The networks are particularly careful during the early evening hours. A planned episode of *The Waltons* was cancelled because the script described Mary Ellen's confused reaction to her first menstrual period. Gelbert explains the problem: "Sex is an enormous subject and the act seems to be the least of it." ABC Program Practices vice president Alfred Schneider has deduced that some people object more to sex and others object more to violence. He has summarized the difference: "Intellectuals; sex—yes, violence—no. Fundamentalists; violence—yes, sex—no."

There seems to be a rather curious connection between where people live and their reactions to sex and violence on television. At a 1980 National Association of Television Program Executives session, a Corpus Christi, Texas, station executive stated that 60 per cent of his station's audience was opposed to or disturbed by sex on television. But a Milwaukee delegate acknowledged, "I don't think I get five letters a month" on the subject. When *The Exorcist* was shown (with warnings) in February 1980, station WCCO-TV, Minneapolis, received 7000 complaint calls and KOIN-TV, Portland, Ore., received 4000 calls. The New York station showing the movie received only 70 calls to complain, and half of these complaints were that the film had been edited; and New York is by far the nation's largest television market.

Public concern has led to studies about people's reactions to television portrayals of sex and violence. In 1972, then Surgeon General Steinfeld told Senator Pastore that, "it is clear to me that the causal relationship between televised violence and anti-social behavior is sufficient to warrant appropriate and immediate action." Two years later, the House Appropriations Committee, with the support of its Senate counterpart, instructed the FCC to supply a report by December 31 of that year, "outlining specific positive actions taken by the Commission to protect children from excessive programming of violence and obscenity."

During the fall of 1974, concern over televised sex and violence erupted when NBC broadcast a made-for-TV movie titled *Born Innocent.* The show was aired on a Tuesday evening at 8:17 P.M. With millions of children watching the segment, the heroine (actress Linda Blair), who was serving time in a female reformatory, was pulled from the shower by several other inmates and raped with the wooden handle of a plumber's helper. To make matters worse, NBC had given the show a lot of publicity. One promo referred to the "sensational star of *The Exorcist.* She's a woman in prison. She's fourteen years old. She's learning fast what you have to learn to survive there." In California, four days after the program had been seen on television, a seven-year-old girl and her friend were attacked and raped with a beer bottle by three teen-age girls and one boy. When questioned, one of the teen-agers said they had conceived the idea from watching *Born Innocent.*

Born Innocent and its aftermath greatly intensified the pressure upon the FCC and the networks to do something about limiting sex and violence on television. The result was the Family Viewing hour. After considerable jawboning by FCC chairman Wiley to the networks, it was agreed that by the fall of 1975, network programs aired before 9:00 P.M. Eastern and Pacific Time would be suitable for young children, except in rare instances and in these cases appropriate warnings would be broadcast. The industry also agreed that programs after 9:00 P.M. would not contain gratuitous sex and violence. Further, if programs that were to be broadcast after 9:00 P.M. might be objectionable to large numbers of people, warnings of that fact would be aired at the beginning of the show. After being accepted by the networks, the Family Viewing hour was adopted into the NAB Code. The independent stations later also agreed to the arrangement.

The Catholic Conference attacked the Family Viewing hour as "too permissive." *Variety* called it the "biggest public relations hype since Evel Knieval fell into the Snake River Canyon." Critics of the plan also argued that because family viewing ended at 8:00 P.M. Central and Mountain Time, children in those time zones would be receiving unequal protection; also children in the Central zone typically watch television later than children in the other zones. The critics cited the Nielsen ratings which indicated that even in the Eastern and Pacific regions, about 25 per cent of all children aged 6 to 11 still watch television at 10:00 P.M.

The creative community was incensed by the networks' action. The Writers Guild, the Producers Guild, the Directors Guild and producer Norman Lear took the Family Viewing hour to court. The grounds were that the action of the networks and the FCC constituted a violation of the First Amendment as well as a violation of the Administrative Procedures Act, which requires agencies like the FCC to go through specific public procedures before trying to implement governmental policy. The plaintiffs argued that the Family Viewing hour was really a form of government regulation because Wiley's role, in their opinion, was indispensable to the action. The judge agreed with the plaintiffs. The case was appealed, however, and the federal appeals court suggested the case should have gone to the FCC in the first instance. The case was still in litigation in the spring of 1980, but the Family Viewing hour was still the policy of the NAB Code, the networks and television stations.

The NAB Code of Good Practices (NAB Television Code), according to NAB executive vice president John Summers, "indicates the areas where broadcasters believe ground rules may be needed to best serve their audiences." There are NAB Codes for both television and radio. The approximately 575 television stations which are members in good standing are allowed to display the Code's Seal of Good Practices on the air.

Even though the Code contains program standards, the NAB Code Board does not have the authority to prescreen programs. Normally, stations, advertisers or the networks—who are guaranteed representation on the Board—bring problems to the Board's attention. In early 1969, Senator Pastore persuaded NBC and ABC to go along with the idea of allowing Code representatives to prescreen programs, in return for certain assurances regarding legislation giving broadcasters greater security of their licenses. CBS refused: "Were CBS to share the responsibility for its program decisions with the National Association of Broadcasters, it would only be a matter of time before the government would go to the Code Authority about our performance—initially to inquire, then to urge. This would spell the beginning of the end of our independence." Ironically, two weeks later CBS fired the Smothers Brothers after disputes regarding network censoring of their weekly comedy/variety series and the *New York Times* asked in an editorial: "Will the Real CBS Stand Up?"

One reason the Code is not vigorously enforced is because an active Code Board, which would really restrict broadcasters' activities, might result in court suits alleging restraint of trade. A federal judge recently underscored the difficulty. "The NAB has no constitutional right to set up a network board to censor and regulate American television," because "the First Amendment requirement of diversity in decision-making does not protect such tie-in arrangements." That ruling is under appeal. In another action, the Justice Department has asked the courts to rule that portions of the NAB Code violate the Sherman Antitrust Act and should thus not be used, because they constitute an "unreasonable restraint of trade and commerce." The specific standards being challenged are those limiting the time for commercials. The Justice Department chose these rather than other Code provisions, such as the prohibition on contraceptive advertising, which would prove even more controversial.

The NAB states the purpose of the Code is to "manifest the desire and determination to set professional standards on the public's behalf." The real, practical value of the NAB Code to broadcasters is that the industry is able to argue that it is regulating itself, and there is thus no need for government to step in. Historical analysis of Code amendments since the beginning of broadcasting clearly reveal that the Code is strengthened when expressed concern and complaints from Congress, the FCC, or the public about a particular practice are sufficiently strong to make government intervention a real possibility.

MAX GUNTHER

There Is a Man Who Can Do Something About Commercials

The NAB Television Code prescribes guidelines for advertising. "Advertising messages should be presented in an honest, responsible and tasteful manner." When deciding whether or not to broadcast a commercial, the station should consider "the characteristic of the medium, its home and family audience, and the form and content of the particular presentation." Should there be "good reason to believe it would be objectionable to a substantial and responsible segment of the community," the commercial should not be put on the air.

The Code also specifies how much advertising the stations may broadcast: no more than 9½ minutes during one hour of prime-time programming or on weekend mornings, no more than 12 minutes during programs designed for children, and no more than 16 minutes per hour any other time for network affiliates; for independent stations the limits are the same except the prime-time limit is 14 minutes. Although most stations usually abide by these limits, there are violations. One monitoring study by advertising agency representatives found that in the first 25 weeks of 1979, the networks exceeded the Code by 30 seconds or more in 56 programs and by 10 seconds in 482 other programs. These figures were almost identical to figures gathered for a comparable period in 1978.

Yet the NAB Code remains the major instrument for regulating advertising practices in the television industry. Max Gunther refers to the Television Code Authority as "this little police force" and describes its practical operation.

This essay first appeared March 27, 1971.

An ad agency produces a television commercial touting a spray-on disinfectant for minor cuts and scrapes. The commercial uses a circus clown as pitchman and is obviously aimed at children. Some TV stations hesitate to accept the ad. They note that the product's own label shouts in large type: "KEEP OUT OF REACH OF CHILDREN." The label also warns: "Not for use on eyes, mouth or other delicate membranes. . . . Do not inhale."

Is it right to pitch such a product at children?

The worried stations take the question to their industry's chief arbiter in such matters: the TV Code Authority of the National Association of Broadcasters. The Code Authority studies the commercial, checks with some physicians, concludes the product could indeed be dangerous in the wrong hands and should not be advertised directly to children. The ad agency and the manufacturer grumble a lot, mutter gloomily about censorship and bullying, then finally back down and withdraw the commercial.

A shampoo manufacturer's commercial has been appearing for some time when stations begin to receive letters from irritated viewers. The commercial claims the shampoo "positively controls dandruff." The viewers say it doesn't. Once again the Code Authority is called in for a decision.

The Code Authority asks the manufacturer and its ad agency to produce evidence backing their claim. The evidence doesn't satisfy the Authority's statisticians. Moreover, the Authority notes another objectionable element in the commercial. A hand protruding from a white doctor-type sleeve appears in the action at one point, indirectly implying that the product enjoys some kind of medical endorsement. The Authority feels this violates the spirit of its "men-in-white" rule, which forbids doctors, nurses or actors dressed as such to tout products on TV.

The Authority asks the manufacturer and ad agency to stop by its offices and discuss revisions of the ad. Two months go by. The manufacturer and agency fail to turn up. Finally the Code Authority swings its biggest stick. A memorandum goes out to the three TV networks and to all stations that subscribe to the Code. The memorandum doesn't directly urge the networks and stations to stop accepting the ad. It says merely that, in the Authority's opinion, the ad "constitutes a violation of certain provisions of the Television Code." The commercial rapidly disappears.

The TV Code and its companion, the Radio Code, represent the broadcasting industry's attempt to police itself so that government agencies and consumer groups won't feel called upon to step in. Although there are some who aren't wholly satisfied with the results, the fact is that the TV Code has managed [since 1952] to keep most of what we see on TV from provoking serious public outrage.

The TV Code is a [37-] page pamphlet of rules and policies defining what is and isn't acceptable in commercials, programming and other matter. Its rules are continually reviewed, adjusted and rewritten as changing times dictate, by a TV Code Review Board, which meets at least twice a year, usually more often. The board has nine members: three from the major networks, six from individual stations around the country. The six are appointed by the president of the National Association of Broadcasters, Vincent Wasilewski.

The job of administering the Code day by day—interpreting and enforcing the rules laid down by the Review Board—falls to a full-time staff group called the TV Code Authority. The chief of this little police force is Stockton Helffrich, who performed similar censorship duties in his previous job as director of NBC's Continuity Acceptance Department. Helffrich calls himself a "reluctant censor," but his group wields a substantial amount of power over commercials. NBC, CBS, ABC and roughly two-thirds of all U.S. television stations subscribe to the Code, officially accepting its provisions as a kind of self-imposed law. If they break the law, the ultimate punishment is expulsion from Code membership and the loss of public-relations benefits that membership can bring. . . .

Stations that don't subscribe to the Code, of course, aren't bound to observe it, but in practice they tend to go along with it in a broad and general way.

There are two main reasons. The first is a practical one. National and regional advertisers don't usually want the trouble and expense of producing two sets of commercials, one for Code and the other for non-Code stations. Thus, nonsubscribing stations carry many of the same ads that subscribers carry: commercials made to Code requirements.

The second reason is ordinary prudence. "In general," says Stockton Helffrich, "the Code expresses the current public feelings about things. It should change every year as society changes. We try earnestly to keep it an accurate reflection: no more and no less puritanical or demanding than the American public itself. In most cases, non-Code stations don't *want* to go much beyond the boundaries set by the Code. The boundaries are sensible. To go beyond them could be risky."

"As a matter of fact," says one ad-agency executive, "many people in this business use the Code as a kind of reference manual even though they aren't officially bound by it. I mean non-Code stations, ad agencies, manufacturers. The Code is a pretty good indicator of what would and wouldn't offend the public in a given year. If our agency wants to do something, but we're nervous about it, we check the latest edition of the Code. If the Code says don't, we usually don't."

For example, Code practice forbids advertising of commercial birth-control products on TV. "We know this subject is discussed more freely today than it once was," says Helffrich. "But the Code Board feels that the climate is not quite right yet for such ads to appear on TV. We feel too big a portion of the viewing public would be offended." As far as Helffrich's office knows, non-Code stations appear to buy this reasoning. No one has yet dared air a birth-control commercial.

It's the same with liquor. The Code allows TV advertising of beers and wines, as long as nobody is shown actually drinking. But hard liquors (defined as any form of booze having more than 24 per cent alcohol content by volume) are out. Very few non-Code stations are known ever to have defied this prohibition. One that did—it aired a bargain sale by a liquor-store chain in a Southern city—was promptly buried in mail from irate viewers. "We now realize," a station executive reportedly said later, over a soothing drink, "that the Code decrees what people are going to get used to on TV. They weren't used to seeing liquor commercials. Buck the Code? No way."

Some national liquor makers and some TV stations would like to see the liquor ban lifted soon. The Review Board has been listening to arguments pro and con but so far continues to uphold the ban on liquor. Meanwhile, national liquor merchandisers have made no attempt to defy the Code by buying time on non-Code stations.

Heublein, Inc., for one, is perfectly content to wait until the Code is amended—which the company thinks will happen sooner or later. "The historical pattern," says Heublein president Stuart Watson confidently, "has been that laws, rules and codes change to accommodate public opinion." The company sees no point in angering people by trying to outmaneuver the Code before that day comes. Heublein, which markets wines as well as hard liquors, not only keeps its liquor business away from non-Code stations but leans over backward to avoid any semblance of Code violation. Its wine commercials are nervously edited to prevent stray aromas of the liquor business from seeping in. "Most of the time," says a spokesman, "we sell our wines on TV by using the individual brand names only, we don't even breathe the word 'Heublein'."

Helffrich believes a major reason for the Code's nearly industry-wide acceptance is that, as Heublein's Watson suggests, it can be counted on to keep in step with the times. "There are very few in the industry who chafe under it or consider it a collection of outmoded bluenose edicts. As the country changes, it changes."

Until 1969, for instance, the Code banned TV advertising of feminine-hygiene products. Alberto-Culver Co. had a feminine deodorant spray that it wanted to promote, and the company argued before the Review Board that the increasingly free-speaking U.S. public was now ready to accept such advertising, if carefully and tastefully presented. The Board voted (though not unanimously) to lift the ban. The Code was amended to say that such products could be advertised in a "restrained and obviously inoffensive manner."

It was then up to Stockton Helffrich and his staff to decide in detail what the phrase meant and apply it to individual cases. "In the normal course of events," he says, "we don't check every commercial before it goes on the air. We just respond to complaints or questions from stations, ad agencies and others. But when a new-product category comes on the air for the first time, we may act as a central clearance agency for a few years. We study and clear everything in that category, and keep at it until a file of case precedents builds up and the meaning of the Code grows clearer."

As the meaning has evolved since 1969, a feminine-deodorant

commercial must obey the following rules (among others) before it can get by the Code Authority.

There may be no reference to sex, direct or implied. No men may appear in the commercial except in a group of people, and no particular man in the group may be pointed out as the product user's husband or boy friend. Nor may the user talk about physical maturity: "I'm a big girl now," and so on.

Cute double entendres are strictly out. Nixed: "I don't sleep with dolls any more." Nixed: "For you are the very air he breathes."

The commercial may not refer to any specific time span over which the product is effective.

Decidedly nixed: dramatizations in which a woman, by using the product, solves some social or emotional problem such as shyness or the Saturday-night lonesome blues.

These rules aren't written in as formal amendments to the Code. Helffrich calls them "guidelines." But since they say what the Code Authority will and won't challenge, such guidelines have just about the same effect as full-dress amendments.

A similar set of guidelines was published to cover certain drug commercials. "With the growing concern over narcotics," Helffrich recalls, "we were getting sensitive to a certain undercurrent of criticism about this so-called 'pill-taking society.' Kids would say, 'Well, our parents take tranquilizers and sleeping pills, so why can't we pop a pill sometimes?' There was no real evidence that pill commercials on TV led to drug abuse, but we could feel the anxieties building up." So the Code Authority decided they'd better regulate themselves before somebody else stepped in and did it for them.

Now commercials pitching sleeping aids, calmatives or stimulants on TV have to follow these guidelines, among others:

Drug-culture phrases such as "turn on" are strictly forbidden.

No drug may be advertised as a "simplistic solution" to personal or emotional problems. Nixed: "When your day wears you down. . . ."

The color of a pill mustn't be emphasized visually nor mentioned at all in the ad copy.

The commercial must make plain that the drug's action is temporary and that it is for occasional use only. In no case must there be any suggestion of dependence on the drug. Sleeping-pill commercials, for instance, may not show an insomniac taking a pill to prepare himself for the next day's activities.

Whatever ills a drug is meant to alleviate, the relief may not be depicted as happening instantaneously or miraculously, and the change from "before" to "after" must be modest. Nixed: a woman feels weary and depressed, takes a pill, becomes the life of a party. . . .

The Code Authority has published similar guidelines covering areas in which doubts and criticisms have been building up. Among them: pet foods, weight-reducing products, toys, acne medicines, insecticides.

Meanwhile, the day-to-day work goes on. Much of it deals with relatively simple questions about the accuracy of advertising claims. For example, a toy maker's commercial claimed that his product had certain advantages over a competitor's. The Code Authority asked the toy maker to come in and prove what his commercial said. It turned out that the claimed advantages depended on the manual dexterity and strength of the child using the toy—and, in tests, only three out of seven children could make the toy work right. The claim was deleted from the commercial.

This kind of work, carried on quietly for nearly [30] years, has so far kept the TV industry relatively free of hard criticism most of the time. But we are in an increasingly critical age, and a once-bland consumerism has suddenly become a powerful new force for broadcasters and advertisers to reckon with. . . . It may be that the Code Authority will need to get tougher. . . .

DONALD H. MCGANNON

Is the TV Code a Fraud?

Some broadcasters have joined the ranks of those who criticize the NAB Code as inefficient and too lenient, especially about advertising practices. Donald McGannon, chairman of Westinghouse Broadcasting Company (Group W), is among the most outspoken of this group.

Do most of the television programs you watch live up to these guidelines?

- Profanity, obscenity, smut and vulgarity are forbidden, even when likely to be understood only by part of the audience.
- The administration of illegal drugs will not be displayed.
- The use of liquor in program content will be deemphasized.
- The presentation of techniques of crime in such detail as to invite imitation shall be avoided.
- Violence and illicit sex shall not be presented in an attractive manner nor to an extent such as will lead a child to believe that they play a greater role in life than they do.

These statements were part of the first Television Code, adopted in 1952 by the National Association of Radio and Television Broadcasters (now the NAB). It was an effort at self-regulation and an attempt to establish a high degree of responsibility for both television programs and advertising. It failed.

We at Group W (Westinghouse Broadcasting Company) resigned from the TV Code in January 1969. We felt it hypocritical to support a code we could not proudly defend. We believe the Code has not been tough enough in dealing with crime and violence on TV;

This essay first appeared January 22, 1977.

we also strongly object to the Code's policy of allowing too many commercials and the advertising of intimately personal products.

As the president of the country's fourth largest broadcast company (after the three commercial networks), I had for years supported the TV Code. Our resignation was an act of frustration over the Code's continuing failure to deal effectively with program and advertising content. We hoped our action would stimulate some positive changes. Unfortunately, it has not. . . .

[Too many] of the prime-time network programs during the past seasons have contained excessive violence and what is termed "mature content."[1] Although I do not object to the use of such material as legitimate plot devices, unnecessary sex, crime and violence are now used simply to "hype" programs that might not otherwise sustain viewer interest.

However, when there are not sufficient program alternatives, it only obscures the issue to say that violence is popular because of the sizable audience it attracts. Walter Lippmann once wrote that "a continual exposure of a generation to the commercial exploitation of the enjoyment of violence and cruelty is one way to corrode the foundations of a civilized society." If we consider the violence and gratuitous sex on TV today as reflection of the American character, we do our peole a great disservice. Programs like *The Waltons,* "Eleanor and Franklin," "Carl Sandburg's Lincoln," "Fear on Trial" and *Family* prove that television need not be violent to be successful.

The [amount of] violence and "adult material" are especially alarming because crime, promiscuity and alcoholism among young people are at an all-time high. I am concerned that the cumulative effect of these programs can only have a numbing effect on the viewer.

In April of 1975, the NAB added a Family Viewing Time provision to the Television Code. The objectives were admirable, but the concept itself is a misconception. The networks' own research shows that millions of children watch TV *after* 9 o'clock, and the NAB action has simply transformed the 9–11 P.M. time period (8–10 P.M.

1. Mr. McGannon recognizes there has been "some diminution" in the amount of televised violence between 1977 and 1980, but "strongly believes" there is still too much violence on television.

in the Midwest) into a virtual ghetto of "nonfamily" programming. This shuffling of potentially objectionable programs from an early to a later time period violates the spirit of the original Code. Far worse, it evades the problem of what goes into the programs that go on the air.

The Television Code's policy of allowing the advertising of intimately personal products is also objectionable. During the Code's first decade, these products were regarded as unacceptable. Since then the industry has done an about-face. Stations now routinely accept commercials for feminine-hygiene products, and there is support for the consideration of contraceptives as "just another product" for broadcast advertising.

Whether these products are undesirable, or whether the public is unaware of their function, is immaterial. Television audiences tune in for programs, not for advertising. It is a medium directed at all members of the family—who have no control over the commercials they see. For that reason, broadcasters must exercise greater restraint over the advertising they allow on the air.

During the 1960s, [an] area of concern was the length and number of commercials. In the early '60s, commercials were one minute long, except for station breaks. As the advertisers' use of television grew, there was a significant increase in commercial content. This stemmed from some expansion of commercial time slots and the introduction of what the industry called the "piggyback" commercial (the inclusion of a second message within the framework of the existing 60-second length). As a result, commercial "clutter" became a chronic complaint, while "piggybacks" were a continuing source of disagreement within the industry.

By the late '60s this had become academic. The 30-second commercial emerged, and it is now the basic advertising unit for television. With the replacement of a one-minute announcement by two 30-second commercials, the commercial content for any given time period has virtually doubled. By allowing this situation to develop, the Code Review Board has fallen short of its responsibility to maintain a reasonable level of commercialization.

Since the local licensee has the ultimate responsibility for what we see on television, some people rightly ask, "Why doesn't the local broadcaster exercise more control?" Unfortunately, the ever-increasing dependence for programming by local stations on the networks is a fact of life in television. Under normal circumstances, a station does not have ample lead time to preview a program, make a judgment about it or obtain an adequate and appropriate substitute, if necessary.

Back in 1952, the first TV Code was administered by a Review Board consisting *only* of local broadcasters. Representatives of the three networks were not included in the Review Board—by design—since their primary role is to supply programs. During its first decade, the Code worked well. But in 1962, the makeup of the Board was altered to include representatives of the networks. This was a significant change, a change I regard as a major factor in the compromises that have made the Code relatively ineffectual during the past decade.

These problems could be resolved by a dynamic, self-regulatory effort conducted in the spirit of the original Code. But the entire thrust that characterized the 1952 Code has changed. The industry's concept of responsibility for "the highest standards of respect for the American home applied to every moment of every program presented by television" (as enunciated in the original Code's preamble) has been replaced with this watered-down statement in the current preamble:

"They [television broadcasters] are obligated to bring their positive responsibility for professionalism and reasoned judgment to bear upon all those involved in the development, production and selection of programs."

Since 1952, television has developed into the most powerful social force in America. During this period, however, the industry has failed to keep pace with the growing complexities of the medium and the society it reflects. If we as broadcasters cannot find a practical method of resolving these issues, I sadly predict that someone else will find it for us.

ERIC LEVIN

Censors in Action

CBS's West Coast Program Practices chief Richard Kirschner has described the censoring of network shows that takes place in his division as "the kind of job that you learn by doing." One editor assigned to the CBS series *M*A*S*H* was told her first day on the job to simply use her "imagination." Eric Levin spent some time with the censors in the CBS Program Practices department and describes how the department operates.

I was sitting in a room full of CBS censors. Four men, three in full beards, none in ties. All laughing. . . .

What do you know, I thought. They laugh. They're human. Censors! With beards.

Censors, as I imagined them, were people with pinched faces and eyes like ball bearings, who drive precisely at the speed limit at all times and never eat ice-cream cones. I did not really believe the stereotype, but, like most people, I had nothing to replace it with. Censors are the Abominable Snowmen of television. Everyone has heard of them and many have been awed by the footprints—but confirmed sightings are rare.

As luck had it, I had sighted one—[CBS's vice president of Program Practices Van Gordon] Sauter, with his beard and pipe—and held on. Sauter happens to be gregarious, so this wasn't difficult. We had lunch, and Sauter said he would be willing to let a reporter observe the workings of his department, listen, watch and ask limitless questions. Months later, here I was, sitting in a room full of CBS censors, on a bright Hollywood morning in summer.

Excerpts have been taken from this essay, which first appeared in two parts, December 10, December 17, 1977.

Summer is the hottest time of year for censors because the series that will have their premieres in the fall are going into production. Scripts arrive daily on desks; Sauter spends a good deal of his time working in Hollywood, instead of network headquarters in New York. The [Program Practices] department directors meet frequently in his office to bring him up to date, iron out problems, set policy. I sat in on several such meetings. This morning had begun with Paul Bogrow, fellow directors Jim Baerg and Jim Revard, and Teri Weissenberger, an editor, walking into the office and sitting down on sofas as Sauter, in a booming, jovial voice, greeted them, "Good morning, good morning, good morning, sports fans!"

They each had in their laps several scripts of a situation comedy. Each, including Sauter, had read the scripts previously. The pace was quick, the mood relaxed.

In the first script, a convict being taken to jail in leg irons tells his captor to go get a good meal and afterward pick him up, waiting at the roadside. "You can't miss me," he says. "I'll be the one with the dangling cuff." "And that ain't all," the cop quips. This, the group agreed, was a lewd reference to the convict's sexual organ. Not much had to be said. Here is the sum of it:

"Page five. Is it just my dirty mind?"

"No, we couldn't figure anything else that would be dangling."

"OK, *that's* going, going, gone."

Next, they looked at a scene in which several characters are discussing the remote possibility of an earthquake when suddenly the ground begins to shake. When the tremor passes, one man says to another, who has frozen in his tracks. "I thought you had to go to the bathroom." He responds. "I just did."

There was one sentence spoken about this line: "That's a little more bathroom than we want to go."

They took up a second script, which happened to feature a prostitute as a prominent special character. "I am not opposed to there being a hooker on this show," said Sauter. "Is everybody else opposed to it?" Mixed emotions. Revard said. "I just worry that she'll be popular and they'll want to bring her back."

"We can control that," said Baerg.

They decided she could stay, but that the sexual gags that follow her through the script, with few exceptions, had to go. One of those they cut: "All the guys back in San Diego say she is the best."

In a third script they faced a similar situation. Here the characters are discussing a rape trial they have read about in the newspapers. Revard said, "This is a valid theme, and they can have it. But it is not a valid source of humor. The jokes have to go." Sauter added, "Agreed. You make the jokes, you diminish the seriousness of the issue."

One line they singled out has a male character asking, "How do you know she wasn't looking for it?" Teri said, "They're going to argue that they are merely representing the typical male-chauvinist response." The group tried to find some alternative wording, less blatant, to suggest to the production company. "'She was coming on'," one of them said, to no response. "'Luring him' doesn't do anything for you, does it?" Teri asked. They shook heads no. Stumped, they decided to let the creative types be creative. Revard, who is known as the house comic, commented, "The usual approach is to milk these themes for every laugh they're worth and then save it with a serious line at the end." . . .

The one Revardian statement that is most a part of his colleagues' vernacular is: "A lot of producers seem to think their show is the only one on the air." That misconception actually points to a principal truth: that the department is responsible for the integrity of everything that appears on CBS, except news. *Everything* else, down to and including commercials. Much as an individual producer regards a season's worth of episodes of his show as a whole, a unified creation, so does Program Practices view the entire prime-time schedule as a whole.

"A couple of seasons ago we found we were getting a lot of scripts with hookers as central characters," Revard says. "The producers didn't know that other producers were doing the same thing. They asked, 'Why can't I have that theme?' How can you tell them, 'We had three of those in here yesterday'?"

"We don't feel that all shows are equally capable of handling all themes," says Bogrow. "If we get a couple of scripts in here with a difficult or sensitive theme, we will often decide to give it to the show where we think it is most appropriate or natural, or where we have the most faith that the writers and directors will handle it well."

The entire season and schedule likewise are the focus when it comes to individual incidents of sex and violence. Sometimes the censors will disallow a line that, taken by itself, they admit is not going to scandalize anyone. But they reason that to leave it in is to invite the producer to throw into subsequent scripts perhaps dozens of lines of the same intensity, and the sum of these over the course of the season, they think, would indeed be offensive.

The concern for the tone of the season can lead to a situation in which a line that is unacceptable in, say, September is allowed to pass in December. If they start the season by "establishing a line just a notch below the maximum we will allow," the department people can be looser later and still hold the overall tone of the series generally where they want it.

Establishing a line is most important with pilots. Whatever level of sex and violence the censors allow in the pilot episode becomes "the ground floor," the taking-off point for the season. Some producers will try to extend the boundaries. Even for those who don't, the only way to discover what Program Practices will actually allow is to submit a script and see what kind of "notes" come back. Therefore, the early scripts each year take on a special importance. . . .

Before I met the Program Practices people I wondered what kind of person would ever take such a job. I asked some people in Hollywood what they thought. "I always had the feeling they are decent people who wish they were doing something else," said a producer.

Before I left, I asked Bogrow, who is considered the most intellectual of the department executives, what CBS looks for in a Program Practices editor. "A lot of things," he replied, "but most of all, intelligence." Anyone who seems even remotely to fit the classic profile of a censor—a prude supercharged with zeal—is automatically rejected. "We don't want anyone who is eager to go out swinging a club on behalf of some personal, absolute moral standard," he said.

Neophyte editors learn the job by doing the job. "We start them on the shows that, in terms of our concerns, we don't expect anything radical or bizarre from, shows like *The Waltons* or perhaps *Barnaby Jones.* The trainee reads the script along with someone more experienced. They each take a copy and separately flag things of concern; then they compare notes."

There is just about no way to prepare specifically for a career in

Program Practices. Not surprisingly, the people who get into it come from all sources. This has always been the case. Thomas Bowdler, the eighteenth-century Englishman from whom we get the verb "bowdlerize," was, among other things, a physician. The censors at CBS include a former film technician, a former script girl and production assistant, a former legal secretary, a former social worker, a former actor. Bogrow, 31, has a Ph.D. in psychology from Harvard. As an undergraduate at Columbia University, he managed the campus radio station. . . .

There are nine editors working on prime-time programs on the West Coast—six women, three men. Some are married, some aren't. In age, they range from their 20s to their 50s, with most being in their early 30s. . . .

When a Program Practices editor at CBS receives a script, there is no bible, digest, constitution or code at hand that explains what to leave in and what to take out.

"There's the Code of the National Association of Broadcasters," says Paul Bogrow, "but that's largely a collection of platitudes. What we work from is an oral tradition."

In the department are a few people who have been working as censors for a decade or more, and they serve as bards to the newcomers. The recounting of the past permissible, and impermissible, seldom proceeds along inductive lines. That is, the oral histories start with specifics—the year, the season, the day, the hour, the type of show, the type of character—and they remain specific. Policy takes the form of "guidelines"; laws are not indelible. "Inflexible" is probably the most dreaded word in the lexicon of the department.

"We had a policy at one time that you couldn't show a person at the moment he was struck by a bullet," Bogrow says. "We thought that would help us avoid brutality on the air. But because it was inflexible, it was self-defeating. The rule stood still and producers got around it. They found ways to follow the letter of the rule but still come up with a ghastly effect. So the rule no longer exists."

In the absence of a rigid code, the editors' personal sensitivity becomes the essential litmus. There are a number of things they are trying to be sensitive to, including the image of CBS, the libel and slander laws, the concerns of pressure groups, congressmen, CBS's affiliated stations, Hollywood writers and producers, and the ethical, cultural milieu of the American living room. "You must have a sense of what is going on," Bogrow says. "I am trying to read the country at every moment."

Additionally, editors must incorporate their own gut feelings into the roily puddle without flushing everything else out. They are always conferring, bouncing opinions and tentative solutions off each other, sifting out a consensus. Meetings involving editors, department directors and department vice presidents are common. "There is no penalty for referring problems up," says Bogrow.

If there were a "Ten Commandments" of program standards, the department's relationship with Hollywood producers would be quite different from what it is. In that case, producers, knowing the rigidity of the rules, would probably save themselves time and trouble by obeying them completely in the first place. But since, as one producer says, "Program Practices' reactions are difficult to predict," the custom is to instruct scriptwriters to give it their best shot, regardless of the censors, and then when Program Practices comes back with what are called "the notes," negotiate, negotiate, negotiate.

It used to be common practice at CBS to call, in the notes, for many more changes than were actually considered important. "That way we had bargaining chips," says an editor. "We could argue, compromise, give up a few things and yet still come out with what was important to us." This system has in large part been abandoned because, as Bogrow explains, "It was an insult to everyone concerned. We were training the producer to resist us and we were rewarding him for it. We also were making our front-line editors into pawns. The producer would ignore the editor and immediately call the vice president and make a bargain. By dropping that system, we have upgraded the job of editor."

Under present procedures, examples of negotiated settlements abound. Here's one: The *Rhoda* people submitted a two-part story for [the 1977–78] season in which Rhoda at last meets a guy she likes. On the morning after the first date, she subtly lets Brenda know that they went to bed. End of Part I. In Part II, they leave town for a weekend together but turn back when it starts to rain. "Part II was not a problem for Program Practices," says Grant Tinker, president of MTM, makers of *Rhoda*. "But they objected strongly to the idea that Rhoda had had a one-night stand. It was too overtly sexual, they thought. We argued it back and forth, and after a week we arrived at a compromise acceptable to both sides. Now we've changed the dialogue slightly so that it's clear they have been dating for three weeks, instead of one night, before they got in bed. The way it's handled, an adult will understand. For those who are too young to catch that sort of thing, it'll be unimportant."

This is a typical case in that the distance traveled between the unacceptable version and the final, negotiated version is small and subtle, a matter of nuance and implication. "We are paid to split hairs," says a member of the department. "We are accused of being nit-pickers. I don't like the pejorative, but it's more or less true. You can't go at this job with a meat cleaver. You need a very fine tweezer."

It is not difficult to find in Hollywood a producer or studio executive who will say, as one said to me, "We often get better scripts as a result of these discussions." This particular person prefers the present system to one "in which rules, carved in stone, are sent down from bureaucrats on high. Individual judgments would be irrelevant, circumstances irrelevant. You'd be in a straitjacket."

On the other hand, argues Allan Manings, co-creator of *One Day at a Time* and former executive producer of *Good Times,* "If there are no firm rules, you don't know what you're fighting against. We did a *Good Times* episode in which two elderly people were living together without being married. It almost didn't get through because one of the characters said the old folks were 'shacking up.' I argued that Judith Lowry had been allowed to say it on *Phyllis*; so why couldn't we say it? Program Practices responded that in our case it was being said by a 15-year-old boy. That, they said, is very different from having it come from an 80-year-old adult. (Program Practices did finally relent on this point and allowed the phrase.) They will admit that they apply different standards to different shows, at different times and places in the schedule. I find it very frustrating to deal with such an amorphous situation."

Van Gordon Sauter says, "There is a different standard for nearly every show because they play to very different audiences, with different levels of expectation. You can't throw a single blanket over the schedule and cover every situation." . . .

"We are," Sauter says, "to some degree, pariahs. You almost get a kind of trench-warfare attitude in this job. You know that you occasionally make decisions that diminish the chances of commercial success for a series. It's hard to sit in a room with close friends and tell them things that will make their lives difficult, and maybe even hurt their careers. But you have to. That's part of the ghastliness of the job. You can't have a vested interest and be an effective ombudsman for the public."

[Leigh] Vance, of *Switch,* like many producers, thinks Sauter and his counterparts are not playing ombudsman to the public so much as to the pressure groups, which, in the producers' view, arrogantly presume to represent the public. "The networks roll over dead at the least objection," Vance remarks.

Of the pressure groups, Sauter says, "They are a part of doing business. Their sophistication and motives are sometimes admirable, sometimes not. But you can't program TV to conform to some ideal vision of a special-interest group. I think we'd then be looking at a world of unreality." . . .

Hollywood Fights Back

In recent years the Hollywood creative community has become increasingly outspoken about the dangers of censorship of television programming, regardless of the source: the networks, the advertiser, the FCC, Congress or the public. Five of television's most important producers were sufficiently concerned that they challenged *TV Guide* to allow them to present their side of the issue.

The producers were David Gerber, whose series have included *Police Story, Police Woman* and *Eischied*; Frank Price, president of Universal Television which has produced more television programs than any other production company during the past ten years, including *Stone, The Rockford Files, The Incredible Hulk, Buck Rogers in the 25th Century, Baretta* and *Kojak*; Aaron Spelling, co-president of Spelling-Goldberg Productions, noted for *Starsky & Hutch, Charlie's Angels, S.W.A.T.* and *Vegas* as well as such non-violent shows as *Love Boat, Fantasy Island* and *Family*; Grant Tinker, president of MTM which, in addition to such comedies as *The Mary Tyler Moore Show, Bob Newhart* and *Rhoda,* produces made-for-TV movies and dramatic series such as *Lou Grant*; and David Wolper, executive producer of *Roots, Chico and the Man* and many documentaries.

The editors of *TV Guide* noted when introducing the article: "Since our purpose was to encourage these major TV-industry figures to express their views fully and freely, *TV Guide* occasionally found itself playing the role of devil's advocate, asking provocative questions in order to draw the participants out."

Excerpts have been taken from this essay, which first appeared August 27, 1977.

GERBER: . . . Although we [are] acting as individuals, we represent a common worry about the pressure groups. At the moment we feel we have lost the violence battle. We feel the networks have thrown in the towel because of their own fears of FCC licensing authority, Congressional investigations, pressure groups and pressure from advertisers.

TVG: How have they thrown in the towel?

GERBER: By going to Washington and stating that television is better because they have gotten rid of so many action shows. The networks are acquiescent to these groups: they want to just keep their profits coming in.

TVG: Have the networks cut down on the number of action shows and also issued instructions for the action shows that remain to be less violent?

GERBER: I don't think they've issued instructions. What we do know is that police shows are off. Any realistic shows are off. Now they're looking for fantasy, escapism and good comedy. We could still do some honest comedies, but our worry is, now that we have lost the battle on violence, next will be sex. They're now looking to see how we're dealing with sex in comedies and mature family dramas.

TVG: You mean the pressure groups?

SPELLING: Yes. Our fear is, if they go after these things in series, they will then go after the mini-series. I think they've already killed the weekly series in terms of any kind of realistic drama. If they go after mini-series, then they go after long forms, and then they go after news. In fact, we were there at a PTA meeting when they worried about how to depict violence on the news. But the mass audience does not seem to be in concert with what the pressure groups claim.

TVG: The genesis of this era of television was the Family Viewing Time doctrine. . . . Family Viewing Time was imposed, theoretically, so that programs that might not be suitable for children could be shown in later time periods.

TINKER: Yes, but we all know that was hokey as hell, because a program that was right in New York at 9 P.M. Eastern Time was wrong in Chicago, where is was 8 P.M. Central Time. It was a totally artificial imposition of rules. What I look at as better rules are those that are hammered out on a case-by-case basis between people of good intent and producer and network working together, and I think that has worked fairly well over the years. There will be the occasional mistake. *Born Innocent* I guess, is the classic example. But the fact that shows like *Born Innocent* are as rare as they are is the proof to me that the system that we had—give-and-take, program-by-program review—really does work, in contrast to some law that everybody adopts.

TVG: Nevertheless, there are many who feel that Family Viewing Time defines for them what they will be presented with before a certain hour, and that is helpful in guarding . . .

TINKER: That's exactly the kind of McCarthyism that we deplore. Who says it's helpful? I'm not saying that. There's a knob on the set. Violence is there, it's on the 6 o'clock news. It's there at 4 in the afternoon if you look at reruns on the independent channels, so who is saying that it shouldn't be on from 8 to 9, when it's on at 4, it's on at 6.

TVG: There is a knob on the set, but a parent does not know necessarily before he gets into a program, what he's going to see.

TINKER: I don't want to take us off the hook entirely. You're absolutely right, and I don't believe that just anything goes. But I think that there are well-intentioned people at the networks and among the producers, and I think that our system of program-by-program review works better than some artificially imposed edict.

WOLPER: OK. Have your family hour from 8 to 9, let's assume that. But now they say we've got too much violence and sex from 9 to 11, too.

TVG: Well, why do you think this has happened? Don't you think that there is a substantially large segment of the population that *is* concerned about too much violence on television?

WOLPER: Or is it the effect of what people are *writing* about violence? Is it the total effect of violence on TV or is it the PTA and the AMA *saying* that people see so much violence that causes more violence in society? . . . Who is going to make the rules of when you can have violence and when you can't? Who's gonna decide this—the PTA, the AMA, the network? Who's gonna say it's OK to have *Roots,* but not *Starsky & Hutch,* it's OK to have one of these, but not this—who's that gonna be? . . .

PRICE: You don't realize what has happened. [First] it was [the] family hour. . . . Next year they'll be saying they don't like fantasy because some report says it makes kids fantasize. And three years from now we'll be talking about something else. Step by step, the pressure groups are eroding television. And the networks don't give a damn because they're gonna sell the advertising time anyway. . . . I think most of us believe that the right way for television to operate is for the audience to be able to make its own choices. There's a heavy filtering process that goes on before those programs get on the air. But once they're on the air, if it's *Starsky & Hutch* that someone wants to watch, I frankly believe that person has the right to watch it, and that my job in supplying a program to another network is to try to come up with something that more people will want to watch than *Starsky & Hutch.* I think there is a free marketplace that potentially can operate. The problem, I think, came about when there were too many cop shows competing. . . .

TVG: There are two facts, it seems to us, that account for everything. Many public surveys indicate a huge per cent of the public is indeed concerned or outraged about televised violence. Second, every index says that violence has increased enormously in the past ten years on television. . . .

WOLPER: Well, now let me tell you what else is up. I can list a lot of changes in ten years. We're probably living in a more violent society. Somebody may say that the number of dope stories on TV is up in the last ten years. Well, I guess ten years ago there were fewer incidents to talk about.

PRICE: I have a great lab experiment I'd like to propose. During a good, long, hot summer, take a few of the major cities like New York or Detroit and eliminate every action program on the air. I wonder whether violence would go up in those communities. I'd like to hear from them—do they want *Starsky & Hutch* taken off the air? . . .

TVG: What's your position on the effects of violence on its viewers?

GERBER: We don't think television violence has any appreciable bad effect on the American public. But we're also asking who has the right to interpret violence and on what basis? When social scientists ask people if they like violence, do they really expect anybody to say yes, we love violence? . . .

PRICE: The reason the antiviolence campaigns are having such an effect now is because the advertising agencies, sponsors and networks don't want to make waves. . . . The networks don't want waves made either. They don't need *Starsky & Hutch* on if it becomes controversial. They'll put on some variety show instead, and they'll still sell the advertising minutes. They'll do very well. The people who get hurt in this kind of thing, I believe, are the creators and the audience, because they don't get a choice in the matter.

TVG: What's the solution?

PRICE: I don't see an immediate solution. I'm looking toward the future here. I don't think anyone sitting at this table wants gratuitous violence on the air. I think that we do want a climate, though, where we can do shows we believe have quality. . . .

TINKER: I think the ideal situation is a natural mix dictated by audience reaction, responsible production and even distribution by the networks. And I think that also means responsibility on the part of critics. . . .

PRICE: Who's going to decide what's violence and what's not?

TVG: It's the responsibility of the networks to make such judgments. And those judgments get passed on to you.

GERBER: You're talking about an industry that is vulnerable to criticism. To this day two or four letters complaining about a show would disturb sponsors and even networks, even though maybe 30 million people are watching it. This system is based upon fear and the making of profits. These groups come along and exert pressures on the networks, who have affiliates with licenses that periodically come up for renewal. So as not to get themselves in trouble with Congressional investigations, they then accede to the pressure groups. They then force us to come up with the kind of programming that is against our very nature as responsible producers.

We're talking about creative integrity being stifled. Police shows are dying without the pressure groups. The Western died that way too. I'm suggesting that the cure is worse than the disease. So we're not just talking about violence and sex, we're talking about a climate of repression. It's already around us; it's already stifling us. Where does it go from there?

TVG: The pendulum has swung too far, but you created that problem.

TINKER: OK, that's exactly right. But Dave said it very well: the cure that is being suggested, as opposed to a natural evolutionary cure, is worse than the sickness. One of the things that hasn't been mentioned here tonight is that we've all got shows we're ashamed of, possibly because they were too violent, too permissive, possibly just because they stank creatively.

PRICE: That's what we should be attacked for.

TINKER: It's unfortunate that this violence uproar is one of those things that takes our eyes off the ball. We should be concentrating on making better shows. This kind of distraction is really injurious to the welfare of the medium. It's not constructive that all these groups are so preoccupied with an unnatural imposition of rules.

TVG: Of course, one of their points is that television is a pervasive and powerful medium, and if it can sell toothpaste and cars, then by constant repetition of violence it can sell that too.

PRICE: You know that this kind of attack, however, has generally taken place against whatever the popular entertainment form of the time was. It was true with regard to the comic books. They were going to destroy the population. It goes back to the movies, which were under attack in the '20s. The dime novels of the 1890s were attacked because children were reading about Western outlaws, and so they would all turn into them. You go back to Euripides, who was driven out of Athens for corrupting the youth with his plays.

Somehow various well-meaning groups have a fear that the depiction of one thing or another is going to corrupt society. I happen to believe that the freer the means of expression and communication, the better off the society is. I believe, in general, in the good taste of the public. It knows to put aside those things that are worthless and to hold on to what's of value. The only way I know for those things to get freely into the marketplace is to have as few restrictions as possible. . . .

TVG: We've heard you talk about your "rights as creative artists" and about the good you're attempting to do. But when it comes right down to it, isn't what you're trying to protect your ability to make money out of television?

PRICE: May I answer that very simply? All of us have been in television quite a while. We're professionals. We ultimately can make any kind of a show that we're allowed to make and that will be reasonably profitable. So I don't think we're defending violence on the basis of economic interests here. We all have the reputations, the backgrounds and the ability to sell programs to any of the three networks and to any independent station. Whether we do violent shows, comedy shows, quiz shows or anything else, we can all succeed. We're here fighting for a cause, not to make money. . . .

WOLPER: Let no one miss the point of all this. In case you didn't hear us, certain television programs that you [once] thought were terrific can't be done today. Certain television shows that *TV Guide* said represented the best in television can't be done today. That is the point we want made.

CHRIS WELLES

The Fairness Doctrine

The FCC regards "strict adherence to the Fairness Doctrine—including the affirmative obligation to provide coverage of issues of public importance—as the single most important requirement of operation in the public interest." Chris Welles explains that whether or not the Fairness Doctrine promotes the public interest is a question about which there is continuing debate.

A doctrine that requires broadcasters to present important public issues "fairly" sounds, on the face of it, like a simple and straightforward affair, about as controversial as *Little House on the Prairie* and almost as American. But, in fact, the FCC's Fairness Doctrine has become an explosive issue. . . .

The problem with the Doctrine is that, while everybody is in favor of being "fair," few people can agree on what fairness means in practice or how it should be achieved and guaranteed. "Even those of us who approve of it agree that the Fairness Doctrine has been a bloody mess," says Thomas Asher, former executive director of the Media Access Project, a Washington public-interest law firm. "It doesn't lend itself to precision and is hard to enforce. It leads to a high volume of litigation and a low volume of public understanding."

The root of the controversy, however, is rather simple: to what extent should the federal government exercise control over the way news and public issues are presented on radio and television? It all boils down pretty much to a question of whom do you trust or, at least, whom do you distrust less, the government or the networks.

This essay first appeared August 30, 1975.

Those who favor the Doctrine fear that the networks will abuse their predominant and privileged position in the nation's news flow. Therefore, they say, broadcasting must be checked by limited federal supervision. Those who oppose the Doctrine fear that federal supervision could easily become unreasonable censorship. They find the networks quite capable of fulfilling their public-interest responsibilities without government regulation. The present debate over the Fairness Doctrine could importantly affect the nature of broadcasting for years to come.

Though the Fairness Doctrine essentially is a philosophical issue, it derives from a technological fact: there is a limited number of frequencies on which radio and TV programs can be broadcast over the air. While there is no practical limit to the number of people who can exercise their right of free speech by publishing newspapers and magazines, only a relative few can transmit over the airwaves, particularly on the heavily watched VHF channels, without causing electronic interference.

A series of laws beginning with the Radio Act of 1927 has developed the idea that, since some people necessarily must be denied the right to use the airwaves, the few who are permitted to use them must be prohibited from monopolizing the viewpoints expressed. In return for the privilege of using the airwaves, broadcasters must adhere to standards of "public [interest, convenience and necessity]" and broadcast a variety of viewpoints in addition to their own. The public's right to be informed thus justifies limits on the broadcaster's right to free speech. Through its power to issue broadcast licenses, the FCC is supposed to ensure that broadcasters live up to these obligations.

The Fairness Doctrine itself was laid down in a 1949 FCC report that was later upheld by Congress and the courts.[1] It decreed that a broadcaster must spend a reasonable amount of time discussing controversial issues of public importance, and do so in a way that fairly reflects opposing points of view. Unlike the Equal Time Rule, which requires broadcasters to grant equal time to competing candidates for political office, the Fairness Doctrine permits the broadcaster to take as strong an editorial stand as he desires—as long as

1. In the Matter of Editorializing by Broadcast Licensees, 13 FCC 1246.

he also reasonably presents the opinions of those with contrary positions.

The scope of the Doctrine's use has been determined by a variety of FCC and court decisions. Its constitutionality was established in the famous Red Lion case,[2] which concerned an attack on a journalist, Fred J. Cook, broadcast over WGCB, a conservative radio station in Red Lion, Pa. When Cook complained, the FCC ordered WGCB to give him air time to reply. The station refused and filed suit. In 1969, the Supreme Court unanimously upheld the FCC. A frequency licensee, the Court said, is a "fiduciary with obligations to present those views and voices which are representative of his community and which would otherwise, by necessity, be barred from the airwaves."

Applying this principle to paid commercials is a tricky problem. A 1973 Supreme Court decision, in a case concerning attempts by private groups to buy air time to advocate political views, helped ease that problem by ruling that broadcasters do not have to sell time to such groups; that a station is not obliged to grant access to the airwaves to every group that demands to purchase time.[3]

In 1967, the FCC forced TV stations to put antismoking commercials on the air to counterbalance cigarette advertising, but [in 1974] the Commission decided that the Fairness Doctrine cannot be applied to ordinary commercials promoting the sale of a product. That applies even if the advertising is false or misleading or the use of the product is a matter of controversy. However, the FCC made it clear that the Doctrine does apply to ads that consist of "direct and substantial commentary on important issues." For that reason the networks have, generally speaking, refused to accept ideological advertising.

By and large, the courts and the FCC have strengthened the Fairness Doctrine. Most rulings have been favorable. But that hasn't deterred an increasingly vocal group of critics, particularly NBC and CBS, who argue that broadcasters should have the same unfettered First Amendment rights as newspapers and magazines. They point out that broadcasting is no longer the restricted medium it

2. *Red Lion Broadcasting Co.* v. *FCC,* 395 U.S. 367.
3. *Columbia Broadcasting System, Inc.* v. *Democratic National Committee,* 412 U.S. 94.

once was. The nation's broadcasting outlets now outnumber daily newspapers by more than four to one. And cable television may soon dramatically expand the number of broadcasters.

Those who oppose the Doctrine are most aroused by its sanction of government involvement in news broadcasting. Fairness in covering controversial issues, NBC chairman Julian Goodman told Congress, "is an essential professional standard for any responsible journalist. But when it becomes a government-enforced doctrine, it automatically gives the government authority to second-guess news judgments and threatens to make it a supereditor for broadcasting." CBS's [president] Arthur Taylor said the Doctrine is "a potential tool for determined and unscrupulous public officials to destroy what is, in effect, the only national daily press that this diverse Nation has."

As an example of this potential, many Fairness Doctrine foes cite incidents revealed by former CBS News executive Fred Friendly. According to Friendly, White House and other Democratic politicians during the Kennedy and Johnson Administrations covertly engaged in "an unsavory project of political censorship" that consisted of using the Fairness Doctrine to harass right-wing radio commentators. Part of that campaign, Friendly alleged, was Fred Cook's challenge in the Red Lion case, which Friendly said was backed by the Democratic National Committee. (Cook has denied the charge.)[4]

Foes of the Doctrine claim that even without specific government pressure, the potential has been enough to inhibit broadcasters, especially at local stations, from putting hard-hitting public-affairs programs on the air. NBC News correspondent Bill Monroe told Congress that when he left a newspaper for a TV news job he was surprised to find "a consciousness of government, an anxiety about it, that robbed TV executives of the same quality of journalistic zest and readiness to take initiatives displayed by newspaper executives." In return for the "limited and sometimes dubious benefits" of the Fairness Doctrine, Monroe said, "we suffer the imposition of blandness, timidity and don't-rock-the-boat fear of government" on the nation's radio and TV stations.

Proponents of the Fairness Doctrine have not been quite as visible as its opponents, but their views are no less firmly held. Exclu-

4. Friendly's charges appear in *The Good Guys, The Bad Guys and the First Amendment* (New York: Random House, 1976).

sive rights to use broadcast frequencies, they point out, remain a government-conferred privilege, and public-interest criteria remain the only means to determine who should be granted that privilege.

Another argument offered by proponents of the Doctrine is that statistics on how many radio and TV stations there are, as opposed to the number of newspapers and magazines, are misleading; that much of the print media consists of small weekly newspapers, trade journals and limited circulation publications; that they are no match for the concentrated power of the TV networks; that lumping TV in with radio simply confuses the issue; that the vast majority of radio stations provide a steady diet of popular music and pay almost no attention to controversial public issues. They also point out that cable-TV is still in its infancy and its long-term effect is hard to foresee; and that its growth has been hindered by understandable opposition from the networks.

Fairness Doctrine supporters worry that television has a much stronger economic motivation, because of advertiser preferences, to broadcast bland entertainment and sports shows than to present controversial public-affairs programs. "I see myself as a libertarian," says Ned Schnurman, associate director of the National News Council, an independent watchdog of press fairness, "but I think the Fairness Doctrine is the only existing assurance that the networks will responsibly discharge their responsibilities regarding news and public affairs."

The Doctrine provides an important guarantee of access to the airwaves by contrary and minority opinions, its adherents argue. "It's a hell of a big stick for us," says Russell Hemenway, director of the National Committee for an Effective Congress, which assists political candidates in challenging incumbents.

Proponents admit the potential for government misuse of its power, but point to the lack of evidence that the power has been used unfairly. None of the incidents related by Fred Friendly alleged irresponsibility by the FCC. "We're not trying to set ourselves up as the national arbiter of truth and objectivity," says FCC Chairman Richard Wiley. He points out that even when challenged successfully on fairness, broadcasters cannot be compelled by the FCC to change or delete programming. They retain almost complete discretion over how, when, and in what form contrasting views are to be presented. (CBS's *60 Minutes* dealt with a rash of fairness complaints about a segment on Jews in Syria by presenting a brief commentary by Mike Wallace summarizing the criticism and giving CBS's rebuttal.)

ABC News president William Sheehan, who favors the Fairness Doctrine, feels that the FCC has behaved quite judiciously in applying it. "I don't think they have any appetite for becoming the editor of last resort," he says. Some observers suggest that, if anything, the FCC has been lax in the Doctrine's application. Of 4300 fairness complaints filed with the Commission during 1973 and 1974, 97 per cent were dismissed out of hand. In only 19 cases did the FCC [require broadcasters to take any action]. And [since the Doctrine was established in 1949, only a handful of] stations have had licenses revoked for fairness reasons.

While some broadcast newsmen agree with Bill Monroe, most questioned did not. William Sheehan says the Fairness Doctrine "has not been an inhibiting factor" in ABC's news coverage. Despite the statements of his superiors, CBS's Mike Wallace, who on *60 Minutes* often tackles controversial issues, says "it hasn't troubled me." Edwin Newman, who narrated and co-authored a 1972 NBC documentary critical of corporate pension plans—which, the FCC rules, violated the Fairness Doctrine—refused to join the network in what was to be a successful challenge of the ruling. "Providing it is reasonably administered," Newman says, "I find nothing in the Fairness Doctrine to object to." To Donald McGannon, [whose] Westinghouse Broadcasting owns seven radio stations and five TV stations, the Doctrine is, if anything, "a goad and an incentive to us to do what we're supposed to do effectively and well."

FCC Chairman Wiley thinks some broadcasters use the Fairness Doctrine as a "shield." That TV broadcasts a paucity of controversial public-affairs shows, he says, "is more due to its own timidity than any kind of regulation. If a newsman is letting the Fairness Doctrine inhibit him, then I suggest he might be in the wrong business."

Clearly, the notion of the federal government as overseer of the nation's radio and TV news and public-affairs programming is an ominous one. Yet, as Fred Friendly has noted, "the power of the major broadcasters is so awesome that the thought of their exercising it totally unchecked is hard to accept." Though the exercise of federal power is relatively visible and under continual outside scrutiny, network power is exercised largely invisibly.

Opinions differ, but it seems to many that the Fairness Doctrine doesn't need to have an inhibiting effect on the honest pursuit of news and public affairs by radio and TV stations. "If you want to go out and report," says Edwin Newman, "you go out and report." And some observers regard the Doctrine as a useful reminder to broadcasters of their public accountability as beneficiaries of federally sanctioned monopolies. From that point of view, it would appear to be a small price to pay for a mechanism that guarantees to outsiders at least a modicum of access to the nation's airwaves.

From another point of view, any infringement of the First Amendment rights of any newsman seems a very high price to pay for what may be a doubtful benefit. The Fairness Doctrine, from this angle, appears to contain at least the seed of government control of the news.

Keep the Fairness Doctrine or dump it? There are problems—and dangers—either way. Americans will eventually have to decide which course seems less risky.

DON KOWET

When Is an Ad an Editorial?

In January 1980, the networks turned down a Mobil Corporation commercial in which a well-dressed man, described by Mobil as a "security-analyst type," told the viewers that to place the profits of the oil companies "in perspective" it should be understood that "over the years, Mobil has earned about the same profit percentages on money invested as the average of all manufacturing industries—and less than for ABC, CBS and NBC."

Mobil's claim, based on figures relating to stockholder's equity and already in print in Mobil newspaper ads, was not really challenged. The networks insisted that their refusal was based on a long-standing policy against airing commercials about controversial public issues—such as oil company profits. Don Kowet explores the arguments surrounding this policy.

In recent years, the three principal networks have been engaging in acrimonious debate with a number of big advertisers. At issue is the networks' reluctance to broadcast a peculiar kind of commercial—one that sells a controversial viewpoint instead of a consumer product. Ironically, this prohibition against controversial-idea ads is now a full-fledged controversy itself, with assertions and rebuttals that echo all the way to the solemn chambers of the Supreme Court.

In the summer of 1976, for example, during a *Today*-show break, NBC's New York station, WNBC-TV, broadcast a commercial for a novel called *Pipeline*. The advertisement used the words "ruthless," "shocking," "recklessness" and "corruption" to describe the building of the Alaska pipeline. It thus ensured, in the midst of the energy crisis, that NBC would get plenty of heat from Mobil Oil.

This essay first appeared February 4, 1978.

Mobil, a participant in the pipeline project and a thinly veiled villain of the book, promptly asked WNBC-TV for time to broadcast a Mobil commercial to rebut the *Pipeline* allegations. WNBC-TV consulted with network lawyers, then rejected Mobil's request because it would be an "editorial" commercial—advocating a particular viewpoint about a public issue—and, therefore, unacceptable. Unable to buy time, the oil company bought space, placing indignant editorial ads in newspapers across the country.

Mobil argued in those ads that WNBC-TV was denying its constitutional guarantee, under the First Amendment, of the freedom of speech. All three networks quickly countered that Mobil was attempting to infringe upon *their* guarantee, under the First Amendment, of the freedom of the press.

"We feel that important public issues should be handled in a responsible way, in news and public-affairs programming," says Rick Gitter, an ABC vice president in charge of Broadcast Standards and Practices. "In other words, there is a forum for ideas, and there is a marketplace for goods. The two should be kept separate."

"Over the past several years," replies Herb Schmertz, Mobil vice president of public affairs, "the oil industry has had an almost impossible time gaining media access to tell its side. The networks," he adds, "are thus denying the American public information. They're failing their obligations under their licensing procedures."

The seed of this bitter debate was planted in 1973. That year, the Supreme Court reversed a lower-court decision (involving the Democratic National Committee and Business Executives' Move for Vietnam Peace), in which the litigants had claimed their right of free speech had been denied when broadcasters refused to sell them time to present their views. On May 29, the Court ruled that radio and TV stations have an absolute right to refuse to sell time for ads dealing with political campaigns or controversial public issues. Writing for the majority, Chief Justice Warren Burger said that the alternative, giving the Federal Communications Commission regulatory power over such advertising, would run "the risk of an enlargement of Government control over the content of broadcast discussion of public issues."[1]

1. *Columbia Broadcasting System, Inc.* v. *Democratic National Committee,* 412 U.S. 94.

The FCC, in turn, interpreted that decision to mean that it was up to individual broadcasters, subject to FCC review, to determine whether an ad or opinion was advocating one side of a controversial issue. At the same time, the Commission warned that any editorial ads broadcast might be subject to its Fairness Doctrine. . . . In other words, the broadcasters might have to give away free air time for replies.

That was all the networks needed to hear. Telling a network executive he might have to grant free time during his broadcasts was like telling a cleric he might have to permit a plug for free love during his Sunday sermons. The networks henceforth felt more justified than ever in measuring proposed ads against their long-standing yardsticks—codes similar to ABC's, which states: "Absent [read: Apart from] special public-interest considerations [read: political campaigns], ABC will not sell time for controversial-issue programs or announcements or for comment on controversial issues."

"Thirty-second spot announcements are simply not the best place to debate issues of public importance," says Ralph Daniels, NBC's vice president of Broadcast Standards Administration. "OK," says an official of the AFL/CIO, which also had a TV ad rejected as controversial, "then sell us *10 minutes.*"

Aside from ads for the AFL/CIO and Mobil, in recent years the networks have refused editorial commercials from: the Stern Law Firm, urging Chevrolet owners to take their cars to dealers for correction of a faulty safety device, and advising consumers to take plain aspirin instead of higher-priced pain killers; Allstate insurance, praising the effectiveness of air bags as safety devices; a consumer group, warning of the hazards of snowmobiling; Phillips Petroleum, advocating offshore drilling; and the Energy Action Committee, in favor of legislation to break up the eighteen biggest oil companies. In each case, the networks argued (a) that the ads were controversial and (b) that the issues raised in the ads were proper to their news programming, where they had already received balance coverage.

The rejected advertisers don't dispute that their messages were controversial, but do deny (a) that the networks thus had a right to bar them from the air and (b) that their points of view had been fairly dealt with in news broadcasts.

"So what if the commercials are controversial?" says Herb Schmertz of Mobil. "Neither the Supreme Court nor the FCC ever said commercials couldn't be controversial. As a matter of fact, the FCC said the networks should start experimenting, to find new ways of increasing the flow of information. And when they say issues of public importance shouldn't be dealt with in 30-second spots," he adds, "well, what are they doing every night on their own news programs? That's all network news is—just a 30-second headline service."

As far as the networks are concerned, this obsession with their news programming poses a dangerous threat to their independence. "Companies claim they're upset with our advertising policies," says one network spokesman. "But they're simply using the editorial-ad issue as a back door to come in and rewrite the news."

The networks are least convincing when they try to defend themselves against charges of being arbitrary in evaluating exactly which commercials are controversial. "We don't allow editorial commercials," says NBC's Ralph Daniels, "but image commercials are quite acceptable."

"It's when, along with promoting his image, the advertiser seeks to get into areas of public debate that the problem arises," adds ABC's Rick Gitter. "Then it becomes a matter of judgment as to what is controversial."

According to NBC's evaluation, the *Pipeline* ad wasn't controversial, but the Mobil reply was. Opinions as bitterly contradictory as those that characterize this controversy permit no easy compromise. Truth, undoubtedly, lies on some unexplored middle ground between them. On the one hand, the movement for editorial commercials was a constructive effort to right the imbalance between broadcaster power and viewer outrage. Congress did initially intend broadcast stations to reflect the diversity of their communities, and thus instructed the FCC to license them to serve the public interest.

On the other hand, the outraged viewers now demanding air time are often multinational corporations or their powerful consumer counterparts, whose claims represent not necessarily the public interest, but special interests. And the final arbiter is often not an individual station manager, but a network executive whose own vested interest, given the utter dependency of his industry on advertising revenues, is to resist selling any air time that might generate free time in response.

Perhaps it will take another decision by the Supreme Court, or a further review of existing court decisions by the FCC, to settle the argument. For there are legitimate First Amendment issues at stake. In the meantime, two immediate measures might help.

"Advertisers should start labeling their editorial commercials as opinion," says Bob Gertenbach, vice president of the Council of Better Business Bureaus, which reviews TV ads for their truth and accuracy. "The best way to do that is with qualifiers," he adds, "such as 'we believe,' 'in our opinion' and the like. These qualifiers would alert the public to the fact that what they're seeing is one subjective judgment."

Nicholas Johnson, the former FCC commissioner, now with the National Citizens Committee for Broadcasting, offers another alternative. "The answer," he says, "lies in a suggestion Mobil made a while back. They wanted to buy two minutes of network time. They would use one minute to express their viewpoint, they would give the other minute free to the strongest advocate of the opposing view." Johnson adds, however, that the networks have already rejected that proposal.

The Thoughts of Chairman Ferris

Charles Ferris, chairman of the FCC, feels that the best way for the Commission to improve the quality of television is to "keep from getting in the way." The marketplace rather than government regulation is the best shaper of broadcast policy. Ferris elaborates in a question-and-answer session with *TV Guide.*

TVG: In [a] speech to the National Cable Television Association, you said you felt that the public was dissatisfied with the diversity of the programming that is now available to them. And yet when there are surveys of people's attitudes toward television, the result always seems to be that most people are generally satisfied. Do you have evidence that there is dissatisfaction?

FERRIS: Well, I don't have a market survey or a Gallup poll or whatever. But I think there is a sense that it could be better. I don't think it's reached the point where people are throwing shoes at the TV screen because the quality of programming offends them. But I think there is a sameness and a blandness to what you find on television, and I think most people agree.

I can understand, as I comprehend the economics of the broadcasting industry, why this takes place and I don't think it's wrong at all. The Commission's decisions back in 1952 [see pp. 402–13] really structured the industry so that it is driven by these economic necessities. You have a lowest-common-denominator psychology driving the programming decisions of the networks.

Excerpts have been taken from this essay, which first appeared July 15, 1978.

Now, how one would develop a system that gives us greater diversity—that's all we're talking about. We're not talking about anything beyond just providing a broader program base so that it would become economical for a station to seek to satisfy 10 per cent of the market, or 15 per cent, rather than 100 per cent. I think if you have that type of economic incentive, with the same forces that drive the decision process now, you'll have a more significant range.

TVG: Are we talking about cable now? Or television in general?

FERRIS: I'm talking about both. The capacity is there in over-the-air broadcasting, or through a wire, or through satellites or other options. It's like being able to have more than three faucets through which all programming flows. What medium transmits it? I don't know. It could be any medium.

TVG: What makes you believe that if we have more outlets we're going to have better programming? Or more diversity? When the Commission decreed that all new TV sets had to be equipped with UHF tuners, everybody said, ah, now we'll have diversity. But it didn't happen.

FERRIS: I don't agree with the implication of your question. We have the outlets that could provide the base for diversity, but UHF is not yet comparable to VHF. But working with the transmitter, the power output, the antenna and its type of reception, the lead-ins and the design of the tuner could improve UHF to that extent.

If we do get to that point, I think you will begin to see the capacity to develop the economic infrastructure for more networks. And we're putting a significant priority on reaching that point. Now this won't happen in my term. But I'm not going to be discouraged, because it's the long term that I'm interested in, rather than the short term and the quick fix. . . .

TVG: When it comes to programming, do you have a definition of "public interest, convenience and necessity," which is, of course, the basis established for your decision making?

FERRIS: I don't think that in the specifics of programming, the government and the Federal Communications Commission have anything to say.

TVG: Not even in the public interest?

FERRIS: Not on specific programming. I don't think any government should be dictating what the content of a specific program is.

We can get involved in the percentages of programming and licensing. You know, that 15 per cent of a station's programming will be public affairs, as opposed to entertainment programming—but not what that 15 per cent or that 85 per cent should contain. However strong my personal feelings are, I don't think it's my job to impose my tastes on an industry and on 200 million people. The ones who prevent us from doing that are Thomas Jefferson and the others who wrote the Constitution and the first amendments. I think the First Amendment is very strict with respect to government dictating program content.

TVG: Does that include advertising content?

FERRIS: The percentage of advertising gets into the quantitative evaluation of the use of the license. So, levels of advertising can be prescribed.

TVG: You do have that power.

FERRIS: Oh, sure. Very definitely.

TVG: Following up on that—just after you became chairman [in 1977], you said that you were inclined toward guidelines that would compel broadcasters to program certain percentages of commercial-free public-affairs programming, perhaps even at specified times. Do you still feel that way? Are you going to do anything about it?

FERRIS: Well, my inclinations are one thing, but everything that we develop is going to be on the basis of a record.

TVG: Are you going to develop a record in this case?

FERRIS: We are, we are. We've assembled an extraordinary staff to investigate the networks from the standpoint of their economic premises, their interrelationships with programmers and how programs are produced, and how the networks affect the licensees, their affiliates. The whole economic premise of this, as well as the broader issues of the societal effects, will be studied. I think the data that will be collected will put us in a position to determine what we should or shouldn't do.

TVG: In addition to your study of the networks, you are also starting an inquiry into children's television. What are you looking for in that area?

FERRIS: As you know, there was an inquiry [between 1971 and 1974] at the Commission, looking into children's programming. That inquiry resulted in a voluntary agreement on the part of the broadcasters to impose certain standards with respect to the types of programming that they would direct to preschoolers and to preadolescents, and to reduce the commercial time in these programs. We're going to look and see how well this is all working. We will update the premises and, again, develop a record as to what should be done, if anything.

TVG: What can you do?

FERRIS: There is a full range of things we could do. We could require that there be less time devoted to commercials. Instead of nine and a half minutes an hour, you could get it down to four. You could even get it down to zero. I think that's well within the capacity of the Commission, to have no commercials in children's programs. But if you do have commercials, you could require that they be bunched. If you have four minutes of commercials in an hour, you'd have two minutes at the beginning of the hour and two at the end and no interruption in between, so that there would be less risk of the children not discriminating between what was taking place and what was the commercial pitch.

TVG: You've talked a lot about deregulation in your speeches. But you have the network inquiry and the children's television inquiry and an inquiry into all-channel tuners and others. Some people might interpret this as pushing for more regulation. Is there an inconsistency there?

FERRIS: I don't think there's any inconsistency at all. I believe in zero-based regulation. I want to go back and find out right from the beginning the value of each rule and regulation to see if it still has validity. If it doesn't, let's get rid of it. I think that the regulatory scheme we have now has, to a great extent, gone stale.

The purpose of regulation should not be to protect the status quo. It's there only to assure that the marketplace forces can work. . . .

TVG: You've said that commercial broadcasting must present more than the survival of the tired, timid and the imitative. But the Commission can't really do anything about that, can it?

FERRIS: Well, I think that the things that we've been talking about for this past hour are exactly what the Commission can do about it. There should be more than just reruns. There should be much more than the simple and the bland on television. I think that's part of the whole psychology of the lowest common denominator. I think one could conclude that much of commercial broadcasting is the survival of the tired. And the timid.

TVG: And the way to cure it is to provide more outlets?

FERRIS: If we had more outlets, we wouldn't have everybody aiming at the lowest common denominator. Instead, they could go for a specialized segment of the audience. Then you'd have a much greater diversity.

TVG: We already have public television, which does provide a certain amount of counterprogramming. But public television, even at its best, doesn't attract a great audience. Anyone starting a network or station obviously has to try to make money. They would have to start competing with the *Charlie's Angels* type of program. If we had twice as many networks, why wouldn't we have six imitative programs rather than three?

FERRIS: Implied in that is a premise that I don't agree with. I've heard from network people that we are at the outer limits of capturing the creativity of our society on television, that everything conceivable to satisfy the dramatic and literary and entertainment tastes of America is being done now. I say that's a lot of bunk.

There's a great deal of creativity in our society that I don't think television is bringing to us. The conclusion that is implicit in your question derives from the basic economic infrastructure of commercial broadcasting as it exists today. I think it would be very different if you had greater capacity for more programming options.

TVG: You have control over the licensing of individual television stations. Do you see the Commission using its role in that area to require stations to provide more than lowest-common-denominator programs?

FERRIS: I don't think we can get into program content. I don't think we should be dictating whether you should have *Charlie's Angels* or you should not have *Charlie's Angels.*

TVG: Speaking of *Charlie's Angels,* are you getting complaints on sexual innuendo in shows?

FERRIS: Some, but not much.

TVG: Do you think the campaign against sex on TV is stirred up by just a few people?

FERRIS: Well, it's awfully hard to say. There's another thing about it. I don't think I should be imposing my views on other people. Still,

I do think someone has to have good taste. To a great extent it depends on the context in which things are done. One of the most significant programs that I can recall watching, and I didn't miss one segment, was *Masterpiece Theater*'s, "I, Claudius." It contained a great deal of violence and sexuality. But the important thing was the context in which it was done. I mean, I sat there with my daughters. We watched it. It was very well done, and no one got embarrassed by watching or found that it was exploitative at all—and it was pretty harsh stuff.

I think most people probably complain about what they see as sexuality or violence for its own sake, the exploitation of sex or violence. But that's another judgment call. If the government had the power to prescribe there, it would have the power to do it elsewhere. And I don't think the government should. . . .

PUBLIC TELEVISION

The first noncommercial educational television license was awarded by the FCC in 1952. By February 1980 there were 267 public television stations on the air. Noncommercial television has been and still is the subject of much discussion and controversy. On one occasion, former educational commissioner of the FCC Rex Lee told the annual convention of the National Association of Educational Broadcasters: "I sometimes wish . . . for every 100 hours of debate about who or what you are, the public could be guaranteed 1 hour of quality programming." Former FCC and Public Broadcasting Service (PBS) chairman Newton Minow has commented that the public broadcasting system in the United States is "the product of history rather than logic."

The goals envisioned for public broadcasting are ambitious and have been frequently articulated. In a letter to the Carnegie Commission, which prepared its first report about public television in 1967, essayist E. B. White wrote:

> Noncommercial television should address itself to the ideal of excellence, not the idea of acceptability—which is what keeps commercial television from climbing the staircase. I think television should be the visual counterpart of the literary essay, should arouse our dreams, satisfy our hunger for beauty, take us on journeys, enable us to participate in events, present great drama and music, explore the sea and the sky and the woods and hills. It should be our Lyceum, our Chautauqua, our Minsky's and our Camelot.

Public television "should be a place where a viewer is exposed to higher quality shows than on commercial television," according to Dick Cavett who has been a talk-show host on both commercial and public television. "Can any network executive afford to be for quality when a stockholder's meeting is coming up and a quality program may mean sacrificing ratings and money? I don't know of a case where that's happened yet." ABC president Frederick Pierce clearly agrees with Cavett, as illustrated by his response to a question about the lack of cultural programming on commercial television: "There's a marvelous thing in this country called public broadcasting and they're supposed to supply alternative programming to that which the commercial networks are doing." National Association of Broadcasters (NAB) president Vincent Wasilewski echoes Pierce's sentiments. Public television should complement private broadcasting "by providing minority taste programming," including all the types of programming "which private broadcasters—whose franchises call for them to serve all the people—cannot carry or can carry in limited amounts."

In January 1967, when there were already 187 noncommercial stations on the air, the Carnegie Commission defined the goal for public broadcasting in its report, *Public Television: A Program for Action.* Public broadcasting should "appeal to excellence in service of diversity." This report, which was the catalyst for the Public Broadcasting Act of 1967, was to "recommend lines along which noncommercial television stations might usefully develop during the years ahead" and to "focus its attention principally, although not exclusively, on community-owned channels and their services to the general public. . . ." President Lyndon Johnson endorsed the Commission's efforts: "I believe that educational television has an important future in the United States and throughout the world. . . . I look forward with great interest to the judgments which this Commission will give."

The Commission adjudged that in order for noncommercial television to attain the goals set for it, "a well-financed and well-directed educational television system, substantially larger and far more pervasive and effective than that which now exists in the United States must be brought into being if the full needs of the

American public are to be served." Furthermore, the Commission was troubled by the term "educational" because it "sounds forbidding" and "calls to mind the schoolroom and the lecture hall." The report recommended that noncommercial television be considered as two separate parts: "instructional television" which would deal "primarily with formal instruction" and "public television" which would be "directed toward the general public." The report specified that public television should incorporate "all that is of human interest and importance which is not at the moment appropriate or available for support by advertising, and which is not arranged for formal instruction."

Although the Public Broadcasting Act was passed largely because of the Carnegie Commission's report, the Act failed to define the purpose of public broadcasting as distinct from educational or instructional broadcasting. Thus noncommercial stations receive no mandate or guidance concerning purpose or operation. This is especially important because of the disparity in ownership of public television stations: approximately one-third are owned by colleges and universities, about one-third by state or municipal school systems and about one-third by community foundations. The result has been public television stations "differing in structure, financing, concept of role and degree of independence," according to Douglass Cater who, as aide to President Johnson, was one of the principal architects of the Act. "In retrospect, we were overly optimistic to believe that public broadcasting in the United States would find its own identity. Too little account was taken . . . of the frailties of the system we were seeking to nurture." Cater pointed out that, "as public broadcasting began the search for its unique role, there were bound to be differing definitions of what that role should be." Public broadcasting is "hardly a system at all, but rather a variety of broadcasting arrangements bearing a common name."

A decade after the Public Broadcasting Act was passed, a second Carnegie Commission evaluated the growth and problems of public television in a report, *A Public Trust.* Although "public broadcasting has managed to establish itself as a national treasure" and is an "absolutely indispensible tool for our people and our democracy," public broadcasting "suffers from chronic underfunding, growing internal conflict, and a loss of a clear sense of purpose and direction."

This second report (published in 1979) stressed a major difficulty for public television: "adequate funding alone is not a guarantee of complete success, but without it, success is unattainable." Public broadcasting is not allowed to carry advertisements, so its funding must come from other sources, such as the federal government and contributions. In the fiscal year 1978, the federal government provided 27.9 per cent of public television's money. The rest of the funding came from the following sources: state governments, 24 per cent; members (public subscribers), 11.5 per cent; businesses and corporations, 9 per cent; state colleges, 8.1 per cent; local governments, 7.2 per cent; foundations, 3.6 per cent; money collected from on-air auctions and marathons, 3 per cent; nonstate colleges, 0.9 per cent; and other sources, 4.8 per cent.

The use of government funds as major support for public broadcasting has met with much disapproval, especially concerning two basic questions: Does federal funding lead to or imply federal control? Is it fair for taxpayers to foot the bill for specialized programming? MIT professor Ithiel de Sola Pool has defined the danger of government support: "In any communications system, the manner in which you fund the system will undoubtedly determine what is produced." Arizona Senator Barry Goldwater, ranking Republican on the Senate communications subcommittee, has urged that "we must get the federal government completely out of public broadcasting and return public broadcasting to the public."

In an article in the *Wall Street Journal,* Benjamin Stein argues that government funding is basically unfair. "Public television represents a subsidy by the lower-middle-class people, who pay the bulk of Federal taxes, to the upper-income groups, and a subsidy of the many to the few. It is income transfer from the poor to the rich, to oversimplify a bit." It is time "for the Government to stop doling out money for the few, and for the television-watching elites to start paying for what they get." Goldwater's counterpart in the House of Representatives, Congressman James Collings of Texas, has also suggested that public television should be a "pay-as-you-go" system.

Although not an advocate of government funding, Newton Minow defends public television from the argument that it is elitist.

> One day . . . I passed a group of hard hats and heard one say, "did you catch that show last night on . . . [public television]?" And another said, "I sure did because I love opera." I never forgot that. The idea that we [public television] reach an elitist audience is a myth and I reject it.

Nevertheless, according to analyses of the audiences who regularly tune in public television, viewers are in the older age groups and typically upscale—in education, income and profession. In fact, station KQED-TV, San Francisco, used the elite nature of its audience in a promotion booklet prepared for prospective corporate underwriters, called, "A Company Is Known by the Company It Keeps."

> Chances are the people you want to think positively about your company are precisely the people who don't watch much commercial television. [M] KQED members are well above average in income, and [are] well educated. Almost three-fourths own their homes—50% own two or more cars. They travel a lot. Over three-fourths of them flew someplace during the year. Of those who vacationed last year, 42% went abroad. They have plenty of disposable income, and they spend it.

Those who support government funding point to other countries who do support public broadcasting systems. Both Japan and Great Britain spend considerably more per person to maintain their systems than the United States spends per person to support PBS. Corporation for Public Broadcasting (CPB) president Robben Fleming asserts: "If you're going to have a public television system, I don't think there is any way of avoiding financing it with tax dollars."

There are other very significant questions about the use of federal funding for public television. Can or even should the money be handed over without any conditions attached? If conditions are attached, what should they be, who should make sure they are met and how should the accountability be monitored and enforced? Should federal funding be limited, for example, to facility construction or improvement and for interconnection of stations? To what extent should nonfederal funds raised by individual stations be matched to the distribution of federal funds? Should a certain portion of federal funds be set aside for local programming, for programming for certain racial minorities, for programming produced by independent producers and so forth?

To have or not to have federal funding is not the only fiscal dilemma for public television. Corporate underwriting has become increasingly important to public television and increasingly unpopular with many critics in recent years. Although contributions from corporations provide only about 9 per cent of public broadcasting's total annual income, all corporate underwriting goes into programming. That money provides either whole or partial support for approximately 45 per cent of all the program hours on public television's national network (PBS). Corporations contribute about 25 per cent of all national programming dollars.

Between 1973 and 1978, corporate contributions to public television increased by nearly 500 per cent. Oil companies contributed more than half. In 1978 the top four corporate underwriters were Exxon ($3,811,000), Mobil ($3,350,000), Atlantic Richfield ($2,280,000) and Gulf ($1,430,000). A large number of the programs funded by these corporations are British imports, such as *Masterpiece Theatre* (Mobil), and thus the Public Television Service has occasionally been dubbed the Petroleum British System.

There is support for corporations entering public broadcasting. Douglass Cater claims that "corporate funding is vital to PBS. If the service had to raise all its money through subscribers, it would be in a real predicament." William McCater, who is general manager of WTTW (Chicago's public television station) states another reason for corporate underwriting: "Our biggest fear is to build a second rate institution. We've learned that the smaller . . . grants have to be turned down because they really don't make anybody happy. This is why we turn to corporate underwriting."

PBS president Larry Grossman responds to critics of corporate funding: "Every source of money is tainted. If you rely on corporations, you're presumed to be pro-business. Government money indicates you're politically slanted, and membership money means you cater to upper middle class viewers. The only way to be totally pure is to be totally bankrupt."

Speaking for the corporations' point of view, Exxon's deputy manager of public affairs Elliot Cattarulla believes that corporate underwriting is "a good thing to do because we're helping to bring something to people that we believe in. To the extent people think better of us for bringing them good television, that's a terrific side benefit." In 1979, Exxon committed $500,000 to help fund 260 episodes of the PBS news program, the *MacNeil/Lehrer Report.* That money could not have purchased even three minutes of advertising during the telecast of the 1980 Super Bowl.

The corporations' underwriting of programs also promotes them. This is an important bonus to public television because on the whole PBS cannot afford to allocate funds for promoting its shows. FCC commissioner Tyrone Brown defined the importance of promotion: "Next to creativity and funding, promotion must be the lifeblood of the public television system." Of the twenty-three individual programs with the largest national audience on public television since 1975, only four had no corporate underwriting.

The Public Broadcasting System and the FCC have rather stringent rules regarding how corporate-underwritten shows can be promoted on public television. The rules do not apply, however, to other types of promotion. Mobil, for example, budgeted $2 million in 1979 to promote its public television offerings and undertook a massive ad campaign in New York City, including posters blanketing bus shelters, suburban railway stations, construction sites and the like. Gulf Oil, in 1978, spent $1.4 million to help underwrite the costs of its *National Geographic Specials.* To promote these programs, Gulf budgeted $1.8 million. The results? Nine of the twenty top-rated public television shows during a four-year period were the *National Geographic Specials*; the top-rated program, "The Incredible Machine" which dealt with the human body, received a 13.9 Nielsen rating.

The problem with corporate underwriting is similar to that of government funding. Ford Foundation consultant Fred Friendly states the difficulty: "What worries me about corporate underwriting is not so much the programs put on the air but the programs the stations don't do enough of because they get a subliminal message of what underwriters will buy. It's not the material left on the cutting-room floor; it's what the stations don't dream about." Mary Perot Nichols, director of WNYC (New York's public station) gives the following example of what public broadcasting faces when requesting corporate underwriting:

> Let's say . . . that you've got someone who can make something arcane, like Renaissance poetry, come alive for an audience who, except for this program, wouldn't know or care about it. So you schlepp around to the most likely prospect and its executive director says, our board is into three-legged dogs this year. What do you do then? Scrap the Renaissance poetry idea? Or salvage it by highlighting poetry about three-legged dogs?

Some feel that corporate underwriting tends to steer programming toward the "safely splendid." Citizen Communications Center director Nolan Bowie has referred to "large corporate grants tied to programs that will re-inforce the image of the giver because of [the] pleasing haute couture of [the] programs." Maryland public television head Frederick Breitenfeld claims that companies asked to underwrite a show typically respond: "We're not into consumerism this season," and suggest they support a program featuring an orchestra that does not play Russian music.

The extent of corporate funding and influence on public television programs has led *Washington Post* television observer Tom Shales to state: "Public television is in the grip of the aristocrats. If we don't force them to let go, it will be theirs forever." Commercial broadcasters also have vocalized a discontent with corporate support for public television. One reason is that corporations are funding these programs rather than buying commercials. Public television actively solicits corporate support and Vincent Wasilewski insists that this kind of activity is, in fact, "commercialization of public broadcasting." He states that this is in reality the "exploitation by corporations of their underwriting basically for advertising purposes."

There are those who suggest that public television's difficulties with funding are not necessarily confined to the source and amount of funds. Rex Lee told the NAEB, "if a commercial broadcaster were to manage his business with the same indecision that plagues public broadcasting, he would possess not a license to print money but a one-way ticket to bankruptcy." Newton Minow answered this charge in a *TV Guide* interview with Neil Hickey in 1978. Although admitting to inefficiency in public television, he pointed out that public broadcasting's budget was typically less than 7 per cent that of commercial television's.

Whatever the financial or organizational problems faced by public broadcasting, it stands accused of not meeting the needs of the public. Critic Jeffrey St. Johns has suggested that a "degree of intellectual dishonesty permeates much of the discussion about public broadcasting. First, there is the quaint fiction that it truly serves the 'public.' In reality it serves an elitist audience of students, academics, intellectuals, professionals and politicians." And Tyrone Brown has told public television decision makers, "if public television is to achieve more realistic government funding levels, your support among the public must be broad as it is deep." Brown stated that Congress must receive "a strong message from a broad based constituency of viewers that public television is *their* television and they want it to prosper."

The demands for public participation in public broadcasting are becoming increasingly strident. Aware of this trend, the second Carnegie Commission report noted: "Expectations of a system that calls itself 'public' are necessarily broad, and perhaps overambitious at a time when many conflicting voices claim to speak for the public interest." Citizen groups, especially groups who claim to speak for racial minorities, point to a paucity of minority programming and minority hiring practices. Congress is being asked to ensure that public stations have effective equal employment programs, to require public stations to grant greater public participation, to provide more opportunities for independent producers, to limit the amount of foreign program offerings and to provide public access to station records and meetings of public broadcasting executives on both the local and national levels.

The push to make public broadcasting a tool of the public has met with some resistance. For example, Jack Lewis, Jr., a San Antonio lawyer who is chairman of the Southwest Texas Public Broadcasting Council (a nonprofit board that holds the license for KLRN, Austin-San Antonio), expressed what could be considered to be a traditional attitude: "The public has nothing to do with the management of this station. . . . The public could care less about what we're doing. They just want a good TV station."

Even though the public is becoming more aware of public television, PBS is not yet a household word. In 1979, the Opinion

Research Corporation of Princeton, N.J., conducted a poll of 1011 persons for *TV Guide.* The question was: "As you understand it, what is public television: How would you describe it?" Thirty-three per cent of the respondents did not know what it was, 44 per cent gave answers which were inaccurate and only 21 per cent had "a reasonably acceptable answer." Two per cent did not respond. After public broadcasting was explained, two-thirds of the respondents indicated that they did indeed watch public television—typically for about four hours a week.

The general figure usually cited for the PBS audience is 2 per cent of all television households. The most popular shows on public television are watched in only 5 per cent of households—the least popular network shows generally get twice that audience. *Paper Chase* was dropped from the CBS schedule because it only reached 23 million people every week.

Although about 20 per cent of American homes cannot get a viewer's signal from a public television station, viewing in the other 80 per cent of homes reached record levels in 1979. By the end of that year, 81 public television stations thought it worthwhile to subscribe to the Nielsen Station Index. In March 1979, a four-week Nielsen study—using the regular Nielsen 1200 metered homes as its sample—indicated that 49.1 million families, or 65.9 per cent of television households, watched public television an average of 9 hours, 7 minutes over the four weeks. These figures were 35 per cent higher than those for 1975. During a week in November 1979, 45.6 per cent of all television homes were tuned into some public television. It was the highest weekly cumulative audience to date.

PBS programming was carried at the same time nationwide for the first time in the fall of 1979. During the first week of the season, viewing rose 24 per cent from the previous year, with a cumulative audience (total audience for the entire week) of 44.1 per cent of television households and a cumulative prime-time audience of 23.4 per cent: 47.5 per cent higher than two years earlier.

The future of public television is "impossible to comprehend, much less to predict," according to the second Carnegie Commission report. Some predict that public broadcasting may not even have a future. Economists suggest that specialized audiences could better be served by a system which caters to and is market responsive to the audience's desires rather than a public system, where decisions are made by bureaucrats. Senator Harrison Schmitt, in his keynote address to the 1979 annual convention of the NAB, pointed to the new technologies (see The Future) and warned that commercial entrepreneurs either already could or may soon be able to fulfill, at a profit, the specialized needs and interests of various audiences.

However, the second Carnegie Commission report stated the importance of retaining a public broadcasting system: "Public broadcasting may well be the only vehicle within the communications infrastructure that will be capable of dispassionate evaluation of programming and new telecommunications services without a constant and chilling eye on the bottom line or the fortunes of a particular corporation."

NEIL HICKEY

Public TV in Turmoil

The clashes between the Corporation for Public Broadcasting and the Public Broadcasting Service over responsibilities and lines of authority undermine the success and perhaps even the existence of public television. In its second report, *A Public Trust,* the Carnegie Commission found "public broadcasting's financial, organizational and creative structure fundamentally flawed. . . . Institutional pressures . . . remain today—despite the best efforts of the thousands within the industry and the millions who support it—out of kilter and badly in need of repair."

Les Brown of the *New York Times,* as well as other experts and critics, has also despaired of the structure of American public television: "The industry's politics are fierce and confusing, and often bizarre . . . there are so many different administrative and operating entities that most of the money donated to the system for programming winds up being used for real estate, housekeeping and conferences." Neil Hickey examines the power struggle between CPB and PBS and some of the other problems that continue to plague public broadcasting.

Two volumes rest on the coffee table in the elegant Washington, D.C., office of Henry Loomis, president of the Corporation for Public Broadcasting. "I tell people who come in here that if they read those two books they'll know everything there is to know about public television in America," Loomis tells a visitor. The books? *Alice in Wonderland* and Machiavelli's *The Prince.*

Excerpts have been taken from this essay, which first appeared in three parts, July 23, July 30, August 6, 1977.

Loomis is only half kidding. Anybody who has followed the tortuous, behind-the-scenes history of public TV since the U.S. government became its patron and benefactor, knows that the Mad Hatter and the denizens of Florentine court life would be right at home in it.

. . . The Carnegie Commission Report [of 1967] and the Public Broadcasting Act of 1967, taken together, created public television as we now know it. That commercial-free TV system has given us some of the best fare ever to appear on American TV screens: *The Forsyte Saga, The Adams Chronicles, Sesame Street, Upstairs, Downstairs, The Great American Dream Machine.* It has also provided many thousands of hours of instructional television aimed at the nation's classrooms during daylight hours. And it has generated a number of high-quality informational programs such as the *MacNeil/Lehrer Report, Washington Week in Review* and *Wall Street Week.*

But underlying such achievements is a turbulent history of ideological battles, personality clashes and jurisdictional disputes that have drained the energies of the participants and kept public television from being what its founders intended: namely, a shining example of a high-class, well-funded, noncommercial TV service doing all the cultural and informational programming commercial TV can't or won't do.

A good deal (but by no means all) of that turmoil derives from a long-standing eyeball-to-eyeball confrontation between the two presiding bodies of public television—the Corporation for Public Broadcasting and the Public Broadcasting Service. It's a controversy with zero sex appeal for the average TV viewer, and indeed probably not one in a thousand is even aware of it. But large sums of taxpayer money ([$152] million in [1980]) are being pumped into public television (PTV), and serious questions are being raised about how those funds—and others contributed directly by private citizens—are being spent. Is the whole rickety, unwieldy, grotesque structure of public television in need of drastic reform? . . .

For the moment public TV is treading water in the same roiled pool where it has lived since President Johnson's Great Society tried to make it a first-class citizen. LBJ spawned the first Carnegie Commission, which made an elaborate study of American PTV and issued a detailed (and much honored) report on how to create a full-fledged national service. The Carnegie Commission spawned the Corporation for Public Broadcasting as an instrument to "receive and disburse governmental and private funds," and to act as a kind of lead umbrella between the bureaucrats and the creative people. And CPB spawned the Public Broadcasting Service as an instrument to distribute programs nationally, in somewhat the way the commercial networks do.

On paper, that sounds like a perfectly workable and potentially harmonious structure. But for complicated reasons, CPB and PBS have developed a cat-dog relationship, with plenty of hissing and growling between them. Or to put it another way, PBS sees CPB as a domineering parent who is squandering part of the family fortune and being stingy with its talented offspring, thus retarding his progress. And CPB tends to see PBS as an undisciplined upstart who doesn't know his place, is undermining family unity by telling tales in public—and is trying to get his mitts on a bigger and bigger share of the family estate.

Disinterested experts on public television agree that the federal money really ought to buy more actual programs than it does. Instead [in 1979 only $14 million] (or about [11] per cent) [was] earmarked for national programs (of the sort that might compare with the BBC's splendid output), and the rest [went] to administration, travel, technical facilities, consultants, support of National Public Radio and direct grants to local television stations.

And there is palpably an unconscionable amount of duplication of effort between the two groups, which strikes many outsiders as extremely wasteful. Each body, for example has [traditionally had] a department for programming, public relations, finance, legal affairs, research and economic development. PBS claims that if some of these functions were combined under one roof, large sums could be freed to create new programs and support older ones.

It's CPB's "intrusion" into programming, actually, that most sticks in the craw of PBS's partisans. They're sure the Public Broadcasting Act never intended the Corporation to get involved with program decisions of any sort, but rather to serve as a conduit for federal funds and a layer of insulation between the government and PTV's creative talent—thus obviating any temptation by bureaucrats to meddle in program content. That "heat shield" function—which must be carried out by the Corporation's [fifteen] board members, who are nominated by the President and confirmed by the Senate—is considered central to CPB's purpose.

As it stands, though, CPB maintains [its own] programming staff headed by a senior vice president who weighs program proposals by outside producers and (with the advice and consent of the CPB board, and in consultation with PBS's own program department) hands out money for projects that look promising.

That's a "totally inappropriate activity for CPB," says Lawrence K. Grossman, president of PBS. "A politically appointed board charged with the job of insulating public funds for a television service should not turn around and become a programmer itself. Those people are in the *worst* position to make program decisions. They're mostly businessmen and lawyers, not broadcasters." Adds Grossman: "Nobody wants a Federal broadcasting system with political appointees in charge. That runs against every tradition we have in this country."

Supporting that general view is McGeorge Bundy, president of the Ford Foundation, who [has] excoriated CPB for its failure "to perceive that its true role is that of the insulating and arbitrating trustee" of public television, and not "the bureaucratic manager. The right place for program decisions," said Bundy, "is as far from the original source of funds, and as near to the consumer, as it is possible to get. If CPB and PBS resolve their differences by this basic guideline, PBS will be the active agent and CPB the trustee and public defender."

That was a powerful endorsement of PBS's position, coming as it did from the man whose organization has plowed [about $300]million into public television since 1951, propping it up whenever and wherever it sagged. Fred Friendly, the Foundation's man who administered many of those bequests, agrees with Bundy. . . . "The Corporation has a big job to do, if they'll do it. But their job is not to duplicate what PBS does. It's to defend the system, to get funds for it, to put a buffer around it, to articulate the goals and purposes of it and to make policy. But there's a territorial imperative that is tugging away at public broadcasting—everybody defending his turf. They've got to stop all this infighting. The territory is the public's and that's why it's called public broadcasting." . . .

Nobody says that all CPB functions are unnecessary. But among people who have closely followed PTV's birth and growth, there's a firm consensus that far too much of the federal appropriation is going into peripheral activities and far too little into what public TV should be all about—programs. And, say the critics, there are too many meetings, trips, reports, consultations and conferences—which, along with the friction between CPB and PBS, sap the energies of the participants. Commercial TV, by comparison—says one expert—is a miracle of efficiency: "The programs may be terrible, but at least the trains run on time."

CPB, naturally, is certain that all its myriad activities lie well within the spirit of the Public Broadcasting Act. "CPB has not exceeded its prescribed role," declared former CPB chairman Robert Benjamin. "Indeed, it has a long way to go to fulfill it fully." Benjamin then said that the "root cause" of strife between the two groups is PBS's "failure to accept the mandated role of CPB. . . . Until that mandate is accepted by PBS or is reaffirmed by Congress or altered by amendment of the legislation, it will remain an insurmountable obstacle to complete harmony among the colleagues in public television."

But students of public broadcasting in America recall that CPB's "mandate" did not protect it, during the Nixon years, from severe White House pressure over what kinds of public-affairs programs, if any, should go on the air. Thus, what we are seeing, dramatized before our eyes, is a power play for the soul of public television. . . .

In essence, CPB contends that it alone is properly positioned to initiate new and experimental types of national programming—of the sort that wouldn't normally emerge through the Station Program Cooperative—as well as shows for the aged, Hispanics, blacks, American Indians and women. (The Corporation normally funds a program for two years, after which it either wins favor with the local stations and is renewed through the Cooperative, gets funding from a private corporation or foundation or disappears from view.)

Says Henry Loomis, "We simply throw more balls into the game and see which ones the stations want to bat out of the park and which they want to continue to play with. For the sake of diversity, we feel we should not only permit but encourage outside producers to get a crack at production funds." PBS agrees in principle, but thinks the program proposals should come through the local stations.

Loomis and his fellows at the Corporation think that if public television is to maintain its discrete character as a broad-based, grass-roots, decentralized television service (unlike commercial TV's concentration of program power in the networks), the three chief functions of PTV must be kept separate: 1) responsibility for what actually gets on the air should remain with the individual stations; 2) the scheduling and distribution of national programs should continue to be the domain of PBS; and, 3) the funding and production of programs should be achieved through a variety of sources—CPB, corporations, foundations and the Station Program Cooperative.

"That, by definition, is a confusing and complicated mix," Loomis confesses, "and doubtless seems inefficient to people accustomed to the methods of commercial TV. We're trying to do something that's never been done." He laughs. "And some feel it never *will* be done."

As early as 1970, members of Congress and the [Nixon] Administration were growing restive over such public-TV offerings as "The Banks and the Poor," a documentary that attacked American's bankers and accused scores of congressmen of conflict of interest; "Castro's Cuba," a sympathetic treatment of the Cuban leader; "Who Invited Us?," a critical inquiry into U.S. intervention abroad; and a segment of *The Great American Dream Machine* dealing with alleged subversive activities of FBI agents.

But the last straw was the hiring of correspondents Sander Vanocur (for $85,000) and Robert MacNeil (for $65,000), both of whom were perceived to be "left-wing, anti-Administration" newsmen. Vanocur's hiring, especially, angered Nixon conservatives because of the former NBC reporter's well-known friendship with the Kennedy family, and his presumed bias against Mr. Nixon. Similarly, McGeorge Bundy, was distrusted by Nixonites because he'd been a high-level adviser to President Kennedy and was now funneling millions of dollars into PTV, much of it for public-affairs shows.

Spearheading the Administration's attack on public television was Dr. Clay T. Whitehead, director of the Office of Telecommunications Policy, who demanded to know whether a federally supported TV system had any right at *all* to broadcast news programs, news analysis or documentaries.

Up until then, federal money to PTV had been increasing substantially and was about to take a great leap forward for fiscal year

1973 from $35 million to $65 million. CPB board members began to feel strong pressure from White House aides to eliminate public affairs from the schedule, at the risk of losing public TV's funding. That attempt did not prosper, and on June 30, 1972—in a move that rocked PTV to its foundations—President Nixon vetoed the pending two-year funding bill. (Eventually PTV had to get along on $35 million in 1973).

The veto came only eight days after a White House meeting at which commercial broadcasters had complained that public television was beginning to compete with them for large audiences, in a way not envisioned by the Public Broadcasting Act. Thus, the veto served two purposes: it was a bow to commercial broadcasters in an election year, and it was a message to PTV's overseers that they could not triumph in any power play with the Administration.

In rapid order, the then CPB president, John Macy, resigned; Loomis was named to replace him; CPB expropriated to itself full responsibility for program selection and scheduling (thus reducing PBS to the operation of technical facilities); and CPB announced that it was ending the funding for such news-analysis shows as *Bill Moyers' Journal, Washington Week in Review* and *Black Journal.*

The "heat shield" had been penetrated. Public TV in America was now heavily controlled by CPB—and heavily influenced by White House interests. A number of station operators, however, rebelled and let it be known they'd never accept such an arrangement, and aimed to fight it. By the spring of 1973, a state of civil war existed in public television, with dire intimations of doom on all sides. At that juncture the attention of Congress, the White House and the public was diverted from PTV's problems by the widening Watergate investigation, particularly the Congressional hearings, which were broadcast in prime time by—ironically—public television.

Station operators banded together to strengthen and reorganize PBS, and indeed to transmogrify it into a power center—as spokesman for the stations—capable of facing up to CPB on almost equal terms. Under pressure from this new PBS, CPB was obliged to retreat from its insistence upon its own hegemony, and a so-called Partnership Agreement was hammered out between them—laboriously, and not without bloodletting.

When the dust had settled, PBS had assurance (among other

provisions) that CPB would not fund any programs that the stations specifically did not want, and that fully 50 per cent of the federal appropriation eventually would go straight to the local stations with no strings attached. That's roughly where the relationship [stood at the start of 1980], although spokesmen for PBS continue to agitate for CPB to get out of programming altogether, and to eliminate the alleged waste and bloat that divert so much of PTV's funding from actual programs.[1]

One CPB board member says, "There's only one essential issue in all of this: whose hand will be on the throttle of American public television—the stations' or a Government-supported agency's? The winner will have a direct line to the best minds in the Nation. Those are the people who watch public television. And that's *real* power. That's a trophy worth fighting for."

Other observers at CPB and elsewhere fear what might happen if PBS became a true "network," with a concentration of both programming and scheduling power in its hands. They suspect that a kind of homogenized national program schedule would result, with insufficient attention to both adventurous, experimental program forms and the needs of cultural and racial minorities—whose tax money, too, goes to public television.

CPB staffers are fond of pointing out that PBS is not the monolith it purports to be; that it is, instead, a loose confederation of stations (many with drastically differing needs) operated variously by state governments, private colleges and universities, local school districts, boards of education and nonprofit community organizations.

Indeed, there [is] evident an undercurrent of impatience among many station people with the PBS leadership's seemingly eternal preoccupation with the CPB confrontation. "We have plenty of problems of our own, at the local level," said one of them. "We'll stand behind PBS in a showdown, but our energies must go into satisfying our own constituencies and boards of directors. And into raising money." . . .

1. The Public Telecommunications Financing Act of 1978 states that "a significant portion of funds" allocated to CPB "shall be used for the funding of production of television and radio programs." In the Conference Report which accompanied the legislation, Congress indicated that by fiscal 1981, CPB "should strive to allocate at least one-fourth of its funds to programming."

In a real sense, the historical conflict between the two principal agencies of public television—CPB and PBS—is one of the less important aspects of the crisis faced by noncommercial TV in America. The CPB-PBS shoot-out is eye-catching and pyrotechnic, to be sure, but in the long run it's only symptomatic of the deeper identity crisis afflicting public TV. Other questions persist.

How, for example, is public television to rise from its current poverty-stricken state to a level of affluence that will guarantee its health and growth into the 1980s and beyond? Should it compete with the commercial networks for mass audiences by emphasizing strong national programming or should it give higher priority to minority interests whose needs are not met by commercial TV? Should the institutions and power centers of public TV be rebuilt from the ground up in the attempt to make the whole system more sane and efficient? How can public television make itself more accessible to people with exciting new program ideas? How can the system expand its coverage beyond the current [80] per cent of American homes that receive its programs and provide service for the millions of other taxpayers who are deprived of them? How will it meld with the approaching revolution in communications technology? . . .

Everybody agrees that the amount of federal money reaching public TV is shameful (Japan spends [about two and a half] times as much per capita on public television as the U.S.)[2] But opinions vary on how to get more. A trust fund created by means of a dedicated tax is the most often mentioned alternative. (The Federal Highway Trust Fund, for example, comes from federal excise taxes on gasoline). The Carnegie Commission [in 1967] suggested an excise tax on television sets; others favor an annual license fee on the use of television sets, a practice common in many countries.

Other proposals: a tax checkoff like that used for financing Presidential campaigns; direct contributions made by taxpayers, added voluntarily to their income-tax payments; an excess-profits fee imposed on commercial broadcasters for their use of the airwaves.

As it happens, President Carter favors none of the above. As a candidate [in 1976 he indicated] that, with few exceptions (such as

2. According to a 1979 Aspen Institute, Japan was spending $6.06 per person on public television versus only $2.46 spent in the United States.

fish and game licenses), he's against "the designation of specific tax funds for a particular purpose." He thinks that "the President and the Congress, if they are working together," should be able to "allot adequate funds to support public television to a substantial degree from tax revenues."

If that is to happen, however, and if federal funding is to take a great leap forward, then PTV stations will need relief from the requirement that they raise two and a half dollars [two dollars beginning 1981] for every dollar of federal money appropriated. "We're already scraping the bottom of the barrel in our fund raising," says one station operator. "We can't possibly keep pace with a major jump in Federal funding." . . .

By 1979, CPB [had] in operation a full satellite distribution system for PBS programs (replacing the current terrestrial one), giving each station the capability of receiving three or more program signals simultaneously instead of only one. It'll make PBS "one of the most efficient and sophisticated" agencies in all of broadcasting, says the Corporation, since it will be better able to serve regional and special-interest audiences, and enhance the program options of every station.

It may also simply add to the chaos, making a coherent national program schedule even more difficult to achieve than it is now. Stations will be receiving up to four programs simultaneously (depending on equipment), but they'll be able to broadcast only one at a time—until cable (or optical fiber) TV provides public broadcasting with multiple outlets into American TV homes. When that happens, a well-founded and enlightened PTV system could truly offer rich and varied TV fare: a children's channel, an instructional channel, a drama and music channel, a sports channel and so forth. That conjoining of satellite and cable technology is one of the most promising and tantalizing prospects for PTV's future. "The satellite is the key to rethinking everything we know about PTV's future," says a White House aide. Regrettably, very little thought has been given so far to what programs might be transmitted over this fancy new system.

Predictions about public broadcasting's long-range future vary widely. One view has it that when cable TV, pay cable, video discs, cassette players and other gimmickry are present in enough American homes, a publicly subsidized program service will be redundant and unnecessary. Others are sure that public broadcasting will not only survive but prevail; that it will become the *dominant* TV system, superseding commercial broadcasting. This latter view supposes that the present financial base of commercial TV will be undermined, perhaps fatally, as the choices available to viewers grow geometrically and audiences are fractionated.

In sum, there is good news and bad news in the public-TV sector. Part of the good news is that more people are watching it than ever before. . . . (Still, in terms of citizen involvement, "it can barely claim the right to be a public institution at all," says Douglass Cater, a founding father of public broadcasting. "Its existence still depends in large degree on support that is [not] deeply rooted in popular appeal.")

The bad news is that public TV will continue to be a nickelodeon medium in a space-age telecommunications world until its first principles are reassessed, its shape redesigned and its future assured. It holds every promise of being a haven of sanity from the mindlessness, the laugh tracks and hard sell of commercial television. Many people, both inside and outside the system, agree with Lawrence K. Grossman's estimate that public broadcasting is "the most exciting and fastest growing area of communications in America today."

Nonetheless, the sentiment persists that American PTV needs to be torn apart—gently—and put back together again. What it surely needs is to address itself as E. B. White suggested [in 1967], not to the "idea of acceptability" but to the "ideal of excellence."

FREDERICK BREITENFELD, JR.

Speeding Down the Wrong Track

To investigate increasing criticism that public broadcasting gives inadequate service to minorities, the Corporation for Public Broadcasting created a Task Force on Minorities in Public Broadcasting. The Task Force reiterated that criticism. One member asked: "What have minorities gained from [the] system? Asians have gotten zero. American Indians have gotten next to zero. Hispanics have done a little better, but not much. Blacks have done the best of all. We have one single national show." According to a study by the CPB, only 5.8 per cent of CPB-funded programs were made by or were of specific interest to racial minorities in 1977–78.

The Task Force recommended in November 1978 that public broadcasting distribute minority programming nationally in proportion to the percentage of minorities in the general population: in 1980, over 14 per cent of the population consists of minorities, and that figure is expected to increase to 25 per cent by 1990. Furthermore, according to the Task Force, the CPB should lease a satellite transponder (channel), controlled by a cross section of minority people, for the distribution of minority programming to local stations.

Frederick Breitenfeld questions the whole concept of minority programming as a tool to help racial and ethnic minorities become integrated with the rest of American society.

All the current programming questionnaires for broadcasters seem to include the same items:

This essay first appeared January 25, 1975.

- What percentage of your programming is for minorities?
- What percentage of your minority programming is locally produced?
- What is the greatest need within the minority community in your market?
- Do you have a system for minority feedback?

Each question assumes more than the one before. We want to help everyone who asks, including the Federal Communications Commission. After all, the FCC itself poses the same questions with the same implicit assumptions: broadcasting licenses are public trusts, and stations must provide programming for minority audiences. Minority programming is essential to any broadcast schedule. The needs of minority audiences must be defined, analyzed and met by broadcasting stations. Minority programming is "in."

But what is it?

One official definition, now in administrative use across the country—at least among public broadcasters—is disturbingly circular: *Minority programs are programs closely identified with the social, economic and cultural experiences of a minority group, and which focus on a need or an interest of the specific minority group with which the program identifies.*

We are asked to list our program offerings that meet the definition, and we try to do it. But it seems strange, somehow, at least for broadcasters who consider themselves educators. We spring from a field in which segregation was declared unconstitutional [in 1954].

To force integration, we send our children across town in buses in compliance with one set of federal regulations. At the same time, promoting separatism, we divide our electronic services in order to satisfy another set of federal regulations.

These past [two and a half] decades have been important to America's social growth. The country was made to realize, at long last, that some of our citizens are getting a raw deal. Some Americans, because of color or origin, had—and still have—a tougher time taking advantage of the alleged equal opportunities that exist in education and commerce.

Those who are being gypped, and are running short of patience, include American Indians, Americans from Puerto Rico, American black people, Americans with Spanish names . . . and others. They are, we are told, the "minority" audiences.

However, will a black dentist respond to minority programming aimed at better opportunities for semiskilled workers? Will an American Indian, unable to get employment at all, watch a sophisticated series on Indian history? Will an Oriental professor of linguistics identify with characters in a drama about an urban ghetto? Will an unskilled laborer of Mexican heritage be helped with a series exploring the roots of Latin music? All programs might pass as forms of "minority" fare, but can "needs and interests" really be defined by ethnic background or race? Probably not. And, in the midst of all this desperate categorizing, what happened to integration?

Those being gypped, for whatever reasons, are mostly *poor people.* They and urban and rural; they are helpless and angry. They need skills and no-kidding fair chance. The only two factors that really count are ignorance and poverty.

Then what is "minority programming"?

Is it a series on the status of women? Is it third-grade music taught by a black teacher? Is it [entertainment shows centered around the lives of members of minority groups such as] *Sanford and Son* or *Chico and the Man*?

Sometimes minority programming is described as "by and for a specific racial or ethnic group, focusing on the experience or self-awareness of that group." The logic is that there is a need to instill pride and a feeling of strength in the people who have been subjects of bigotry over the years. It's good logic, and the cause is laudable. But it screams for separatism, and segregated schools cannot be far beyond.

If we insist that people of only one race or national background should write, produce, act in and watch a program before it is "minority" programming, we are endorsing segregation. Some programming will be for you and some for me . . . and sooner or later, someone will describe them as "separate but equal." While we bicker over it, poverty and ignorance will lie unchanged.

Why, then, do we insist that there is a "minority" program type? Why do we count up the "minority programming" hours? It may be because broadcasters must assure themselves (and the FCC), that they are not bigoted, that this is indeed a land of equality, and that we are erasing sins of our predecessors from the public ledger.

As we try to right the obvious wrongs, as we try to make our programming responsive to our communities and responsible to our constituents, we need reassurance. So we concoct "minority programming" to try to measure our good faith, whether we have it or not.

For the public broadcaster, there are many minorities. A surgeon enjoys learning about both music and the latest in anesthetic devices; an unskilled laborer is in need of a high-school diploma; an industrialist needs a brushup on business arithmetic; a city dweller wants help in getting his apartment fixed; a parent is ignorant of the latest techniques in helping deaf children.

These minorities overlap with every program. These are the audiences for whom we should design "minority programming," and they watch with different skin colors.

It's helping people, and what we call it doesn't matter. Let's just do it.

ROBERT MACNEIL

25 Years of Public Television

Despite acknowledged difficulties and many diverse criticisms, public television, according to PBS president Larry Grossman, "has introduced new standards of television excellence to this country. We have come late and we have taken risks. Yet our record demonstrates that no other institution in American life has given people so much value for so little." Robert MacNeil discusses the achievements and potential of public television.

. . . Since the first noncommercial station (KUHT-Houston) went on the air on May 25, 1953, public television has grown from an earnest experiment in televised education to a national network presenting a full range of programs. It now claims to command the occasional attention of more than half the American TV-watching population. . . .

No other broadcasting organization is quite like it, and many people would say "Thank God." If it had no other distinction, public television could claim to have invented the most fiendishly complicated system of local accountability ever to spring from the minds of fanatical democrats.

But it works—just. It is a monument to diversity, peopled by a collection of types quite unlike the commercial breed: the foundation hustler, the cranky academic, the tidy bureaucrat, the creative misfit, the Rotary smiler, the urgent feminist, the minority nag, and frustrated preacher, the fringe documentarian, the ubiquitous conference-goer. What they all have in common is zeal, an overfondness

This essay first appeared March 18, 1978.

for committees perhaps, but a genuine belief that American television can and should be better than it is.

They have shown an alternative. The further commercial TV has descended to the lowest mass taste, the higher public television has ascended to indulge those excluded. As the commercial people have homogenized the majority, public television has identified and programmed for minorities. It has shown that television need not insult the intelligence of the nation.

Kenneth Clark's *Civilisation,* Jacob Bronowski's *The Ascent of Man* and Alistair Cooke's *America* have expanded the possibilities of the medium as they have expanded people's experience.

It has opened the riches of the opera, ballet and the concert hall in *Great Performances, Wolf Trap, Live from Lincoln Center* and *Evening at Pops.*

It has addicted millions to a high standard of serial drama in *The Forsyte Saga, Elizabeth R, Upstairs, Downstairs* and other imported mini-series, creating the climate for the form that ABC employed so successfully with *Roots.*

It has given our children an alternative to constant sales pitches by toy makers and cereal manufacturers with *Sesame Street, The Electric Company, Mister Rogers' Neighborhood* and *Zoom.*

In public affairs, it has repeatedly carved out new forms. Starting with *News in Perspective* in the '60s, it has brought a parade of alternatives to commercial news: *Washington Week in Review, Wall Street Week,* coverage of Congressional hearings, state legislatures and city councils, new forms in local news with the *Newsroom* format, our own *MacNeil/Lehrer Report, Bill Moyers' Journal, The Great American Dream Machine.*

Through all these programs public television has offered an alternative to the chief tool of commercial television—the shrinking attention span.

Since prestige is a real commodity to commercial broadcasters, public television, even with its tiny ratings, causes just strong enough tremors of anxiety occasionally to stimulate protective imitations. It has served as a nursery for seedlings commercial television may later find feasible to transplant. It has been a shop window for foreign, mostly British, broadcasters, demonstrating that American TV's obsession with ratings is not the only way the game can be played.

It would distort reality, however, to vaunt all these achievements without looking at public television's failures. They do not erase the achievements, but they show how much the institution has to grow to fulfill its potential.

Public television has not proven itself viable enough to command really adequate resources. Consequently, it has not devoted enough to publicizing its own existence. Its advertising voice is a weak mew in a hurricane of commercial promotion. So it remains largely invisible to the mass audience and it has not broken through the threshold of credibility in audience share. The average public-television station commands no more than 3 to 4 per cent of the available audience, not enough to create a political constituency for a permanent, adequate system of funding.

But there are further twists to this vicious circle. Public television suffers from chronic internal schisms. It can't make up its mind what it wants to be when it grows up.

On December 28, [1977] I had the privilege of sitting as the PBS correspondent with those from NBC, CBS and ABC to interview President Carter. Although it was not the first time we had been included, Mr. Carter made a point of welcoming what he called "the four major networks." There were probably as many in public television who shuddered to hear that as there were people who sighed with happiness. In the received wisdom, "network" is a nonword. It stands for everything wrong with commercial television: central control and mass taste. By trying to preserve local control, public television has failed to concentrate its resources into critical masses needed to create enough programs of national appeal that would build its audience. Millions of dollars have been poured into equipping and staffing local stations but that has produced very few scintillating local programs that the nation wanted to share.

In my view, public television will be a success when, in any local market, the public station attracts enough audience—say, 10 per cent—to be the spoiler in the ratings game. That will be the threshold of credibility.

It may be that public television is doomed to remain the larvae spinning cocoons from which profitable commercial butterflies emerge. But Americans deserve more from this incredible medium. Television is perhaps the most important development in the technology of mass communications since the printing press. Where would our civilization be if that technology were managed exclusively by those who run commercial television? Our great libraries would look like airport bookstalls—the occasional Faulkner reprint among the volumes of popular escapism. Public television's mission is to recapture some of that ground.

[Since 1953], it has demonstrated the promise: it has only begun to fulfill it.

NEIL HICKEY

An Apple for the Television?

The first Carnegie Commission report defined instructional television, as distinct from public television, as programming "which calls upon the instinct to work, build, learn and improve, and asks the viewer to take on responsibilities in return for a later reward."

Public television stations invested approximately $58,180,000, or 17 per cent of their total expenditures, in instructional television (ITV) in fiscal 1979. The bulk of this money, more than $47 million, went to instructional programming on the elementary and secondary school level. Neil Hickey reviews the progress of American instructional television.

Five characters in a TV series tumble across the screen, punching, pushing and yelling. The children watching the program grow animated. Aha! More TV violence leading children astray?

No. These viewers are seated in a fourth-grade classroom at the Waverly Park School in East Rockaway, Long Island. The TV characters they are watching with such intense interest are part of an instructional television (ITV) series called *Inside/Out*. Its purpose is to "help children achieve and maintain well-being."

The 15-minute program—an episode called "Getting Even"—places youthful actors in a conflict situation that deals with such behavior as secretiveness, rejection and vengefulness.

After the program, teacher Michael Greenfield discusses the program with the class, asking questions that induce these 9-years-olds to think for themselves. He carefully avoids lecturing or moralizing. "How would you have solved the argument, Linda? What are the consequences when someone is bossy, Andy?"

This essay first appeared July 29, 1978.

A lively discussion ensues. The kids raise their hands, eager to offer a related experience, an opinion, a solution.

After class, four youngsters talk about the series. They all agree *Inside/Out* is interesting, and that they learn most from the discussion period. "It's helping us make our own decisions," one says.

For these suburban grade-schoolers, at least, instructional TV is obviously making an impact.

Some educators are still reluctant to enter the Age of Supermedia, but most would agree that the best classroom TV programs can perform impressive feats of education that grow out of the nature of the medium. The camera can go anywhere. It can introduce students to artists, scientists, authors and legislators whom they couldn't meet any other way.

Such electronic techniques as microphotography, slow motion, freeze frame and animation can imprint lessons effectively on children's minds. The capability of editing video tape and film makes it possible to contrast, compare and select images that dramatize points in vivid, visual terms.

"Television is perhaps richer and denser than any other instructional medium," says social scientist Dr. Wilbur Schramm. "Literally hundreds of studies have now shown television used effectively for teaching at every level . . . for almost every subject in the formal curriculum. No other medium has been tested so widely. . . . Where these varied uses of television have been measured, they have almost invariably shown learning gains, often large ones."

In Lincoln Heights, Ohio, the largest all-black city in the United States, an elaborate TV-instruction system was initiated [in 1972] after tests showed that 75 per cent of the students in the Lincoln Heights Elementary School were scoring lower in reading and mathematics than was appropriate for their ages. During the very first year, reading scores in the second and third grades—the main target grades—improved remarkably. By the third year, most students were reading at levels that were appropriate to their IQ scores, and some were doing much better than that.

Ever since the early 1950s, instructional-television programs have been available in one form or another to schools that want to use them. Their quality has ranged (as one teacher puts it) from "arrant junk" to "scrupulously crafted, expensively produced shows of great worth"—with the huge majority falling somewhere in between.

But for complicated reasons, the whole subject of classroom TV has long been a quagmire of misinformation and misimpressions, as well as a battleground of contending viewpoints. A dedicated core of True Believers in TV teaching continue to wage an uphill fight against inertia—and sometimes hostility—on the part of some teachers, principals and school boards.

Until [November 1977], educators had only a few vague notions about how much ITV is being used in the United States, by whom, and what the attitudes toward it are on the part of teachers and school administrators. Then the Corporation for Public Broadcasting (CPB) and the National Center for Education Statistics (NCES) released the results of a two-year, $250,000 survey—the first ever done nationwide on TV in the schoolroom—that provided some answers.

Thirty-two per cent of elementary and secondary schoolteachers [used] ITV "regularly," said the study, and 15 million out of 45 million students [were] exposed to it. ("Regular use" was defined as using 75 per cent or more of all the lessons in at least one series.)

Other findings: 72 per cent of teachers [reported] that ITV [was] available to them in one form or another, and the most-often-mentioned delivery system [was] over-the-air broadcasts from their local public-TV station; 37 per cent [had] access to video-tape recorders, but only one-quarter of those [used] them "regularly" and almost half [used] them "seldom or never"; TV sets for classroom use [were] available to 97 per cent of teachers who could utilize instructional programs if they chose to.

The survey also showed that a surprisingly large number of teachers have either a "don't know" or "don't care" attitude about classroom TV. Half the teachers surveyed agreed that "teachers don't make enough use of instructional television," but fully 44 per cent had no opinion at all about that assertion. Fifty-four per cent of the teachers disagreed with the statement that "the personal relationship between student and teacher is lost when instructional television is used," but a third weren't sure how they felt about that; and while 52 per cent of teachers disagreed that "children watch enough television at home—they don't need to watch more in school," almost 40 per cent were ambivalent on the subject.

Thus, the CPB/NCES survey was a mixed bag of good news and

bad news. Many ITV advocates choose to interpret its findings as proclaiming that ITV is "alive and well" in the U.S., and claim to be pleasantly surprised that even *that* many teachers and students were using it. Others have been quick to point out that—because of the definition of "regular" in the survey—a teacher could spend as little as one per cent of his [or her] time using TV and still be included in the 32 per cent of teachers who use it "regularly." Still, "It's the first positive indication we've had," says Dave Berkman, an official of HEW's Office of Education, "that TV may be making some minimal inroads into the schools."

ITV's road has never been smooth. Bennie Lucroy, former director of Mississippi's ITV network, says: "You still have to convince some parents that it's OK to have a TV set in the classroom. They say, 'I'm sending my child to school to be taught, not to watch television all day.' Certain expectations about teachers are rooted in tradition, and parents think their children should go through basically the same process as they did. That makes change very hard to come by in education."

Moreover, many teachers themselves are of two minds about ITV. Some feel threatened by it, as regards both their egos and their pocketbooks. [Said] one: "Teachers tend to be independent spirits who are proud and proprietary about their roles in the classroom. Many simply refuse to surrender any part of that sovereignty." Similarly, some teachers object to expenditures (from already overburdened school budgets) for expensive ITV programs, video-tape recording (VTR) machines, color-TV sets and study guides—money that might otherwise go into teachers' salaries. And they wonder if classroom TV might jeopardize their very jobs, now that the effects of a declining birthrate have turned the teaching profession into a buyers' market.

The latter fear is ungrounded, say the experts. "Over the years we've learned that TV doesn't replace anybody," says Lee Sauser, director of educational services for the Public Broadcasting Service in Washington. "It's a marvelous motivator; it can hold children's attention and stimulate their interest and curiosity." But without a knowledgeable teacher trained in the use of ITV, she insists, classroom TV just can't be effective. (Only 17 per cent of teachers have had *any* training in the use of ITV, according to the CPB survey.)

Actually, it's less fear or hostility than simple ignorance about instructional television and its availability that prevents ITV from fulfilling its manifest destiny. One of the "best-kept secrets in education," says Shirley Gillette, of New York's PBS outlet, WNET, is that most public-TV stations broadcast a daily diet of instructional shows during school hours that can be utilized at the flick of a switch. One school administrator asked her what "special hookup and equipment" he'd need to receive over-the-air ITV programs, and had to be told, gently, that all he had to do was switch on the TV sets on his school building.

To mitigate that kind of confusion, a dedicated, valiant corps of "utilization specialists" (of which there are fewer than one hundred in the entire country) regularly fan out from public-TV stations and some state boards of education to publicize ITV among principals and teachers. "Sometimes it's like rolling a rock uphill," says one of them.

One problem is that many of those educators sampled instructional programs years ago, found them (quite rightly) to be dreadful and have disdained ITV ever since. But in recent years, the quality of classroom TV has improved dramatically from the distant days when a "talking face" on the TV screen was the typical ITV show.

Now, groups like the Agency for Instructional Television (AIT) in Bloomington, Ind.; the ITV Co-op in Falls Church, Va.; and others create expensive, custom-tailored, scrupulously designed, researched and produced programs such as *Inside/Out, All About You* (a course in anatomy, physiology and health care), *Cover-to-Cover* (which encourages a love for reading), *Alive and About* (a nature-study and conservation series) and *Whatcha Gonna Do?* (which draws students into decision-making situations).

The Children's Television Workshop makes *The Electric Company,* the single most used program in schools. (CTW's other popular success, *Sesame Street,* is for preschoolers and is thus not technically an ITV program, although some schools use it as such.) Programs by the score also emerge from such sources as the Great Plains National Instructional Television Library in Lincoln, Neb.; the Encyclopaedia Britannica Educational Corp. in Chicago; and Western Instructional Television in Los Angeles.

Ironically, the same medium that's so often accused of sabotaging the literacy of America's children is the one that—when transported to the classroom—offers genuine hope of stemming the precipitate erosion in the basic skills of reading, writing and arithmetic. A 1975 study by the U.S. Office of Education indicates that 22 per cent of Americans over 17 [were] totally illiterate and that another 32 per cent [were] only "marginally literate." [November 1977] tests in New York City showed that 40 per cent of all public-school sixth graders were reading below their level, and 53 per cent were behind in math. Forty-two per cent of ninth graders were two years behind in reading. It's worse among black students: nationwide, nearly 42 per cent of 17-year-old black Americans are functionally illiterate. (Studies show that poor black children watch even more television than their white coevals.) City University in New York spends about $30 million a year on remedial instruction—teaching college-level students how to read, write and reckon.

Those appalling figures are an incentive to ITV's True Believers to spread the gospel of classroom TV and to proclaim their conviction that it can go far toward mitigating the nagging problems of hammering home to children the essential skills. "TV in the schools is probably on the threshold of its maturity," says AIT's Edwin Cohen. "We have every right to expect this, since it is now [over] 25 years old. Nobody questions any more that it can do a job that schools will value."

THE FUTURE

"By 1990 you're not going to recognize television as it is today," according to California Congressman Lionel Van Deerlin, chairman of the House Subcommittee on Communications. Van Deerlin further predicts that new technological developments "will transform not only the face of broadcasting but the lives of Americans as profoundly as the Industrial Revolution." The official publication of the American Film Institute, *American Film,* refers to the "video revolution, long forecast by pundits . . . hard upon us, made manifest by the burgeoning of cable systems, pay television channels, a dizzying array of videocassette recorders . . . and the emergence into the marketplace of the videodiscs."

New technological developments will provide vehicles of experimentation, "a kind of video off-off-Broadway," in the opinion of producer Norman Lear. He feels that in time "channels will exist for the eleven million people who are interested in opera on TV and even for the eleven thousand people who may want to see a show about polishing skis. . . . There won't be the money to spend on 80,000 patrons that the networks spend on 40 million . . . the poverty will force innovation."

CBS Broadcast Group president Gene Jankowski has been skeptical about how much innovation the new video outlets will encourage, given the current experience with cable and pay cable. "Beyond sports, what do all these extra signals provide? For the most part, old movies and off-network reruns, and even some dusted-off, old

Public Broadcast Systems material. If we announced a comparable schedule, someone would be calling for a Congressional investigation, and the critics would be looking upon television as the light that failed." As for those who promote the new video form, in November 1979, Jankowski called them "doom and gloom sayers, who would have you believe that television as we know it is a member of an endangered species."

Despite Jankowski's pronouncement on the new video apparatus, CBS Incorporated announced in February 1980 that it was creating CBS Video Enterprises. The new division will manufacture, produce and market programming for video tapes and video discs. And in May 1980, CBS announced that by 1981 it will initiate CBS Cable which will produce and distribute original programs for cable operation. The new CBS division will operate independently of the CBS Broadcast Group and CBS Video Enterprises.

ABC also is trying to ensure itself a piece of the new video market through the formation of ABC Video Enterprises. When ABC's founder and board chairman Leonard Goldenson announced the new division, he told his stockholders, "new forms of distribution have appeared at so rapid a rate that even the cloudiest crystal ball suggests a revolution in viewing patterns." Goldenson emphasized that "the important fact to remember" about new technologies such as pay cable, video discs, video-cassette recorders, is that "they are means of distribution. They can be no more popular than the material that they distribute. And at present they have a substantial need for programs to distribute—programs of all kinds: news, information, instruction, entertainment." Goldenson thinks the new venture could be very profitable because of ABC's "special expertise in identifying and producing programs that people want to watch."

NBC has not been excluded from the push into new technologies. NBC's parent company, RCA, announced in 1979 that its satellite division (RCA American Communications) would offer to build and maintain Earth stations at its own expense for all commercial television stations in the United States. Not a company to take chances, RCA is assuring itself a significant portion of satellite traffic should producers eventually be able to bypass NBC and get their programs directly to the local stations via satellite transmission. RCA is also developing a video-disc system which is scheduled for market release in 1981. CBS has agreed to supply video discs for that system through CBS Video Enterprises.

Variety pointed out in the lead story of a December 1979 issue: "In a sense, it's a matter of change or be left behind." In the preceding months, according to *Variety,* "virtually every one" of its issues had been "filled with stories of new companies getting into production, setting up home video divisions, forming alliances with pay cable firms, and the like." These observations are certainly borne out by the current market. In late 1979, Warner Cable proposed a cable system for portions of New York City that would provide more than 120 separate television channels. Fifteen different major brands of video-cassette recorders are now available and more models are expected by 1981. With video discs coming on the market too, some experts believe the consumer will be faced with too many choices in the very near future.

The effects of the so-called video revolution remain to be seen. Enthusiasts predict that television owners of the future will use their sets rather than watch them. The question will no longer be, "What's on TV tonight?" but rather, "What would we like to put on TV tonight?" Newton Minow predicts a "radical upheaval" in mass communications during the next twenty-five years. "There'll be so many paths into the viewer's home that McLuhan's 'medium is the message' will be turned on its head. The message will be what counts and it will have to satisfy the individual viewer's capacity to select and choose." Much is made of the potential for vastly increased choices in our means of education, communications, convenience and enjoyment. Sylvester "Pat" Weaver, president of NBC in the 1950s, recently stated: "We had the potential for turning the common man into the uncommon man. TV people should want to help inform, enrich and enlighten as well as entertain. . . . In the 1980's, we will have another chance." Syndicated columnist Harriet Van Horne, however, foresees some problems:

> Our people are becoming less literate by the minute. As old habits decline, such as reading books and thinking thoughts, TV will absorb their time. By the twenty-first century our people doubtless will be squint-eyed, hunchbacked, and fond of the dark. Conversation will be a lost art. People will simply tell each other jokes. . . . The chances are the grandchild of the Television Age won't know how to read this.

Others fear that people will become "video junkies" and wrap themselves up in an "all-electronic cocoon, lighting up their three-dimensional wraparound screen" with little contact with the rest of society.

Even the television industry has expressed concern about the social effects of the video revolution. Head of 20th Century-Fox Television Sy Salkowitz has said that the new technology being produced may result in "something quite pleasant" or the industry may be "unknowingly infecting people with a cancer." Richard Frank of Paramount Pictures has a similar view: "No one has any concrete answer for how television will finally evolve, which technologies will endure and which will fall by the way, and finally, what effects a 'communications revolution' will have on society."

NEIL HICKEY

Will the Network System Survive?

Each network currently orders 2000 hours of original prime-time programming a year, which costs an average of over $500,000 an hour. "Only the national distribution which the networks have enables us to do that," according to NBC president Fred Silverman. "It will be years, if ever, before other technologies will come close to delivering the kind of audience that would justify those costs or require that kind of volume." In a 1979 speech to the Academy of TV Arts and Sciences, Silverman declared that in spite of "dreams of cable outlets, magnetized bubble gum wrappers and 48 other technologies," the networks will continue to be the primary markets for program suppliers.

Bruce Owens, the Department of Justice economist most directly involved in communications, sees the encroachment of new technologies somewhat differently. "Cable and pay [television] and superstations and video recorders and discs will eventually chip away at network power. . . . And some year we will all notice they're [the networks] gone." Neil Hickey enumerates some of the threats facing the networks because of the new technologies.

"It's *Die Götterdämmerung,*" said one expert observer. "The twilight of the gods. After 30 years of Government-sanctioned monopoly, commercial-television broadcasting is now faced with an array of adversaries who insist there are better ways to serve a nation's communication needs." Another veteran of many broadcast wars, Rev.

Excerpts have been taken from this essay, which first appeared November 6, 1978.

Everett Parker (who heads the United Church of Christ's Office of Communication), says that what we're beginning to see, in the industry's panic to achieve ever-higher profits and ratings, is "the dinosaur's last throes of agony." Louis Friedland, president of MCA-TV, puts it a bit more cautiously: "There are many who now believe that the networking system has a limited existence. In the next 10 years, television networks and stations will be subjected to every kind of stress."

Commercial TV's predicament is not unlike that of a powerful country—having conventional armed forces—under siege by hordes of highly motivated guerrillas. Some of those guerrillas are easily identifiable: they have names like cable TV, home video recording, video discs, video games and pay cable. Others are more shadowy but just as threatening: well-organized citizen groups with powerful grass-roots support (National PTA, Action for Children's Television, National Citizens Committee for Broadcasting, among many others) who know all the sensitive pressure points (e.g., license challenges, advertiser boycotts) by which change can be effected.

And in Washington, the Carter Administration is thought by broadcasters to have fostered a regulatory climate that is more friendly to entrepreneurs of the new technologies than to themselves.

But it is Representative Lionel Van Deerlin (D-Cal.) who is forcing the TV industry into its most painful self-examination in years. As chairman of the House Communications Subcommittee, he wants to revise the [1934] Communications Act (which does not even mention television) to make it more consanguine with the communications revolution that is even now being born. He is at pains to persuade broadcasters that it is in their own best, long-term interests to help "adjust old law to new needs" by cooperating in the creation of a new act that would deal with satellites, cable and pay-cable TV, fiber optics, computers, lasers (and other new hardware), thereby plotting an orderly communications policy for the twenty-first century. He also points out that the authors of the 1934 Act intended that broadcasting serve the *local* needs of American communities, but that networks now dominate television so thoroughly that they provide 67 per cent of what their affiliated stations put on the air.

Van Deerlin's efforts at reform have met the massed resistance of broadcasters who are fearful that such tinkering might (as they put it) "seriously impair or destroy a system that has successfully fulfilled its mandate to the public." And they intend to marshal their vast lobbying resources in Washington to (in Van Deerlin's words) "keep the gold in Fort Knox." Their fervid defense of the status quo doubtless will succeed for a time, but disinterested experts are certain that broadcasting's structure is destined for a slow but sure evolution into new forms over the next few decades. The outlines of that structure are only now coming into view.

Satellites and cable, in conjunction, will be near the heart of the new systems. Satellite transmission over long distances is far more flexible and cheaper than either microwave relays or land lines. Cable television now serves about [16] million American homes ([20] per cent of the total TV homes). A study by the Young & Rubicam ad agency foresees 30 per cent penetration of U.S. homes (with the potential for 20 per cent more) by 1981.

Already we are witnessing the birth of so-called "superstations" (like WTBS in Atlanta) that distribute their signals via satellite to regional networks of cable systems, giving those cable subscribers yet another viewing choice.[1] That phenomenon is bound to grow, says Daniel Aaron, chairman of the National Cable Television Association. Actually, any speculator with a program to sell and some money to invest can reach [over 2000] cable systems (those equipped with Earth stations) by satellite if he chooses, and that figure is mounting as more cable operators decide they want the entertainments available via satellite.

Principal among those attractions at the moment is pay cable, and the largest pay-cable company (Home Box Office, with [about two-thirds] of the market) also happens to be the world's largest private satellite-communications network, beaming movies and some custom-made programming to almost every state in the Union.[2] Altogether, the pay-cable industry [has more than 5 million subscribers]. . . .

1. By March 1980, WTBS had over 7.3 million subscribers via satellite in 48 states.

2. By March 1980 Home Box Office had a network of more than 1700 affiliates.

Those numbers may be unimpressive by commercial-TV standards, but they represent a fragmenting of the mass audience, which is the commodity networks sell to advertisers. Other examples of that erosion abound. [Millions of] video games were sold in 1977 to families who chose to play electronic hockey rather than watch television. Public television attracted more prime-time viewers than [ever] before, and [in 1978] PBS unveiled a fancy and flexible new satellite distribution system for its programs (which [in] 1980 allows it to "feed" up to four shows at a time to its stations) that's more sophisticated than anything the commercial networks now employ.

Similarly, an ad hoc "fourth network" called Operation Prime Time, consisting of a consortium of [over 100] stations (both independents and network affiliates), [looms] as an alternative, for both viewers and advertisers, to the three-network output.[3] Not only Operation Prime Time but other program producers as well are concocting still more first-run TV fare and formats—some of it to run 52 weeks a year—for any station that wants to buy into it. Says one station manager: "The networks are exerting subtle pressure on us, through our affiliation contracts, to abjure this 'unsanctioned' programming and get back on the plantation. They see it as another crack in their dike." . . .

"It's a very exciting time" in television says Frank Price, president of Universal Television, the biggest supplier of TV shows, because the winds of change are definitely blowing. Alternative outlets for producers are about to expand dramatically. Companies like Universal are nearing the day when they will be creating programs directly for pay cable, either on a pay-per-program basis or for outfits (like Home Box Office) that charge a monthly rate.

Says producer David Gerber: "As these new systems grow, we'll have the flexibility to make the kinds of programs we want rather than designing product for a three-network market." A drama or musical special could earn $40 million in one night alone, he points out, by charging $4 per set to 10 million homes. "The network system as we know it is in for some large-scale alterations," says Gerber. "They're going to have to compete for ratings not only

3. Operation Prime Time plans to broadcast nine specials, including three four-hour mini-series in 1980.

among themselves but with the new systems that will be drawing off tremendous numbers of their audience."

Another alternate outlet for producers will be the video disc—long-playing video recordings of dramas, operas, ballet, Broadway musicals and other entertainments that you'll collect and play like phonograph records through your TV set. . . .

Many other guerrillas are lying in the weeds: Hollywood moviemakers talk of beaming new films straight to local stations and cable systems via satellite, bypassing the networks; in Japan, broadcasters are experimenting with direct satellite-to-home TV transmission via rooftop antennas; AT&T and others are developing home terminals to expand enormously the flow of entertainment and information into American homes; Warner Cable is offering a two-way feedback TV system in Columbus, Ohio, that serves its subscribers a menu of thirty channels; owners of home video players (Betamax, Selecta Vision, etc.) can buy or rent all manner of cassettes containing theatrical movies and other entertainment and instruction, as an alternative to broadcast fare; [manufacturers are attempting to devise] a new TV tuner that will give UHF stations near parity with VHF. . . .

Still, television's transformation will proceed at glacial pace for the present, gathering some momentum in the 1980s. Nobody can divine its ultimate shape. But it's certain that today's 20-year-olds will enjoy a far saner, more multifarious communications environment than anything we know today. The needs of that formless beast, The Mass Audience, no longer will be the medium's dominant concern. The public will be addressed, at last, in all its variety, potentiality and dignity rather than as an immense herd of dimwitted sheep to be delivered to the highest bidder.

DAVID LACHENBRUCH

The 3-Billion Dollar Gamble

The dominance of the three networks has been enhanced because UHF (Channels 14 through 83) stations have never been fully competitive with VHF (Channels 2 through 13) stations, and about two-thirds of American television households receive only three of the VHF stations. Representative Van Deerlin suggests that UHF stations gaining even near parity with their VHF counterparts "could change the economics of television as much as anything in the last two decades."

Broadcasting reported in 1979 that UHF stations, although still underdogs, had "turned the proverbial corner" and "finally come into their own." *Broadcasting* added that UHF stations "had done it largely alone, with little help from others and over tremendous obstacles placed in their way."

One of those obstacles was the television allocation scheme, labeled by *Fortune* magazine, "the engineering botch of the century." David Lachenbruch reviews the problems UHF has had and discusses some of the attempts to help UHF since 1962.

Outside of the television industry, few people remember the all-channel law of 1962, but its effects have been significant. Depending on how you look at it, it was either (a) a heroic attempt to provide the nation with far better choice in television viewing, greater diversity of programs and more local expression on the air, or (b) a classic attempt by government to bail out a failing industry at public expense. However you look at it, it has added an average of $20 to the retail price of every television set manufactured since April 1964, for a total of nearly [$3.75] billion spent by American consumers.

This essay first appeared in two parts, November 1, November 8, 1975.

This massive subsidy was paid by television-set buyers to provide equipment that would enable them to tune in the ultra-high-frequency (UHF) channels, 14 through 83. Whether you use it or not, what you paid for is that second tuning dial on your set. If you have a portable, you also paid a little extra for the loop antenna used to pick up UHF channels the same way a rabbit-ear picks up VHF.[1]

When the all-channel law was passed, UHF broadcasting was in imminent danger of extinction as the result of a colossal goof by the FCC in 1952—the "intermixing" of VHF and UHF stations within the same communities.

In 1946, when postwar television started, there were thirteen channels (Channel 1 was taken away in 1948 and earmarked for other services). Channels 2 through 13 were assigned pretty much to those intrepid television pioneers who applied for them, so long as they weren't close enough geographically to cause interference with other TV stations on the same or adjacent frequencies.

It quickly became apparent that television was neither a toy nor a fad, but the mass communications and entertainment medium of the future—and also a gold mine for those who got in on the ground floor. Applications for stations began to pile up. It was obvious that some kind of master plan was needed to provide multichannel TV service to all parts of the nation. On September 30, 1948, with fewer than one hundred stations on the air, the Commission declared a "freeze" on grants of all new stations while it tackled the problem of providing equitable nationwide distribution of television channels.

There seemed to be no way that the twelve very-high-frequency (VHF) channels could supply the kind of service the FCC had in mind—to provide a choice of channels to every community in the United States. Since the start of TV, engineers had been experimenting with "upstairs television" in the ultra-high band. It worked, but it had some definite limitations as compared with VHF. The signal required much more power to carry the same distance. It reacted differently to various types of obstructions, such as mountains and buildings. And little was known about building TV sets which could pick up the UHF (ultra-high-frequency) signals.

1. All television sets manufactured after July 1, 1978 have been required to have attached UHF antennas if they have antennas included. Prior to that date, viewers often had to fasten a UHF loop antenna (which generally was packed in the bottom of the carton) to the set in order to adequately receive UHF stations.

But there was no place to go except up. As the freeze dragged on, the Commission and Congress held hearings on how to integrate these new channels into television. Meanwhile, those stations already on the air—all VHF, of course—were reaping a golden harvest of advertiser dollars as the result of the increasing numbers of sets owned by viewers lucky enough to live in areas where they were broadcasting.

Bearing in mind the differences between UHF and VHF, as well as VHF's huge head start, there were many proposals to help UHF overcome its handicap. One idea was to reserve the UHF channels for color television (a system that worked very well, but much later, in England). Another was the assignment of UHF channels principally in areas with flat terrain, VHF to serve more mountainous areas and city canyons.

One of the most cogent pleas, as it now turns out, was made by Dr. Allen B. DuMont, who then headed the DuMont Television Network, running a poor fourth in ratings.[2] He argued that, insofar as possible, VHF and UHF channels should be "nonintermixed"—that is, some areas should be all VHF, others all UHF. He explained that this would eliminate the unnatural advantage enjoyed by the older Channels 2 through 13 and provide for equality among all channels in a given area, permitting the growth of four networks with equal access to the public, as well as public broadcasting.

But the DuMont plan raised the hackles of the existing VHF broadcasters (108 were on the air by the time the freeze was thawed in 1952). DuMont's proposed geographical table of television allocations, if it had been adopted, would have forced twelve of them to move to UHF to accomplish nonintermixture—and they'd have none of that. They were the pioneers who embraced television when

2. The DuMont network, with WABD (Channel 5) in New York as the flagship station, operated from 1946 to 1955. Its most popular programs included Bishop Fulton J. Sheen's *Life Is Worth Living,* Jackie Gleason's *The Cavalcade of Stars* (later moved to CBS and changed to *The Jackie Gleason Show*), and *Monday Night Boxing*. DuMont was unable to obtain a full complement of five VHF owned and operated stations and eventually was forced to produce inexpensive variety, quiz and game shows. The network had increasing problems getting its network programs cleared in the major markets on a regular basis. By 1954 DuMont had lost $4 million and only three or four of its weekly programs were fully sponsored for the 1954–55 season.

others were belittling it, and they didn't feel they should be penalized by being banished to the higher, unknown frequencies.

When the FCC finally ended the freeze on July 1, 1952, it rejected the DuMont plan and all others which took into account the differences between UHF and VHF, and issued a table of allocations which mixed V and U channels in most areas but tended to give major cities the most VHF channels. It didn't require the changeover of any VHF stations to UHF, and was anchored on the east by the seven existing VHF stations in New York, and on the west by the seven in Los Angeles. This table provided for 70 UHF channels in addition to the 12 VHF and contained geographical assignments of 2051 proposed stations, of which 1445 would be UHF.

In 1950, RCA had built an experimental UHF transmitter in Bridgeport, Conn., to prove that upstairs television could provide acceptable service. It showed that UHF indeed was adequate, and even superior to VHF in some relatively unimportant ways ("UHF goes 10 feet deeper into the Holland Tunnel than VHF," quipped one top RCA scientist). But the tests also revealed that UHF needed far more transmitter power than VHF to provide an equally snow-free picture. When it finally ended the freeze and authorized UHF broadcasting, the FCC recognized this problem and authorized UHF stations to radiate as much as one million watts from their antennas, compared with 360,000 watts for VHF Channels 7 to 13 and 100,000 for Channels 2 through 6.

After the freeze came the TV gold rush as thousands of entrepreneurs sought to make their fortunes through the Midas magic of television. Many were radio-station owners, newspaper owners, movie producers and distributors and theater owners, along with used-car dealers, real-estate agents, widget manufacturers and morticians—all intent on proving to the FCC that they could serve the public while making millions in television. Where they could, they applied for VHF channels, which were quickly oversubscribed. Elsewhere they signed up for UHF.

The first UHF station went on the air with amazing speed and resounding fanfare. KPTV, assigned to Channel 27 in Portland, Ore., bought RCA's experimental Bridgeport transmitter and turned it on September 1, 1952, just 60 hours after it had arrived by air.

By the time the first UHF test pattern lit up on KPTV, there were more than 20,000,000 television sets in use in the United States—virtually none of them able to tune in UHF channels. To receive the new channels with an existing set, the viewer had to add a converter or have his service technician install a UHF "strip" in his set's tuner, usually along with an outdoor UHF antenna. The TV-set manufacturers rushed into production of all-channel sets with two dials—one for VHF and the other for UHF.

Although UHF stations were allowed to broadcast with a million watts of power, nobody knew how to build that powerful a transmitter at the time the freeze ended. The insensitivity of early UHF converters and UHF-equipped TV sets, combined with low transmitter power and lack of UHF experience by TV-set installers, often made it difficult to receive an adequate picture.

But many of the new stations faced a far more serious problem—competition from established VHF outlets. VHF stations had none of UHF's transmission or reception problems—but, more important, many had already built up large audiences of viewers with VHF-only sets. The most important ingredient in a television station's success was a network affiliation. Given the choice of a VHF or a UHF affiliate, the networks invariably chose the VHF.

Could UHF have succeeded on a nonintermixed basis? There is enough proof to answer yes. Some UHF outlets were successful from the start, and those were all in areas with little or no VHF competition. There simply was no television until UHF came along, so UHF *was* television. In those nonintermixed areas—such as Peoria, Youngstown, Akron, Allentown-Bethlehem, Wilkes-Barre, Scranton, Fresno-Bakersfield—the public and the networks quickly embraced UHF. The signals may have been harder to pick up than VHF, but there was no VHF so who knew the difference? The program's the thing, and a network program looks exactly the same on UHF as on VHF.

But in the intermixed markets, trouble began to show up quickly. Station WROV-TV on Channel 27 in Roanoke, Va., was the first to throw in the towel, turning off the juice in June 1953 after trying for only three months, blaming its problems on the lack of UHF sets in the area, failure to get a network affiliation because of VHF competition, and "limited and poor reception." It was to be the first of many.

At the end of 1954, 122 intrepid UHF broadcasters were on the air, but by the middle of the next year, 49 had given up their ghosts, and 106 potential UHF station owners took the hint, deciding not to build and returning their permits to the FCC. By 1960 there were only 75 UHF survivors. Pioneering KPTV had given up in 1957 as the result of VHF competition; only its call-letters now remain—on a VHF station.

There was trouble in televisionland. In 1957, an FCC survey showed 397 reporting VHF stations made total profits of $92,800,000 before taxes, while 88 commercial UHF stations aggregated a loss of $3,500,000.

As the situation threatened to deteriorate from an emergency to a debacle, the FCC came under increasing pressure from the surviving UHF broadcasters and their congressmen to do something. It had already attempted a number of patchwork measures: It increased the permissible power of UHF stations from one million to five million watts. To encourage major broadcasters—particularly the networks—to take an interest in UHF, it changed its "multiple-ownership" rules, which had permitted any one entity to own no more than five stations, upping the number to seven so long as no more than five were VHF. CBS and NBC took advantage of this new rule, each adding two UHF stations. But even network ownership couldn't salvage the situation. The networks found their own stations clobbered in the ratings and soon put them off the air.[3]

There seemed to be only one thing to do: unscramble the egg. The FCC bit the bullet and proposed an elaborate program of "de-intermixture," in effect adopting Dr. DuMont's idea (although the DuMont network had perished, a victim of intermixture). By this time, de-intermixture would have resulted in the shifting of powerful stations from VHF to UHF. The VHF broadcasters put the heat on their congressmen. Now, congressmen don't like to run afoul of

3. NBC owned UHF stations in Buffalo, N.Y. (1955-58) and Hartford, Conn. (1956–58). CBS also owned a Hartford UHF station (1956–58) as well as a UHF outlet in Milwaukee, Wis. (1956–59).

broadcasters in their home districts—particularly VHF broadcasters —and soon there was a clamor from Congress for [the] FCC to drop its de-intermixture proposal. In exchange, the FCC was offered the all-channel bill, to build up the UHF audience without hurting VHF broadcasters.

The all-channel bill would simply transfer the burden of UHF's success to the public by giving the FCC the power to require the inclusion of UHF capability in all future television sets. The manufacturers had already been burned by UHF and were shy about providing all-channel capability on their own. When UHF broadcasting began, about 20 per cent of all sets being produced had UHF tuners in anticipation of a UHF boom, but these started piling up in warehouses, and the proportion fell to as low as 5½ per cent.

TV-set makers screamed that the legislation would add from $20 to $75 to the cost of sets and deprive buyers of "freedom of choice." Their trade association pointed out that 92 per cent of viewers lived beyond the range of UHF stations and the tuners in their sets would be useless. One set maker put it this way: "If the government can tell us what to make, let them tell us how to sell it." But three set manufacturers were remarkably silent about the all-channel bill. They were RCA, GE and Westinghouse. They happened also to own VHF television stations.

The all-channel bill made sense. People weren't watching UHF because their sets didn't have UHF tuners. UHF stations weren't being built because there was no potential audience. The bill could break the vicious circle and in ten to twelve years (the life span of a television set) the "UHF problem" would evaporate—or so it seemed then.

When President Kennedy endorsed the all-channel bill in a special consumer message to Congress, the "compromise" was sealed. The FCC dropped de-intermixture in exchange for the new law, which gave it the authority to rule that all television sets be "capable of adequately receiving" all channels. "Adequately" turned out to be the key word. . . .

Every set built or imported since April 30, 1964, has been capable of "adequately" receiving all channels. The FCC first defined "adequately" by establishing a minimum figure for internally generated electronic "noise" permitted in UHF tuners. It has been redefining it ever since.[4]

Optimists believed that the all-channel rules would solve all of UHF's problems over the ten-to-twelve-year replacement cycle for television sets by putting UHF on an equal footing with VHF as older sets were gradually replaced with new receivers. The television-set industry began grinding out sets with two channel selectors, one for VHF and one for UHF, and the public paid the extra $20 or so at retail.

It soon became apparent that you could force a viewer to buy a UHF tuner but you couldn't make him touch it. Many owners of the new sets didn't even know what that extra knob was. [As has been noted], in 1964, about 90 per cent of the population couldn't have tuned in a UHF station if they tried.

Even where there were UHF stations on the air, problems showed up. The UHF tuner was less sensitive than the VHF—and more difficult to tune, since it had a continuous radio-type dial designed to cover 70 channels as opposed to the neat click-into-place 12-channel tuner for VHF. In many places where VHF channels could be picked up on rabbit-ears, UHF reception required a special antenna. Where outdoor VHF antennas were used, separate UHF antennas with their own lead-in wires were usually needed, and most of the new "all-channel" antennas simply didn't work well on UHF.

Nevertheless, the glimmer of hope provided by the all-channel law encouraged more stations to open up shop in UHF-land. Of course, their owners would have preferred VHF, but there was no more room on those channels. By the beginning of 1970, there were 176 commercial stations on the UHF band (compared with 501 on VHF), and all together they managed to lose $45,500,000 that year, while the VHFs raked in nearly $332,000,000 in profits before taxes. But UHF's big growth was in noncommercial public TV. As 1970 started, 106 of these public stations were on UHF, compared with

4. It is generally estimated that a reduction of 3 decibels (dbs) in noise results in a virtual doubling of the quality of the television picture. In 1964 the FCC set the permitted noise figure at 18 dbs. Not until 1978 did the Commission act to amend that figure: by October 1981 manufacturers must reduce noise in new sets to 14 dbs; by 1982 the level is expected to be 12 dbs.

only 80 on VHF. Of the channels reserved for noncommercial TV, more than 80 per cent are in the UHF band.[5]

In 1970, the broadcasters were back at the FCC, arguing that it hadn't adequately defined "adequately." UHF stations were harder to tune than VHF channels on the same set. So the Commission established a set of "tuner-equality" rules and gave set makers until mid-1974 to gradually phase in sets which tuned UHF as easily as VHF.

As a result, most of the new television sets on the market today have tuners that click into position for each one of the 70 UHF channels. Some have much more elaborate electronic tuners, which use the same knob or push buttons for VHF and UHF, and don't differentiate at all between the two types of channels. These electronic tuners still are quite expensive and are found principally in high-priced sets.

After all the huffing and puffing, the all-channel law finally has started to pay off. [By 1980] in the nation as a whole, some [94] per cent of all television homes [had] sets with UHF tuners—whether they [used] them or not. [As of March 1980 there were 229] commercial and [162] public UHF stations on the air. In its [1978] financial survey, the FCC reported [almost three-fourths] of the UHF stations had made it into the black.[6]

Network-affiliated UHF stations in areas where there was little VHF competition were profitable almost from the start, as were a few independents with innovative programming. William L. Putnam, who heads WWLP on Channel 22 in Springfield, [Mass.], and WRLP on Channel 32 in Greenfield, Mass., says the [Springfield] station has been profitable [since 1955]. "I am not a UHF broadcaster," says Putnam. "I am a broadcaster. By the force of circumstances, I have had to live with the poorer qualities of UHF." The formula for UHF success? "Very high power helps. Local programming helps. Being lucky comes first—and there's nothing as important as having patient stockholders. The all-channel law has wrought

5. As of March 1980, 127 VHF channels and 528 UHF channels were reserved for noncommercial use.

6. While UHF income (profits) and revenues are growing at a faster percentage rate than those of VHF stations, in 1978 only 10 per cent of total station revenues went to UHF stations.

wonders—very slowly—but the tuning capability is now available." WWLP originates its own programs three hours a day and carries some NBC shows. Both stations emphasize sports, telecasting Red Sox and Bruins games from Boston.

Sports have turned out to be the salvation of more than one UHF station. In Philadelphia, viewers can't watch the Phillies or the Flyers without twiddling the UHF knob. Many UHF stations cater to minorities. In New York, Los Angeles, Chicago, San Antonio and San Francisco, there are channels programmed almost entirely in Spanish. Although the networks still prefer VHF, they have signed up UHF stations in areas where there aren't enough Vs to go around. . . .

There's still a broad difference of opinon whether more should be done by the government to build up UHF. FCC commissioner Robert E. Lee, who has been charged with overseeing the development of UHF since the passage of the all-channel law, credits that legislation with vastly improving the status of "upstairs" broadcasting, and adds: "The Government helps a new industry get started, but after a while it's got to be on its own."

The fact remains that there are 1200 UHF channel assignments available throughout the country but only [391 were occupied in February 1980]. Public television can offer a real nationwide service only if UHF succeeds because more than half its stations are UHF.[7] After a long silence on the subject, the Public Broadcasting Service has entered the battle. President Hartford Gunn kicked off the noncommercial stations' active lobbying effort [in 1975] when he told a PBS membership meeting: "UHF broadcasting has failed to meet its potential. It has been branded as an also-ran in the race with VHF. It has failed to attract the needed attention of Government officials who are in a position to effect change. And, most tragic of all, it has evoked apathy from the countless viewers who, for one reason or another, experience great difficulty in obtaining satisfactory reception."

Gunn's speech became the kickoff for a new organization of commercial UHF and public broadcasters—the Council for UHF Broadcasting (CUB). CUB has been collaring FCC commissioners,

7. In March 1980, more than 60 per cent of public television stations were UHF. As of that date there were 162 UHF and 105 VHF public stations on the air.

Federal Trade Commission members, senators, representatives, White House staffers—any government officials who will listen—calling attention to the need for UHF and urging further rescue efforts.

CUB has recuited the powerful National Association of Broadcasters, the Association of Maximum Service Telecasters (a VHF broadcaster's group), PBS and the Corporation for Public Broadcasting to join it in pushing a program of government and private action: (1) Stricter FCC standards for UHF tuner performance. (2) An eventual requirement that single-knob VHF-UHF tuners be standard in all sets. . . . (3) Government testing of antennas for operation on UHF, the results to be widely publicized. (4) An industry crash program to improve efficiency of UHF transmitters. (5) Public-relations programs on how to install and tune UHF sets, sparked by on-air announcements on VHF stations.[8]

The growth of cable TV has been cited as a new threat to the existence of UHF, since, being a closed-circuit system, it can provide vast numbers of channels without using any of the valuable radio-frequency spectrum. Actually, cable has helped some UHF stations and hurt others. Since CATV systems are required to carry all local channels, they automatically bring UHF stations into equality with VHF by eliminating antenna and reception problems and by converting the UHF frequency to an unused VHF channel. But in smaller towns and cities, the cable means more competition for UHF, since it often brings in extra channels from outside the area.

If UHF succeeds, it could mean local stations with local programs in almost every community in the United States. It could mean the availability of public-TV channels to virtually the entire population. It could mean a fourth commercial network.

But at this moment, the underused UHF band is in danger of disappearing entirely. The radio-frequency spectrum is a valuable natural resource—as real and as limited as oil or uranium—and it's being eyed greedily by other radio services which desperately need electromagnetic elbow room. Already, 15 channels have been lopped from the UHF broadcast band in major urban areas to relieve the shortage of frequencies for mobile communication services used by

8. By early 1979 the National UHF Broadcasting Association, an organization of UHF broadcasters, was also involved in these and other efforts to strengthen UHF.

police, taxicabs and so forth. With more than 800 UHF broadcast assignments lying fallow, it's only a matter of time before strong arguments will be made for more efficient use of these frequencies.

[During the fifteen years between April 1964, when] the all-channel rules went into effect [and March 1979], the public bought [180,000,000] television sets with UHF tuners. This [$3.7 billion] investment dwarfs the UHF broadcasters' [$378,187,000] in [property] and equipment and their [1978] gross revenues of [$510,300,000]. Although the three-billion-dollar gamble shows some signs of beginning to pay off, UHF is still far from a strong and established nationwide television service. It does show more promise than at any time in the past. But is it too late?

DON KOWET

High Hopes for Pay Cable

Cable television is now a reality in approximately 9000 American communities. By spring 1980, to serve the roughly 15 million cable households, various specialized cable networks had been or were being formed: these included a network for people over 50 and another for young children, a 24-hour news network featuring a two-hour newscast in prime time, an all-sports network, a Spanish language network and an entertainment network for blacks. National Cable Television Association president Tom Wheeler refers to cable as "video publishing" or "narrowcasting" as opposed to broadcasting. "We're moving to the point where we're breaking the audience to smaller and smaller markets and programming to them." Wheeler, noting that two-thirds of the nation's television viewing is confined to only one-third of the television households, says, "we're going for that two-thirds who turn off their sets because they don't like what's there. We're going to give them an option."

In March 1980, *Broadcasting* featured a special report titled "The Gold Rush of 1980: Prospecting for Cable Franchises." The report stated that, "With a few notable exceptions, every major metropolitan area in the country is in some stage of the cable franchising business," and cited pay cable as a major propellant for the "wave of franchising activity." This "wave" leads many observers to predict that by about 1990, 50 per cent of all television viewers will be watching cable television, and that as many as three-fourths of these viewers will be pay-cable customers. There were more than 5 million pay-cable subscribers in the United States by March 1980, and new customers were signing up at the rate of 100,000 per month. Some pay-cable experts project that by 1985, one pay-cable system linked by satellite could reach nearly 15 million customers. Don Kowet explores the growth and bright future of pay cable.

This essay first appeared June 10, 1978.

On November 8, 1972, as Sterling Manhattan Cable was about to transmit Home Box Office's inaugural program to a test group of 365 subscribers in Wilkes-Barre, Pa., a sudden rainstorm toppled the microwave antenna on Manhattan's Pan Am Building. Barely ten minutes before air time, the antenna was hoisted upright. The broadcast proceeded as scheduled, but that didn't keep industry oracles from interpreting the mishap as an omen. It wouldn't be long, they warned, before this latest effort at pay cable would topple, too.

Instead, over the next six years, a funny thing happened to pay cable on the way to oblivion. HBO's 365 subscribers swelled to more than a million, on 500 cable systems, in 46 states and Puerto Rico. Beginning as a penny-ante hobby for its parent, Time Inc., in 1977 HBO suddenly turned into a profit center, controlling (with a subsidiary) about 80 per cent of a pay-cable industry worth $14.2 million in revenues monthly. Cable systems in cities and towns across the country now have the option of signing up for HBO's movie/entertainment/sports package, or for programming devised by Viacom's Showtime, as well as several more modest regional packages built around sports.

Aroused by this unanticipated flurry of activity (and profitability), industry seers are again scanning pay cable's future. . . .

Significantly, it was in the largest city of all that the pay-cable idea was revived. In the early months of 1972, Sterling Manhattan Cable was merely one of a thousand or so CATV (Community Antenna Television) cable systems that had sprouted up across the country to afford viewers in "fringe" areas either improved TV reception or *any* TV reception. Sterling's predicament was that only in the narrowest sense could Manhattan be characterized as a fringe area. A viewer haunted by ghosts on one channel could exorcise them by switching to another of the many channels available—or turn off the set altogether.

To lure more basic cable subscribers, Sterling decided to resuscitate the idea of pay cable (which had died most recently in the mid-1960s, on the West Coast), offering, for an additional monthly fee of $8 to $10, a separate channel full of uncensored movies, plus sports—all without commercial interruption. To test it out, an experimental group was set up in Wilkes-Barre.

But the new venture was no overnight sensation. By the end of 1972, subscribers numbered only 1395, *all* of them still in Wilkes-Barre. Two years later, subscribers totaled a still modest 57,000 on 42 cable systems, in four Northeastern states. Then, in 1975, something elevated not only HBO and Sterling, but the whole cable industry, into a loftier orbit. On September 30, 1975, HBO transmitted to its subscribers an Ali-Frazier heavyweight title fight, live from the Philippines, via "the bird"—a Western Union Westar satellite, poised 22,300 miles over the equator. (Afterward HBO switched to an RCA American satellite.) The impact of satellite service (and the subsequent introduction of smaller, cheaper Earth receiving station) on pay cable was startling. By the end of the following year, 1976, HBO's subscribers had climbed to nearly 600,000, on 262 affiliated systems, in 40 states.[1]

The advantages conferred by using the satellite are twofold. First, long-distance signal distribution via satellite costs less than distribution by traditional land lines. According to Ralph Graff of RCA, an hour's worth of time on AT&T phone lines between New York and Los Angeles can cost [twice] as much as [the cost] for the same amount of time on a satellite. Furthermore, via satellite it costs no more to broadcast to thousands of receiving stations than to just one point.

"Before the satellite," says Gerald Levin, HBO's chairman, "there were an isolated 3500 cable systems across the country. Immediately, with the satellite, we had the potential of a national network, with millions of homes across the country available."

The next hurdle was legal, not technological. Since 1970, the Federal Communications Commission had imposed regulations limiting the quantity and kinds of programming that cable operators could broadcast. Designed to protect commercial television, these rules prevented pay-cable operators from showing any movie that was between three and ten years old or any specific sporting event that had been aired on commercial TV during the previous

1. According to Home Box Office general counsel Peter Gross, by March 1980, HBO had "well over" 4 million subscribers and its programs were being viewed in all 50 states, Puerto Rico and the Virgin Islands on over 1700 affiliated cable systems.

five years. On March 25, 1977, the U.S. Court of Appeals (District of Columbia) ended these restrictions, plus rules that prohibited a pay-cable channel from broadcasting commercials, or devoting more than 90 per cent of its schedule to sports and films.

"Not only did it give us a lot more films to choose from," says HBO's Levin, "it gave us the freedom not to be artificially denied a particular film merely because it was a certain age. . . .

Emboldened both by HBO's success in using the satellite and by the U.S. Court of Appeals' "HBO Decision," a host of fledgling contenders were soon queuing up at RCA and Western Union, buying time on an Americom or Westar. Some are nonpay networks, such as UPI's 24-hour news service and UA-Columbia's advertiser-supported Madison Square Garden Sports package. Others, such as Hollywood Home Theatre's Fanfare, are pay packages, delivering sports and movies tailored to a specific region. However, the most ambitious pay-cable challenger is Viacom's Showtime.[2] The battle between HBO and Showtime will be fought in the arena of programming.

Currently, HBO's fare consists of about 60–75 per cent movies, 15 per cent other entertainment, and 10–25 per cent sports (college basketball, with an occasional track meet or boxing bout).

Showtime, according to Viacom president Ralph Baruch, offers (for $7.00 to $10.50 per month above the basic cable fee) a schedule of approximately 85 per cent movies, with most of the remaining 15 per cent devoted to other entertainment. . . .

At least one powerful sector of American industry is already casting covetous glances in the direction of basic cable and its pay offspring. William Donnelly, a vice president at the influential Young & Rubicam advertising agency, believes that "it's fair to estimate a 30 per-cent penetration [of all TV homes in the U.S.] by cable on Christmas Day 1981. We say that advertisers at that point will start becoming interested on a broad scale."

Will some of those future ad dollars be funneled into pay cable, allowing companies like Showtime and HBO to reduce subscription rates, while increasing their programming investment?

"I would be very strongly opposed to that," says Ralph Baruch. "I

2. By March 1980, Showtime claimed over one million subscribers nationwide.

don't believe the American public is ready to have pay cable and, in addition, be besieged by commercials."

HBO's Gerald Levin agrees, but others think a combination of pay cable and commercials is not only possible but inevitable. Ernest Sauer, president of Satori Productions, a pay-cable production company, predicts that commercials will "most definitely" appear on pay-cable channels "when the industry is consolidated or interconnected enough." By the mid-1980s, Sauer says, pay cable will resemble European television, with four- to six-minute blocks of advertising between programs.

Aside from an enormous influx of advertisers' dollars, and the lower costs that might result by replacing bulky copper cables that must be connected to each home with "optical fibers" (hair-thin glass strands that transmit voices and images with light impulses), some industry observers pin at least modest hopes for future expansion on pay-per-view (with the subscriber paying only for those programs he chooses to watch). However, at least with regard to cable, the program suppliers are doubtful about pay-per-view's prospects.

"How," asks Baruch, "do you persuade the viewer to pay $2 to $3 a program above the basic cable fee, when he was paying $8 to $10 a month above the basic cable fee for a whole lot of programming?"

While pay-cablers debate the merits of pay-per-view and flat-fee, [an increasing number] of TV stations are reviving a method of delivering pay TV fundamentally different from both. These over-the-air pay TV stations broadcast, without cable, a scrambled signal, which can be unscrambled only by a subscriber in possession of a decoder box.[3] . . .

However, the men at HBO and Showtime are content to place their bets on their tandem of flat-fee pay cable and those small high-flying spheres.

3. Only 15 applications for pay television were granted by the FCC between 1960 and October 1979, when the Commission released its rule that limited each city to only one STV station. By March 1980, there were about 60 applications pending with the FCC for STV authorization, most in major metropolitan areas. STV stations are required to carry free television programs for several hours each day, and most offer their pay programs during prime time and on weekends. The average fee charged customers for STV service has been about $20 per month. KBSC-TV, Corona, Cal. (a suburb of Los Angeles) is the largest over-the-air pay-television operation in the nation. By March 1980, the station had almost 250,000 STV subscribers.

"We see Earth stations proliferate," says Gerald Levin. "We see equipment costs decline enough for small cable systems to afford satellite service; we see other program suppliers follow our path to the bird. And we become surer," he adds, "that the only ceiling to this business is 22,300 miles above our heads."

DAVID LACHENBRUCH

Will It Play in Columbus?

By the beginning of 1980, more than one thousand of the newer cable systems had the capacity for two-way television communication. The Warner Cable Corporation has developed a two-way cable system that combines cable television with computer terminals in the home: the system is called Qube and was introduced in Columbus, Ohio. Warner's chairman Gustave Hasuer feels that Qube "is not even cable television as we know it. It is the next step, a supermarket of electronic services." David Lachenbruch describes Qube's operation.

On November 12 [1977] Otterbein College engaged Marietta College in a football contest—not in itself a particularly noteworthy occurrence, except, perhaps, to students and alumni of the two schools. It's not even important who won or lost—what's important is how they played the game. They played it with a television audience kibitzing every play. By pressing buttons on their "home terminals," viewers became Saturday-evening quarterbacks instead of the Monday-morning variety. They actually were able to "vote" on which play they thought the quarterback should call next, and they saw their responses tabulated on the screen before the play began.

It's not known whether this majority rule had any influence on the play actually called. What is known is that the viewers watching what certainly seemed to be a very unhistoric football game were

This essay first appeared December 24, 1977.

part of what was hailed as the first large-scale American use of "participatory television." For their efforts, viewers who participated received a bill for $2.50.

The viewers were residents of Columbus, Ohio, who subscribe to a new type of cable-TV service called "Qube," developed by Warner Cable Corporation, a subsidiary of the Warner Communications entertainment conglomerate. (Nobody at Warner will say exactly what, if anything, the name means, but "QUiz the tuBE" is as good a guess as any.) It's undoubtedly the most elaborate cable system operating in the United States and, in fact, is a pilot project that Warner hopes to adapt to other areas if it succeeds in Columbus.

Qube is a marriage between television and the computer. Four central computers are used to "sweep" the cable system every six seconds, making a record of which sets are turned on and what channels they're tuned to—a sort of instant Nielsen rating. The computer automatically bills viewers who watch individual "pay-per-view" programs. It can tally the results of a survey or poll of viewers and display them on the screen within seconds. Using Qube, Warner says subscribers are able to give elected officials their opinions, take college-course quizzes at home, compete from their living rooms against game-show contestants on their screens or against other viewers, order merchandise from stores—all by pushing little buttons on their home terminals. [By early 1979], Qube subscribers [were] offered fire, burglary and other emergency alarm services (at extra cost).[1]

In addition to its back-talk aspects, Qube, which began operation on December 1 [1977], brings 30 channels of television, entertainment, information and education into its subscribers' homes in a community where only four TV channels can be received ordinarily. The 30 channels are divided into three groups: "T" channels for regular TV, "C" for community programming and "P" for premium shows. Qube is being offered to about [175,000] homes accessible to Warner's cable in Columbus and carries with it Warner's hopes for big-city cable TV. Traditionally successful in smaller communities isolated from TV stations, cable has been a flop in larger cities

1. Other services which may someday be offered by Qube include home energy-management programs, information retrieval, shopping at home, electronic banking and perhaps even voting through the television set.

where many regular channels are available. But Warner Cable chairman Gustave Hauser is betting Qube will be different.

Warner Communications admits to having poured at least [$15 million] into Qube so far, and some observers think it has [more than $20 million] tied up. To develop this pilot project, it tapped some top TV, show-bix and educational talent. Qube's president is Lawrence B. Hilford, veteran movie and TV programming executive. Children's programs are in the hands of Dr. Vivian Horner, formerly of Children's Television Workshop, which developed *Sesame Street* and *The Electric Company*. Qube's principal local programming venture—*Columbus Alive*—is the brainchild of Michael Dann, the long-time CBS programming vice president, who later became a consultant to Children's Television Workshop.

Whenever a subscriber turns the set on, it automatically tunes to *Columbus Alive* on Channel C-1. Mike Dann unabashedly admits that the show is a steal from the original *Today* show, which he helped create for NBC. *Columbus Alive,* according to Dann, is intended to bring the immediacy and excitement of live programming back to TV—at the local level—and at the same time establish a feeling of intimacy between viewer and box.

"People will watch this for the same reason they watch parades," says Dann. "They'll see their neighbors. And we'll continually ask questions. How many people are making peanut butter sandwiches today? How many tuna? We'll tally the results right before their eyes." *Columbus Alive,* as originally conceived, was a fantastically ambitious undertaking, starting at 6:30 every morning and running all day with original, live programming. But by the time Qube service started, it was cut down to about three hours a day—to be gradually expanded, Hauser says.

Among the regular features of *Columbus Alive* is "Going Once, Going Twice," a sort of televised tag sale in which viewers with interesting things to sell make cameo appearances and are provided by the computer with a list of subscribers who made tentative bids from their home terminals. Other features, some yet to be inaugurated, are scheduled to interview local people and visiting celebrities, ask the audience questions about community affairs and sports, take requests from viewers for a teen-age record-dance party and let subscribers participate in local quiz and game shows.

Columbus Alive runs commercials, too, and some could be as long as 10 minutes—but they're commercials with a difference. A local newspaper asks viewers' attitudes toward its various features. A travel agency's commercial will open by asking viewers which of five vacations spots they'd like to learn about—the location getting the most votes to be the subject of the rest of the commercial; viewers then push a button if they want to receive a brochure. A department store is expected to sponsor long live commercials with special demonstrations, such as the application of makeup.

Running 12 hours daily, seven days a week on Channel C-3 is *Pinwheel,* a sort of TV baby sitter for preschoolers that boasts "no commercials and no violence." It features both new material shot especially for the Columbus audience and segments purchased from other sources. There are now 160 hours in the can.[2]

Another "C" channel is designated Selected Audience Programs and is for rent to organizations wishing to reach specialized portions of Qube's subscription list. For example, it could beam special courses to physicians or lawyers. The computers can determine which subscribers' homes are eligible to receive the program, automatically excluding those unqualified. The channel is also expected to find use in audience research, such as closed-circuit tests of TV commercials, the home audience immediately expressing its opinion via the response buttons.

How much will all this cost the subscriber? Well, after paying an installation charge of $19.95 for new viewers, or $9.95 for those already hooked to the existing Warner Cable system in Columbus, there's a monthly charge of $10.95, which includes unlimited use of "T" and "C" channels. For a one-time fee of $10, the subscriber can add five channels of stereo music piped to his own FM stereo receiver; also thrown in are simulcast channels for *Columbus Alive* (broadcast in stereo) and for premium TV concerts or films with stereo sound.

2. In March 1979, Warner Cable inaugurated satellite transmission of a new cable young people's network, Nickelodeon. Nickelodeon runs 13 hours on weekdays, 14 hours on weekends, and includes the *Pinwheel* program for preschoolers. Nickelodeon is available to any cable network at a cost of 10 cents per subscriber per month with a 30 cents-per-subscriber charge if the service is used on a pay basis.

But that's only the beginning. Neatly itemized on the subscriber's monthly bills are all the "P" (for "premium") programs viewed. "P" also stands for "pay," and unlike most other pay-cable operations in which the viewer pays a monthly fee to watch all programs, Qube charges per program viewed. First-run movies are $2.50 to $3.50 each and are shown over and over so viewers can catch them at convenient times. *Movie Greats,* on a different channel, [costs] $1 [per movie]; all have been previously shown on commercial TV, but Qube presents them uncut, without commercials. Channel P-10 is the naughty channel—R-rated movies at $2.50 to $3.50 each, available only to customers who elect beforehand to receive them (the computer delivers a blank screen on P-10 to those who don't).

Warner is producing a few of its own special premium shows for Qube—such as a series of nightclub performances taped in New York and a nightclub tour shot in Paris. Opera, ballet and symphony will be available, as well as rock concerts. Channel P-6 is all sports—high-school, college and pro contests not on regular TV. Channel P-9 is called *College at Home* and provides credit courses in such subjects as anthropology and accounting. *Better Living,* Channel P-5, features noncredit courses, such as writing, speed reading and backgammon.

The ultimate in viewer participation will be Channel P-8, called *Qube Games.* The Qube people are a little indefinite about this one, except to say it will consist of contests of skill played by viewers for a small entry charge, probably around 75 cents. The computer may pick the top twenty or so scores for prizes, or there could be tournament finals to pick a grand winner.

Heavy viewers of "P" channels obviously can run up quite a hefty bill. If a family watches one movie, one special and one sports event a week, an opera or rock concert every month and takes one course, the monthly bill can total around $60, including the regular $10.95 fee. On the other hand, the viewer isn't required to watch any premium programming at all. In fact, he can eliminate all temptation by removing a special key from the home terminal, locking out all pay programs.

But Warner obviously is betting that viewers will dip broadly into the premium column to finance the freebies on the other channels. Live programming, such as that scheduled for *Columbus Alive,* is very expensive, and budget overruns may be responsible for the drastic cutback in the original dawn-to-dark plans for that show. . . .

Suppose nobody watches the expensive live programming on *Columbus Alive*? "That's the beauty of the system. If we have stuff nobody's watching—out! We'll find out right away—we don't have to wait. We'll ride with the public. A year fron now we'll have a totally different product mix."

Qube obviously wasn't designed for Columbus alone. "It's a prototype," says Hauser. "It's like the space program—we don't know what the spinoffs will be."

Most broadcasters and many cable-TV operators are skeptical about Qube's prospects. But they'll be watching it closely. And Warner is betting millions of dollars that people will spend a lot of money on per-program viewing, and that they really *do* want to talk back to the television set—paving way for Qubes not only in Columbus, but perhaps in cities as large as New York.

[Warner has invested an estimated $100 million in constructing Qube-type installations in Houston and suburban Cincinnati. These systems will have 36 channels and are expected to begin operations in 1980. In December 1979, Warner announced its desire to install a Qube service in three of New York City's five boroughs. If New York approves, Warner would build a $400 million cable system with a capacity of over 120 television channels.

Although by the start of 1980 Qube in Columbus continued to be unprofitable, with subscriptions from only about 40 per cent of its potential market, Warner's Hauser considers it a proven success. He claims the losses should be regarded as the costs of research and development and that if Warner wanted to make the system profitable it could do so by cutting costs. But this would not serve the cause of exploring new avenues for cable. Moreover, Qube has given rise to a number of new businesses for Warner Cable, including the Nickelodeon cable network for children's programs.

Half of Warner Communications was purchased by American Express for $175 million in late 1979. Noting that Warner and American Express have combined annual sales of $6 billion, Hauser indicated, "With our joint resources, we can develop these sophisticated two-way systems faster than if we did it alone."]

NEIL HICKEY

The Video-Cassette Supermarket

The *Wall Street Journal* has called the video-cassette recorder (VCR) "the glamour product of the late 1970s" which "bears the seeds of radical change in the way people spend their leisure time." It will have a "marked impact on the television industry, particularly on the three commercial networks."

Along with being able to record television shows for delayed watching, the VCR owner can also acquire prerecorded cassettes. More than 10,000 titles are available: they cost anywhere from $45 to $100 and can be purchased from mail order houses. One can even rent prerecorded material by phone from a nationwide chain of Fotomat stores. Charts of the best-selling cassettes are now included in *Billboard*, the music industry's top-selling trade magazine. As of March 1980, pornographic movies were the most popular purchases: *Deep Throat, The Devil in Miss Jones* and *Behind the Green Door* were the leading films and cost about $100 each. But for every prerecorded cassette sold, six blank video tapes were being purchased for recording shows off the air.

Video recorders have not sold as briskly as had been hoped in 1977 when they first came on the market. Although 1979 sales were 16 per cent higher than in 1978, by spring 1980 fewer than 2 per cent of TV homes had VCRs. They are expensive: the first VCRs sold for about $1300 and, although the prices have gone down, it is still rare to find one for under $700. Manufacturers are attempting to break down this barrier with new models that are streamlined and scaled down to sell for under $700. The consumer will find, however, that different cassettes match up with different types of systems. The formats for the Beta and VHS systems are incompatible. At the beginning there were also three other systems on the market—all with incompatible formats: they are no longer being retailed.

This essay first appeared June 17, 1978.

The VCR market is very complex. *Television Digest* describes the purchaser's choices: "Today, a consumer shopping VCRs has to choose from 15 different major brands offering one of 2 formats in home or portable decks, with both programmable and non-programmable tuners and operated at 7 different speed standards." The consumer's decision will become even more complicated later in 1980: "In addition to expected stripped-down models, we'll be seeing smaller & lighter units in both home & portable models, more VHS & Beta with improved visual-fast-forward & -reverse, new program-location features and more full-function wireless remotes—all of which will further serve to depress value of inventories."

According to several 1980 industry projections, by 1985 VCRs will be in at least 12 per cent of the nation's TV households. Neil Hickey describes what the American consumer can expect to find when shopping for a video-cassette recorder.

There was George C. Scott in his *Patton* uniform and Barbra Streisand caparisoned for her role in *Hello, Dolly!* and Robert Redford as he appeared in *The Hot Rock*; and near those photographs in the newspaper advertisement was the headline: "Introducing major motion pictures you view at home any time you want." Strung out below in neat columns of type were the names of fifty 20th Century-Fox movies—*The Longest Day, The French Connection, M*A*S*H, The Bible, The King and I*—being offered for sale on video cassettes at prices from $49.95 to $69.95 each.

The advertisement (which appeared in newspapers [in March 1978]) was, in fact, mildly historic. It was the first time a major motion-picture company had opened its vaults to the owners of those newfangled videotape machines. And it signaled the start of a new chapter in the burgeoning do-it-yourself home-video market that is giving TV fans more control than ever before over what shows they watch and when they watch them. . . . During the 1980s, say the experts, the little record-and-playback attachment that's being turned out by RCA, Sony, Magnavox and others will be a staple in millions of American homes.

So far, VCR manufacturers have keyed their sales pitch to the machines' capability of recording one program while the owner watches another, and of preserving programs automatically (with the aid of a timer) while the owner isn't at home. But the day is fast approaching when most consumers will purchase the VCRs chiefly because of the wealth of high-quality prerecorded material they can buy, rent and swap.

Already there's a smorgasbord of prerecorded fare for sale to anybody who owns or has access to a VCR, and the list is growing daily (*hourly,* say some in the industry). A company called Cinema Concepts, Inc., in Chester, Conn., for example, will sell you Charlie Chaplin's *The Gold Rush,* or D. W. Griffith's 1915 masterpiece *The Birth of a Nation,* or *The Blue Angel* with Marlene Dietrich, or Jean Renoir's *Grand Illusion* or *The Phantom of the Opera* with Lon Chaney, Sr.—as well as old one-reelers by W. C. Fields, Harold Lloyd, Buster Keaton, Our Gang and a spate of more recent adventure and horror films, cartoon packages (Bugs Bunny, Porky Pig, Daffy Duck) and sports.

From Entertainment Enterprises International in Coral Gables, Fla., you can choose from a list of 125 films, including *The Outlaw* with Jane Russell, Shirley Temple in *The Little Princess* and Bruce Lee in some of his kung fu movies. Several companies offer horror tapes (*The Blob, Son of Blob, Astro Zombies, Master of Horror*) and the inevitable sex movies with titles like *The Swingin' Stewardesses, Danish Delights, Naughty Co-eds, Voluptuous Vixens,* and (so help us) *Sexual Freedom in Brooklyn.*

One of the richest troves of video fare in the United States belongs to Time-Life, and it's described in an elaborate catalogue that lists programs (for sale or rent) in the fields of travel, fine arts, self-improvement, religion, philosophy, entertainment, music and social studies, as well as a group of blockbuster series from the BBC. Most of those [in early 1978 were] aimed at institutions that [could] afford the stiff prices, and not at individual VCR owners. Thirteen-part series like *Civilisation, The Ascent of Man* and *America,* for example [went] for $4250 each; *Ten Who Dared* [for] $3000 and *The Tribal Eye* (in seven episodes) [for] $2000. But [then] Time-Life took one giant step toward joining what it calls (in a letter to VCR owners) the "home-entertainment revolution." VCR users are a "select, discriminating group who want programs of lasting value and the highest quality," said the letter, "not just something taped off the air . . . but professionally recorded programs with which to start permanent home-video libraries."

Having said that, Time-Life offered for sale (at $299) a Whitman's Sampler of eight video cassettes containing highlights from *Civilisation, The Ascent of Man, The Fight Against Slavery, Europe: The Mighty Continent, Ten Who Dared, America, Rose Kennedy Remembers* and *Life Goes to the Movies.* If the experiment prospers, says Time-Life, it will make other programs available for home use.

In Salt Lake City, a mail-order video supplier called Sports World Cinema offers a long list of tapes about skiing, tennis, football, motorcycling, boating, auto racing, skateboarding, hot-air ballooning, snowmobiling, mountaineering, bicycling and gliding. In Cranbury, N.J., another mail-order firm called Discotronics runs a video-tape exchange that works much like a rental library: owners mail in their taped movies and, for a fee, receive another in return. Other suppliers have similar exchange deals. Most programs are available from suppliers in both half-inch and three-quarter-inch cassettes, and in the several "formats"—Beta, VHS—used by VCR manufacturers. Full compatibility of tapes and players does not yet exist, so buyers are required to specify their needs.

And illegal tapes abound. A VCR user in Brewster, N.Y., points with pride to a shelf laden with such recent theatrical hits as *The Turning Point, Annie Hall* and *The Goodbye Girl,* all purchased on the thriving underground tape market. Says he: "I can pick up the phone and get a tape cassette of any movie ever made," although such major hits as *Star Wars* and *Close Encounters of the Third Kind* sell for $500 and up. . . .

The increasing availability of software for VCRs, combined with the machine's so-called "time-shift" capability (to record off the air for later viewing) is expected to alter the public's notions about what "prime time" in television really is. "With books and records, prime time is when you feel like using them," says one enthusiast. "It'll soon be the same for TV."

Home video is still in knee pants, as an aspect of the TV business. But experts are sure that as high-quality software becomes more abundant, sales of video recorders will rise to meet the supply. And vice versa. Producers inevitably will create original entertainment programs, including "first-run" feature films, specifically for video cassettes as soon as the VCR market is broad enough to support them. Says Andre Blay, president of Magnetic Video Corporation, the distributing company that struck the deal with 20th Century-Fox for the sale of their movies on cassettes: "When 10 million machines are in use, a producer who received $5 per tape as his share of the gross could ear $10 million by penetrating just two million of those homes. You could make a pretty good movie for $10 million."

Others speculate that creators of VCR entertainment might put commercials on some tapes as an added revenue source and a means of reducing the cost to buyers; and that those plugs could be for products that can't be (or generally aren't) advertised on regular TV, such as hard liquor and cigarettes. (The FCC has no regulatory authority over video software.)

So the possibilities for home video are intriguing. "This is very definitely a revolution and is going to change the viewing habits of the entire country and eventually the world," says Ron Obsgarten, operating manager of Video Warehouse. That may be putting it too strongly.

Or it may not.

DAVID LACHENBRUCH

What Looks Like a Phonograph Record, Works on a Laser Beam and Shows Jaws?

The video cassette will soon have competition from the video disc. RCA board chairman Edgar Griffiths has referred to plans for a "memorable introduction" of an RCA video-disc system in "every city and town" in the first quarter of 1981. SelectaVision players—selling for less than $500—will be supported by a catalogue of discs that will cost from $15 to $25 each. According to Griffiths, RCA's venture is the largest single investment in a consumer product in the company's history. The project is "considerably larger than color television" and will be supported by "the most comprehensive advertising, promotion and publicity campaign ever put behind an RCA consumer product."

When color television first appeared on the market, RCA and CBS, Inc. fought a fierce battle over which company's color system would become the industry's standard. RCA won. The two companies also had competed over whose long-playing record would become that industry's standard when long-playing records first appeared. In the second instance, CBS, Inc. was the winner. In the emerging video-disc market, RCA and CBS, Inc. have joined forces. RCA has licensed CBS to manufacture and distribute Selecta Vision discs. Griffiths predicts that by 1990, video-disc players will be in 30 to 50 per cent of all color television homes, with five to six million players and 200 to 250 million discs being sold each year; the new industry will be "bigger than the broadcast industry, two and one-half times the record industry."

This essay first appeared November 25, 1978.

RCA's SelectaVision will not be the first video-disc system in this country. David Lachenbruch describes the Magnavision video-disc player made by Philips and the entertainment available on MCA Disco-Vision records.

You'll [soon] be able to buy a 12-inch disc that resembles a platinum LP, drop it on a turntable and watch *Jaws* in incredibly high-fidelity color on your own TV set (and listen on your stereo, if you wish).

The video-disc age is dawning, courtesy of an alliance between the world's largest manufacturer of TV sets and one of America's top entertainment factories. [The video disc is] scheduled to fan out through the country and to be available nationwide in 1980.

[In March 1980], the Magnavision video-disc player [was selling for $795]. An ever-expanding catalogue of Disco-Vision records [ranged] from [$16 to $25] for major movies (more for special attractions such as opera) down to as little as [$6] with [some] discs priced lower per hour than conventional hear-only LPs. Movie discs contain up to two hours of picture and sound (one hour per side). Others hold a half-hour per side, and their moving pictures can be stopped and held, played in slow motion, speeded up or even shown backward. Each such record can hold up to 54,000 still pictures per side, and any individual frame can be located rapidly by push button—which gives the video disc important potential as an educational tool. A slide show of all the world's great art masterpieces could be recorded on just one side. If you watched each slide for five seconds, starting Sunday at 8 P.M., without stopping to eat or sleep, it would be 11 o'clock Wednesday night before you saw them all.

The parents of the video disc are the global Netherlands-based electronics combine N. V. Philips Gloeilampenfabrieken (that jaw-breaker means "light-bulb factory"), whose companies are estimated to produce some 6,000,000 color sets a year; and MCA Corporation, better known through its subsidiaries, Universal Pictures and Decca Records. In 1974, Philips purchased Magnavox as its American launching pad for the video disc. For the time being, Philips is making the players, MCA the records, but each company plans eventually to build both.[1]

The Magnavox player is a slick, futuristic-looking gadget slightly larger than a record player. It is simply attached to any TV set's antenna terminals. You merely place the shiny MCA Disco-Vision record—which glows like a rare gem with reflected rainbow colors—on the turntable, close the lid, and push the start button. Then incredible magic begins. The turntable almost instantly revs up to 1800 rpm. A low-powered laser shoots its pinpoint beam to the disc. The disc reflects it back to a mirror-and-prism system where the beam is split in two. One of the beams conveys picture and sound information to the player's electronics, while the other keeps the pickup arm on the correct microscopic "track," which is spaced 65/1,000,000ths of an inch from its neighbors.

No pickup ever touches the disc—only a beam of laser light—so theoretically there's never any record wear. In addition to the color picture, the disc contains two high-fidelity sound tracks. The player can be connected to any stereo system to play back programs whose sound is recorded in stereo or you can play it through your TV sound system. A disc can have two separate sound tracks—a switch on the player determines which one is heard. (MCA has made a demonstration disc of *Columbo* with the detective talking in both English and Japanese.)

This is the system Philips calls VLP (for Video Long Play). How MCA became involved is one of the most fascinating stories in the history of technology: it acquired a small electronics lab and invented the same disc system at almost exactly the same time as Philips. The two companies eventually agreed to merge their systems. For MCA it was a partnership with the world's largest manufacturer of consumer-electronics products. And Philips gained a zippy show-biz partner that owns the world's largest film library of 11,000 feature movies and is a leading producer of television shows and phonograph records.

1. In September 1979, MCA and IBM announced the formation of a 50-50 video disc and player partnership called Disco-Vision Associates (DVA). MCA and IBM indicated that DVA would be involved in the industrial video and computer markets rather than the consumer market, at least for the time being. MCA announced it would retain MCA Disco-Vision as a consumer disc marketer.

MCA Disco-Vision's initial catalogue [includes] at least 200 titles, of which about half [are] feature films—not only from Universal, but some Warner and probably some Disney movies, some pre-1948 Paramount oldies (MCA owns 700 of these) and selections from the prestigious American Film Theatre. Topping the premiere catalogue [are] such films as *National Lampoon's Animal House, Jaws, American Graffiti* and *The Sting*; and American Film Theatre's *The Man in the Glass Booth* and *Luther.* At a somewhat lower price [are] landmark made-for-TV movies, including the pilots for *The Six Million Dollar Man* and *Kojak,* plus *Duel* (the first movie directed by Steven Spielberg). Documentaries from TV, including Jacques Cousteau's undersea sagas and the British *World at War,* cooking instructions, educational shows, golf lessons with Gene Littler, tennis and swimming instructions and a film version of the book *Total Fitness in 30 Minutes a Week* [are] tested at various prices. . . .

In the nostalgia department, MCA owns all but one of the Marx Brothers features and [has launched] them on their video-disc career with *Animal Crackers.* There [is] also *The Bride of Frankenstein, Buck Privates* with Abbott and Costello, and a hybrid of the two called *Abbott and Costello Meet Frankenstein.* . . . "Fortunately," says MCA president Lew Wasserman, one of America's great showmen, "manufacturing costs are so low that we can test all sorts of prices and marketing techniques." He estimates that every television series is good for two video-disc albums—how about "'The Best of *Lucy* . . . Gleason . . . *Dragnet*? Would you pay $2.95 for these?" Wasserman asks, sort of rhetorically.

When enough players are in use, original productions could be developed specifically for video discs. Even now, Wasserman says, "We're discussing making a group of new films especially for discs, with supplementary exhibition in other media, such as theaters and TV." Eventually, he predicts, movies will be released to video disc immediately after their theatrical premieres—or even before. "Our research shows that *Jaws* didn't reach 50 per cent of its potential audience despite its being [among] the most successful [films] in history."

Discs will be available from the dealers who sell the players, or by mail. A toll-free number listed in the Disco-Vision catalogue connects callers with the Spencer Gift Company, an MCA subsidiary, which ships discs directly to them, charging their credit cards.

MCA Disco-Vision's video-disc plant in Carson, Cal., will [be able to produce up to 12,000,000 records a year]. Disco-Vision president John Findlater estimates that any disc must sell about 10,000 copies to break even. . . .

[Other companies that are introducing their own video-disc players include RCA, which has had its SelectaVision system under development since 1964, Zenith and Universal-Pioneer. By 1981, Pioneer, which is partly owned by MCA's Disco-Vision, hopes to sell its players for $749; RCA and Zenith for under $500. The Pioneer player will be compatible with the Magnavox machine discussed above, and Disco-Vision is expected to supply software for both. RCA and Zenith will use a different (incompatible) system developed by RCA.]

Another system that uses 10-minute discs has been marketed [since 1975] in Europe by Telefunken with unspectacular results. LP video discs have been demonstrated by Matsushita, JVC and Sony of Japan and Thomson-CSF of France. There's no interchangeability among any of these, and a hodgepodge of nonstandard and incompatible systems could result if they all came to market.

What's the difference between a video-disc player and a home video-cassette recorder, or VCR? About the same as that between a phonograph and a tape recorder. Home VCRs . . . cost more than disc players and are more versatile, since they can make their own programming from television broadcasts or home cameras. Prerecorded cassettes are available, but movies cost from $49.95 to more than $100 because of the inherently expensive nature of tape and of the process of making tape duplicates. Video-discs, with far better picture and sound quality, can be stamped out in large quantities at a labor and material cost of about 40 cents each. To make it at all, the video disc must succeed as a mass medium, with its players in millions of households, making necessary the development of reasonably priced programming in large quantities. VCRs can exist without such huge popularity—they don't depend on availability of special programs.

Regardless of what happens in the home, the future of the video disc seems assured in industry and education. Special versions with built-in minicomputers, or coupled to external computers, are flexible tools for programmed learning and data storage. MCA and its Japanese affiliate already have a dozen contracts with government and industry to develop specialized systems. It's understood that the White House is experimenting with the disc's tremendous storage capabilities and easy indexing for use in Presidential briefings. . . .

The total amount [that will be] invested by Philips, MCA, RCA and others in video-disc development can only be guessed, but it undoubtedly [will exceed one] billion dollars. This could pay off as a fantastic new medium that revolutionizes our lives as television did a generation ago—or it could lay a magnificent, full-color stereophonic egg. Broadcasters, moviemakers, record companies, publishers, TV-set makers will be watching for clues.

NEIL HICKEY

Read Any Good Television Lately?

CBS News president William Leonard has observed, "What's going to change is that [television set]. That box is going to be able to store and retrieve. . . ." The merging of electronic communications and computers has resulted in video technologies that present printed alphanumeric material on a cathode ray picture tube. Neil Hickey discusses two of these technologies: teletex, an over-the-air video technology combining printed words with television; and viewdata, a more sophisticated distribution method that links the television set with the telephone system.

Videotex, Viewdata, teletext, CableText, Prestel, Viewtron, Telidon, Teletel, Telset, Inteltext, and Bildschirmtext, Ceefax, Oracle, Antiope, Captain.

Perhaps you've never heard *any* of those terms, but stick around. All of them relate, in one fashion or another, to startling new ways of using your television set for more than just picking up *Laverne & Shirley*. And what *is* this magic new ingredient?

Print. Good old-fashioned printed pages that will appear right on the face of your TV screen. And if the smart money is right, this new kind of television will change your life in some important and even profound ways.

It's all part of what's now called the Information Explosion—which, at the moment, is little more than a firecracker. But it will grow into the multimegaton range in the next decade, fueled by hundreds of millions of dollars already being committed in the

This essay first appeared February 16, 1980.

United States, Great Britain, West Germany, Japan, Canada, Holland, France, Australia, Sweden and elsewhere.

How, precisely, will it work? Your garden-variety TV set, equipped with a special decoder, will be the display terminal for a theoretically infinite amount of information that can be summoned up at the touch of a key-pad device: news, sports results, stockmarket prices, classified advertising, weather, traffic reports, reviews, radio and television logs and reviews, real estate listings, job-hunting information, travel schedules, cooking, gardening and crafts advice, and home-study courses in every imaginable subject. The TV screen also could become an encyclopedia and dictionary, as well as the "note paper" for an electronic mail and message service and a convenient way to communicate with the deaf. Two-way capability will allow voting, public-opinion polling, retail buying and selling, banking and credit transactions, game playing and home computing.

All those services will arrive in your home via two main bits of gadgetry, the generic names for which are teletext and viewdata. Teletext is older, having been pioneered by the British Broadcasting Corporation a half-dozen years ago, and is now in full operation in Great Britain, where 42,000 homes are equipped to receive it. It's simple and cheap to operate and—best of all—free to the consumer (except for the cost of the decoder). It's transmitted over the air encoded on an unused, or "blank," space on an ordinary TV signal. Teletext allows the viewer to choose from about 800 "pages" of printed material that are continually being broadcast (invisibly until requested) right along with regular programs.

In Britain, two teletext services are available to viewers: one called Ceefax, from the BBC; and Oracle, from Independent Television (ITV), the commercial network. A few years ago, an American broadcast executive named Arch L. Madsen, president of Bonneville International Corp., which owns station KSL-TV in Salt Lake City, studied Ceefax in London, was enthralled by its prospects and promptly got permission of the BBC (and the Federal Communications Commission) to test a similar service in the U.S.

Ever since, broadcasters, newspaper publishers, electronics-equipment manufacturers and government officials "have been visiting us in droves," says Madsen, eager to know how this new tool will affect their lives and fortunes. Teletext "adds a whole new dimension to over-the-air broadcasting," Madsen claims. And he's pretty sure that eventually it will produce enormous advertising revenues for broadcasters who have the vision to get in on it.

CBS conducted its own tests at station KMOX-TV in St. Louis, where they studied British teletext systems and a French one called Antiope.

The second main distribution method for televised print—viewdata—uses ordinary telephone lines instead of over-the-air transmission. A viewer simply places a phone call to a viewdata computer in which is stored, for easy retrieval, all manner of useful information and services. He is charged for the phone call, and charged also (automatically) for many of the pages that then appear on the TV screen (the specially equipped set is connected to the telephone by an adapter).

Those pages are placed in the computer by companies, called information providers, that pay to have their services included in the data bank. Thus, the viewdata computer is a kind of warehouse in which the information providers rent space and from which the viewers purchase goods, services and information as their needs require. Currently, the British viewdata system is fed by about 160 information providers, including the British Library, the British Medical Association, Barclays Bank, Reuters, the English Tourist Board and the *New York Times.*

Unlike teletext, viewdata is a complete, two-way, "transactional" device that makes the consumer the master of his own communications needs, including the sending and receiving of printed messages and the purchase of products. Also, viewdata's capacity is theoretically unlimited, as against teletext's current ability to broadcast, in Britain, a menu of up to 300 pages.

As with teletext, the British were the pioneers of viewdata, which is called by the brand names Prestel in Great Britain and Viewdata in the United States. In Britain, the post office operates the telephone service, and back in 1970 a post-office employee named Sam Fedida dreamed up the first viewdata system as a scheme to increase the number of phone calls made daily by Britons, and hence increase the post office's revenue. (It was averaging a meager 1.5 calls per day per instrument.)

In the process, Fedida and the post office took the first few steps toward creating the world's first universal data base: a reservoir in which all the information that a nation needs to function socially, politically, culturally and economically could be stored, and then retrieved by every member of the society.

Last June, the General Telephone & Electronics Corporation, the nation's second-largest telephone company, obtained a license to offer viewdata services to the public in the U.S. and Canada. In July, RCA announced it had been testing viewdata systems and might proceed with in-home tests in 1980. The Knight-Ridder Newspapers chain has set up a subsidiary called Viewdata Corp. of America, Inc., to operate a service, which they're calling Viewtron, as a hedge against the day when viewdata may constitute a threat to the economic health of newspapers. In late spring, 150–200 families in Coral Gables, Fla., will get the Viewtron service as a test of how consumers will use a TV information-retrieval system.

Recently, twenty-two of America's largest communications companies (including AT&T, CBS, RCA, Dow Jones and Texas Instruments) chipped in to produce an expensive marketing and technical study on how viewdata may effect each of them in the future. And abroad, viewdata systems are sprouting like weeds in West Germany (where it's called Bildschirmtext), Japan (Captain), Finland (Telset) and Canada (Telidon).

None of which surprises Sam Fedida, who took time out at his London office recently to demonstrate Prestel to *TV Guide*. "This will have tremendous impact in the home," he said. "We'll be able to get information *when* we want it, and thus be able to make decisions better and quicker than ever before. And this will be a very important source of revenue for the information providers."

As one indicator of the system's profitability, Fedida points out that if three million viewers in Great Britain spent an average of only $100 a year on Prestel, the gross annual revenue would be $300 million. And that average would probably be much higher in the U.S., he claims, because Americans have more to spend and are more likely to experiment with new things.

Right now, TV sets equipped to receive viewdata and teletext signals are fairly expensive: $2000 in Great Britain for a set fully equipped to receive viewdata. The experts are sure, though, that when new sets are mass produced with both teletext and viewdata capability, the cost may be as little as $25 to $50 more than the ordinary price of the set.

TV set manufacturers have been quick to detect in all this the greatest potential boon to their business since the introduction of color. Obviously, if people in great numbers want these home-information services, they'll eventually decide to junk their present sets and buy new ones that are properly equipped. That fact helps explain the current interest of RCA (which makes TV sets) and GT&E (which owns Sylvania). In Britain, the entire TV set industry is busily manufacturing the new sets.

Some observers (including a number of network executives) claim that home-information systems are Buck Rogers stuff that won't be economically viable for many years, and besides, the public may never want that kind of service anyway. "That's what all those monks who were copying manuscripts back in the 15th century said when they first heard about printing," says Paul Zurkowsky, president of the International Information Association. "The future shock will be momentous."

Still, obstacles do exist. One of the toughest is the need for electronic standards that would allow TV set makers to proceed confidently with the manufacture of this new generation of sets and assure compatibility not only domestically but globally, so that—for a long-distance phone call—viewers in the U.S. could tap data banks elsewhere in the world.

Also, teletext constitutes a potential bone of contention between networks and local stations over control of that valuable piece of electronic real estate—the vertical blanking interval—on which teletext is transmitted. KSL's Madsen is adamant that it belongs to the stations themselves and that they have 100 per-cent-ownership rights to the ad revenues that might result, including a share of the newspaper industry's $4-billion-a-year income from classified advertising.

Networks, for their part, tend to be appalled at the prospect of viewers switching off national commercials to watch local teletext news and advertisements. Nonetheless, networks are presumptively on the prowl for new sources of income, in the face of intimations that their economic base will soon grow rickety under pressure from cable TV, pay TV, video discs and the like. They're eager to position themselves (in the view of one insider) to take best advantage of teletext when it starts to gather force—and that could mean a pitched battle with their own affiliates over the lifeblood of both of them: the advertising dollar.

A French television executive speculated recently that by the mid-1980s the home-information-service industry will be a multibillion-dollar business that will help redefine what television is. The investment firm Kidder, Peabody & Co., Inc. says that TV computer services "to the home via telephone or satellite communications provide an exciting potential market, in our view."

Maybe they're right and maybe they're wrong, but the fuse has definitely been lit and pretty soon we'll know just how big a bang this information explosion will be.

DON KOWET

Keep Your Eye on the Bird

New York Times television columnist Les Brown feels that "when commercial television enters the satellite age, it's a wholly different ballgame." The television satellite age has begun, and *Washington Post* planning vice president Christopher Burns does not underestimate its importance: "None of the technologies we now envisage will effect TV as profoundly as satellite broadcasting."

By March 1980, more than 2000 cable systems had Earth stations and an estimated 10 million cable homes were receiving programming via satellite. According to RCA Communications Satellite Division president Andrew Ingles, "our biggest surprise was the *size* of the cable market. . . . I don't think anyone anticipated how big it would have been." Market analysts expect the satellite business to get even bigger: to grow to nearly $2 billion by the mid-1980s—from about $100 million in 1978.

Space shuttles will enable satellite companies to extend the lives of their "birds" (now about seven years) by allowing the satellites to be retrieved from orbit for repair. The use of satellite for television transmission will increase with the realization of RCA's plan to build and maintain Earth stations at all American commercial television stations. The size of the satellite Earth station has decreased from 100 to 15 feet in diameter between 1970 and 1980, and the cost has dropped to as low as $10,000. One trade journal reported that a firm in Atlanta was "stamping out satellite earth stations like Detroit stamps out fenders."

Don Kowet discusses how satellites already in use are affecting American television broadcasting.

This essay first appeared December 9, 1978.

Eight months elapsed before Queen Isabella learned that her investment in Columbus had paid a dividend; almost two weeks passed before anyone in Europe knew that Lincoln had been assassinated. Yet it took only 1.3 seconds, via satellite, for Neil Armstrong to take his "giant leap for mankind"—off the moon and onto hundreds of millions of TV screens.

A worthier payoff from America's 73-billion space lottery than five-year flashlights and ball point pens that write upside down, satellites are subtly revising the pace and pattern of global communications. Since Early Bird (the first commercial communications satellite) was launched in 1965, the worldwide consortium called Intelsat has grown from five members to 102, spanning the alphabet from Afghanistan to Zambia, serving, via its ten satellites, 120 nations on six continents. Film of international news and sports used to be lugged by plane from country to country; now billions (an estimated one out of every five persons on Earth) can see live lunar landings, and Presidents, grinning as broadly as China's Great Wall, in *front* of China's Great Wall, and famous Olympic athletes and infamous foreign wars. And the Pentagon and Kremlin use satellites to spy on each other.

As Intelsat serves whole countries, domestic systems are now servicing states, cities and even smaller geographic entities, beaming TV and telephone to remote areas in Algeria, Brazil, Canada, Malaysia, as well as in the Soviet Union. Five hundred and eighty miles above the U.S., government-funded and NASA-launched "landsats" prospect for precious minerals and scan parched land for portents of water; "metsats," though guilty of providing TV weathermen with their mystifying maps, exonerate themselves by detecting the eyes of hurricanes only fifty miles wide.

Meanwhile, whirling 22,300 miles above the equator, [six] commercial broadcast satellites—[three] owned by RCA and [three] by Western Union—are humming the tune all American commercial broadcasters may soon dance to.

Already, RCA's Satcom I is a switchboard-in-the-sky for the following major cable-TV services: Home Box Office and Showtime, pay-TV purveyors that transmit movies, specials, etc.; Madison Square Garden's 135-game orgy of forechecks and free throws (the Rangers, the Knicks); UPI's Newstime sight-and-sound news service; "Christian theme" programming from three religious broadcasters (Christian Broadcasting Network, PTL Network and Trinity Network); and "superstation" WTCG (recently joined by WGN-TV, Chicago), which has found devotees for Atlanta's sports teams throughout the Southeast and in Idaho and as far away as Hawaii.

In the noncable, broadcast spectrum, Western Union's Westar II transmits programming of SIN, which sounds like a cloven-hoofed plot to thwart the three religious broadcasters but is merely an acronym for the Spanish International Network, delivering [100] hours a week to its [ten] affiliates.

Packagers, such as Hughes Television Network and Robert Wold Co., Inc., purchase satellite time in bulk, getting bargain rates for their own "custom networks." The time not used to distribute Wold's programming goes into providing an interconnection service for clients, such as [ABC-TV, to distribute its early-morning *Good Morning America*]. On Westar I is the ITNA (Independent TV News Association)'s [21-] station news service. But Westar I's superstar is, without a doubt, the world's first authentic national satellite TV network—the Public Broadcasting Service.

On March 1, 1978, PBS cut the AT&T telephone lines to 24 of its member stations in the Southeast and connected them to Western Union's Westar I satellite. An additional 31 stations began receiving their PBS fare via Westar as of May 31, [1978], and by [December 1978] all 277 PBS stations [were] airborne, fed not only from headquarters near Washington, D.C. but from five geographically dis-bursed transmitting stations as well. An intriguing feature of this system [is] its capacity to beam to its interconnected stations four programs *at the same time.* (Each Westar satellite has 12 "transponders" or TV channels, and PBS has leased [four] on Westar I.)

"On one channel," says Ed Hymoff, director of communications of the corporation for Public Broadcasting (PBS's parent and patron), "You might have the *MacNeil/Lehrer Report,* going out from Washington, live. At the same time, on a second satellite channel, we might send out the Panama Canal hearings that stations could take live instead of *MacNeil/Lehrer,* or tape for later use. On a third channel, the Native American Consortium in Lincoln, Neb., might put up a program on the American Indian, using their regional 'uplink' [transmitting station], that PBS affiliates in Maine, in upstate New York, in the Southwest—wherever they have Indians—might want to take . . . and so on."

Aside from giving PBS more diverse programming, the satellite [gives] PBS less costly programming. "Believe it or not," says former CPB president Henry Loomis, "the operating costs of the four TV channels on the satellite are cheaper than the single TV channel we had with the AT&T interconnection." (The three-to-four-channel satellite network will cost from \$9.3 to \$12.8 million annually over the next ten years while conventional networking for basically one channel will cost from \$11.1 to \$18.2 million.)

However, while the satellite will allow *more* programming (and often a more vivid signal) critics point out that no technology can guarantee *better* programming. "I don't write any better with an electric typewriter," says CBS News vice president Bill Leonard "Even with a better mousetrap you still need cheese."

Leonard's cynicism about satellites permeates the three commercial networks. Currently, none is using satellites for [continuous] program distribution, although each is using [them] for a laundry list of special purposes (at least 700 hours per annum apiece, to bring West Coast-produced shows to the New York distribution center, plus live sports and news events).[1]

"The systems we have now do the job on an economic basis that is acceptable to us," says Frank Smith, formerly CBS's vice president of operational resources (and now the network's sports chief).

"But if AT&T came back and boosted its rates from \$55 [per mile per month] to what we considered an exorbitant amount," says ABC's director of TV network services, John Gilmore, "we might very well go into satelliting. Right now, though, why should I gamble the large capital investment it would take to go up in the air, breaking with the phone company, if it's just as cheap to stay on the ground?"

Others, however, suspect a different reason behind the networks' fear of flying. "The networks want to keep their local affiliates

1. In May 1979, NBC affiliates were told that the NBC network was developing a satellite transmission capability. Richard Sonnenfeldt, NBC vice president for operations and technical services, likes the flexibility which the satellite's multiple transponders provide. Sonnenfeldt claims, "We're quite determined to get into it, to get into it fast, but we know it will take a long time to install."

locked into a network schedule to guarantee their advertisers a certain mass audience," says William Houser, director of CPB's satellite project. If many of the network affiliates ever installed their own Earth-receiving stations, the umbilical cord binding them to network headquarters might be severed.

An even more ominous threat to the networks, the telephone company and the stations is "direct-to-home" satellite broadcasting. NASA itself has four communications satellites in orbit, plus one jointly owned with the Canadians. Until now, these satellites have been used, according to NASA's former director of communications, Sam Hubbard, "to perform experiments in delivering public services [such as coordinating medical services in Alaska, etc.]." Yet these high-power satellites (and new ones that will be piggybacked into orbit via the Space Shuttle) offer a unique potential: the power to eliminate the need for large, costly Earth-receiving stations. "We have already proved," says Hubbard, "that, with our satellites, we can put studio-quality TV into a receiver that will fit into your attic." . . .

STEPHEN BANKER

Beaming All Over

In August 1979, the Communications Satellite Corporation (COMSAT) announced its intention to institute direct satellite-to-home pay-television services, perhaps as early as 1983. ABC and the National Association of Broadcasters have filed complaints with the FCC, arguing that the venture is illegal because it is not within the scope of the corporation's charter. According to NAB senior vice president Erwin Krasnow, COMSAT's plan "would change the very character of this country's broadcast system" by diverting programming from the "traditional" system. Stephen Banker describes the plan and its implications for local television stations.

The affluent customers of Neiman-Marcus, who in the past have been urged to buy a vault built deep within a mountain, or a cunning pair of his and her submarines, [in] Christmas [1979] are being tempted with a $36,500 satellite receiver. The new catalogue from the Texas-based department store announces not your old-fashioned daddy-longlegs rooftop TV antenna, but a "dish" that can "pick up 100 channels . . . even from the back of beyond."

Such advertising, though aimed at the very rich, dramatizes the fact that it is already possible for individual homeowners to hook their TV sets to a satellite floating thousands of miles away. And as for price, $36,500 is considerably less astronomical than the $5 million or so a receiving dish, or "Earth station," cost as recently as the mid-'60s, when the Communications Satellite Corporation (COMSAT) first made commercial satellite links among nations a reality.

Early experiments quickly showed the value of TV by satellite. Its pictures are sharp and clear, retaining remarkable definition in the

This essay first appeared December 6, 1979.

round trip through space. In fact, both satellite and cable are better sending devices than the tower of the local station.

Still, most viewers probably will prefer cable to satellite TV, if the programming is equally attractive. A coaxial cable, no thicker than your little finger, can provide dozens of crystal-sharp channels.

But millions of Americans live in far-flung areas where there is little hope of getting cable, now or in the near future. It's estimated that even by 1985, only one-third of the country will have been hooked to cable, leaving COMSAT or other satellite-to-home broadcasters a hefty potential market of at least 60 million households without an auxiliary TV service. For these relatively remote households, signals by satellite could be ideal, since distances of a few hundred miles are negligible to an orbiting spacecraft.

Today, Earth stations measuring some 15 feet across are already in wide use—by local public-television stations receiving their network feeds; by cable systems plucking first-run movies, the U.S. Congress in action and other fare from the sky; and by hotels gathering entertainment for their guests.

As satellite-to-home telecasting gets more sophisticated, it is also becoming miniaturized and affordable to the middle class. Canada and Japan have started experiments with home dishes that will cost $300–400 in mass production. And [in] summer [1979] COMSAT announced plans to establish a direct-broadcast satellite system for the United States, providing from two to six noncommercial channels. Subscribers would pay a monthly rental fee for a 2½-to-3-foot dish, tunable only to COMSAT's own frequencies. The company hedged on the exact cost, but word is out that installation and deposit would run about $150, with monthly charges to range from $25 up, depending on how many of the channels the consumer orders. The company estimates that service could begin by 1983.

Part of COMSAT's apparatus is an "addressable" box—a small device connected to your TV set that transforms the coded signal into a normal picture. From its home office, COMSAT can turn your channels on and off as it pleases—ON, if you spend an extra amount for a special broadcast; OFF, if you haven't paid your bill on time.

Of critical importance: there must be a clear line of sight between the dish—rooftop, back yard, or wherever it is installed—and the precise point in the sky where the satellite is in orbit. The picture on your screen will be close to studio quality, but any interference between dish and satellite—a heavy rainstorm, say—can interrupt the reception. The signal cannot travel through hills, trees or buildings.

COMSAT's announcement of its plans brought a heated reaction from government agencies as well as from the broadcasting and cable industries. Around Washington, COMSAT was condemned for undermining American broadcasting and, at the same time, praised for delivering the space age to the ordinary citizen.

The truth, as usual, is not so dramatic. The first reaction from many observers was that 1983 is a considerable error on the side of optimism. Just building the satellites could take up to three years—*after* Congress and the Federal Communications Commission (FCC) give the green light. And the legislative and regulatory processes will be stretched to the limit by some very high-priced lawyers who are already brandishing monkey wrenches over the machinery.

As for the programs themselves, COMSAT plans to commission its own rather than merely rebroadcasting the offerings of the major networks or local stations. Exactly what their programming will be is currently under discussion. A company spokesman did say that one channel is likely to be devoted to sports and another to entertainment, probably first-run movies. But something ambitious or revolutionary is needed if COMSAT is going to compete with less costly systems. In fact, the competition for shares of the audience is already sharp. Most threatened and therefore most adamantly opposed to home-satellite reception are the over-the-air broadcasters. They foresee satellites bypassing their elaborate local operations and delivering the product directly to the customer.

"This is a plan for a national system of broadcasting, which is the antithesis of the American system of 'localism'," says A. James Ebel, president and general manager of KOLN-TV in Lincoln, Neb., and chairman of the ABC-CBS-NBC Network Affiliates Satellite Transmissions Committee.

Not surprisingly, Thomas Bolger, the chairman of the board of the National Association of Broadcasters, anticipates lengthy hearings. "We'll have ample opportunity," he says, "to express our opinions to the Congressional and agency leadership before any final decision is made." Another NAB source says, with emphasis, "We intend to participate fully in the regulatory process."

A group with an ambivalent response is the National Cable Television Association (NCTA), whose own growth has been delayed and limited by the broadcasters. One industry-sponsored study warns of "direct competition." But NCTA's young president, Thomas Wheeler, welcomes the new blood. "Let 'em come," he says. "It would be stupid of us to oppose COMSAT, because we have been the cutting edge of competition in communications, and COMSAT is a further example of that."

Wheeler anticipates a day when cable and satellite join forces. "Where cable exists, we play together. Where we don't exist, they go direct to home. We are compatible."

The FCC, which must finally approve the COMSAT venture, is the largest question mark. Chairman Charles Ferris assured *TV Guide* that the FCC "will not retard a technology that can provide greater diversity to the American people." But Ferris had already told the *Washington Post* that "to allow new technology, like immediate satellite transmission of television signals . . . would have an unsettling and disrupting effect on the marketplace."

"The regulatory process," says Jonathan Miller, managing editor of the newsletter *Satellite Week,* "normally restrains the introduction of new technology and protects status quo operators."

Other problems as yet unresolved include the allocation of transmission frequencies that will make the smaller dish possible, and the assignment of favorable satellite "parking spots." These matters must be coordinated with the claims of other countries.

So the technology for satellite-to-home telecasting is on hand, but it won't happen without a sheaf of legal and political permissions. Let us, nevertheless, peer over the bureaucratic clouds to see what wonders direct-broadcast satellites could achieve.

Since a satellite 22,240 miles in space can "see" a third of the Earth, a mere three satellites can interconnect the whole world for a firm realization of Marshall McLuhan's "global village." Languages are beamed to their appropriate areas on separate audio lines.

"And there may be," writes science-fiction writer Arthur C. Clarke, who first predicted the communications satellite thirty years ago, "even more dramatic changes, for good or bad, that no one can foresee today—any more than Samuel Morse or Thomas Edison could have imagined that one day a quarter of the human race would watch the same pictures and hear the same sounds."

The room for growth in satellite-to-home TV is almost unlimited. James Martin notes in his book *The Wired Society* that "if as much money were spent on such satellites as on television stations in the United States today, the satellites could broadcast *hundreds* of channels to home receivers."

The broadcasters know this and resent it. KOLN-TV's A. James Ebel fears that the satellite people will "skim off the cream," not bothering to discharge the traditional "responsibilities" of the industry, such as local news, weather, traffic, etc. Former FCC commissioner Nicholas Johnson points out that 90 per cent of all television programming in the United States is put together in New York or Los Angeles. "Stations take either network feeds or syndication packages. Local material is mostly done on the cheap. If the local stations want to survive," says Johnson, "they have five years to make themselves indispensable."

Some observers think the cable industry has a real opportunity here. Without the costly superstructure of a local station, [more than 4000] cable companies could put together (as a few have already done) local news teams and service organizations. Thus the new order could eventually be satellites instead of networks, and cable systems instead of affiliates.

But "free" television is not about to wither away, however altered it may be. The salvation of local stations may well be local advertising, while that of the networks will probably be what NBC president Fred Silverman calls "nonfiction" broadcasting. After all, the chief information source for a majority of Americans is television news. And if network and local-station news aren't enough, entrepreneur Ted Turner, with his Atlanta superstation already carried nationwide by a combination of satellite and cable, [started] a round-the-clock cable news service in [June] 1980.

It may be well into the middle or late 1980s before the American home-video operator gets his dish, his decoder and his first monthly invoice from COMSAT. By that time, the cable industry expects to offer 30 channels or more on most installations. The networks and their affiliates, the public stations and the independents will still be around. And looking farther ahead, a successful COMSAT experiment would surely call forth a new variety of star wars, with other corporations rushing to send up a more powerful generation of satellites. "To accommodate the profusion," *Horizon* magazine predicts, "*TV Guide* may look like a telephone book."

ISAAC ASIMOV

Our Race with Doom

In the not too distant future—possibly in a decade or two—satellites will most likely provide the bulk of the world's communications. John E. Fox, vice president of Satellite Business Systems, points out that "for the first time we have the potential of eliminating the distinction between local and remote. No one is smart enough to say where that will lead."

Isaac Asimov outlines the important role television and the satellite can play in sensitizing the world's population to our common destiny, and the need for unified action against the significant problems and dangers we all share.

Mankind is plunging wildly toward catastrophe—and within a generation, perhaps. Many prophets tell us this in anguish. The world population is wildly rising, our environment is deteriorating, our cities decaying, our society disintegrating, our life-quality declining.

How to halt it? How can we determine the necessary actions and then take them when the large majority of the Earth's population is indifferent and is utterly concerned only with the immediate problem of the next meal? Or, if their eye is lifted to a further horizon, it is to become chiefly concerned with the hate and fear of some near neighbor.

To rally the different peoples of the world—different in language, religion, culture and tradition—against the overriding problems that threaten to turn all the world into a desert, what weapon do we have?

The traditional weapon is force. Let one of the world's peoples, one coherent group, kill or conquer all the rest, make itself the one

This essay first appeared June 5, 1971.

power to be considered and then take what measures are necessary to save the world!

But that won't do, for the nature of war is such that even if we could bring ourselves to advocate world conquest, the very process of conquering the world will destroy it and leave no room for any solution but death.

What else? As an alternative to force there is persuasion. Mankind must somehow be talked into saving itself, into agreeing to turn its combined strength and ingenuity toward a program for keeping the Earth fit for life.

But there is so little time, and mere persuasion has so rarely worked. . . . Unless some new weapon of persuasion can be found.

Such a weapon exists. It is television.

Of all forms of communication, television is the most forceful and immediate. It is not incomplete as radio and photography are; it is not remote, as books and printed periodicals are; it is not necessarily contrived fiction, as movies are. Television fills both eye and ear, in the full range of color and tone, and can deal with matters that are happening at the very moment.

Television has already shown its force. The Vietnam War [was] the first to be played out on television, and war has lost its glamour at least partly because it becomes distasteful when taken unfiltered. The whole nation has been sharing experiences; every corner of the land is aware of the drug scene. We all become, in a way, more neighborly since we share even in trivia, recognize the same ubiquitous faces and become aware of the same advertising catch phrases.

And television is as yet in its kindergarten stage. Its influence on society now is only a hint at what it could be when it comes of age.

There is a limit now to the number of television channels available in any community; a limit to the reach of any television station. The sharp limits leave room for little or no flexibility, and only that can be offered which will please a multitude—which usually means mass entertainment at the common denominator.

Cable television is extending those limits, increasing the possible flexibility, making it easy for more channels to reach more people. The real jump, however, will come with the expansion of communications satellites. By using objects in outer space as relays, signals can bounce from any one spot on Earth to any other, and the number of possible channels, stretching across a broad band of wave lengths, becomes virtually unlimited. . . .

When sufficiently sophisticated satellites in sufficient numbers are placed in orbit, electronic communication will for the first time become personalized. Though television stations could still be offering mass programs to a mass audience, it will also be possible for any man on Earth, individually, to reach any other.

The printed word, in a computerized space-relay world, could be transmitted as efficiently as the spoken word. Facsimile mail, newspapers, magazines, books, could be readily available at the press of a button—anywhere.

The world will be tiny indeed, and we will all be neighbors, electronically. It is simple to hate an abstraction, to cry down death upon some bunch of faceless foreigners somewhere. It is much harder to do the same to the pleasant foreigners with whom we could be speaking at any time—arguing our case and listening to theirs.

To be sure, national leaders are, in a sense, doing this now, but what they can do is limited as long as each must consider the public opinion of an isolated people who might well each have been deliberately exacerbated against the other out of power-politics considerations. Defusing the situation then becomes difficult unless low-level contact is possible. Consider how suddenly tension between Mainland China and the United States seemed to lessen once the Chinese invited an American ping-pong team into their nation and treated them in friendly fashion.

With massive personalized communication, the world will more and more share its problems and experiences. We live in a world, today, in which all parts will be dragged down to ruin, if any major part is. None of us will ever escape if we don't feel this unity-of-destiny with heart and soul; and television-in-its-adulthood will make sure we feel this.

As communication improves and becomes more intensive, mankind will find it less necessary to live together in huge clusters. In a world of automation, it will be information that will have to be transported from point to point, not human bodies—and information can be moved electronically at the speed of light.

With unlimited numbers of television channels, conferences can meet in the form of images. The actual bodies, belonging to those images, fed with facsimiles of any necessary documents, can be anywhere on Earth. For more and more purposes, men can stay where they are and send their images.

This is not to say that people might not want to be together for personal or psychological reasons; or that they might not want to travel for fun and excitement. The point is that people will have less and less reason to travel when they *don't* want to.

The result will be that transportation facilities will feel lessened strain. People will no longer have to live in groups so that they might reach each other. They can spread out.

In a world in which every person is, or can be, in instant touch with anyone else, we have, in effect, what has been called a "global village" and, under such conditions, cities are unnecessary.

Again, this does not mean that some people won't choose to live together, just because they want to. Still, the cities will decrease in size and become more livable for those who stay, while much of the population will spread out into the relatively empty areas, enjoying physical space *without* cultural isolation.

What about education? With a flexible electronic system in control, education can become infinitely more detailed and personal. And it need not be confined only to the "advanced" nations. With mass electronics, the submerged mass of peasantry in Asia, Africa and South America can, essentially for the first time, get the information they need—information the whole world needs to make sure they get.

The population of the have-not nations can grow up learning about modern agricultural methods in the most dramatic possible way—each for himself. They can learn the proper use of fertilizers and pesticides, proper hygiene, proper techniques for population control.

The beamed wavelengths, bouncing off satellites, can bypass clogged social setups, slip around decaying tradition, overcome the weight of illiteracy. The *whole* world, *all* of mankind, can receive the strong push into the approaching twenty-first century that it must have. Nor must we underestimate the force of the push. Radio, movies, and kindergarten-television have already, in a mere half-century, made astonishing progress toward Westernizing (even Americanizing) the world. What then will the communications revolution, grown to maturity, succeed in doing?

What of world government? Many consider it necessary if mankind is really to take action against its overwhelming problems; yet world government seems out of the question. There are too many conflicting interests; too many differences; too much hatred.

So it seemed when the infant American republic was born. The thirteen original states were more spread out in stagecoach days than the whole world is now, and the distance between Boston and Savannah was as great in culture as in miles. But canals, and then railroads, knitted the country together and a single government became a practical possibility as well as a theoretical ideal.

Let mass electronic communication work, then, and become an intellectual "railroad net." Let the man on the banks of the Zambezi or the Orinoco have an equal chance at equal information with the man on the banks of the Thames or the Hudson, and there will come a morning when mankind will realize that for quite a while its governing units *had* been acting in a common cause and that while there were many nations, there was already the essence of world government.

Let's summarize: Television plus communications satellites will mean that, for the first time in history, the planet can be a cultural unit. And that means that for the first time in history it will have the capacity, and *perhaps* the will, to be an action-unit against global problems. And maybe we will then survive.

Naturally, the communications revolution will not take place overnight. It will not be here tomorrow. It will not be here, in full, by the year 2000.

But then mankind may not be destroyed overnight either.

What we face is a race. As the arteries of mass communication begin to spread over the Earth, there will be a push toward efficient education, decentralization, world unification and, on the whole, toward a stiffening of action against the deteriorating situation.

In the same period, however, there is almost sure to be a continued rise in population, a continued increase in pollution, a continued suicidal devotion of man's efforts to dozens of hostile military machines, and all this will keep the situation deteriorating.

Which will win out?

My guess is that by 2000 the power of communication may still not have reversed the tide, but that the misery will not have deepened as greatly as it would have otherwise. Men will (we can hope) be more aware by then of the nature of the race, of the terror of the doom, of the possibility of rescue. There will be a greater push toward developing the intricate television network that will create the global village.

If so, the forces of communication and unification may gain the upper hand and—not without considerable pain and struggle—produce a new human civilization that will look back upon these days we are living through now as a Dark Age.

Yet on the other hand, it is also possible that the inertia of indifference, the dead weight of tradition, the dark shadow of hate and suspicion may be too much for the developing communication network to overcome. In that case, we are probably doomed.

No man can, as yet, surely predict the outcome of the race, but each of us, whether we do it consciously or not, will pick his side. I am on the side of world communication, world understanding and world union.

And you?

ALVIN TOFFLER

And on Our Tricentennial . . .

The individual, personalized television of the future to which Isaac Asimov refers has been termed, "Indi-Video," by Alvin Toffler. The author of *Future Shock* discusses the potential effects of indi-video upon society by the year 2076.

What we call television today is no more than a primitive forerunner of video systems that could turn out to be the electronic spine of tomorrow's society. TV today is essentially an entertainment medium and, as such, peripheral to our lives. Tomorrow we might well base much of our economy and our political system on what we still anachronistically call "the tube." In short, television may move out of our living room and into our living.

In the 1950s, when TV was still new in the U.S., science-fiction writers used to speculate about bigger and bigger screens. They pictured suburbanites scrimping and saving to buy giant "four-wall" units that surrounded the viewer. Years earlier, Aldous Huxley had imagined movies that presented us not only with sights and sounds, but with smells and tactile sensations as well. He called them "feelies" and the same reasoning could naturally be applied to TV. Basically, such forecasts suggest that we might get more of the same—thus, bigger screens, clearer images, more sensory involvement, etc.

Much more daring speculations, however, start from the idea that we will make "leaps." For example, one might explore ways in which television actually could bypass our ears, eyes and other sense organs, and transmit images directly into the brain through electrodes that activate those portions of the brain that control "seeing"

This essay first appeared June 28, 1975.

or "hearing" or "smelling." It is already many years since Dr. Jose M. R. Delgado implanted tiny radios in animal brains and controlled behavior by transmitting signals to them. So the notion of bypassing the sense organs and feeding TV images directly into the brain and nervous system of the "viewer" isn't as wild as it might once have been.

Today we already have linked television with biofeedback devices to help viewers regulate their own pulse rates and brain waves. Futurist Bill Rojas has even speculated about the possibilities of combining video with various drugs to produce bizarre new effects. Listen, for example, to this possible script of the future:

"OK, all you quiz freaks out there! Ready for the fun? Have you taken your little yellow pills this morning? Fine. Great. That means we can get on with the show. Those of you who take our little pills—only pennies for a full 30-day supply—will see things on the screen that nobody else can see. All those squiggles and snowflakes or flickers that go by so fast and seem meaningless to other folks are visible to you and you alone. So YOU can participate in our quiz and complete for the big, Big, BIG experiences!"

While such technological fantasies may be either titillating or horrifying, another breakthrough that could have even deeper consequences lies closer at hand.

Right now television, in every country, is a tool used by "them" to influence "us." The "them" may be advertisers selling a product, politicians pushing a party line, or celebrities offering their views. But the messages flow in only one direction.

Now imagine a system in which each of us becomes not merely a passive viewer, but also a sender—a system that permits each of us to communicate privately with others. Imagine, in short, a video equivalent of the lowly telephone.

The telephone is far more deeply wired into our lives than television. Our jobs depend on telephones, not television. Our homes, our communities, our love lives and friendship patterns are all profoundly affected by the telephone. And while television is inherently totalitarian, treating each of us as a digit in a Nielsen rating, rather than as an individual, the telephone is inherently democratic. No network or advertising agency or government commissar determines who will use the telephone, when, or for what purpose.

Today video pioneers—inventors, electronics engineers, artists, filmmakers, some in big companies, others so-called "software radicals"—are hastening the day when the "modern" television catches up with and outstrips the "old-fashioned" telephone. They are working on two-way cable systems, on cassettes, on advanced electronic switching systems, on picturephones, on information banks and computer ties, all of which could ultimately lead to drastic, potentially positive changes in our society. They are putting together the pieces of a system that might be called "Indi-Video"—individualized communications through video.

In their early stages, all industrial societies develop powerful mass communications machinery: mass entertainment, mass news distribution, not to mention mass education, all of which go along with the mass production and mass distribution of goods.

What is happening now—as industrial societies break down and a new, more advanced superindustrial society emerges—is a powerful process of "demassification." Instead of uniform, standardized societies, with uniform, standardized tastes, fashions, ideas, values and ideologies, we are becoming more richly diverse. Instead of a "mass market," economists are discovering that we really represent a changing mix of "minimarkets."

Indi-Video is "demassified television." It is the communications part of the superindustrial revolution. It permits a vast, rich diversity of messages to pulse through society. While we will no doubt continue to use mass communications for some limited purposes—we may even permit one network to survive—Indi-Video fits the needs of a fast-emerging future.

Thus behind the work of many Indi-Video pioneers lies the dream of a society of smaller, decentralized communities in which virtually everyone has, and makes use of, tiny, cheap video cameras, employing them as casually and for as many different purposes as we now use phones or electronic calculators. The more Huxleyian visionaries imagine the day when we can each ring up our friends or co-workers and transmit not merely pictures in full color and in perfect clarity, but also eventually the appropriate smells, tastes and tactile sensations.

Advanced Indi-Video systems, as they develop, could completely alter not merely personal communications but also the way we work. Many jobs do not require the actual presence of the worker. With the right kind of television-computer-cable hookups, most of us could happily stay home and work. We could control machines, inspect finished products, enter figures in a column, demand a raise, hold a union meeting or enjoy a coffee break with our co-workers without ever setting foot outside our own front door.

This could, of course, almost at a stroke, eliminate the maddening rush hour from our lives. It could eliminate the enormous waste of human and nonhuman energy burned up in this daily two-way movement of workers to their jobs. It could make large urban centers obsolete. While the metropolises of the world might survive for special functions, their populations would thin out and, instead of new industrial cities springing up, Indi-Video would permit us to live further apart—yet still enjoy close communicational contact.

But the most far-reaching aspect of this Indi-Video dream has to do with politics. Today, as parliamentary democracy comes under attack in country after country, the partisans of the emergent communications-based society see in it the possibilities for a revival of genuine grass-roots democracy.

Even people who live far apart could, in effect, participate in electronic town meetings, flashing a light to ask for the floor, turning their Indi-Video cameras on themselves as they speak, and thus transmitting their own views, hopes, fears, smiles and scowls to their fellow citizens. The system, linked to computers, would make instant voting possible. It would also make it possible for a voter confused about some issue, to call up on his or her private screen computer-banked images showing in explicit detail what the effects of a "yes" or "no" vote might be.

We have already had the first experiments with these forms of electronic democracy and political action. In England, mothers who tried to get community action to slow down traffic at a busy intersection used video cameras to document in dramatic form the difficulties their kids had in crossing the street. They then showed these tapes on TV screens in nearby pubs until they had won enough political support to do something about the problem.

In the Netherlands, a leading politician has suggested that television stations show pictures of "Amsterdams of the Future" and semifacetiously called for citizens to turn on a light when they see one they prefer, to douse a light when they see images they do not like. Their opinions, he said, might be registered by measuring the increase or decrease in the consumption of electricity at that moment. In Germany, an experimental TV program called *Orakel* polled samples of the viewing public for their opinions on pollution. Their responses were computer-analyzed on the spot and were fed into the program for discussion by officials, businessmen, consumerists and others.

In Washington state recently, as part of a statewide experiment in "anticipatory democracy," ordinary citizens drew up eleven alternative sets of goals and strategies for the state to pursue over the next ten years. Working with the state planning agency, which took as its slogan "You don't have to be an expert to know what you want!," the group arranged for these alternatives to be presented on television stations throughout the state and asked their fellow citizens to vote on them through 1,400,000 ballots provided by their local newspapers.

Clearly, in the German, Dutch and American examples we see efforts to give viewers a choice, to make "feedback" possible. These efforts are still hampered by the one-way character of today's television. Indi-Video would remedy that problem. Everyone would be able to respond instantaneously—not by turning on a light or clipping a ballot from a newspaper—but by pressing a button, or by actually using his or her own Indi-Video unit to comment, or to add his or her own ideas, images and proposals for a worthwhile future.

Anticipatory democracy—grass-roots participation in setting goals for the future—is, in my view, the necessary next stage in the development of democracy, with or without advanced electronic communications. What the Indi-Video enthusiasts tell us, however, is that the new electronics could help make anticipatory democracy work.

We ought to have learned by now that all technologies carry "side effects" with them. Sometimes these side effects are adverse or even dangerous. No one can say for sure what problems Indi-Video could produce along with its apparent benefits. Would many of us choose to live out our lives in an "electronic womb" cut off from direct, face-to-face experience of other people? What effect would the increasing diversity of messages have on our nervous systems and on our modes of thinking? On psychological development? How would we deal with privacy?

No one as yet can answer these questions. What we do know is that television systems of the future will bear only the remotest resemblance to their forerunners of today. And we need to begin thinking now about what changes we—not the broadcasting networks, the engineers, the scientists, the advertisers, the politicians or pundits, but *we*—want for tomorrow. For the way we communicate with one another is almost as important as how we breathe.

List of Contributors

ISAAC ASIMOV is Professor of Biochemistry at Boston University School of Medicine. In his "spare time" he writes books: as of May 1980 he had published two hundred sixteen books of science fiction, mystery, mathematics, history, literature, humor, biography and every branch of science.

STEPHEN BANKER is the publisher of the audiocassette series, Tapes for Readers, located in Washington, D.C. As a broadcaster, he narrated the John F. Kennedy funeral for CBS Radio and the departure of Richard Nixon for National Public Radio.

SALLY BEDELL has been a *TV Guide* staff writer since 1977. She is a former reporter for *Time* magazine and the author of a forthcoming book on prime-time television in the 1970s.

LIZA BERCOVICI is assistant counsel of the House Interstate and Foreign Commerce Committee. She was formerly a reporter for the *Washington Post* and *Daily Variety.*

THEODORE BERLAND is a free-lance writer. He has written several *Living with . . .* books, including *Living with Your Teeth, Living with Your Ulcer* and *Living with Your Eye Operation.*

JOHN BIRT is the controller of features and current affairs at London Weekend Television. He has worked in British television since 1966 as a reporter, producer and editor.

DANIEL J. BOORSTIN has been the Librarian of Congress since 1975. A former professor of history at the University of Chicago and director of the Smithsonian's National Museum of History, Technology and Science, he was awarded the Pulitzer Prize for his trilogy, *The Americans.*

FREDERICK BREITENFELD, JR., is executive director of the Maryland Center for Public Broadcasting and visiting professor at Johns Hopkins University. He has served on the faculties of both Catholic and American universities in Washington, D.C., and has worked professionally as an actor, a musician, a writer and a high school teacher.

DAVID BRINKLEY is the well-known, Peabody Award-winning news commentator. A former newspaper reporter, he became a newswriter for NBC in 1943, the network's Washington correspondent in 1951 and the co-anchorman of the *Huntley-Brinkley Report* in 1956.

DAVID CHAGALL spent ten years in the Roper Organization directing marketing research studies for top U.S. corporations before turning to full-time writing. Now an investigative reporter for national magazines, he is a regular contributor to *TV Guide.*

BARRY COLE is adjunct professor at the Annenberg School of Communications of the University of Pennsylvania and a member of that university's School of Law faculty. A former consultant to two chairmen of the Federal Communications Commission and the House Communications Subcommittee, he has twice received the annual book award of the National Association of Educational Broadcasters.

EDWIN DIAMOND heads the News Study Group at the Massachusetts Institute of Technology. A journalist and critic, he is also senior editor of the *Washington Journalism Review* and contributing editor of *TV Guide*'s sister magazine, *Panorama.*

MELVIN DURSLAG has been a sportswriter since 1940, much of that time as a columnist for the Los Angeles *Herald-Examiner* and King Features Syndicate in New York. He first began contributing to *TV Guide* in 1960 and is now a contributing editor.

EDITH EFRON is author of *The News Twisters* and collaborator with William E. Simon on *A Time for Truth.* She has been a *TV Guide* staff writer, a *Time-Life* correspondent and assistant women's editor for *Look* magazine.

MAX GUNTHER is a free-lance writer. The author of eighteen books, he was formerly a contributing editor to *Time* magazine.

PAUL HEMPHILL is senior editor of *Atlanta* magazine. He is the author of hundreds of magazine articles and four books, including *Long Gone,* which is being made into a motion picture.

NEIL HICKEY has been *TV Guide*'s New York bureau chief since 1964. The author of a number of books, he is a former newspaper reporter and editor of the *American Weekly Sunday Magazine* and *True* magazine.

DICK HOBSON has worked at several of Hollywood's major television production studios. He has written extensively about television in a number of national magazines and at one time served as a *TV Guide* staff writer.

PAUL L. KLEIN is president of PKO Limited, a television production company. He has been research manager of a major advertising agency, vice president of audience measurement and later executive vice president of programming at NBC. In 1970 he founded the world's first independent pay-per-program TV firm.

DON KOWET has been a *TV Guide* staff writer since 1977. A former managing editor of *Sport* magazine, he is the author of nine books.

LOUIS KRONENBERGER, one of our leading drama critics for almost half a century, was drama critic for *Time* magazine between 1938 and 1961. He has edited about forty textbooks on literature and drama, taught at a number of major universities and has written several books of his own, including *A Month of Sundays* and *Company Manners.*

DAVID LACHENBRUCH is editorial director of *Television Digest* with *Consumer Electronics* and a contributing editor to *TV Guide* and *Panorama.* A prolific writer on television technology, he is a frequent contributor to consumer magazines and the author of *Videocassette Recorders: The Complete Home Guide* and the forthcoming *Color Television: A Look Inside.*

ERIC LEVIN is an assistant editor of *People* magazine. A former newspaper reporter, he was a staff writer for *TV Guide* from 1973 to 1978.

JAMES LIPTON is the author of *An Exaltation of Larks* and has produced *The Mighty Gents* and *Monteith and Rand* on Broadway. He has been writer/producer for several important TV specials, including President Carter's inaugural concert and Bob Hope's birthday celebration.

LEE LOEVINGER is a partner in the law firm of Hogan & Hartson in Washington, D.C. He was formerly a commissioner on the Federal Communications Commission, assistant attorney general in charge of the antitrust division, and a justice of the Minnesota Supreme Court.

BOB MACKENZIE has been a contributor to *TV Guide* since 1972 and a contributing editor and resident program critic since 1977. A former TV critic for the *Oakland Tribune,* he has been the writer-host of various public television programs and in 1980 received the National Headliner Award in journalism as the nation's best magazine columnist.

ROBERT MACNEIL is co-anchorman and executive editor of the *MacNeil/Lehrer Report* seen on public television every weekday evening. A Canadian citizen, he has been a correspondent for the Canadian Broadcasting Company, the British Broadcasting Company, NBC and the Reuters News Service.

MARTIN MALONEY is a professor and former chairman of the Department of Radio-Television-Film at Northwestern University. He has written extensively about mass media in books and professional journals and is the author of hundreds of radio and television scripts.

JOHN MARIANI is a New York writer whose work has appeared in the *New York Times, Saturday Review* and various journals. He also teaches communications at the college level.

MARTIN MAYER has been a free-lance writer since 1954 and is the author of twenty books, including *Madison Avenue USA, The Schools* and *About Television.* A former associate editor of *Esquire* magazine, his "About Television" column is a regular feature in *American Film* magazine.

DONALD H. MCGANNON is the chairman of the board of the Westinghouse Broadcasting Company. A television executive since 1952, he has been the recipient of the two highest awards given by his peers—the distinguished service award of the National Association of Broadcasters and a special Emmy award.

ARTHUR C. NIELSEN, JR., is the chairman and chief executive officer of the A. C. Nielsen Company. He is a director of a number of corporations and has served on various federal governmental advisory committees.

MAL OETTINGER is a writer and editor for the International Communications Agency. He has been a reporter for *Broadcasting* magazine, the Washington editor of *Television/Radio Age* and Washington news information coordinator for NBC.

MERRILL PANITT is editorial director of *TV Guide, Panorama* and *Seventeen* magazines. A former Philadelphia television columnist, he became *TV Guide*'s first managing editor in 1953 and was editor of the magazine between 1956 and 1973.

MICHAEL RYAN is an associate editor of *People* magazine and the author of *Climbing*. He was formerly a staff writer for *TV Guide* and executive editor of *Boston* magazine.

JOE SALTZMAN is chairman of undergraduate studies at the University of Southern California's School of Journalism and a freelance newspaper and magazine writer. A senior writer-producer of documentaries at KNXT, Los Angeles, for more than ten years, his television programs won more than fifty national and local awards.

ARTHUR SCHLESINGER, JR., is Schweitzer Professor of Humanities at the City University of New York and was a special assistant to the President from 1961 to 1964. The noted historian is author of fourteen books and was awarded the Pulitzer Prize for History in 1946 for *The Age of Jackson* and the Pulitzer Prize for Biography in 1966 for *A Thousand Days: John F. Kennedy in the White House.*

LEMUEL B. SCHOFIELD is vice president and general manager of WROC-TV, the NBC affiliate in Rochester, New York. Previously a broadcast lawyer, he was manager of WRCB-TV, Chattanooga, Tenn., when his *TV Guide* article was written.

HARRY SKORNIA is Professor Emeritus of Radio and Television at the University of Illinois, Chicago campus. A past president of the National Association of Educational Broadcasters, he is the author of several books on television, including *Television and Society* and *Television and the News: A Critical Appraisal.*

ALVIN TOFFLER has been a well-known futurist since his award-winning *Future Shock* was first published in 1970. A former associate editor of *Fortune* magazine, he is the author or editor of seven books, a contributor to ten more and has written for most of the nation's important periodicals.

ELLEN TORGERSON (SHAW) has been a *TV Guide* staff writer since 1976. She was formerly an aide to Los Angeles mayor Tom Bradley and a reporter for UPI.

RICHARD TOWNLEY is a writer and columnist. He has been a reporter, editor and critic for newspapers, radio and television since 1958.

ARNOLD TOYNBEE, the distinguished British historian, was a professor of international history at London University for thirty-six years. He will presumably be best remembered for his classic twelve-volume *A Study of History.*

JOHN WEISMAN is the Washington bureau chief of *TV Guide.* He is the author of *Guerrilla Theater: Scenarios for Revolution* and, most recently, *Evidence.*

CHRIS WELLES is a free-lance writer specializing in business, finance and the media. He is a contributing editor to *Esquire* and *Institutional Investor* and director of the Walter Bagehot Fellowship Program in Economics and Business Journalism at the Columbia Graduate School of Journalism.

Index